Organized Labor in Venezuela 1958–1991

Organized Labor in Venezuela 1958–1991

Behavior and Concerns in a Democratic Setting

Steve Ellner

A Scholarly Resources Inc. Imprint
Wilmington, Delaware

The paper used in this publication meets the minimum requirements of the American National Standard for permanence of paper for printed library materials, Z39.48, 1984.

Scholarly Resources Inc.
104 Greenhill Avenue
Wilmington, DE 19805-1897

Library of Congress Cataloging-in-Publication Data

Ellner, Steve.
    Organized labor in Venezuela, 1958–1991 : behavior and concerns in a democratic setting / Steve Ellner.
        p.   cm. — (Latin American silhouettes)
    Includes bibliographical references and index.
    ISBN 0-8420-2443-3
    1. Trade-unions—Venezuela—History—20th century. 2. Labor movement—Venezuela—History—20th century. I. Title. II. Series.
HD6652.E43   1993
331.88'0987'09045—dc20   92-44554
                                                       CIP

To Janet, Peter, Susan, Rebecca, and Cypress

About the Author

Steve Ellner earned his Ph.D. in Latin American history from the University of New Mexico in 1979. He is currently full professor of economic history at the Universidad de Oriente in Puerto La Cruz, Venezuela, where he has been teaching since 1977. In addition to writing over twenty journal articles and book chapters, Professor Ellner is the author of *The Venezuelan Petroleum Corporation and the Debate over Government Policy in Basic Industry* (1987) and *Venezuela's Movimiento al Socialismo: From Guerrilla Defeat to Innovative Politics* (1988), and he is coeditor of *The Latin American Left: From the Fall of Allende to Perestroika* (1993). Professor Ellner is also a regular contributor to *Commonweal*.

Contents

List of Abbreviations and Acronyms, **ix**
Preface, **xi**
Introduction, **xv**

CHAPTER 1   From Labor Consolidation and Unity to Fragmentation, 1958–1963, **1**

CHAPTER 2   Economic Recovery and Boom, 1964–1979, **37**

CHAPTER 3   Economic Contraction and Crisis in the 1980s, **65**

CHAPTER 4   The CTV's Strategy, Analysis, and Internal Organization, **95**

CHAPTER 5   Ideological Currents and International Affiliations, **113**

CHAPTER 6   Worker Fragmentation and Transformation in the Oil Industry, **131**

CHAPTER 7   Labor Militance in the Steel and Textile Industries, **149**

CHAPTER 8   *Cogestión* and the CTV's Financial Interests, **175**

CHAPTER 9   Labor Legislation and the Workers' Movement, **197**

Conclusion, **221**
Selected Bibliography, **233**
Index, **239**

List of Abbreviations and Acronyms

AD	Acción Democrática (Democratic Action)
Aifld	American Institute for Free Labor Development
ANDE	Asociación Nacional de Empleados (National Association of Employees)
Atiss	Asociación de Trabajadores de la Industria Siderúrgica (Association of Workers of the Steel Industry)
BTV	Banco de los Trabajadores (Workers Bank)
Cacref	Corporación de Ahorro y Crédito Fedepetrol (Corporation of Savings and Credit Fedepetrol)
Causa R	Causa Radical (Radical Cause)
CDN	Consejo Directivo Nacional (National Directory Council)
CEN	Comité Ejecutivo Nacional (National Executive Committee)
CGN	Consejo General Nacional (National General Council)
CGT	Confederación General de Trabajadores (General Confederation of Workers)
CLAT	Central Latinoamericana de Trabajadores (Latin American Workers Central)
Codesa	Confederación de Sindicatos Autónomos (Confederation of Autonomous Unions)
Copei	Comité de Organización Política Electoral Independiente (Committee of Independent Political Electoral Organization)
Coracrevi	Corporación de Ahorro y Crédito para la Vivienda (Corporation for Housing Savings and Credit)
CSU	Comité Sindical Unificado (Unified Union Committee)
CTV	Confederación de Trabajadores de Venezuela (Confederation of Workers of Venezuela)
CUTV	Central Unitaria de Trabajadores de Venezuela (United Center of Workers of Venezuela)
CVG	Corporación Venezolana de Guayana (Venezuelan Corporation of Guayana)

FCU	Federación de Centros Universitarios (Federation of University Centers)
FCV	Federación Campesina de Venezuela (Peasant Federation of Venezuela)
Fedecámaras	Federacíon de Cámaras de Industria y Comercio (Federation of Chambers of Industry and Commerce)
Fedepetrol	Federación de Trabajadores Petroleros (Federation of Petroleum Workers)
Fedetransporte	Federación de Trabajadores del Transporte (Federation of Transportation Workers)
Fetrahidro-carburos	Federación de Trabajadores de la Industria de Hidrocarburos (Federation of Workers of the Hydrocarbons Industry)
FTC	Frente de Trabajadores Copeyanos (Federation of *Copeyano* Workers)
FVM	Federación Venezolana de Maestros (Venezuelan Federation of Teachers)
IAN	Instituto Agrario Nacional (National Agrarian Institute)
ICFTU	International Confederation of Free Trade Unions
ILO	International Labor Organization
IMF	International Monetary Fund
Inaesin	Instituto Nacional de Altos Estudios Sindicales (National Institute of Higher Trade Union Studies)
IVSS	Instituto Venezolano de Seguro Social (Venezuelan Institute of Social Security)
MAS	Movimiento al Socialismo (Movement toward Socialism)
MEP	Movimiento Electoral del Pueblo (People's Electoral Movement)
MIR	Movimiento de Izquierda Revolucionaria (Movement of the Revolutionary Left)
ORIT	Organización Regional Interamericana de Trabajadores (Interamerican Regional Organization of Workers)
PCV	Partido Comunista de Venezuela (Communist party of Venezuela)
Pdvsa	Petróleos de Venezuela (Petroleum of Venezuela)
Sidor	Siderúrgica de Orinoco (Orinoco Steel Works)
SNTP	Sindicato Nacional de Trabajadores de la Prensa (National Union of Press Workers)
Sutiss	Sindicato Unico de Trabajadores de la Industria Siderúrgica (Single Union of Workers of the Steel Industry)
URD	Unión Republicana Democrática (Republican Democratic Union)
UTIT	Unión de Trabajadores de la Industria Textil (Union of Workers of the Textile Industry)
WFTU	World Federation of Trade Unions

Preface

Labor studies in Venezuela, in comparison to elsewhere in Latin America, are in an embryonic stage, despite the major role that trade unions have played since the outset of the nation's modern period in 1936. Reliable literature on the democratic years since 1958 is particularly scarce and focuses almost exclusively on the relations between the labor movement and political parties. Autobiographies of outstanding labor leaders are also notably absent, and the one lengthy account of an important trade unionist, which was based on interviews conducted and transcribed in the early 1980s, has not been published to date.[1] The labor press is highly deficient; most significant, national labor organizations have failed to develop mechanisms of distribution for their publications, which thus lack input from rank-and-file trade unionists.

Coverage in the mass media is mainly limited to the positions of worker representatives on political issues, particularly those related to political parties. This imbalance reflects the high degree of politicization of organized labor, as well as the inordinate importance that national labor leaders attach to a narrow range of labor concerns. They especially harp on government-decreed wage increases while inadvertently downplaying specific legal reforms and contractual benefits, which receive little airing at the national level. The failure of top labor leaders to defend forcefully a wide diversity of proposals was clearly demonstrated during the public debate over the new Labor Law, which was introduced in congress in 1985. While the business sector mounted a well-devised campaign in opposition to twenty-odd articles of major importance, trade union leaders announced their endorsement of the proposed law but refrained from pointing out shortcomings for fear that public criticism would only play into the hands of labor's adversaries.[2]

The main objective of this study is to present a balanced account of organized labor in order to fill various lacunae in the field. In addition to evaluating the relationships among unions, political parties, and the state, this book deals with a multiplicity of themes: organized labor's internal structure, its financial interests, its role in the international labor movement, its long-term strategy, the workers' struggle in important sectors, the objectives and application of the model of worker participation in decision making, the relationship between contractual benefits and labor legislation, and the role of the smaller confederations and independent federations in the labor movement. Information is derived mainly from in-depth interviews with important labor leaders, lawyers, and company spokesmen; nonpersonal archival material; and the press.

Over one hundred lengthy interviews were conducted for this study, of which forty-one were taped. Copies of the cassettes, consisting of forty-eight hours of interviews with leading trade unionists and several prominent labor lawyers, have been deposited in the Archivo de la Palabra (Oral History Department) of the Biblioteca Nacional, the Instituto Nacional de Altos Estudios Sindicales, and the Butler Library of Columbia University in New York. I believe that it was worth making the trade-off between quoting labor leaders in the text, on matters that receive little coverage in the media, and forfeiting information that they may have withheld as a result of the use of a cassette recorder. Certain questions relating to international affairs and internal party matters were not taped, and the interviewees were assured that their answers were strictly "off the record."

After considerable thought, I decided against complementing the institutional focus with a bottom-up history of the labor movement in which workers were "allowed to speak for themselves." Under certain circumstances, such a combined approach is viable, as Charles Bergquist has cogently argued.[3] In the case of Venezuela, however, the groundwork for a comprehensive history of organized labor has hardly been laid. The dual approach was unrealistic, given the vastness of the terrain that needed to be covered and the space limitations of a single-volume work. The richness of the untapped primary sources that were used was another reason to concentrate on institutional history. It is my hope that some of the questions and conclusions formulated in this volume will be useful to researchers who employ a nonelitist approach to examining issues related to gender, race, rural origins, and professional formation, to name but a few of the avenues of inquiry that scholars need to pursue in depth.

Having worked on this study for five years, I naturally have numerous people and institutions to thank for their support. The Howard Heinz Endowment and the Consejo de Investigación of the Universidad de Oriente (UDO) provided stipends that covered my travel expenses. I would especially like to extend my gratitude to Lucas Alvarez Martínez, coordinator of the Comisión de Investigación of the UDO in Anzoátegui, for the interest he took in my research. It would be dishonest to exclude mention of my students in the seminar "Sindicalismo y Fuerza Laboral," which I have taught for five semesters at the UDO. The opportunity to discuss labor-related themes in class and respond to provocative questions and comments from students helped to clarify issues in my own mind and made the task of writing all the easier. In addition, some of the information gathered by my students and the ideas they presented in class proved useful.

I also would like to express my thanks to those who facilitated my access to, and daily work in, several archives in Caracas. The sixteen volumes of material on the Venezuelan labor movement, located in the archive of the workshop Movimiento Obrero Latinoamericano (MOLA), were an invaluable source. Although a large number of scholars (myself included) belong to MOLA, the moving force behind this project was Dick Parker of the Universidad Central de Venezuela (UCV). In 1986 the director of the Centro de Estudios del Desarrollo, Heinz Rudolf Sonntag, gave me permission to read the numerous transcribed interviews—most of them containing over one hundred pages—that were conducted with leading Venezuelan figures in the early 1960s as part of the study *Conflictos y consenso*. This material, which at the time was the source of considerable controversy,[4] is not open to the general public. The archival staff of the state oil company Petróleos de Venezuela was extremely helpful in showing me formerly classified material related to industrial relations prior to the nationalization of the industry in 1976.

Needless to say, I am grateful to the approximately one hundred labor leaders I interviewed in various parts of the country. Several, in particular, were unstinting in their efforts to provide me with the information I was seeking: Pedro Méndez of the oil workers' federation (Fedepetrol); Arturo Tremont, formerly of the National Committee of the metal workers' federation (Fetrametal) and president of the Frente de Trabajadores of the Movimiento al Socialismo; Johnny Díaz Apitz, trade union undersecretary of the Frente de Trabajadores Copeyanos; and Rafael Castañeda of the National Committee of the Confederación de Trabajadores de Venezuela. I also benefited from the opportunity to participate in the series of roundtable discussions in 1991, organized by the Office of International Relations of the Labor Ministry, that were designed to facilitate the preparation of a report on labor relations in Venezuela undertaken by the International Labor Organization. Finally, Susan Berglund of the history department of the UCV showed utmost care in reading each chapter and providing useful suggestions, criticisms, and comments on both style and content.

It seems appropriate to end this study in 1991, because on May 1 of that year the new Labor Law went into effect. The law substantially alters the rules of the game for trade unions, starting with a provision that grants them the right to organize at the national level. Other unprecedented events in the recent past—not the least of which was the election of the former president of the steel workers to the governorship of the state of Bolívar—clearly indicate that the early 1990s mark the onset of a new era for organized labor. The study of the period since 1958 thus puts in relief the changes that are currently taking place, as well as the challenges that the labor movement will face in future years.

Notes

1. Carlos Arturo Pardo was interviewed by Rafael Dum in Caracas prior to the former's death in October 1982.

2. Antonio Rios, press conference, May 6, 1989, Barcelona.

3. Charles Bergquist also argues, however, that "an edifice of political, economic, and 'old' social and cultural history" is a prerequisite for creative new labor history. "Latin American Labour History in Comparative Perspective: Notes on the Insidiousness of Cultural Imperialism," *Labour/Le Travail* 25 (Spring 1990): 193–94. See also idem, "What Is Being Done? Some Recent Studies on the Urban Working Class and Organized Labor in Latin America," *Latin American Research Review* 16, no. 2 (1981): 203–23.

4. Rodolfo Quintero and Orlando Araujo, "Interviene la C.I.A. en las investigaciones sociológicas que se realizan en Venezuela?" *Nuestra Economía* (Caracas) 5 (1968): 33–40.

Introduction

The Venezuelan labor movement has played a central role in the construction and consolidation of the democratic system since the outset of modernization in 1936, and particularly in the recent democratic period beginning in 1958. The political strike has been a potent weapon in the struggle. An oil workers' strike in May 1950 shook the regime, whose strongman was Lt. Col. Marcos Pérez Jiménez, and a general strike on January 21, 1958, helped topple it. Subsequent work stoppages were effective in defending the nation's fledgling democracy. During the critical months after January 1958, labor leaders were more persistent than politicians in promoting unity of all organizations and individuals opposed to a return to military rule. This position was essential to the preservation of the new political system.

The protracted attempts to establish democracy were not without a high quota of personal sacrifice. Virtually all top labor leaders were persecuted during the repressive years immediately after 1936, and even more so during the military dictatorship from 1948 to 1958 in the form of imprisonment or exile. One of the outstanding martyrs of the latter period was the workers' leader Luis Hurtado, who "disappeared."

Since 1958 organized labor's restraint has been seen as a major factor contributing to the stability of the democratic system. During the 1960s and 1970s a relatively low level of strike activity gave the Venezuelan military little motive or justification to step into the political scene. In contrast, military coups quenched sharp class conflict in one Latin American country after another during these years. Venezuela was one of the few nations on the continent exempt from widespread disturbances and frequent general strikes in the face of the economic crisis of the 1980s, at least until the latter part of the decade. When the Venezuelan labor movement called a general strike on May 18, 1989, one of its main declared objectives was to counter rumors of an imminent military coup.

This historical behavior has led social scientists to view Venezuela—its labor movement, its other institutions, and its polity in general—as fundamentally different from the rest of Latin America. *Venezuelan exceptionalism* postulates that modern Venezuela has been characterized by relative stability, low levels of political violence, the absence of internecine social conflict, and noninterventionist armed forces. Some writers attribute these propitious traits to the nation's status as an oil exporter, whereas others emphasize statecraft and the leadership skills of the two main establishment parties, Acción Democrática (AD) and the social Christian Copei.

Many scholars argue that oil's displacement of coffee and cacao as Venezuela's principal export products shaped the nation's social and political structure and favored harmony over confrontation. The oligarchy was weakened by the internal migration from rural areas generated by oil production revenue. The concomitant depreciation of land value mitigated the conflict between peasants and landholders that produced extended bloody clashes in Mexico, Bolivia, Colombia, and elsewhere. Export industry workers (the main sector influencing the workers' movement in all Latin American nations at the time of industrialization) lacked an anticapitalist mentality due to oil's stability in the international market, which ensured against sharp cutbacks in the work force and downward pressure on wages. The oil workers were also small in numbers and removed from urban centers, thus further reducing the potential for a strong worker challenge to the existing system.

The middle sector grew as a result of the ample opportunities provided by both the oil enclaves and the government bureaucracy, enlarged by the nation's substantial oil revenue. Middle-class leaders took the initiative in creating multiclass parties in the form of AD and Copei, both of which helped to contain and channel social discontent. This model became dominant because the oligarchy, peasantry, and working class lacked cohesion and were not locked in hardened struggles that would have induced them to form their own parties. Government revenue derived from oil helped soften the impact of other phenomena, such as urbanization and nationalization, that produced sharp conflict elsewhere in Latin America. In short, economic and political stability, interclass alliances, and abundant resources contributed to Venezuela's unique development at least as far back as 1958.[1]

Other scholars question the assumption of the "staple" theorists regarding the primacy of oil, but they agree that Venezuela's salient political features are qualitatively different from its continental neighbors. They give democratic leaders credit for learning from the mistakes of the 1945–1948 period of AD rule, which was characterized by sectarianism, and for uniting around interparty pacts that excluded the Communist party. Their categorization of leadership as a major independent variable is demonstrated by Diego Abente's statement that "the Venezuelan political system . . . has nothing inherently stable except its leadership's ability and will to preserve it." Political parties, which are frequently criticized for overstepping their natural boundaries and dominating civil society, are lauded by these writers for playing a central role in maintaining stability. Daniel Levine attributes political party hegemony to the power vacuum created by the extreme debilitation of the oligarchy during the civil wars of the nineteenth century and the dislocations generated by the oil industry in the early part of the twentieth. Nevertheless, he adds that Venezuela's "success" is primarily a tribute to the acumen of its leaders and suggests that, in this respect, the nation's political processes are more comparable to Europe's than Latin America's.[2]

Venezuelan exceptionalists have been particularly concerned with the role of business interests and labor. The government is seen as enjoying a relative autonomy vis-à-vis powerful economic interests and, in particular, the nation's main business organization, Fedecámaras. One political scientist, René Salgado, has actually denied that Fedecámaras exerts a strong influence on public decision making, at least since the early 1970s. Salgado maintains that the windfall in oil revenue in the 1970s insulated the state from business pressure, especially after 1976 when the nationalization of the petroleum industry provided the government with financial independence. He also argues that prohibition on the reelection of the nation's president upon expiration of his period enhances his imperviousness to lobbying efforts.[3] Other scholars point to Fedecámaras's weakness as an interest articulator, as demonstrated by its tendency to react vociferously against measures that already have been proposed rather than putting forward its own initiatives.

Moisés Naim wrote that "the omnipotence that some critics assign to the private sector and that some businessmen try systematically to project vanishes in the light of its dependence on the public sector."[4] Ironically, Naim's assertion was confirmed by a major scandal that broke out in 1989 when he was minister of development. The illegal sale of preferential dollars by the government agency Recadi led to judicial actions against numerous top businessmen, while prominent officials of the previous administration who also were implicated were left untouched until, subsequently, public pressure mounted in favor of their conviction.[5]

The overwhelming influence of AD and Copei in the Confederación de Trabajadores de Venezuela (CTV), the nation's main labor confederation, over an extended period sets Venezuela apart from most other Latin American nations where leftists have successfully vied for control of organized labor. Furthermore, the AD-dominated CTV has frequently domesticated radical labor movements and leaders by absorbing them, leading some analysts to praise the confederation for its ideological pluralism. In contrast, in Peru, Colombia, and other countries where nonleftists have at one point enjoyed considerable worker backing, there are two or more major confederations, each one clearly identified with a particular ideology or political party.

The ties between political parties and organized labor, while strong throughout the continent, are particularly tenacious in Venezuela where independent trade unionists have been absent from the leadership of traditional sectors of the working class. AD labor leaders have played a central role in internal party affairs—perhaps being equaled only by the *peronistas* in Argentina—thus fortifying the union-party nexus. The extreme centralism that characterizes Venezuelan political parties, and AD in particular, also militates against trade union autonomy. According to various political scientists, labor weakness is both a cause and effect of party domination. On the one hand, the atomization of the labor movement in the form of *sindicatos de empresa* (plant unions) facilitates party control. On the other hand, confidence in the party's ability to deliver the goods discourages labor leaders from pursuing a strategy of worker mobilization.[6] The passivity of the labor movement and the co-optation of radicals have often been attributed to the material well-being and resources derived from oil. Labor leaders and even leftists during the 1970s and early 1980s declared that class confrontation was not the Venezuelan way, since general prosperity was conducive to consensus and harmony. The president of the CTV pointed out that, prior to the economic crisis of the late 1980s, impending strikes were frequently averted by the intervention of the Finance Ministry, which provided subsidies to companies to help pay wage hikes demanded by the unions.[7]

Exceptionalism is further evident in the Venezuelans' class identification and behavior, both of which differ markedly from other developing societies. For instance, no correlation exists between electoral participation and social classes—at least none existed in the early 1970s at the time of the survey analyzed by Enrique Baloyra and John Martz in their *Political Attitudes in Venezuela*. The poll also showed that as many as 57 percent of Venezuelans considered themselves middle class and only 4 percent working class, thereby demonstrating that workers do not feel "trapped in their own class," a point that is corroborated by other surveys.[8]

Historically, low levels of social conflict and relative economic and political stability are related to other national characteristics that strengthen the plausibility of the exceptionalism thesis. Thus, for instance, the high degree of racial intermixture, which has reduced racist attitudes to a minimum, helps explain the absence of intense ongoing confrontations.[9] For its part, stability is responsible for the small number of Venezuelans who emigrate.

Venezuelan exceptionalism is more than just an abstract theory. The notion that their country is different from its neighbors pervades the general attitudes of Venezuelans and even influences government policy. When the problem of the foreign debt shook Latin America in the 1980s, for instance, the Venezuelan government declared itself in favor of a go-it-alone approach. Official spokesmen pointed out that close association with other debtor nations whose economic prospects were less auspicious would tarnish Venezuela's image in the international banking community and discourage new loans.[10] The exceptionalism thesis also manifests itself in the widespread belief that the Venezuelan military is radically different from its counterparts elsewhere in Latin America as a result of the democratic commitment and institutionalist orientation of its officers.[11]

This study examines the applicability of the exceptionalism thesis to the Venezuelan labor movement. The book's central argument is that, while grounded on solid historical evidence, Venezuelan exceptionalism has led both scholars and trade unionists to misleading conclusions. Many of them exaggerate the degree of internal cohesion of the labor movement and fail to probe beyond stated goals and appearances. Furthermore, generalizations about the historical behavior of the working class are made on the basis of trends that are largely due to transitory factors.

Most important, the exceptionalism thesis has proved to be a poor predictor of the political problems and social turmoil that have confronted the nation in the context of the severe economic crisis of the late 1980s and early 1990s. Implicit in the writings of the exceptionalists is the notion that the factors that contributed to the nation's stability were ongoing and would thus continue to play an important role in the face of acute challenges besetting the nation. Given oil's unique qualities as a third-world export commodity, Venezuela should be less subject to destabilization in the course of a continental or worldwide economic recession than its neighbors. Likewise, it is assumed that Venezuelan political culture, which was shaped by the learning experience of the *trienio* period (1945–1948), insulates the nation from political strife. These explanations provide little help in understanding the daily and often violent expressions of discontent by students, the urban poor, and certain sectors of organized labor, as well as the restlessness in the armed forces in recent years.

The book's nine chapters deal with different aspects of the exceptionalism thesis. The first three chapters trace the chronological development of the labor movement. The avoidance of sharp labor conflict and the CTV's maintenance of unity, once the leftists were purged from the confederation in 1961, are seen as largely the outcome of two circumstantial events: the repression and isolation of the Left as a result of the guerrilla struggle in the 1960s and the prosperity induced by oil price hikes in the 1970s.

The first three chapters also describe economic trends since 1958. Chapter 1 covers the provisional presidency of Admiral Wolfgang Larrazábal in 1958 and the constitutional rule of AD's Rómulo Betancourt (1959–1963); both regimes were characterized by economic recession and acute social and political conflict. Chapter 2 takes in the administrations of Raúl Leoni of AD (1964–1969), Rafael Caldera of Copei (1969–1974), and Carlos Andrés Pérez of AD (1974–1979), which were initially years of economic recovery and then, after 1973, of rapid growth and prosperity. Chapter 3 encompasses the terms of Luis Herrera Campíns of Copei (1979–

1984), Jaime Lusinchi of AD (1984–1989), and Carlos Andrés Pérez (1989–), a period of economic contraction and crisis.

Chapter 4 examines distorted self-perceptions influenced by exceptionalism that are manifested in the way the AD labor leaders who control the CTV view labor's historical role and their relations with the party as well as with the rest of organized labor. The gap between the image that the CTV attempts to project and its real motives is also discussed in Chapter 5 on ideological and international linkages. Here, it is argued that the CTV's efforts to promote itself on the international stage are designed, at least in part, to enhance the confederation's prestige, which is parlayed into concrete benefits and favors. Chapter 6 attempts to determine the veracity of the widely held view (which also bears the mark of exceptionalism) that the most important sector of the working class, the oil workers, abandoned its militant tradition after 1958 in exchange for extraordinary material benefits. The major exceptions to generalizations regarding labor's passive behavior are the combative steel and textile workers' movements explored in Chapter 7. The gulf between unstated and overt goals is again discussed in Chapter 8, which focuses on the CTV's financial investments and the model that it advocates of worker participation in company decision making. A similar differentiation between rhetorical and authentic objectives is made in Chapter 9, which deals with the labor movement's positions on the most controversial aspects of the nation's labor legislation.

The CTV's favorable image and prestige are also the product of the experiences of hardened struggle and self-sacrifice of its main leaders prior to 1958. Most of them, including those who would subsequently become CTV presidents, emerged following the long-standing dictatorship of Juan Vicente Gómez (1908–1935). They participated in organized labor and politics during the three governments that promoted a gradual liberalization of the political system: Eleazar López Contreras (1936–1941), Isaías Medina Angarita (1941–1945), and the AD rule from 1945 to 1948. They also played an important role in the resistance to the military regime that governed between 1948 and 1958.

The CTV presidents during the first three decades of the modern democratic period belonged to this "old school" of seasoned trade unionists. Their training was in traditional industries, and they were thus not ideally suited to attract professional and service industry workers to the labor movement. The first three chapters trace their administrations.

Jose González Navarro, who was named president of the CTV in 1959, was a founder of the shoe workers' movement in 1936. As president of the workers' federation of the Federal District, he attempted to foment general resistance to the November 1948 military coup. González Navarro joined the left-leaning Movimiento Electoral del Pueblo (MEP) in 1967, a split off from AD, and consequently was not reelected at the CTV's congress in 1970. He was replaced by Francisco Olivo, a pioneer of the woodworkers' movement who claimed to have been influenced by the anarcho-syndicalist thinking of his Spanish-born kin. Following his death in 1974, Olivo was succeeded by José Vargas, who had belonged to the cigar workers' union and served after 1945 as secretary of grievances of the workers' federation of the Federal District. Vargas was wounded in an encounter with the special police force during the Pérez Jiménez dictatorship, after which he joined González Navarro and Olivo in the publication of *C.T.V.* in Mexico. Vargas also died in office in 1983 and was replaced by Juan José Delpino, who had played a leadership role in the 1950 oil workers' strike and subsequently served seven years in prison. Unlike Olivo and Vargas, Delpino maintained an extremely critical stand toward AD governments and resigned in 1989 for reasons that were never clarified. All four CTV presidents had joined AD at the time of its founding in 1941 and occupied important positions within the party while also serving in the national congress.

AD's historical dominance in the CTV is illustrated in Table 1. In seven of the nine congresses since the CTV's founding in 1947, AD has had a majority of delegates. Only from 1967 to 1970 was the party's control placed in doubt as a result of the MEP division. Copei, for the most part, has maintained the number-two position, holding between 14 and 22 percent of the delegate strength since the CTV's 1964 congress. Following the erosion of MEP's original influence (including the return of González Navarro and Delpino to AD), the party settled into third place. Nevertheless, these statistics regarding party influence are misleading, since AD's strength is greatest in predominately rural states. The Left has enjoyed greater worker backing in strategic industrial sectors than its meager representation in the confederation's leadership would indicate. Furthermore, over the past two decades, small radical leftist parties (such as those that control the steel and textile workers' unions discussed in Chapter 7) have made important inroads. In some cases, these smaller parties have advanced at the expense of the more moderate MEP, as has happened in the oil industry in recent years. The three other Venezuelan labor confederations controlled by Copei and the PCV are discussed in Chapter 4. Although their worker following is limited, they have influenced the CTV's positions in certain respects.

Two opposite viewpoints attempt to explain the role that the CTV leadership plays in the context of the political and economic crisis of the early 1990s. Social democratic writers assign AD labor leaders a vanguard status in their own party, and the CTV a similar position in society as a whole due to its advocacy of far-reaching socioeconomic models and its resistance to the government's neoliberal policies. At the opposite extreme, members of the far left depict the CTV as unresponsive to its constituency and undemocratic.[12] An accurate evaluation of these antithetical positions requires more than just an overview of recent events or an analysis of stated objectives. On the contrary, it is necessary to look at the strategy that the CTV has implemented to achieve long-term goals, its relations with political parties and the state, its response to the transformations in the work force and the economy, and its participation in labor struggles since 1958. The pages that follow examine the labor movement from this perspective.

Notes

1. Terry Lynn Karl, "Petroleum and Political Pacts: The Transition to Democracy in Venezuela," *Latin American Research Review* 22, no. 1 (1987): 63–94; Charles Bergquist, *Labor in Latin America: Comparative Essays on Chile, Argentina, Venezuela, and Colombia* (Stanford: Stanford University Press, 1986), pp. 206, 273; Moisés Naim and Ramón Piñango, "El caso Venezuela: una ilusión de armonía," in *El caso Venezuela: una ilusión de armonía*, 3d ed., ed. Moisés Naim and Ramón Piñango (Caracas: Ediciones IEASA, 1986), p. 554.
2. Diego Abente, "Politics and Policies: The Limits of the Venezuelan Consociational Regime," in *Democracy in Latin America: Colombia and Venezuela*, ed. Donald L. Herman (New York: Praeger, 1988), pp. 138, 149; Daniel H. Levine, "Venezuela since 1958: The Consolidation of Democratic Politics," in *The Breakdown of Democratic Regimes: Latin America*, ed. Juan J. Linz and Alfred Stepan (Baltimore: Johns Hopkins University Press, 1978), pp. 102, 105; idem, "Venezuela: The Nature, Sources, and Future Prospects of Democracy," in *Democracy in Developing Countries: Latin America*, ed. Larry Diamond, Juan J. Linz, and Seymour Martin Lipset (Boulder: Lynne Rienner Publishers, 1989), pp. 266, 281; Luis J. Oropeza, *Tutelary Pluralism: A Critical Approach to Venezuelan Democracy* (Cambridge, MA: Harvard University Press, 1983), pp. 6–17.
3. René Salgado, "Economic Pressure Groups and Policy-Making in Venezuela: The Case of FEDECAMARAS Reconsidered," *Latin American Research Review* 22, no. 3 (1987): 91–105.
4. Moisés Naim, "La empresa privada en Venezuela: Qué pasa cuando se crece en medio de la riqueza y la confusión?" in *El caso Venezuela*, p. 177. See also José Antonio Gil Yepes, *The Challenge of Venezuelan Democracy* (New Brunswick, NJ: Transaction Books, 1981), chap. 7. Samuel Moncada discusses the strategy designed by Fedecámaras to overcome business weakness vis-à-vis the state during the 1945–1948 period. See idem, *Los huevos de la serpiente: Fedecámaras por dentro* (Caracas: Alianza Gráfica, 1985), pp. 122, 278.
5. *New York Times*, August 16, 1989, pp. D-1, D-5; *Wall Street Journal*, August 24, 1989, pp. A1, A6.
6. Humberto Njaim, "Acceso y exclusión en el sistema político venezolano," in *Sistemas electorales, acceso al sistema político y sistema de partidos*, 7 vols. (Caracas: Consejo Supremo Electoral, 1987), 3:119–20; Luis Salamanca, "La incorporación de la Confederación de Trabajadores de Venezuela al sistema político venezolano, 1958–1980" ([unpublished paper] Instituto de Estudios Políticos, UCV, 1988), p. 184.
7. Juan José Delpino, interviewed by Marcel Granier, TV Channel "Radio Caracas," May 15, 1989; Carlos Eduardo Febres, "El movimiento sindical: actor social o gestor institucional?" in *El caso Venezuela*, p. 297.

8. Enrique A. Baloyra and John D. Martz, *Political Attitudes in Venezuela: Societal Cleavages and Political Opinion* (Austin: University of Texas Press, 1979), pp. 14, 65, 224; Kenneth M. Coleman and Charles L. Davis, "Diffuse Support in Venezuela and Mexico" (unpublished manuscript, May 1983), chap. 4: 37.

9. Scholars and Venezuelans in general have often denied the prevalence of racist attitudes. See Winthrop R. Wright, *Café con Leche: Race, Class and National Image in Venezuela* (Austin: University of Texas Press, 1990).

10. Steve Ellner, "Venezuela: No Exception," *NACLA: Report on the Americas* 23, no. 1 (May 1989): 9.

11. The view that Venezuela was largely exempt from the social and political disruptions that afflicted other Latin American nations was internalized in the armed forces. The military was ill prepared for the disturbances that convulsed the nation during the week of February 27, 1989, and its clumsy response resulted in the death of hundreds, if not thousands, of innocent bystanders. Subsequently, top officers failed to attach sufficient importance to intelligence reports regarding conspiratorial activity in the army, which found expression in an attempted coup on February 4, 1992. The social makeup of the Venezuelan armed forces is markedly different from that of its neighbors. Modest entrance requirements, such as a mere high school diploma, have allowed a large number of members of the lower-middle class (although not the marginal class) to enter the ranks of the officer corps. Nevertheless, as is the case of the exceptionalism thesis in general, contrasts with the military in the rest of the continent are sometimes overdrawn. Thus, for instance, an article in the Spanish edition of *Military Review* written by political scientist Francisco Rodríguez Landaeta, professor at the Altos Estudios de las Fuerzas Armadas, claimed that military exchange programs with other Latin American armed forces, which in general have a "low level of political culture," contaminated Venezuelan officers with authoritarian ideas to which they would otherwise have been impervious. See "Con excepción de Venezuela, militares latinoamericanos tienen poca cultura política," *El Nacional*, February 10, 1992, p. A-2; and Teodoro Petkoff, "Fuerzas Armadas: economía y política," *El Ojo del Huracán* 9–10 (November 1991–February 1992): 14–15.

12. These two viewpoints are discussed in Steve Ellner, "Organized Labor's Political Influence and Party Ties in Venezuela: Acción Democrática and Its Labor Leadership," *Journal of Interamerican Studies and World Affairs* 31, no. 4 (1989): 115.

1 From Labor Consolidation and Unity to Fragmentation, 1958–1963

The Formative Years of Organized Labor

The twenty-seven-year regime of Juan Vicente Gómez in the early part of the century was long enough, and the government ruthless enough, to eradicate the traditional opposition, which was grouped around regional caudillos and other conservative figures. When Gómez passed away in 1935, the field was wide open for a new breed of young political leaders who were ideologically committed and who belonged to the emerging middle sectors and working class. These activists exhibited a sense of boldness by establishing political parties, at a time when the very word had radical implications because it implied internecine conflict and organized opposition.

The two governments that ruled Venezuela for the next ten years were headed by generals who had formerly sworn loyalty to Gómez and retained many of the traditional attitudes and values of that era. Not only did these governments fail to open regular channels of participation for organized labor, but also they forced labor leaders to conceal their political commitments and pretend to be "apolitical" in accordance with legal requirements. Nevertheless, the governments promoted modernization and guided Venezuela through a transition that included the opening up of democratic liberties and practices. Furthermore, the Labor Law of 1936 legalized unions, without tying them to a corporatist structure of tight government control. One recent study characterizes the ten-year period as "incorporationist" on the basis of the welfare provisions and the mechanisms for resolution of labor disputes created by the state.[1]

By 1944–45, AD had gained control of the labor movement from the Communist party (PCV). AD was a typical Latin American populist party in that it defended a radical program of income redistribution, its long-term goals were not clearly defined, and it based its popular appeal to a considerable degree on the charismatic qualities of its *jefe máximo*, Rómulo Betancourt. Perhaps even more so than other Latin American populists, AD leaders promoted the belief that the nation's destiny was closely tied to the party, and instilled in their followers a sectarianism that generated interparty rivalry at all levels. In organized labor, AD coined the phrase "to divide is to locate," which meant that the creation of parallel unions identified with individual parties should be encouraged in order to give workers the opportunity to choose between contrasting ideologies. This view led to the splintering of the labor movement after 1944 and was symptomatic of the close ties between unions and parties that have always characterized organized labor in Venezuela.

AD's impatience with the gradual liberalization process after 1936 led it to participate with junior military officers in a successful coup on October 18, 1945. During the *trienio* of 1945 to 1948, AD was able to extend its support among popular sectors and gain absolute control of the worker, peasant, and student movements. AD's self-assurance as a result of its position in power and the massiveness of its following led it to spurn formal understandings—both with the PCV, to its left, and Copei, to its right— throughout most of the *trienio*. Furthermore, government officials and AD national leaders failed to restrain rank-and-file members who participated in street clashes with Copei militants, thus hardening the opposition of the latter party. The tenseness of interparty relations contributed to the coup against the AD government on November 24, 1948, which ushered in nine years of military rule.

The trauma of persecution and exile after 1948 convinced leaders of all four political parties (AD, the PCV, Copei, and Unión Republicana Democrática—URD) to put aside differences and form a united front against the dictatorship. Scholars emphasize the importance of the *trienio* as a learning experience that convinced politicians to avoid sectarianism and political intransigence. However, the same conclusion was reached by labor leaders who, during the years immediately before and after the overthrow of Marcos Pérez Jiménez, achieved even more solid forms of unity.

By the 1960s economic growth and industrialization had thoroughly transformed the working class, which, outside of the oil industry, had been predominately artisan three decades before. Economists and historians differ as to which government deserves credit for import substitution: that of the early 1940s, which encouraged national production in order to alleviate the scarcities brought on by World War II; the *trienio*, which authorized credit to promote economic expansion; Pérez Jiménez, who ensured stability and a friendly climate for foreign capital; or the post-1958 AD administrations, which implemented a policy of high tariffs in certain sectors.[2] Undoubtedly, the process was gradual and all four regimes contributed to it in different ways. In any case, the changes in the economy and the makeup of the work force convinced most labor leaders of the need to modernize the structure of the labor movement, which was viewed as excessively decentralized and lacking technical capacity.

The Role of Labor in the Struggle against Pérez Jiménez

In the years immediately following the overthrow of President Rómulo Gallegos in November 1948, the proscribed AD played a leading role in the struggle against the military regime. Much of the hopes of AD leaders centered on the oil workers' movement in the state of Zulia and the Oriente region. Not only did the Venezuelan economy revolve around petroleum production, but also the oil workers had always constituted a vanguard in organized labor. The legacy of the oil workers' strike of 1936, which galvanized nationalist sentiment and united the entire nation, encouraged resistance leaders to look to the petroleum industry.

On May 3, 1950, a strike broke out in the states of Zulia and Anzoátegui, led by prominent members of the aboveground PCV and middle-level AD labor leaders. The conflict was sparked by the refusal of the companies to negotiate a wage readjustment in the second year of the 1948 oil workers' contract, as was allowed for in that agreement. Despite the bread-and-butter demands that were put forward, the strike immediately assumed insurrectional overtones. The government reacted by laying siege to the workers' quarters in an effort to starve the workers into submission. Although the strikers returned to work after ten days without having achieved their objectives, the struggle set a precedent for unity that would be embodied in interparty agreements in the final years of the dictatorship.[3]

Another important confrontation, which occurred in the town of Turén in the state of Portuguesa, was organized by AD in coordination with a revolt at the air force base of Boca del Rio in September 1952. The rebels consisted mostly of peasants who were incensed at the land encroachment of a local hacendado, himself a military officer, and the forceful conditions that he imposed on his workers. After the insurgents seized the local police headquarters and a National Guard post, the rebellion was ruthlessly put down. The incident is significant because, unlike in other Latin American countries, the Venezuelan rural population does not have a tradition in this century of resorting to arms.[4]

The failure of the oil workers' strike and of subsequent military plots, the assassination of the maximum leader of the AD underground, and the capture and death of his successor all contributed to the demoralization of the movement against the dictatorship. The lull between 1953 and 1956 encouraged the regime to intensify its efforts to construct its own labor movement, which in 1956 found expression in the Confederación Nacional de Trabajadores (CNT). In an additional attempt to legitimize its rule, the regime granted important concessions to the popular classes, specifically the amplification of social security benefits and, of greater significance, the construction of low-income housing (*superbloques*), which helped eradicate the shantytowns in Caracas and elsewhere. Various historians who are not particularly sympathetic to Pérez Jiménez have pointed in recent years to the populist and nationalistic dimensions of his rule in an effort to explain the relative passivity of the working class during this period.[5]

By 1956 the four principal parties in Venezuela—AD, the PCV, Copei, and URD—put aside their mutual animosities. In June of the following year, they formed a united front that was embodied in the clandestine Junta Patriótica. Several meetings were held in the house of retired military officer Gen. Rafael Arráez Morles in the district of El Paraiso in Caracas. The junta created the Workers Committee, which consisted of four important leaders: Dagoberto González (Copei), Eloy Torres (PCV), Américo Chacón (AD), and Vicente Piñate (URD). The committee published a manifesto that demanded the abolition of the CNT, the removal of the minister of labor, and the enforcement of the Labor Law.

In the weeks following an abortive military uprising on January 1, 1958, resistance to the dictatorship intensified. Opposition leaders addressed multitudes in slum neighborhoods and outside factory gates, and police were attacked in hit-and-run operations. Several newspaper strikes were organized by the junta in conjunction with the Sindicato Nacional de Trabajadores de la Prensa (SNTP), the Venezuelan Linotypist Association, and the Union of Workers of the Graphic Arts, which were among the few legal labor organizations not controlled by *perezjimenistas* (Pérez Jiménez's followers). A general strike call issued by the junta on January 21 was widely obeyed in Caracas and elsewhere. Several marches originating from distinct parts of Caracas converged on the center of the city.

The strike resulted in hundreds of casualties but failed to spur discontented military officers to action. As a result, the junta considered ending the work stoppage, but finally decided to extend it for several days, while ruling out an indefinite strike. On the evening of January 22, Pérez Jiménez prepared a speech in which he was to announce the launching of a spectacular public works program, but after being informed of the defection of several of his top loyal generals to the side of the military conspirators, he decided to flee the country.

The role of labor and other sectors of the population in the overthrow of the dictatorship has been the source of considerable debate. The fact that Pérez Jiménez decided to leave Venezuela only after learning of the extent of the conspiratorial movement within the armed forces lends itself to the thesis that January 23 was predominately a military affair. Many accounts of the events leading up to January 23, on the other hand, emphasize the diversity of the sectors that participated in one form or another in the struggle against Pérez Jiménez.[6]

Several leftist writers accept this balanced view and maintain that the workers failed to play the central role that Marxist theory assigns them.

They point out that the Workers Committee was in contact with business representatives, who supported the general strike and opposed the dictatorship for reasons of their own. Furthermore, the general strike was called surprisingly late in the struggle against Pérez Jiménez and only after other sectors such as the Church, university students, the U.S. embassy, and a significant part of the military had clearly distanced themselves from the regime.[7] One prominent leftist who participated in the underground states that the resistance to the dictatorship met with general apathy in important workplaces targeted by the insurgents.[8] Those who downplay the decisiveness of worker opposition are in general agreement with the thesis that the relative passivity of the working class in recent history is due to Venezuela's privileged status as an oil exporter, which has endowed the nation with a relative degree of prosperity and economic and political stability.[9]

1958 and the Reemergence of Nonofficial Labor Unions

Immediately following the overthrow of Pérez Jiménez, the Workers Committee transformed itself into the Comité Sindical Unificado (CSU). Its aim was to reestablish the CTV, which had been dissolved by the dictatorship nine years earlier. The CSU played a crucial role in defending the Junta Militar headed by Admiral Wolfgang Larrazábal, which ruled Venezuela until the national elections in December 1958. For one week following the flight of Pérez Jiménez, the labor movement took over civic responsibilities from the police force, which was completely absent from the streets of Caracas. During coup attempts in July and September, the CSU called general strikes. Bus drivers used their vehicles to block roads in a strategic area of the capital in order to obstruct military movements. In one document the CSU promised to lift the strike only after the Junta Militar had "taken all the measures it can to put down the conspiracy once and for all and inform the general public of the names of the officers . . . as well as the civilian elements in and out of the government who are plotting against democracy."[10] At a mass rally at the time of the July military threat, the president of the construction workers' union, Juan Herrera, announced labor's willingness to take up arms to defend the nation's nascent democracy. Herrera and other AD labor leaders were intent on avoiding a repetition of November 1948 when AD balked at arming the workers in the face of military threats.[11]

Party and labor leaders backed by the general populace, which took to the streets of the capital, successfully demanded the exclusion of two *perezjimenista* officers from the junta and the incorporation of civilians. The removal of *perezjimenistas* and other unpopular persons from positions of authority became a general rallying cry that was reflected in demands put forward by organized labor. The CSU called for the expulsion of *perezjimenistas* from labor unions and the complete reorganization of the Labor Ministry in order to dismiss proemployer functionaries who sympathized with the former regime.[12] In addition, the CSU complained of certain government officials who favored granting legal status to political organizations recently formed by *perezjimenistas*, including one called the Unión Cívica Electoral led by trade union agents of the previous dictatorship.[13]

Union leaders were generally pleased by the willingness of Larrazábal and his advisers to discuss labor problems personally with them. Not only did the government accept the reconstitution of hundreds of labor organizations proscribed under the Pérez Jiménez regime, but also their property, which had been confiscated during the dictatorship, was returned. In addition, Larrazábal reestablished relations with the International Labor Organization (ILO), which had been severed by Pérez Jiménez due to its attempt to investigate freedom of organization in Venezuela.

At the urging of the government the CSU and the business organization Fedecámaras drew up the Pacto de Avenimiento Obrero Patronal in April 1958. Designed to reduce labor conflicts for the sake of easing the transition to democracy, the pact called for the creation of labor-management commissions to settle industrial disputes and for the signing of industrywide contracts to standardize working conditions and benefits. In subscribing to the pact, business representatives committed themselves to avoiding layoffs when possible and recognizing the right of workers to organize unions. The CSU considered the possibility of accepting the postponement of new labor contracts, but this provision was not included in the final document.

The spirit of the pact reflected the widespread feeling among labor and political leaders—including those belonging to the PCV and the Junta Patriótica—that social harmony was a sine qua non for the survival of the nation's fledgling democracy.[14] Even the PCV accepted the need for labor to moderate its demands in order to commit business interests to the defense of the new regime. In the early months of 1958, several labor conflicts among textile workers, iron workers in the Guayana region, and automobile workers at a General Motors plant in Caracas threatened to spill over to other sectors as a result of the pent-up demands accumulated in the course of the nine-year dictatorship. Nevertheless, by the end of the year the minister of labor announced that there had been only fifteen strikes in the course of 1958. He went on to point out that although the ministry's efforts to implement the system of conciliatory commissions included in the pact had not been successful, numerous contracts contained provisions for voluntary arbitration.[15]

Decree 440 issued by the Junta Militar in November was also intended to ensure labor peace. It stipulated that industrywide collective bargaining—either at the regional or national level—would be mandatory when businessmen, the government, or the majority of the workers in the industry, as represented by their labor leaders, requested it. In the event that labor and management failed to reach an agreement, the contract was to be decided by arbitration. The arbitration clause was opposed by labor representatives on the commission that drew up the decree, but it was unexpectedly included in the final draft.[16]

The disturbances of unemployed workers that broke out in 1958 contrasted with the restraint and disciplined behavior of the labor movement in defense of the country's nascent democracy. These protests were not organized by established political and labor groups such as the CSU and the PCV, which were anxious to avoid obstacles to the upcoming elections. Nevertheless, party spokesmen—including those of the more conservative Copei—and the CSU agreed that it was incumbent on the government to provide work for the unemployed. The Larrazábal administration attempted to alleviate the problem by implementing the Emergency Plan, which employed a large number of workers in public works. The plan, however, was a stopgap measure and did not involve long-term projects. The unemployed workers themselves demanded permanent jobs and even suggested state-run industries as a solution. In one demonstration in Barcelona, unemployed workers called on the government to operate an abandoned coal mine in nearby Naricual in order to generate employment.[17]

Venezuela's four political parties, which dated back prior to the installation of the Pérez Jiménez dictatorship in 1948, enjoyed, to one degree or another, support in the labor movement. All four were represented in the CSU, which was headed by an independent, Gustavo Lares Ruiz. AD had the largest labor following, but the party was divided into three factions: an Old Guard, headed by former President Rómulo Betancourt; a middle generation known as the ARS Group; and the radicalized youth wing, which had played a major role in the final stage of the struggle against Pérez Jiménez. The PCV was the second largest party in the labor movement nationwide and the largest in Caracas; it had always exerted great influence among the oil workers and had controlled the textile workers' movement since before 1948. URD, headed by Jóvito Villalba, was somewhat to the left of AD, although ideologically ill defined. Copei, whose standard-bearer was Rafael Caldera, attempted to discard the right-wing label that was often attached to it, but made no effort to conceal its staunch anticommunism.

Although a consensus prevailed among politicians throughout 1958 that unity was imperative for confronting the right-wing threat, labor leaders were more insistent and went further in their support of it. They took the initiative in interviewing leading political figures in order to select an independent who would be acceptable to all parties as a presidential candidate for the December 1958 election. This formula, which the CSU labeled "patriotic," was also supported by the AD's youth group and the PCV.[18] One top AD labor leader, Pedro Bernardo Pérez Salinas, publicly criticized the political parties for playing into the hands of pro-Pérez Jiménez rightists by failing to subordinate their own interests and agree on a unity candidate.[19]

AD's Old Guard raised a series of doubts and objections regarding the "Supra-party" approach promoted by the labor movement and, in the process, contributed to the defeat of the proposal for an independent candidate. In private, Betancourt argued that at this critical juncture the political parties should be fortified and their positions clearly defined. These objectives would best be served by choosing party leaders as presidential candidates.[20] Furthermore, Betancourt warned against "popular frontism" in which all the parties, including the Communists, supported a common candidate. In a departure from the pro-unity rhetoric in vogue at the time, Betancourt pointed out that the Communists rejected democratic goals and that their interests in foreign affairs were contrary to those of Venezuela and thus should be excluded from any interparty alliance.

Betancourt was reluctant to be the first politician to announce his presidential candidacy and, for some time, actually denied interest in running for the position. At that moment, Betancourt's nomination would have appeared to be sectarian and contrary to the spirit of unity. The scenario changed when URD launched the candidacy of Provisional President Wolfgang Larrazábal under the slogan "pluralistic unity," which meant that unity should not preclude interparty electoral rivalry. In the face of URD's unilateral decision, Betancourt argued that AD had the right to select a candidate of its own. In the December election, Betancourt received 49 percent of the vote; Larrazábal, who was endorsed by the PCV as well as by URD, received 36 percent; and Copei's Caldera received 16 percent. Shortly after the presidential contests, one pro-AD commentator labeled URD's go-it-alone electoral strategy "ingenuous." "Had it not been for URD's 'pluralistic unity' . . . AD would not have chosen Betancourt to run because it [his nomination] would have been openly contrary to the true spirit of unity, which called for one single presidential candidate."[21]

One ominous sign for the president-elect was Larrazábal's triumph in Caracas, revealing Betancourt's unpopularity in the capital. The day after the elections a turbulent crowd gathered in the city's downtown El Silencio to protest the results. The ensuing disorders led to rumors that Betancourt's assumption of power would be blocked. Top leaders of the PCV (who, along with URD, scored especially well in Caracas in the congressional contest) addressed the throng in an attempt to calm tensions.

The multitude consisted largely of unemployed workers. The president-elect made a special appeal to them and called for a halt to the migration of the jobless from the nation's interior to the capital in search of opportunities under the Emergency Plan. Betancourt made reference to an entire town in the state of Mérida, which, "like one of those biblical exoduses of starvation and desperation," had moved to Caracas. He added, "Have confidence in me. Rest assured. I promise you that we will eliminate the scourge of unemployment in Venezuela."[22]

Organized labor's general stance in 1958 and specifically its decision to sign the Pacto de Avenimiento provoked considerable discussion among trade unionists in subsequent years. AD leader Manuel Peñalver stated that the pact facilitated labor's principled strategy of "renouncing immediate gains and discussing and settling specific problems by way of consensus [with management] in order to provide a firm foundation free of social agitation" for the democratic government.[23] In contrast, leftist trade unionists would reconsider the moderate positions that they had assumed in 1958 and would denounce the pact for burdening the workers with economic hardships that were not matched by management. Not only did business interests score economic gains under the Larrazábal administration—such as the cancellation of public debts incurred under Pérez Jiménez—but also they counted on an environment of class harmony in the workplace during a period that would have otherwise been characterized by sharp struggle.[24] The leftists would also question their naive and un-Marxian practice in 1958 of distinguishing between "responsible" capitalists, who were flexible in their dealings with employees, and "irresponsible" ones, consisting mainly of foreign companies that opposed the democratic system and provoked their workers into going on strike.[25]

1959: Betancourt's First Year

The coalition government formed by Rómulo Betancourt, consisting of members of AD, Copei, and URD in cabinet and gubernatorial positions, was designed to facilitate the consolidation of the democratic regime. Betancourt excluded the PCV from the alliance, despite the insistence of URD leaders that it be open to all parties. The acute challenges faced by Betancourt during his five-year presidency continuously placed in doubt the survival of his government. Military unrest was exacerbated by the election of Betancourt, whom many officers feared would promote AD penetration of their institution and curb its decision-making authority.

In addition, the downturn in oil prices and the restriction on oil imports in the United States produced a contraction in the economy and forced the government to adopt austerity measures that aggravated social tensions. On the political front, popular energies released by the overthrow of Pérez Jiménez were stimulated by the triumph of the Cuban Revolution, which especially appealed to the youth wings of AD, URD, and the PCV. In fact, Fidel Castro visited Venezuela just weeks after coming to power and addressed a mass rally celebrating the first anniversary of January 23, 1958, where he pledged Cuban support for the Venezuelan revolutionary process.[26] Internally, the Betancourt administration encountered challenges from two sources: URD, which from the outset threatened to withdraw from the coalition and harshly criticized government policies, and the AD Youth and ARS factions, which offered leftist critiques of the positions defended by the Old Guard.

The labor movement played a major role in confronting the military conspiracies. Prior to completing its first year, the Betancourt administration was menaced by General Jesús María Castro León, who in 1958 had been forced to resign as minister of defense due to his involvement in military intrigues. As a warning to the plotters, organized labor called a fifteen-minute symbolic strike that was respected throughout the nation; even fishermen participated and motorists beeped their horns in support. Only in the conservative state of Táchira did the Church-run radio station continue to broadcast, criticizing the strike for producing economic losses. The labor movement defended the record of the Betancourt government in opposition to "the national and international campaign designed to discredit" it. At the same time, labor demanded from the government "greater activity, audacity, and resolve in solving the problems of the popular sectors," and called on it to deepen its reforms as the best strategy for confronting the military threat.[27] Organized labor also denounced the decision of a military tribunal to absolve various officers who had been implicated in the abortive coup of September 1958.

Labor leaders met with business representatives in order to cooperate in the defense of the democratic regime against the various coup attempts during the first two and one-half years after Pérez Jiménez's overthrow. Particularly important were the plans of the Chamber of Radio and Television to broadcast the labor movement's call for a general strike in the case of a military coup.[28] A precedent for such joint efforts had been set prior to January 23, 1958, in the negotiations between Fedecámaras and the Junta Patriótica, and the tradition was reinforced by the Pacto de Avenimiento Obrero Patronal.

This collaboration led labor and political leaders to view business interests—sometimes referred to as the "progressive national bourgeoisie"—as a natural ally in the struggle for democracy and economic reforms. AD's "Labor Thesis" of 1958 approved of "transitory alliances between workers and management in defense of industries facing extinction as a result of competition from foreign capital."[29] The PCV also favored a strategic agreement between organized labor and the national bourgeoisie, although at least one prominent Communist worker leader, Rodolfo Quintero, criticized some trade unionists for being hasty in their efforts to arrive at such a pact.[30]

During Betancourt's first year in office, the number of unemployed workers in the nation's major cities continued to rise, and the tactics they employed in street protests became increasingly belligerent. From the outset the police used tear gas and opened fire on demonstrators, wounding and killing scores. Many of the unemployed were from rural areas and had migrated in search of the construction jobs created by the Pérez Jiménez government's ostentatious public projects in the nation's capital and, subsequently, by the Emergency Plan. As a reaction against Pérez Jiménez's exaggerated emphasis on construction activity, the Betancourt administration restricted credits in that sector. In addition, one of the government's first decisions was to abolish the Emergency Plan, which had come under heavy criticism for being ill conceived, and for representing a dole for idle workers and easy profit for contractors.

The labor movement was pressured from both sides in the dispute over the problem of unemployment. On the one hand, the CSU was aware that the disturbances played into the hands of right-wing military conspirators, although there was little evidence to support the claim that *perezjimenistas* were acting as the principal instigators. On the other hand, the CSU recognized that the protesters represented a part of its constituency.[31] The CSU and the construction workers' union in particular were accused of turning their backs on the unemployed, a charge that labor leaders denied.[32] Under the Emergency Plan, the CSU established a committee to interview unemployed workers and remit them to government offices. In addition, the CSU called for the issuance of a special card for unemployed workers that would make them eligible for certain social benefits.

The construction workers' movement, headed by Juan Herrera, was particularly critical of the unemployment protests and maintained that they were infiltrated by *perezjimenistas*.[33] Herrera insisted that all actions organized by the unemployed had to be channeled through the labor movement. In answer to criticism that his union should actively support these mobilizations, Herrera argued that most of the unemployed were not construction workers and lacked building skills. He added, "We can attend to our affiliates who are unemployed, but we are not going to convert the union into a national Employment Agency."[34]

PCV and URD labor leaders criticized the Betancourt administration for abruptly terminating the Emergency Plan without offering viable alternatives to deal with unemployment. While recognizing the potential danger that the disorders posed to the nation's democracy, both parties defended the right of unemployed workers to protest and denied that their movement was "*golpista*."[35] Due to their large following among the urban poor in Caracas, URD leaders believed that a far greater number of the unemployed protesters belonged to their party than to those of their rivals.[36] Eloy Torres, at the time a leading PCV trade unionist, has stated, "We were in agreement with the marches [of the unemployed] but with certain limitations. We condemned the excesses ... and told our followers to carry out these protests within the existing democratic order."[37]

Actually, leftist youth belonging to AD, URD, and the PCV did not follow this cautious advice and often goaded the unemployed into physical resistance to security forces and even acts of violence. PCV adult leaders criticized Communist Youth members, particularly in the nation's capital, for their lack of discipline and "unconscious violations of our norms and organizational principles."[38] This breach between the PCV's established leadership and its youth wing, which first surfaced in the unemployment protests, would find its maximum expression a few years later when the party took up arms against the Betancourt government. The Communist Youth avidly supported the guerrilla struggle despite the serious reservations of the party's adult leaders, including those in the labor movement.

The internal cohesion of the CSU reflected the spirit of unity that survived in the labor movement even after the development of the center-left polarization in the rest of the society. The CSU's National Executive Committee, in which each of the four main political parties was represented by one labor leader, duplicated the Junta Patriótica's structure, which had proved so successful in the overthrow of Pérez Jiménez. The CSU drew up electoral regulations for its constituent unions that avoided the internal discord and parallel unionism characteristic of organized labor in the years prior to 1948. In each union, proportional representation was granted to all parties with a significant following. The CSU urged that unions devise a single "united slate" based on the estimated following of each party to avoid the "small fisures" often resulting from electoral contests.[39] These agreements were possible because, as one prominent labor leader recalled, "Everybody knew how much support each party had in their union."[40]

Several hundred parallel unions created before 1948 were amalgamated in 1958 and 1959.[41] Mergers in the oil industry where interunion rivalry had provoked considerable conflict in the 1940s proved especially significant.[42] In addition, Copei dissolved the Comité Pro-Federación de Trabajadores de Venezuela (Cofetrov), which was formed in 1950 to coordinate social Christian labor unions and which survived the Pérez Jiménez regime despite its failure to gain legal status.

Interparty friction was not entirely eliminated in the labor movement. Thus, for instance, AD labor leaders instructed their delegate in the CSU to determine whether the PCV's display of party banners in the May Day Parade "means that the Communist Party has decided to abandon its unity policy."[43] Of greater significance was the dispute over party representation in labor unions and federations. AD trade unionists objected to the erroneous interpretation of the CSU regulations regarding proportional representation whereby all four parties received at least one seat on the Executive Committee of labor organizations, regardless of whether or not they had a significant worker following. AD labor leaders frequently protested that "political elements without any force or support among the workers . . . are given representation [in unions] for the sole purpose of obeying a party interest in [maintaining] unity."[44]

In one sharply contested incident, *Copeyano* peasant leaders withdrew from the Federación Campesina de Venezuela (FCV) and demonstrated in the streets to protest their underrepresentation in the federation's Executive Committee. The matter was brought to the attention of Rafael Caldera, who in turn met with AD political leaders. The FCV president, Rámon Quijada, at first rejected party interference in the matter, for which he was branded a "caudillo" by his *Copeyano* rivals. Subsequently, Quijada bowed to political pressure and granted Copei, URD, and the PCV one additional representative each on the federation's Executive Committee.[45] The dispute set a precedent for future left-wing schisms in AD. Quijada and other labor leaders regarded AD as a leftist party and resented political manipulations that increased the representation of trade unionists belonging to Copei, a party they considered both tied to the nation's oligarchy and lacking worker support.

The Third CTV Congress

The Third National Congress of Workers, held in Los Caracas outside the nation's capital in November 1959, marked a milestone in the efforts of the Venezuelan labor movement to achieve unity. In its most significant decision, the congress reestablished the CTV, which had been disbanded after the military coup of 1948. In addition, despite the AD affiliation of a majority of the delegates, the congress passed a number of bold and far-reaching resolutions asserting the independence of the labor movement from the government.

Fifty-two percent of the congress's nine hundred delegates belonged to the governing party, 23 percent were Communists, 15 percent were members of Copei, and 10 percent were members of URD. The CTV's Executive Committee, created at the congress, consisted of seven AD trade unionists, three Communists, and two members each of Copei and URD. Labor leaders have frequently lauded the Third Congress. Former Communist Eloy Torres stated that "not only was it the most important congress organized by the Venezuelan labor movement but it was marked by loftiness in the expression of labor unity as was shown . . . in the Executive Committee of the CTV which consisted of members of all the political currents."[46]

In addition to unifying organized labor in Venezuela, the Third Congress called for the creation of a neutral Latin American organization to overcome the three-way organic split between pro-U.S., Communist, and Christian democratic labor movements. This idea originally had been put forward by the leftist-controlled, but internationally unaffiliated, Central Unica de

Trabajadores (CUT) of Chile.[47] In one speech at the congress, Marcel Bras of the pro-Communist World Federation of Trade Unions (WFTU) highlighted the proposal's importance by suggesting that it could serve as the first step in the unification of the three worldwide labor bodies.[48] AD trade unionist Pedro Bernardo Pérez Salinas pointed out at the congress that the decision to sponsor a conference in Caracas to unify the continental labor movement would only have credibility if the Venezuelan workers' movement overcame internal differences and served as a model of unity.[49]

The Third Congress approved several proposals designed to strengthen the labor movement. The delegates voted in favor of the creation of a permanent strike fund and the development of mechanisms to transmit information to counter adverse publicity in the commercial media. In addition, the congress called for the establishment of single nationwide unions (*sindicatos únicos por rama de industria*) to represent all the workers in a given industry, although up until then the government had refused to recognize the legality of such organizations. Support also was expressed for extending labor's representation beyond the Social Security board to all state decision-making bodies.[50]

Many of the resolutions adopted at the Third Congress challenged the policies of the government and Fedecámaras. The congress advocated revision of the controversial oil concessions granted by Pérez Jiménez in 1956 and the obtainment of oil royalty in kind rather than money in order to penetrate international markets. Both of these policies had previously been defended by AD but abandoned by the Betancourt government.[51] Other far-reaching labor demands for the time included the forty-hour work week, job security for public employees, and the establishment of a minimum wage. The congress also warned that the Pacto de Avenimiento was conditional on the good behavior of management and did not rule out strikes. "The workers' struggle," stated one resolution with Marxist overtones, "is an objective law of society . . . and cannot be regulated or paralyzed by any accord."[52]

José González Navarro was chosen CTV president at the congress, despite endorsements for Augusto Malavé Villalba and Pérez Salinas, both of whom previously had a higher ranking in the Venezuelan labor movement. While González Navarro had headed the federation of labor unions in the Federal District in the years prior to 1948, Malavé Villalba had been secretary-general of the CTV and Pérez Salinas its president. Unlike González Navarro, who consciously spurned close international connections, both Malavé Villalba and Pérez Salinas had served on the staff of the Organización Regional Interamericana de Trabajadores (ORIT) during the Pérez Jiménez dictatorship. In fact, Malavé Villalba had been a secretary of ORIT's precursor organization, the Confederación Interamericana de Trabajadores, and had attended the founding conventions of both ORIT and its parent body, the International Confederation of Free Trade Unions (ICFTU).[53]

Betancourt made known his preference for Malavé Villalba, whom he hoped would draw the CTV into ORIT.[54] However, not only did the Third Congress name González Navarro CTV president, but also it ruled out affiliation with any international organization. This decision seemed "ungrateful" to some AD leaders, including Betancourt, especially in light of the generous financial donations that ORIT had granted the "CTV-in-exile" during the Pérez Jiménez years.[55]

Serafino Romualdi, who headed the AFL-CIO's Latin American affairs department, sharply criticized the Third Congress's failure to define itself in the context of the East-West Cold War struggle. Romualdi censured its decision to establish fraternal relations with the progovernment Confederación de Trabajadores de Cuba (CTC) at a time when President Betancourt was becoming openly hostile to the Castro regime. Most important, he expressed concern regarding Communist representation in the CTV's governing committee.

Following the overthrow of Pérez Jiménez, Romualdi had reluctantly accepted interparty unity in organized labor as "inevitable under the momentum generated by the collaboration in the underground struggle." However, he insisted that this understanding be of a "transitory character."[56] By the time of the Third Congress, however, Romualdi questioned power-sharing in the labor movement, an arrangement that he pejoratively termed "popular frontism." He wrote to Betancourt, with whom he had a close personal rapport dating from the 1940s, "If the Popular Front is to be rejected at the political and governmental level, why not reject it also in the labor field?"[57] Romualdi opposed the concessions that AD labor leaders made to their rivals, reducing their representation in the CTV to less than the majority they had in delegate strength at the congress.

Betancourt and his closest AD allies in the labor movement shared Romualdi's apprehension of the Communist presence in organized labor and viewed unity as an expedient to overcome the right-wing military threat. He wrote to Romualdi stating that "I share your preoccupation concerning the progress of the popular front slogan, behind which one can easily discern the tactic of the Trojan Horse . . . but as far as AD is concerned there is no possibility whatsoever that we may be fooled by this melody."[58] Many other AD worker leaders, however, viewed unity as a strategic goal and the expression of an underlying political commitment. The president of the Third Congress, Juan José Delpino, articulated this position when he implored the nation's political parties to follow the lead of the labor movement and close ranks in order to facilitate the consolidation of the democratic regime.[59]

The *Copeyano* delegation, which was more uniformly in agreement with Romualdi's staunch anticommunism, entertained serious differences with the congress's majority. The *Copeyanos* refused to endorse one resolution, which extended moral support to a convention of Chilean women that was allegedly subject to Communist influence. They also rejected the proposed "Pact for the Defense of Democracy" on grounds that by taking in the PCV it implicitly "considered Communists a democratic and progressive force."[60] The *Copeyanos* particularly objected to the congress's utilization of Marxist language and concepts in its positions on such items as *cogestión* (worker participation in company decision making). Although the *Copeyanos* obtained approval for a resolution in favor of *cogestión* in a commission at the congress, it was voted down on the floor. The *Copeyanos* rebuked such AD leaders as Ramón Quijada for making common cause with PCV delegates in opposing *cogestión* on grounds that it "would impede the true objective of the revolutionary Venezuelan workers' movement: the realization of the revolution that would lead to the implantation of a socialist society."[61]

In another important difference, the *Copeyanos* coined the slogan "trade union liberty" in opposition to the *sindicatos únicos*. The *Copeyanos* defended dual unions as a basic worker right and a hedge against undemocratic trade unionism. In future years the CTV would discuss at great length and modify the positions on *cogestión* and *sindicatos únicos* that it had adopted at the Third Congress.

Division within the CTV, 1960–1963

A few months after the Third Congress underscored the need to maintain unity, the labor movement fell prey to the same internecine struggle that was tearing apart the rest of the nation. The ensuing confrontations, both in and out of the labor movement, would set the stage for the initiation of the armed struggle in 1962. In arriving at its decision, the Left was influenced by the persistence of violent street protests, URD's withdrawal from the ruling coalition in 1960 as a result of Betancourt's hostile policy toward Cuba, and the rift in the ruling AD that gave rise to the Movimiento de Izquierda Revolucionaria (MIR) in 1960 and the ARS Group in 1962.

The leftists, however, committed two basic errors in judgment. First, they overlooked the relative passivity in the nation's interior, which contrasted sharply with the convulsive setting in the nation's capital. Second, they mistook urban disturbances for labor unrest, without distinguishing between a discontented, amorphous urban mass (which Betancourt pejoratively called a "lumpen subclass"[62]) and the organized working class.

An additional mistake was that the leftist insurgency followed too closely on the heels of the military plots sponsored by *perezjimenistas*. Shortly after leftists supported the mobilizations undertaken by organized labor in opposition to the *golpistas*, they called on the nation to join them in the struggle to overthrow the government. In fact, turbulent demonstrations of the unemployed in January 1960, which were abetted by members of the youth factions of political parties, occurred nearly concurrently with the CTV's call for a nationwide ministrike in opposition to the military threat posed by Castro León. The inappropriateness of the timing was underscored in a declaration by the left-leaning FCV: "In the current historical stage that the country is living, conditions are not ripe for a popular uprising. . . . The extemporaneous call for a leftist insurrection will only engender a reactionary coup d'état."[63]

Although the AD division in 1960 mainly involved the party's youth faction, it took in two members of the CTV's Executive Committee: José Marcano, president of the white-collar workers (the Asociación Nacional de Empleados—ANDE), and Américo Chacón, president of the Bank Workers Union. Marcano, Chacón, and other future MIRistas criticized the interference of AD politicians in the party's Labor Bureau and singled out several AD labor leaders for failing to respect the bureau's tradition of noninvolvement in internal, factional struggles. In one document the leftist trade unionists pointed out that, as a result of this partisanship, "We [AD worker representatives] have lost our moderating authority [in AD] and consequently labor leaders are no longer viewed as such in the Party, but rather as simple political militants." The leftists considered these alignments to be at odds with the tradition whereby the Labor Bureau was represented at party conventions by its own *delegados natos* (nonelected delegates), who were presumed to be neutral on issues related to factional conflicts. The document supported the concept of "double militancy," whereby AD trade unionists were not subject to party discipline in matters pertaining to their respective labor organizations. The leftists also defended their right to adhere to Marxist methodology, even though it was not officially accepted by AD.[64]

The leftist faction of AD harshly criticized the signing of the 1960 oil workers' contract, which averted an imminent strike. The attention of the entire labor movement was focused on these negotiations, as demonstrated by the numerous declarations of solidarity by other labor organizations and political parties. Eloy Torres, for instance, declared at the CTV's Third Congress that "the triumph of the oil workers will be a triumph for the entire nation against its principal enemy."[65]

The most important and thorniest issue under discussion was the union's inclusion in its proposed contract of a clause granting *estabilidad absoluta* (job tenure), whereby management was prohibited from laying off workers without just cause. (The concept is discussed in detail in Chapter 9.) The oil workers had first put forward the demand in the early 1940s; company resistance to it nearly produced walkouts at the time of the collective bargaining agreements of 1946 and 1948. Prior to the signing of the 1960 contract, in assemblies held throughout the nation, oil workers expressed their determination to achieve *estabilidad absoluta*, as did union leaders belonging to all four political parties. The sudden turnabout of AD labor leaders in Fedepetrol gave rise to speculation that they had been instructed to drop the *estabilidad absoluta* demand by President Betancourt (who in turn was pressured by the oil companies) due to fear that a paralysis of the industry would undermine the nation's political stability.[66] AD leftist Domingo Alberto Rangel, who as legal adviser to Fedepetrol proposed the mass mobilization of workers in defense of the *estabilidad* clause, criticized the contract in a celebrated article in *La Esfera* that hastened the MIR split.[67]

Shortly after the division in AD, MIR attacked the conservationist policies of Minister of Mines Juan Pablo Pérez Alfonzo for being responsible for the cutbacks in oil production and resultant mass layoffs in the industry. According to the MIRistas, Pérez Alfonzo's efforts to limit output had enabled the Arab nations to displace Venezuela in markets in the United States, Brazil, Argentina, and elsewhere.[68] In future years, Venezuelan leftists would refrain from linking the problem of unemployment with oil production reduction, which they would support as part of a strategy to fortify OPEC.

In an effort to counter the nation's acute economic crisis, the Betancourt administration implemented a series of fiscal and monetary policies that weighed heavily on the popular classes. A 35.5 percent devaluation of the bolívar was coupled with curtailment of certain expenditures, including the elimination of the Emergency Plan in 1959 and the 10 percent reduction of salaries for public employees (pejoratively referred to as the "Hunger Law") in 1961. In addition, the "Emergency Measures" in 1962 empowered the executive to postpone collective bargaining agreements in the public sector for several months; the following year the government granted bonuses to state employees in return for union acceptance of an additional deferment on the signing of contracts. These measures were attacked by leftist labor leaders belonging to the PCV, MIR, and URD who called two abortive general strikes to protest the Hunger Law.[69]

The Betancourt administration and the government party dealt harshly with their leftist opponents. Security forces frequently opened fire on street demonstrators and rounded them up to send to special work colonies in remote parts of the Guayana region. Leftist trade unionists who vied with AD and Copei leaders for control of individual unions received a similarly unmerciful treatment. Armed bands attacked assemblies of leftist workers and, in some cases, took over union halls by force. One shooting at a union meeting in the oil town of Lagunillas in November 1960 left one PCV worker dead and Luis Pinto, a top Communist labor leader, an invalid. The incident was condemned in a joint communication from all political parties, with the exception of AD, in the state of Zulia.[70]

Some of the bands consisted of AD worker cadres, while others were of a more obscure origin.[71] One of the most notorious bands was under the command of construction workers' leader Juan Herrera, who had been denounced as early as the 1940s by *Copeyanos* for organizing "shock troops" against his trade union rivals.[72] After 1958 his bands were known as *"los cabilleros de Juan Herrera,"* because they were equipped with *cabillas* (metal rods) used in the construction industry. These assaults were particularly unjustified since leftist trade unionists, unlike their comrades in the student movement, were generally critical of the decision to take up arms against the government.[73]

The two most important labor conflicts of the period—the walkout of telephone workers in November 1960 and public transportation workers in January 1962—were interpreted by the Left as evidence of the insurrectional mood of the working class. Both conflicts, however, developed to a large degree independently of the direction of leftist trade union leaders. The two strikes set off intense street battles between students and slum dwellers, on the one hand, and police, on the other. They resulted in hundreds of casualties, including dozens of deaths.

The telephone workers' union of the state-run Cantv in Caracas protested against the threatened mass dismissal of employees who mostly belonged to URD, which had held the top executive positions in the company prior to the party's decision to leave the governing coalition. Moderates and moderate leftists, such as González Navarro and URD-labor head Vicente Piñate, initially supported the strike but later questioned its subsequent radicalization.[74] Students celebrated their annual "Students' Day" on November 21 in slum dwellings in an effort to rally popular support for the telephone workers, and the leftists called an unsuccessful general strike; telephone connections were cut throughout the city, including those in the presidential palace of Miraflores. The conflict was finally resolved at the national executive level in negotiations with Secretary of the President Ramón J. Velásquez, who promised that Cantv would refrain from discharging workers.

The strike of public transportation workers first broke out in the traditionally conservative state of Táchira and was organized by nonleftists, many of whom were *perezjimenistas* and *Copeyanos*. The conflict quickly spread to Caracas and elsewhere. The workers criticized the government-decreed increase in the price of gasoline and demanded the abrogation of the Civil Responsibility Law, which obliged drivers to insure themselves against transit accidents. The Betancourt administration insisted that it lacked authority to alter the law. Nevertheless, the Communications Ministry reached a settlement with the unions whereby it pledged to seek congressional modification and to suspend enforcement of the law for three months.[75] Despite the understanding, the violence continued. Although many workers were unwilling to settle for anything less than the law's immediate repeal, they were no longer the principal protaganists in the struggle once it spilled over to the streets in the form of violent clashes with security forces.

The transformation of the telephone, transportation, and other worker conflicts into disorders involving students led to accusations against leftist trade unionists that they were undermining the nation's democracy and making common cause with *perezjimenista* conspirators. In December 1960 the General Council of the CTV met to consider a report submitted by confederation President González Navarro. The report charged MIR and PCV labor leaders with "raising unrealistic demands in collective bargaining, inciting a campaign of disrepute against [rival] trade unionists and the CTV, promoting illegal strikes and demonstrations against the will of worker representative organizations, stimulating insurrection, denying all the positive aspects of the government, and coinciding objectively speaking with the Right against the constitutional government."[76]

The council adopted a resolution, which was drafted by Copei, condemning the leftists and convoking a special CTV congress to consider disciplinary measures against them. A slim majority of thirty-four delegates (twenty-seven belonging to AD and seven to Copei) voted affirmatively, while twenty-six (fifteen Communists, eight URDistas, and three MIRistas) opposed the motion. Nevertheless, had it not been for severe government measures taken against the Left, the outcome may have been different. Seven members of the General Council (four MIRistas, two PCVistas, and one URDista) were in jail at the time while another, who belonged to AD, was opposed to the resolution but did not attend the meeting.

Throughout 1961 elections were held to name union authorities and delegates for the CTV's Fourth Congress. The PCV, MIR, and URD usually put up united slates, while AD and Copei occasionally did the same. As a result of these contests, the rough parity in the CTV leadership between the Left, on the one hand, and AD and Copei, on the other, was altered in favor of the latter. AD won control of thirty-three of the thirty-six CTV-affiliated federations. International observers belonging to the AFL-CIO and other pro-U.S. organizations closely monitored the elections and, along with pro-AD writers, hailed the results as evidence that the Left had lost favor with the nation's working class.[77] Nevertheless, they overstated their case since they failed to acknowledge that most of the electoral battles were closely contested,[78] and that repression was directed against the Left in those unions where its chances of winning were the greatest. Leftist leaders and commentators committed the opposite error in judgment, insisting that the electoral results favored the PCV and MIR, and placed in doubt AD's continued control of organized labor.[79]

The CTV's Fourth Congress, which took place in Los Caracas in December 1961, was boycotted by leftist trade unionists who objected to the decision to move up the date of the meeting by one year. The congress expelled PCV and MIR leaders who belonged to the CTV's national leadership, a procedure subsequently copied by the confederation's affiliate organizations. The congress refrained from taking measures against URD labor leaders on grounds that insufficient evidence existed linking them with the insurrectional movement.[80]

The *Copeyanos* were the great victors at the congress. With the Left absent, 70 percent of the delegates belonged to AD and 30 percent to Copei. The resultant Executive Committee of the CTV consisted of seven AD members and four *Copeyanos*. This improved representation for Copei led some leftists to claim that the *Copeyanos* had assumed a hardened stance in hopes of accelerating the division and reaping benefits.[81] Copei had called for the expulsion of the Left at a time when many AD labor leaders were reluctant to consider such a stringent measure. In addition, the *Copeyanos* favored severance of relations with the Cuban CTC and not just the "freeze" that was finally agreed upon.[82]

Nevertheless, on the issue of international affiliation, Copei's plans were thwarted at the Fourth Congress. Several months prior to the congress, CTV Secretary of Organization Augusto Malavé Villalba complained that, while leftist trade unionists were tightly linked to pro-Communist worldwide labor organizations, the Third Congress's position in favor of neutrality had left the CTV "isolated."[83] At first, Copei's proposal to seek membership simultaneously in ORIT (which was pro-AFL-CIO) and the pro-Christian democratic Confederación Latinoamericana de Sindicalistas Cristianos (Clasc) was accepted. Nevertheless, after Malavé Villalba conferred with ORIT's parent organization, the ICFTU in Berlin, AD ruled out affiliation with Clasc,[84] and the CTV ended up limiting its membership to ORIT.

Many AD labor leaders were uncomfortable with the expulsions decided upon at the Fourth Congress and the polarization process that united them with the allegedly right-wing Copei against the Left. Some suspected that the bloody confrontations with leftist trade unionists, in the words of Eloy Torres, were "designed to force those in the [AD] Labor Bureau who vacillated to decide once and for all" on sanctions against PCV and MIR labor leaders.[85] The Left, for its part, tended to underestimate differences within the Labor Bureau and erroneously attacked AD labor for championing the austerity measures taken by the Betancourt administration. In fact, the reservations of AD trade unionists toward Betancourt's policies provided an important antecedent for the division in 1967, in which about half of the party's national labor leaders split off to form the left-leaning MEP.

The AD Labor Bureau accepted in principle the need to undertake sacrifices during the economic crisis and criticized the leftists for placing heavy demands on companies without taking into consideration their ability to pay.[86] At the same time, however, party labor leaders questioned certain austerity measures that cut into the purchasing power of workers and found themselves midway between the positions of the government and the insurgent Left. They proposed that public employees who earned less than 600 bolívares per month be exempted from the 10 percent salary decrease decreed by the Hunger Law, and that the tax on gasoline not be applied to low-quality octanes.[87] At the CTV's Fourth Congress, AD leaders opposed the devaluation of the bolívar and called for salary increases for public employees and the initiation of collective bargaining, which had been deferred by the Emergency Measures. In his speech at the congress, González Navarro pointed to these proposals in an attempt to refute the Left's claim that the CTV had been converted into an appendage of the state.[88]

The AD-dominated CTV supported other positions that represented an implicit leftist critique of the Betancourt administration: the opening of trade with the socialist bloc at a time when relations with those nations were strained; a law regulating foreign capital, which was not promulgated until after Venezuela joined the Andean Pact in 1973; and the revision of the Reciprocal Commerce Treaty with the United States, which Betancourt had criticized at the time of its approval in 1952 but as president decided to leave intact.[89] Particularly significant were the statements of CTV President González Navarro demanding that the government try right-wing conspirators in special tribunals and confiscate their property, at a time when the Left harshly criticized Betancourt for being overly lenient toward the plotters.[90]

PCV and MIR labor leaders maintained that their expulsion from top leadership positions in the CTV and affiliate unions violated organizational regulations. Purporting to represent a majority of the nation's organized workers, the leftists set up the "CTV-No Oficialista," which they claimed was the true CTV. To eliminate the denominations CTV-No Oficialista and CTV-Oficialista (controlled by AD and Copei) to the advantage of the latter, the Betancourt administration offered to extend legal recognition to the leftists in exchange for acceptance of a new name.[91]

The CTV-No Oficialista, which had put off the calling of a national convention for several months due to fear of government repression,[92] was able to hold a congress in March and April of 1963 at which 945 delegates converted the organization into the Central Unitaria de Trabajadores de Venezuela (CUTV). The founding CUTV congress called for the incorporation of certain clauses of existing labor contracts into the nation's constitution in order to extend the benefits enjoyed by privileged sectors of the working class to all workers. In addition, the CUTV's Declaration of Principles left open the possibility of entering into alliance with the clandestine Left as well as carrying out joint actions with other progressive organizations.

Former Communist Horacio Scott Power of URD was chosen president of the CUTV. However, URD had ill-defined and at times stormy relations with the Left, and it balked at authorizing its trade union members to join the CUTV. URD had preferred the selection of the more moderate Rafael Castañeda and Pedro Brito to form part of the CUTV's Executive Committee, rather than the leftist Power.[93] Nevertheless, the CUTV Executive Committee achieved a degree of pluralism with the naming of Hugo Soto Socorro (ARS), Américo Chacón (MIR), and Rodolfo Quintero (PCV) as national secretaries. Although the pro-leftist FCV decided not to join the CUTV, its president, Ramón Quijada, offered his organization's support.

The CUTV's loss of influence among workers in future years would encourage leftists to examine the events leading up to their decision to split off from the CTV and establish separate labor organizations. Eloy Torres, among others, would argue that the expulsion of PCVistas and MIRistas from the leadership of CTV unions and the violence unleashed against them left the two parties with no alternative but to set up the CTV-No Oficialista and then the CUTV.[94] Nevertheless, Torres would become one of the foremost advocates of the strategy of "boring within" the CTV and affiliate unions and, in effect, shunting aside the CUTV.

Others, however, maintained that the leftists had committed a grave error in opting for dual unionism in 1962 and 1963. Laureano Torrealba, the PCV's secretary of trade union affairs after 1962 who subsequently joined AD, has stated that the Left should have stayed in the CTV despite the expulsions since "when Communists are kicked out the door of labor unions they re-enter through the windows."[95] Martín J. Ramírez, another leading Communist who, unlike Torres and Torrealba, remained in the CUTV, maintained that it was simply not possible for leftists to have worked in CTV federations because "we were met with guns." However, he added that they should have concentrated their efforts on CTV union locals in order to explain their positions to the rank and file.[96]

Some writers, including several who are not particularly sympathetic to the leftist cause, maintain that the Left's efforts to foment militant protests were well conceived prior to 1962. After that date, however, the mass movement was on the ebb, and the Left's response should have been to moderate its tactics rather than escalate them in the form of guerrilla warfare.[97]

A second critique of the Left, which has not been put forward until now—at least in written form—can be added to this one. Due to the simultaneous expressions of discontent among students, workers, peasants, the marginal class, and military officers, the Left failed to evaluate accurately the political leanings of each sector and determine the social basis behind the violent demonstrations in opposition to the Betancourt administration. The Left misinterpreted and overestimated its influence, specifically in the case of organized workers. Although these years were characterized by growing worker unrest, far more dramatic were the disturbances unleashed by students and the urban poor in ghetto areas and elsewhere. These mobilizations eclipsed the industrial conflicts involving strategic sectors of the working class. Recent urbanization had aggravated the problem of unemployment in Caracas (which was one third that of the entire nation) and increased the disparities between workers in the formal economy and the marginal class.

Although AD's support in the slum dwellings of large cities was modest and its following in the student movement was practically nil, the government party dominated organized labor. In the all-important petroleum industry, for instance, leftists enjoyed considerable backing but were unable to mobilize workers in opposition to the 1960 contract, despite its elimination of the *estabilidad absoluta* clause. Furthermore, the overwhelming majority of workers who backed the leftist parties did so in hopes of achieving bread-and-butter gains rather than promoting revolutionary change.

Pedro Ortega Díaz, a labor lawyer and member of the PCV's Political Bureau, has stated, "Our major error was to assume that support in the labor movement [for the PCV] was in favor of the armed struggle. On the contrary, it was support for the demands we formulated, for our program, for what we had just accomplished, for our heroic struggle . . . in the overthrow of the dictatorship, and because we were defending democracy."[98] Thus, the nonrevolutionary vision of the Left's worker followers and the organized strength of its adversaries, rather than sheer repression—as has been the case with abortive political strikes against more repressive regimes in Latin America—were what spelled the failure of the various leftist calls for a general strike in opposition to the Betancourt government.

In summary, the impetus in favor of labor unity that originated in the struggle against the military dictatorship was not sustained after the threat of *perezjimenismo* largely subsided. The 1958–1963 period set the stage for the fragmentation of organized labor, which would represent a major liability for decades to come. Among the factors that contributed to this divisiveness were the AD-Old Guard's strategy of isolating and destroying the Left's political and labor influence; the pressure of U.S. labor leaders, headed by Serafino Romualdi, who also urged the expulsion of the leftists from the CTV; the Left's error of boycotting the CTV's Fourth Congress in 1961; and the unwillingness of many labor leaders, such as Juan Herrera, to extend full-fledged support to unskilled unemployed laborers, many of whom ended up following the lead of ultraleftist youth. The partisan division of labor organizations would gradually limit the possibility of developing an entirely autonomous labor movement on the basis of a more critical stand. Organized labor from then on—although far from quiescent—would depend a great deal on political parties and their agenda.

Agrarian Reform and the Peasant Movement

Two outstanding characteristics of the peasant movement in Venezuela have set it off from its counterparts in other Latin American nations. First, Venezuelan peasant struggles in the twentieth century never assumed the violent dimensions that they did in Mexico, Colombia, Peru, and elsewhere. This relative tranquility is related to the absence of strong pressure on the land from wealthy interest groups due to the insignificance of Venezuela's agricultural exports. Large landholders accepted government takeover of their holdings when, as a result of petroleum's displacement of coffee and cacao as the nation's leading export, they were unable to pay back loans from the state-run Banco Agrícola y Pecuario (BAP) in the early 1930s. Depreciated land value also limited the resistance to the confiscation of property of those accused of graft in 1936 and again in the 1945–1948 period. The resultant extensive public domain served as the basis for agrarian reform programs and thus cushioned tensions between peasants and large landowners.

The second important feature is the organic link between the peasant movement and the rest of organized labor. The FCV, in recognition of its large constituency, was traditionally granted 10 percent representation at CTV congresses. Governments elsewhere in Latin America have prohibited the affiliation of peasant organizations with trade union confederations in order to limit labor's clout. Even the left-leaning Lázaro Cárdenas separated the peasant movement from the Mexican Confederation of Workers in the 1930s.

The relative passivity of the Venezuelan peasantry explains in part the government's willingness to accept its participation in the CTV. Another explanation is that AD was in power at the time of the birth of the CTV in 1947 and at its rebirth in 1959, and in both instances the party enjoyed overwhelming influence in the FCV. The FCV's main national leaders were AD trade unionists who committed themselves to labor organizing in the countryside.

Nevertheless, the FCV's rhetoric and program diverged in significant ways from AD's positions. FCV leaders occasionally invoked the possibility of resorting to violence if agrarian reform were blocked.[99] Such language was virtually tabu for AD political leaders, who were intent on refuting charges of extremism against the party. In addition, at the time of the FCV's founding in 1947, AD peasant leaders argued that a thoroughgoing program of land distribution should be the party's most important goal due to the fact that the latifundio system was the nation's premier economic institution.[100]

This order of priority was not accepted by all party leaders. Pedro Torres, the FCV's secretary general after 1959, wrote that "I had to engage in time-consuming internal struggles in my own Party, so that people would realize the importance of the peasantry and what being a champion of the Agrarian Reform implied."[101] FCV President Ramón Quijada and other AD members in the federation's leadership opposed Betancourt's imposition of Carlos Luis Barrera (a trade unionist from the state of Lara) as the party's national agrarian secretary during the *trienio* on grounds that he lacked ties with the peasant movement.[102] Quijada, who for a long time maintained a position independent of the three factions in AD, declared in 1962 that his two-decade struggle to organize the peasantry had been "*al margen de* [divorced from] AD."[103]

The internal debate in AD centered on two different concepts of agrarian reform. The reform proposed by President Betancourt and promulgated in March 1960 was principally designed to distribute uncultivated land in order to increase agricultural production. An important aspect of the reform was the effort to settle peasants on virgin land, much of which was in remote areas. As a first step to satisfying peasant demands, the government was to distribute public property or attempt to purchase privately owned land. When these procedures were insufficient, uncultivated land would be expropriated and, after that, pasturage. Only after the Instituto Agrario Nacional (IAN) could demonstrate that these options had been exhausted could it proceed to distribute cultivated acreage, paying off the land in bonds and the rest of the property value as well as the mortgage in cash. Following passage of the agrarian reform, AD insisted that the holdings of "productive and capitalistic agricultural companies" be left intact and only "unproductive and feudal lands" be targeted for expropriation.[104]

An additional objective of the agrarian reform was to put an end to the land invasions that shook the countryside in the years following the overthrow of Pérez Jiménez. This agitation was concentrated in the central region where vacant fertile land was the least available. Betancourt, in his dramatic speech announcing the initiation of the agrarian reform (at the site of the Battle of Carabobo, which virtually ended the War of Independence), declared that his government did not "tolerate the violent seizure of lands, because in the system based on law which exists in Venezuela nobody is authorized to take justice into his own hands."[105] Indeed, after 1962 when the land takeovers subsided, land distribution and agricultural assistance were sharply curtailed, much to the disapproval of AD peasant leaders.[106]

The FCV insisted that the point of departure of the agrarian reform be the destruction of the latifundio system through expropriations and its replacement by small- and medium-sized holdings. The FCV pointed out that with 80 percent of the agricultural population landless, the underlying problem in the countryside was a *social* one—that is, satisfying peasant land aspirations—rather than an *economic* one—that is, increasing agricultural production. At the FCV's 1959 congress, Ramón Quijada argued that capitalist agriculture was just as exploitative of the peasantry as feudal relations. He added that the defenders of rural capitalism, despite their support for the agrarian reform, were "more dangerous" than semifeudal interests because of their enormous financial resources and their predominant influence within the government.[107] To stave off the consolidation of capitalism, the FCV favored giving preference to peasants in the distribution of expropriated land and temporarily banning the reselling of parcels granted under the agrarian reform. In addition, the federation called for the transformation of rural workers on capitalist estates into small property holders.[108]

FCV leaders denied that small- and medium-sized agricultural production was inherently inefficient. They pointed out that the *conucos*, which were based on subsistence agriculture, were part of the latifundio system. Once the *conuquero* received a land title and was freed of semifeudal obligations, he would utilize more advanced agricultural methods in order to produce staple crops.

The FCV's positions represented an implicit critique of the agrarian reform and its shortcomings. The reform did nothing to halt capitalist expansion in the countryside. In addition, FCV leaders belittled the importance of the colonization schemes, which figured so prominently in the reform, on the basis that they diverted attention and resources from the main goal, which was the destruction of the latifundio system. Other important demands put forward by the FCV were not incorporated into the reform. This was the case with the FCV's call for a ban on foreclosures of peasant property and the resolution passed at the CTV's Third Congress, at the urging of peasant delegates, stating that the government should limit the size of all agricultural holdings, regardless of whether or not they were efficiently exploited.[109] In addition, Quijada's insistence that the program of land distribution be implemented within a period of two years was not heeded by the architects of the agrarian reform.

The FCV demanded participation in all agrarian agencies in order to ensure that government programs of technical and financial assistance and land distribution favored small- and medium-sized farms and not capitalist enterprises. The CTV's Third Congress recommended that peasant representation be established at 40 percent. The final draft of the agrarian reform, which allowed one FCV delegate to sit on the IAN's National Directorate, omitted a proposed clause that stipulated that peasants would be represented in all local commissions in charge of land distribution.[110] FCV leaders complained that the IAN and the Ministry of Agriculture (MAC) often favored large-scale producers because they were in a better position to arrive at technical decisions than were peasants.[111] The FCV reached an agreement with the BAP, which was under the direction of Reinaldo Cervini (a left-leaning businessman), whereby peasant representatives served as brokers in the authorization of credit. The program was harshly criticized by various AD leaders and government officials on grounds that it was tantamount to an "emergency plan," whose objective was to subsidize and placate peasants rather than stimulate production.[112]

Despite his fiery rhetoric and outstanding differences with the government, Quijada for some time was aware of the importance of maintaining party discipline as well as the danger of precipitating political conflict.[113] In the congressional debate over the agrarian reform, Quijada voted against a proposition submitted by Communist delegate Eduardo Machado that would have limited the size of agricultural estates. While admitting that the labor movement had previously embraced the same position, Quijada argued that conditions were not ripe for such a radical reform and denied that it was a sine qua non for the destruction of the latifundio system. Pragmatic considerations also led him to accept the agrarian reform as a good start, while upbraiding the Left for its harsh criticisms of the law. The FCV president sharply attacked "pseudo-socialist" leftists for their support for land invasions and their position that the state should hold on to titles of expropriated property in order to pave the way for the socialization of agriculture.[114]

Quijada's flexible approach was also demonstrated by his willingness to put aside his opposition to the principle of the gratuity of distributed land. Gratuity was defended not only by other political parties, but also by Quijada's peasant leader rivals in AD. Quijada strongly felt that the agrarian reform would generate wider support and be more effective if the peasants were charged a minimum fee for the land they received.

Quijada's adherence to the FCV's positions led him into open conflict with the IAN. He challenged the reliability of the institute's statistics on land distribution and objected to the scant expropriation of cultivated land. Quijada's clash with the government and the Old Guard of AD came to a head in December 1961 when he refused to send peasant delegates to the CTV's Fourth Congress, which was boycotted by the Left. The CTV's decision to intervene in the FCV split the federation, with about half of its leadership initially siding with Quijada. The more moderate, progovernment AD peasant leaders defended the "integral" thrust of the agrarian reform, which meant, in effect, that land distribution had to be carried out in tandem with the costly process of creating a rural infrastructure (for example, roads and hospitals), thus ruling out extensive expropriation over a short period.[115]

Quijada joined the ARS faction of AD, which put forward a thorough critique of the agrarian reform. Not only did the ARSistas consider the IAN's efforts to promote colonization schemes misplaced, but also they argued that all expropriated property should be paid for with bonds rather than in cash.[116] In the 1963 presidential election, Quijada switched his support to the candidacy of Arturo Usler Pietri but plainly failed to deliver the peasant vote. These brusk political realignments, as well as the government's channeling of rural programs through the rival FCV, undermined Quijada's peasant following and led to the disbandment of the federation that he headed.

Many AD leaders ascribed Quijada's break with the party to personal ambition. Betancourt was convinced that Quijada was set on becoming director of the IAN,[117] whereas Armando González, who succeeded him as FCV president, has stated:

> Quijada was an individual who traditionally identified with . . . the Old Guard. But he did not feel satisfied with the concessions which were granted him and the power that he had to manage—according to his fancy—the IAN and other [government] bodies . . . and so he joined the ranks of those who left the party. He believed that on leaving [the party] all the peasants would leave with him.[118]

This version has misled historians, who play down the concrete issues that lay behind the ARS split.[119] The model embraced by the FCV under Quijada's leadership was not shared by the Betancourt administration and AD's Old Guard. Furthermore, the FCV's insistence on direct participation in the programs carried out by the IAN, BAP, and MAC obeyed a pragmatic imperative. The FCV was convinced that the thrust of the agrarian reform was ill defined; it was necessary to exercise control over the agencies in charge of the implementation of agrarian policy in order to ensure that the federation's two basic objectives were accomplished: destruction of the latifundio system and allocation of desirable land and adequate financial and technical assistance to the peasants. Indeed, these same stated goals were continuously defended by Armando González and other FCV leaders who remained loyal to AD.

Notes

1. Ruth Berins Collier and David Collier, *Shaping the Political Arena: Critical Junctures, the Labor Movement, and Regime Dynamics in Latin America* (Princeton, NJ: Princeton University Press, 1991), p. 22.

2. Steve Ellner, "Venezuelans Reflect on the Meaning of the *23 de Enero*," *Latin American Research Review* 20, no. 1 (1985): 253.

3. For accounts of the 1950 oil workers' strike see Héctor Lucena, *El movimiento obrero petrolero: proceso de formación y desarrollo* (Caracas: Ediciones Centauro, 1982), pp. 427–31; and Rafael Dum, "Huelga petrolera nacional de mayo 1950," in Alberto J. Pla, Pedro Castro, Ramón Aizpúrua et al., *Clase obrera, partidos y sindicatos en Venezuela, 1936–1950* (Caracas: Ediciones Centauro, 1982), pp. 403–47.

4. For accounts of the Turén uprising see Agustín Blanco Muñoz, "Turén: una masacre controversial," *El Nacional*, October 13, 1982, p. C-10; ibid., September 29, 1981, p. D-2; and *Noticias de Venezuela* [published by the PCV in Mexico], no. 21 (March 1953): 16.

5. José J. Hernández, Edgar Ravel, and Margarita López, "El comportamiento del estado frente a las clases trabajadoras durante el período 1948 a 1958" (Paper presented at the Second Conference of the Taller Movimiento Obrero Latinoamericano (MOLA), October–November 1980); Fredy Rincón N., *El nuevo ideal nacional y los planes económico-militares de Pérez Jiménez, 1952–1957* (Caracas: Ediciones Centauro, 1982).

6. For the thesis that assigns the principal role to the armed forces and minimizes the importance of other sectors in the events leading up to January 23, see Hugo Trejo, *La revolución no ha terminado . . . !* (Valencia, Venezuela: Vadell Hermanos, 1977). For the various viewpoints regarding the participation of diverse sectors in the overthrow of the dictatorship, see Ellner, "Venezuelans Reflect on the Meaning," 244–56.

7. Eloy Torres [CTV secretary of organization after 1959], interview, October 29, 1986, Caracas. Articles critical of the Venezuelan military regime appeared with increasing frequency in the U.S. commercial press in 1957. The U.S. State Department made plans to break diplomatic relations with Pérez Jiménez and favored the naming of César González, Venezuela's ambassador in Washington, as provisional president. See Gerónimo Pérez Rescaniere, "Secretos del 23 de enero," *El Nacional*, January 23, 1988, p. A-4.

8. Teodoro Petkoff, *¿Socialismo para Venezuela?* 3d ed. (Caracas: Editorial Fuentes, 1972), p. 139.

9. Idem, *Del optimismo de la voluntad: escritos políticos* (Caracas: Ediciones Centauro, 1987), pp. 58–59.

10. Ramón J. Velásquez, "Aspectos de la evolución política de Venezuela en el último medio siglo," in *Venezuela moderna: Medio siglo de historia, 1926–1976* (Caracas: Editorial Ariel, 1979), p. 218.

11. *Tribuna Popular* [PCV newspaper], July 19, 1958, p. 13; Juan Herrera, interview, May 5, 1976, Caracas.

12. *Frente Sindical* [published by the CSU] 2 (October 4, 1958): 3; "La Federación de Trabajadores de la Industria Gráfica de Venezuela a la clase trabajadora del país," 1958, MOLA Archive, located in the National Congress, vol. 10, 1958–1960 (hereafter cited as MOLA Archive, followed by volume number).

13. *El Nacional*, June 21, 1958, p. 48. Many of the demands put forward by labor following the overthrow of Pérez Jiménez were aimed at individuals. Of the seventy-eight petitions that unions introduced in the Labor Ministry in 1958 as a prerequisite for going on strike, twelve called for the removal of heavy-handed supervisory personnel. See Ministerio del Trabajo, *Memoria y Cuenta*, 1958, pp. 239–49.

14. *Tribuna Popular*, March 8, 1958, p. 21; "Declaraciones del Partido Comunista de Venezuela" (Caracas, February 1958), in *Enero 23 de 1958: reconquista de la libertad por acción del pueblo y de las fuerzas armadas* (Caracas: Ediciones Centauro 82, 1982), p. 290.

15. Ministerio del Trabajo, *Memoria y Cuenta*, 1958, p. 9.

16. Alejandro Cruz Villegas [1960s–1980s, CUTV secretary-general], interview, February 13, 1987, Caracas; Francisco J. Camacaro [provisional CUTV president], interview, October 27, 1986, Caracas.

17. *Ultimas Noticias*, January 15, 1959, p. 41; ibid., January 16, 1959, p. 46; *El Nacional*, January 6, 1959, p. 34.

18. Vicente Piñate [CTV secretary of finance after 1959], interview, November 24, 1986, Caracas; *Tribuna Popular*, July 5, 1958, p. 4.

19. *Frente Sindical*, October 4, 1958, p. 3.

20. Vicente Piñate, interview, November 24, 1986, Caracas.

21. *Ultimas Noticias*, January 16, 1959, p. 4.

22. *El Nacional*, January 10, 1959, p. 33.

23. Manuel Peñalver, "No existe conquista social o económica que no tenga huella cetevista," in *CTV: 50 años de historia, 1936–1986* (n.p., n.d.), p. 37.

24. Cruz Villegas, interview, February 13, 1987, Caracas.

25. *Tribuna Popular*, July 12, 1958, p. 13.

26. The following day, Castro addressed the National Congress where he stated, "In other countries one could fear that the revolution could retrocede, but I am sure that will not happen here." *Ultimas Noticias*, January 25, 1959, p. 2.

27. *El Nacional*, January 13, 1960, p. 26.

28. Eloy Torres, interview, October 29, 1986, Caracas.

29. "Tesis Sindical" [ratified at AD's Ninth Congress in 1958], MOLA Archive, vol. 10.

30. *Tribuna Popular*, August 5, 1959, p. 4. Quintero belonged to a dissident faction in the PCV in the 1940s that questioned the applicability of the orthodox theory of revolution in two stages in underdeveloped countries. See Steve Ellner, "Factionalism in the Venezuelan Communist Movement, 1937–1948," *Science and Society* 45, no. 1 (Spring 1981): 52–70.

31. Rafael Castañeda [after 1958, member of Executive Committee of the Federación Unificada de Trabajadores of the Federal District and URD labor leader; 1980s, member of CTV Executive Committee and AD national deputy], interview, December 11, 1986, Caracas.

32. *A.D.* 40 (February 7, 1959): 5.

33. *El Nacional*, January 12, 1960, p. 33.

34. *A.D.* 42 (February 21, 1959): 21.

35. *Tribuna Popular*, January 31, 1959, p. 2.

36. Centro de Desarrollo (Cendes) of the Central University, *Conflictos y consenso*, interview no. 064, interviewee no. 186, 1963(?) (hereafter cited as Cendes C. C.). [I was given permission to review these in-depth interviews with nationally prominent figures in the early 1960s under the proviso that the names of the interviewees not be revealed.]

37. Eloy Torres, interview, October 29, 1986, Caracas.

38. PCV leaders complained that the Communist Youth members who entered the party at the time of the events of January 23, 1958, "have not really assimilated what the party is and its principles." *Tribuna Popular*, February 7, 1959, p. 5, and March 6, 1959, p. 11.

39. Ibid., May 29, 1959, p. 20.

40. Martín J. Ramírez [after 1959, CTV vice president], interview, October 23, 1986, Caracas.

41. Eloy Torres, *Ideología y sindicalismo* (Caracas: Cantaclaro, 1970), p. 63.

42. *El Nacional*, June 18, 1959, p. 41.

43. *A.D.* 52 (May 9, 1959): 16.

44. Ibid., 64 (August 1, 1959): 19; ibid., 69 (September 5, 1959): 18.

45. Interview no. 071, interviewee no. 023, February 3, 1964, Cendes, C. C.; Dagoberto González (*Copeyano* labor leader; CTV secretary of labor after 1959), interview, Caracas, February 12, 1987.

46. Eloy Torres, interview, October 29, 1986, Caracas.

47. Robert Jackson Alexander, *The Venezuelan Democratic Revolution* (New Brunswick, NJ: Rutgers University Press, 1964), p. 240. The CTV's proposal was accepted by the CTAL and CLASC but rejected by ORIT, which refused to meet

with the Communist-led CTAL. See "Que presenta el Comité Ejecutivo de la CTV al Consejo Central, que comprende el período del 23 de noviembre de 1959 al 16 de diciembre de 1960," MOLA, vol. 11.

48. *El Nacional*, November 20, 1959, p. 20.

49. Ibid., November 17, 1959, p. 12.

50. CTV, *III Congreso de Trabajadores de Venezuela: recopilación de informes, acuerdos, resoluciones y recomendaciones* (Caracas, 1960), n.p.

51. Steve Ellner, *The Venezuelan Petroleum Corporation and the Debate over Government Policy in Basic Industry, 1960–1976* (University of Glasgow Occasional Paper 47, 1987), pp. 11, 12.

52. *El Nacional*, November 16, 1959, p. 42.

53. CTV, *Un venezolano universal: Augusto Malavé Villalba* [pamphlet] (Caracas: August 1975), n.p.; Manuel Alfredo Rodríguez, "Florida Cristal," *El Nacional*, January 30, 1990, p. A-4.

54. Julio Cacique [metal workers' leader], interview, February 22, 1987, Caracas.

55. Pérez Salinas, interview, October 22, 1986, Caracas.

56. Serafino Romualdi, *Presidents and Peons: Recollections of a Labor Ambassador in Latin America* (New York: Funk and Wagnalls, 1967), p. 488.

57. Ibid., p. 492.

58. Ibid., p. 488.

59. *A.D.* 81 (November 28, 1959): 7.

60. FTC, *Tesis sindical de COPEI aprobada por la VII Convención Nacional del Partido . . .* (April 1960), p. 6.

61. "Convención Nacional de COPEI: tesis sindical (April 8–12, 1960)," *F.T.C. Boletín Informativo del Frente de Trabajadores Copeyanos* 2 (May 1960): 5; Dagoberto González, interview, February 12, 1987, Caracas.

62. Juan Bautista Fuenmayor, *Historia de la Venezuela política contemporánea, 1899–1969*, vol. 12 (Caracas: Miguel Angel García, 1985) p. 317.

63. *La Esfera*, October 26, 1960, p. 2.

64. "Bases para discusión sobre la actitud del movimiento obrero dentro de Acción Democrática," Caracas, September 5, 1959 [mimeographed], MOLA Archive, vol. 10.

65. Torres, *Ideología y sindicalismo*, p. 73.

66. Sulpicio Ventura Quero [*Copeyano* labor leader; Executive Committee of Fedepetrol], interview, December 10, 1986, Caracas; *El Nacional*, November 21, 1959, p. 36; ibid., January 7, 1959, p. 30; Moisés Moleiro, *El partido del pueblo: crónica de un fraude*, 2d ed. (Valencia, Venezuela: Vadell Hermanos, 1979), p. 210.

67. *La Esfera*, March 10, 1960, p. 13; Amalio Belmonte Guzmán, Dimitri Briceño Reyes, and Henry Urbano Taylor, *Ensayo sobre historia política de Venezuela (1917–1968)* (Caracas: Academia Nacional de la Historia, 1981), pp. 136, 140.

68. *Izquierda* [MIR newspaper] 5, "Editorial," June 10, 1960, n.p.

69. Magarita López Maya and Nikolaus Werz, *El estado y el movimiento sindical (1958–1980)* (Caracas, Cendes, 1981), pp. 30, 52. Despite these austerity measures, Betancourt carried out ambitious plans to promote industrialization. Some historians have lauded Betancourt for "sowing the seeds of petroleum" in the industrial sector rather than favoring the agricultural export sector. See, for instance, the paper presented by Bernard Mommer at the symposium "Rómulo Betancourt: Historia y Contemporaneidad," Caracas, February 23, 1989. The fact is, however, that during Betancourt's rule (1959–1964) the goal of industrial development was

accepted by all major currents of political opinion. Venezuela was almost completely lacking in agricultural exports and thus there was little support for a conservative position in opposition to industrial growth.

70. Eleazar Díaz Rangel, *Reportajes* (Caracas: Asociación Venezolana de Periodistas, 1965), p. 62; Luis Pinto, interview, May 20, 1976, Puerto La Cruz.

71. Moleiro, *El partido del pueblo*, p. 214.

72. *Copei*, June 25, 1948, p. 7; *Frente* [periodical of the Frente de Trabajadores Copeyano] 34 (July 1986): 6.

73. López Maya and Werz, *El estado y el movimiento sindical*, p. 28. Rodolfo Quintero, Cruz Villegas, and other top Communist labor leaders were opposed to the guerrilla struggle from the outset. Quintero, interview, April 28, 1976, Caracas.

74. Piñate, interview, November 24, 1986, Caracas; César Olarte [MEPista, CTV secretary-general], interview, February 3, 1987, Caracas.

75. *Le República*, January 24, 1962, p. 2.

76. Julio Godio, *El movimiento obrero venezolano 1945–1980*, 3 vols. (Caracas: Ildis, 1980–1985), 2:230.

77. Andrew McClellan [inter-American representative, AFL-CIO], interview, Washington, DC, December 19, 1974; Alexander, *The Venezuelan Democratic Revolution*, pp. 241–42; Godio, *El movimiento obrero*, 2: 246.

78. John D. Martz, "The Growth and Democratization of the Venezuelan Labor Movement," *Inter-American Economic Affairs* 17, no. 2 (Autumn 1963): 13–15; Cruz Villegas, interview, February 13, 1987, Caracas.

79. Moisés Moleiro, *La izquierda y su proceso* (Caracas: Ediciones Centauro, 1977), p. 51; Torres, *Ideología y sindicalismo*, p. 108.

80. *Frente* [Special Edition entitled "Historia del movimiento sindical socialcristiano en Venezuela"], May 1983, pp. vii–viii.

81. Torres, interview, October 29, 1986, Caracas.

82. Dagoberto González, interview, February 1, 1987, Caracas.

83. *La República*, June 1, 1961, p. 6.

84. *Frente*, May 1983, p. viii.

85. Torres, *Ideología y sindicalismo*, p. 136.

86. "Informe que presenta el Comité Ejecutivo de la CTV al IV Congreso de Trabajadores" (December 8, 1961), p. 4, MOLA Archive, vol. 11, 1961–1963.

87. *La República*, May 24, 1961, p. 22.

88. "Informe que presenta el Comité Ejecutivo de la CTV," p. 6, MOLA Archive, vol. 11; "Importante documento de la C.T.V.," *Ceteve* 1, p. 11, MOLA Archive, vol. 11; Confederación de Trabajadores de Venezuela, *Antecedentes y testimonios de los congresos de la CTV*, 4 vols. (Caracas: Inaesin, n.d.), 3: 13.

89. Pérez Salinas, "Notas sobre la plataforma económica de la C.T.V.," *Cruz del Sur* [Caracas] 5, no. 49–50, (August–September 1960): 41–43; interview no. 094, interviewee no. 184, 1963 (?), pp. 58–59, Cendes C. C.

90. The AD youth faction that formed MIR also criticized Betancourt for assuming a weak position in the face of the right-wing military threat and refusing to purge the armed forces of *perezjimenista* officers. At the time of the split in AD, there was some conjecturing that González Navarro would join MIR. See Gehard Cartay Ramírez, *Caldera y Betancourt: Constructores de la Democracia* (Caracas: Centauro, 1987), p. 245; and Manuel Caballero, *Las Venezuelas del siglo veinte* (Caracas: Grijalbo, 1988), p. 170. At the CTV's Third Congress, Betancourt responded to the Left's warnings regarding conspiratorial activity by discarding the possibility of a coup and stating that the "unjustified rumor [regarding a coup] constitutes a danger for the still unstable economic situation in Venezuela." Rómulo Betancourt, "Clausura del III Congreso de Trabajadores," in *La revolución*

democrática en Venezuela (Caracas: n.p., 1968), pp. 160–61. Robert Alexander argues that Betancourt dealt harshly with the military plotters. See Robert Jackson Alexander, *Rómulo Betancourt and the Transformation of Venezuela* (New Brunswick, NJ: Transaction Books, 1982), pp. 472–76. The severe treatment accorded the allegedly right-wing conspirators during the uprising in Barcelona (known as the *barcelonazo*) lends itself to Alexander's contention. For an opposite version that contrasts the government's ruthless handling of left-wing street protests with its laxness toward right-wing military plotters, see Fuenmayor, *Historia de la Venezuela política* 12: 306–26.

91. Cruz Villegas, interview, February 13, 1987, Caracas.

92. *Clarín* [leftist newspaper], March 25, 1963, p. 13.

93. Interview no. 116, interviewee no. 173, April 1964, Cendes, C. C.

94. Torres, *Ideología y sindicalismo*, p. 136.

95. Laureano Torrealba, interview, October 27, 1986, Caracas.

96. Martín J. Ramírez, interview, October 23, 1986, Caracas.

97. Godio, *El movimiento obrero venezolano* 2: 245.

98. Pedro Ortega Díaz, interview, April 22, 1989, Puerto La Cruz.

99. Ramón Quijada, "Discurso en la instalación del Primer Congreso Campesino" (1959?), in Ramón Quijada, *Reforma agraria en Venezuela* (Caracas: Editorial Arte, 1963), p. 129.

100. Idem, "Proyecto de Tesis Agraria para el Partido Acción Democrática" (1945), in Quijada, *Reforma agraria*, pp. 33, 46.

101. Pedro Torres, "Prólogo," in ibid., p. 10.

102. Armando González, interview, January 29, 1987, Puerto La Cruz.

103. *La República*, January 8, 1962, p. 8.

104. *El Nacional*, May 10, 1960, p. 29; Belmonte Guzmán, Briceño Reyes, and Urbano Taylor argue that the Agrarian Reform facilitated the implantation of large-scale capitalism in the Venezuelan countryside. See *Ensayo sobre historia política*, p. 122. Luis Llambi and Andrew L. Cousins deny that medium-sized capitalist agriculturalists in contemporary Venezuela emerged from the subsistence-level peasantry, as was supposed to have happened under the Agrarian Reform. See their "Petty Capitalist Production in Agriculture: Lessons from Five Case Studies in Venezuela, 1945–1983," *Latin American Perspectives* 16, n. 3 (Summer 1989): 86–120.

105. Fuenmayor, *Historia de la Venezuela política* 12: 230.

106. Interview 108, interviewee 070, November 27, 1963, pp. 64, 140–43, Cendes, C. C.

107. Ramón Quijada, "El campesino ante la Reforma Agraria" [speech, May 30, 1959], in Quijada, *Reforma agraria*, p. 68; AD, "Tesis Agraria," in *Acción Democrática: doctrina y programa* (Caracas: Secretaría Nacional de Propaganda, 1962), p. 180.

108. Armando González, "Inauguración del I foro nacional sobre trabajo rural" [July 23, 1969], in Armando González, *Grava de una misma cantera* (Caracas: Editorial Arte, 1977), p. 392.

109. Quijada, "El campesino ante la reforma agraria," p. 70; idem, [speech, February 1961], in Quijada, *Reforma agraria*, p. 78; Godio, *El movimiento obrero venezolano* 2: 214.

110. Torres, *Ideología y sindicalismo*, p. 47.

111. Interview no. 108, interviewee no. 070, November 27, 1963, pp. 66–67, Cendes, C. C.

112. FCV, "Manifiesto del Consejo Directivo Nacional de la Federación Campesina de Venezuela," in Quijada, *Reforma agraria*, pp. 199–209.

113. Quijada, interview, October 15, 1977, Cumaná.

114. *A.D.* 75 (October 17, 1959): 15.

115. John Duncan Powell, *Political Mobilization of the Venezuelan Peasant* (Cambridge, MA: Harvard University Press, 1971), pp. 194–96.

116. Interview no. 184, interviewee no. 094, n.d., pp. 40–41, Cendes, C. C.

117. Alexander, *Rómulo Betancourt*, p. 450.

118. Armando González, interview, January 29, 1987, Caracas.

119. Elsewhere, I have argued that the ARS split had an important programmatic content. This is especially evident in the case of Quijada, who championed a model of small- and medium-sized agricultural holdings that was rejected by leading members of AD and the Betancourt administration. See Steve Ellner, "Political Party Dynamics and the Outbreak of Guerrilla Warfare in Venezuela," *Inter-Amercan Economic Affairs* 34, no. 2 (Autumn 1980): 15–16. The members of AD's "Old Guard" and even those like Luis Beltrán Prieto F. and Jesús Paz Galarraga, who later formed MEP, argued that the ARS split centered around personalities rather than issues. Interview no. 062, interviewee no. 177, October 25, 1963, Cendes, C. C.

2 Economic Recovery and Boom, 1964–1979

The Administration of Raúl Leoni, 1964–1969

At AD's Thirteenth National Congress in July 1963, trade unionist Francisco Olivo, speaking in the name of the Labor Bureau, formally proposed Raúl Leoni as candidate for the upcoming presidential elections. Leoni had always maintained close ties with AD labor leaders; as labor minister during the *trienio* period of 1945 to 1948 he had facilitated the fourfold increase in the number of labor unions. President Rómulo Betancourt adamantly, but unsuccessfully, opposed the nomination of Leoni on grounds that it would preclude renewal of the governing coalition due to Copei's reservations concerning his links with AD labor. Leoni was elected in December with 33 percent of the vote; Caldera received 20 percent; Jóvito Villalba, 18 percent; Uslar Pietri (whose supporters would subsequently found the Frente Nacional Democrático—FND), 16 percent; Wolfgang Larrazábal, 9 percent; and Raúl Ramos Giménez (of ARS), 2 percent.

Leoni invited URD and the FND to join his cabinet. Many AD labor leaders, along with the party's secretary-general, Jésus Paz Galarraga, hailed the exclusion of the allegedly right-wing Copei from the Leoni administration as a sign that it would assume a leftist orientation; some optimistically predicted that it would become a "workers' government."[1] While readily accepting URD as a coalition partner, these same AD leaders were wary of the role that the FND would play, due to its conservative positions on economic policy.[2]

Two important, albeit gradual, trends worked to the benefit of Leoni during his term in office. The economy recovered from the contraction of the late 1950s as import substitution policies contributed to the growth of traditional industries.[3] In addition, the guerrilla movement, which reached its apex in the months preceding the 1963 elections, lost momentum as the PCV called for a negotiated solution under the slogan "Democratic Peace."

Leoni's five-year rule was characterized by labor peace. It was the only presidential period since 1936 in which no important labor conflicts took place. The average number of man-hours lost per year due to strikes was only 34.1 percent of those registered during the Betancourt presidency (excluding 1959, for which statistics are not available). Leoni himself boasted of the prevailing labor harmony, which he maintained stood in sharp contrast to the terrorist activity perpetuated by the insurgent Left.[4]

Two laws enacted by the Leoni administration in 1966 were acclaimed by the CTV, but have since been questioned by opposition parties as benefiting the labor bureaucracy without enhancing the standard of living of rank-and-file workers. The Law of Workers' Representation provided the labor movement with a seat on the board of directors of all state-run companies and institutes, a setup designed to lead to *cogestión* (workers' participation in management decision making). AD leaders had rejected *cogestión* as a deceptive arrangement at the CTV's Third Congress in 1959, but subsequently their attitude changed. CTV president González Navarro pointed out at the confederation's Fifth Congress in 1964 that organized labor had gone beyond the "economistic" stage "exclusively limited to the formulation of bread-and-butter demands"[5]; shortly thereafter *cogestión* became a labor movement catchword.

The Workers Bank Law provided the legal basis for the CTV-controlled Banco de los Trabajadores (BTV). Impetus for the BTV came from the "Inter-American Conference of Labor Ministers" in Bogotá in 1965, which called for the creation of similar banks throughout the continent, as well as from the AFL-CIO after the CTV affiliated with ORIT. A loan of 27 million bolívares from the AFL-CIO, which was channeled through the state-run Venezuelan Development Corporation, facilitated the founding of the BTV. The Venezuelan government also extended capital by purchasing the bank's "Class B" stock, which provided it with less input in decision making than the "Class A" stock held by the CTV and its affiliate organizations. Malavé Villalba, who maintained close ties with international labor, was named the first president of the BTV. (Chapter 8 examines *cogestión* and the BTV in detail.)

A third major law promulgated in 1966 reformed the nation's social security system. Venezuela first established obligatory social security in 1940 at a time when developed countries were beginning to do the same. The coverage, however, was limited to workers in the capital region with monthly salaries under 600 bolívares and was mainly oriented around health care. By 1966 most other Latin American nations had established more comprehensive systems. The 1966 law extended the service throughout the entire nation, took in previously uncovered workers (including public employees with regard to certain benefits), and added provisions for retirement and incapacitation.[6] Organized labor, employers, and the government had two seats each on the Instituto Venezolano de Seguro Social (IVSS), which was under the jurisdiction of the Labor Ministry. In keeping with its modest participation in the political and economic life of the nation, the Labor Ministry did not use IVSS patronage as a lever to promote the personal ambitions of labor ministers, as was the case in Brazil, prior to the 1964 military coup, and other nations where they had considerable power.[7]

During the Leoni presidency, *Copeyano* labor leaders, grouped in the Frente de Trabajadores Copeyanos (FTC), began to assume a more critical stand in the CTV. Their position was shaped by the decision of *Copeyano* political leaders to distance themselves from the government under the slogan "Autonomy of Action," once it became evident that they would not form part of the ruling coalition. In addition, with the subsidence of the leftist threat to the democratic regime, leading *Copeyanos* modified their vehement anticommunist rhetoric and began to emphasize other issues.

A lengthy document drafted by *Copeyano* trade unionists dated October 18, 1966, signaled a new emphasis on the assertion of labor autonomy. The FTC upbraided AD labor leaders for taking cues from the party and the government and failing to comply with CTV electoral regulations, and hinted at their mismanagement of union funds. The *Copeyanos* also criticized AD trade unionists for refusing to join them in submitting legislation to the National Congress, which the CTV was on record as supporting. In particular, the FTC called for enactment of laws granting job security to employees in the private and public sectors (known respectively as the *Ley de Estabilidad Laboral* and *Ley de Carrera Administrativa*).[8]

URD's decision to join the Leoni administration paved the way for the party's return to the CTV. At the time, URD labor leaders stated that their reaffiliation with the confederation was conditional on passage of a true agrarian reform and the liberation of political prisoners and that the CTV and CUTV should attempt to reach an understanding.[9] URD trade unionists refrained from disbanding the oil workers' federation Fetrahidrocarburos, which they had founded along with leftists in opposition to the AD-dominated Fedepetrol. With the systematic purging of Communist and MIR workers from the oil industry, URD was left in complete control of Fetrahidrocarburos. In subsequent years, Fetrahidrocarburos joined the CTV (thus creating an anomalous situation of dual unionism at the federation level within the same confederation) and drew up labor contracts with Fedepetrol for collective bargaining, a practice that leftist oil worker leaders had previously opposed.[10]

Of the 762 delegates who attended the CTV's Fifth Congress in November 1964, 70.6 percent belonged to AD, 14 percent to Copei, 12.5 percent to URD, 1.6 percent to the FND, and 1.3 percent to the left-leaning Fuerza Democrática Popular (FDP). In his opening address, González Navarro underscored the central role that the CTV and the armed forces had played in the consolidation and defense of the democratic system. Speeches were also delivered by Arturo Jauregui, secretary general of ORIT, and Eduardo García, of the Christian Democratic Clasc.

During the latter period of the Leoni administration, differences in AD surfaced, producing the party's third division in the decade. A near majority of AD labor leaders, including González Navarro, sided with the faction headed by Paz Galarraga, which founded MEP in 1967. As in the case of ARS in 1962, the schism was set off by a dispute involving personalities. AD's National Directive Committee, prodded by Rómulo Betancourt from abroad, refused to recognize the triumph of Luis Beltrán Prieto Figueroa, whom Paz supported in party primaries for the presidential election of 1968.

A number of concrete economic issues galvanized tensions between Paz's followers and the Betancourt and Leoni administrations. The future MEPistas in the labor movement staunchly opposed the guerrilla struggle but felt that the Betancourt government went too far by accommodating elite interests in order to shore up the democratic system and face the economic crisis. They were particularly disappointed with the performance of President Leoni because they had thought he was aligned with them in the party and was in debt to them for their unswerving support when he was AD's presidential candidate. As the insurgent movement abated, they argued that the government was no longer dependent on powerful economic groups and could thus take a bolder approach. They chafed at Leoni's failure to revoke the Hunger Law (1961) by increasing the wages of government employees by 10 percent. González Navarro and other AD labor leaders took issue with official statistics that showed that all salaries in the public sector had been restored to their pre-1961 levels.[11]

The CTV supported the nationalization of basic industry and other nationalist economic policies, which Paz pronounced himself in favor of and over which he clashed with official policy on several occasions.[12] While the CTV called for a government monopoly on the sale of gasoline, Leoni failed to fulfill a campaign pledge to reserve 33 percent of the internal market for the state-run Venezuelan Petroleum Corporation.[13] Secretary-General Paz was in agreement with the memorandums that he received from party labor leaders protesting the appointment of business representatives to cabinet posts that formulated economic policy.[14] Many of the demands regarding economic policy and worker benefits that had been put forward by AD labor, including *estabilidad absoluta* for employees in the public and private sectors, were incorporated into Prieto Figueroa's program for the 1968 elections.[15]

In addition to economic issues, political differences relating to the insurgent Left and socialism separated the future MEPistas and those closely identified with Betancourt, and were reflected in the MEP split. In contrast to the attitude of AD hard-liners, the future MEPistas in the labor movement had been reluctant to accept the expulsion of leftists from the CTV. Later, Paz took the initiative in interviewing representatives of the clandestine Left in order to put an end to the armed struggle.[16] Following the MEP split

González Navarro, who continued as CTV president until 1970, would attempt to reach an agreement with leftist trade unionists to reunify the labor movement. On the ideological front, Paz was successful in getting AD to accept the democratic socialist label at its national convention in September 1965, albeit in timid form. This definition was accepted by most party labor leaders, and subsequently would be given greater emphasis by MEP.

During the Leoni period the CUTV lost most of its influence in organized labor. The refusal of government labor inspectors—allegedly following orders from the Labor Ministry—to process contracts introduced by CUTV unions undercut the confederation's labor support.[17] Of greater importance was the guerrilla struggle that obstructed the work of leftist trade unionists. Most MIR and PCV labor leaders were critical of the Left's decision to take up arms and objected to its tendency to exaggerate the political importance of rural areas and play down worker struggles.[18] Nevertheless, the intransigence of leftist parties reflected itself in the rhetoric employed by the CUTV. During these years, the CUTV attacked the CTV for betraying the working class and condemned certain labor laws as serving reactionary interests. CUTV spokesmen, for instance, called for the revocation of Decree 440, despite its mixed character (it restricted the right to strike but at the same time facilitated industrywide collective bargaining).

At first, the CUTV leadership took in trade unionists of diverse parties; it was headed by Horacio Scott Power, a URD member who was expelled from the party in early 1964. At the CUTV's founding congress—which was referred to as the "Fourth" Congress, since at the time of the division in the labor movement the leftists claimed to represent the true CTV, which had previously held three congresses—the confederation's national committee was chosen by consensus. At its Fifth Congress in 1967, however, the Communists took advantage of their majority and insisted on a winner-takes-all rule for the top positions in the confederation's leadership—an arrangement that the MIRistas opposed. The Communist slate, headed by Cruz Villegas, defeated the slate led by José Marcano of MIR who was supported by Power. As a result, the CUTV became increasingly viewed as a Communist labor movement.

During the latter years of the 1960s, labor organizations were more closely identified with political parties than ever before. While the CUTV fell under PCV domination, Fetrahidrocarburos became exclusively URD, with nearly all the members of its national committee belonging to that party. In addition, with the founding of MEP in 1967, many labor unions that had previously been led by AD trade unionists split in two. In subsequent years, labor leaders would discuss at length the harm that parallel unionism had inflicted on the labor movement. Some leftists would urge greater efforts to reunite the CUTV and the CTV, and would subsequently leave the former to join the latter, where the great majority of organized workers were grouped. National leaders of the CTV, while generally spurning negotiations with other confederations, called for greater centralization of the labor movement in order to eliminate parallel structures.

The Administration of Rafael Caldera, 1969–1974

The triumph of Rafael Caldera in the 1968 presidential elections with 29 percent of the vote was made possible by two occurrences. The AD division in 1967 splintered the vote of Copei's main rival party. In addition, Caldera was able to increase his vote over that of 1963 by 9 percentage points due in large part to Copei's efforts to move away from its image as a champion of oligarchic interests and anticommunism. Among Caldera's principal rivals were Gonzalo Barrios of AD, who received 27 percent; Miguel Angel Burelli Rivas, who was supported by URD, the FND, and the FDP, with 22 percent; and Prieto Figueroa of MEP, with 19 percent.

During his first eighteen months in office, Caldera faced formidable challenges in the form of mobilizations of workers and students and the obstruction of his program by the opposition in congress. With only 27 percent of the voting power in the Chamber of Deputies compared to 31 percent for AD, Copei was forced to come to terms with other parties, as AD had done over the last two presidential periods. Caldera attempted to name members of AD and other parties to cabinet positions, including González Navarro for the post of labor minister, but in all cases these offers were turned down.[19] Throughout this period AD made common cause with MEP and other left-leaning parties in congress by assuming leftist positions on economic policy. The president's problems were compounded by the unpopularity of his finance minister, Pedro Tinoco, who was the key formulator of economic policy. Tinoco, himself a banker who was linked with Rockefeller interests, drew up a retrogressive tax reform bill that included provisions for a sales tax.

Caldera recognized that the flurry of strikes in 1969 was due to the demands that had built up in the course of the decade.[20] Now that the economy had begun to pick up, the sacrifices and stringent measures imposed by the previous two administrations seemed unnecessary. The decline in guerrilla warfare removed another rationale for austerity policies. Indeed, upon taking office and over the objections of AD's secretary-general, Carlos Andrés Pérez, Caldera legalized the PCV, granted amnesty to Communist and MIR leaders, and abolished the Digepol, a special police force that had been accused of consistent violations of human rights.

Relations between the Caldera administration and the labor movement started off on a bad note as a result of a polemical exchange between Labor

Minister Alfredo Tarre Murzi and CTV spokesmen. Tarre Murzi questioned the ethical conduct of CTV and FCV (the Peasant Federation) leaders and called on both organizations to collaborate with his ministry in investigating union finances for the purpose of "impeding a general corruption of the labor movement."[21] Tarre Murzi also pledged to extend the CUTV and the Christian democratic Codesa (Confederación de Sindicatos Autónomos) their due recognition and to cease viewing the CTV as the sole representative of the working class. His comments drew a sharp response from CTV leaders who decided to boycott a reception organized by the government for labor representatives in commemoration of May Day. Even FTC representatives were irked by Tarre Murzi's remarks.[22] These reactions would set a precedent, whereby labor leaders of diverse parties would generally set aside political differences and come to the defense of the CTV when they felt that accusations against the confederation represented outside interference in its internal affairs.

A two-week strike of public schoolteachers in November 1969 combined bread-and-butter issues with professional demands such as the reduction of classroom size to a maximum of thirty students. The CTV, to which the Federación Venezolana de Maestros (FVM) belonged, backed the teachers, as did the CUTV and Codesa. Nevertheless, the CTV's support was qualified by its offer to play the role of mediator in the dispute. During the strike, many schools were taken over by the police. In reaching a settlement the Venezuelan state tacitly recognized the right of teachers to form a union, go on strike, and sign a contract (although it was called a *convenio* rather than *contrato*). The government granted the teachers virtual *estabilidad absoluta*, an achievement that the leftist CUTV hoped would spread to other sectors of the working class.[23] The inclusion of an *estabilidad* clause in the collective bargaining agreement would be a stepping-stone to one of the most important pieces of legislation of the Caldera administration—the *Ley de Carrera Administrativa* (1970)—which guaranteed public employees job security and other rights.

A second major strike broke out in December 1969 at Sidor, the state-run steel plant in Ciudad Guayana. The Executive Committee of the Asociación de Trabajadores de la Industria Siderúrgica (Atiss), which represented Sidor workers, was headed by Communists who had won the union elections the year before, and included several MEPistas. Atiss's main demand was the payment of sixty days' wages as a Christmas bonus (known as *utilidades*, or profit sharing, which is calculated on the basis of the company's earnings). Sidor had originally offered sixty days of *utilidades*, but then reduced its offer to between forty and forty-five. During the strike the National Guard surrounded Atiss's headquarters and launched hundreds of tear gas canisters to disperse workers. Atiss's call for a general strike throughout the region did not elicit a widespread response. The strike settlement, which was drawn up by the CTV, provided the steel workers a few concessions, but set *utilidades* at forty-five days and thus represented a defeat for the union.

Leaders of political parties with influence in organized labor assumed widely varying stands with respect to the steel workers' conflict. AD, which claimed Sidor as one of the major achievements of the government of Rómulo Betancourt and which had a dominant position on the company's board of directors, opposed the strike and threatened to withdraw from Atiss to form a parallel union.[24] The FTC also criticized the union, although less forcefully. MEP and several smaller left-leaning parties supported the steel workers. Nevertheless, CTV president González Navarro, who belonged to MEP, upheld a neutral and at times vacillating position. He faulted Atiss for failing to consult the CTV before going on strike and pointed out that Sidor, as a state-run company, should receive special treatment. González Navarro, along with fellow party member José Mollegas, president of Fetrametal with which Atiss was affiliated, called on the government to step in to settle the dispute.[25] The Communist-led CUTV pointed out that the workers' cause was just, but that the strike was not completely legal.[26]

PCVista Eloy Torres, who had played a leading role in the strike (shortly after his release from prison, where he spent six years for his participation in the leftist-inspired military uprising in Carúpano in 1962) has stated that "we gave the conflict a character that was overly aggressive and the government was thus able to isolate the strikers." Torres pointed out that the workers at Sidor were young and lacking political experience and were thus prone to engage in "ultraleftist" tactics, although the PCV leadership, which he represented, shared much of the responsibility. One of their principal errors was calling a general strike without counting on sufficient support in the labor movement.[27] Indeed, since the early years of the Betancourt administration—and up until May 18, 1989—general strike calls have not met a wide response and labor leaders have usually limited themselves to threatening their use in order to scare management and the government into making concessions.

During Caldera's first year in office, the relationships among the labor branches of AD, MEP, and Copei were ill defined. On the one hand, AD and MEP labor leaders in congress drafted the *Proyecto de Ley de Estabilidad en el Trabajo*, which outlawed layoffs without just cause, except in cases where mass firings were justified on economic or technological grounds. On the other hand, AD created parallel unions to represent iron workers in the state of Bolívar, bank employees in Caracas, white collar employees who belonged to ANDE, and in other sectors that were dominated by MEPistas.

AD trade unionists were particularly unhappy with the pact between MEP and Copei, which allowed MEPista Carlos Piñerua to displace a leading AD founder of the oil workers' movement, Luis Tovar, as president of Fedepetrol at its Fourth Congress in 1969. AD threatened to set up a parallel oil workers' federation and called on the government to intervene in contract negotiations in order to avoid an impending strike in the industry. In response to another MEP-Copei agreement in the Workers Federation of Zulia (Fetrazulia), AD set up a rival federation headed by Hugo Soto Socorro (who, as a member of the ARS Group, had belonged to the Executive Committee of the CUTV). Naturally, relations between *Copeyano* trade unionists and those of MEP and AD were equally troublesome due to the hardened opposition of the latter two parties to the Caldera administration.[28]

Prior to the CTV's Sixth Congress in 1970, both MEP and AD trade unionists were confident that their party was the largest in the labor movement. The representation at the congress was as follows: AD, 34 percent; MEP, 32 percent; Copei, 19 percent; URD, 12 percent; and FDP, 1 percent. MEP and Copei trade unionists discussed the possibility of extending the agreement that they had reached in Fetrazulia and Fedepetrol in order to occupy the top positions in the CTV's Executive Committee. Copei union leaders were particularly interested in delivering a heavy blow to AD; since the issuance of the *Copeyano* document of October 18, 1966, they considered AD to be their principal adversary in the labor movement. AD and Copei politicians, however, urged the labor leaders of their respective parties to reach an agreement in order to avoid passing control of the CTV to the left-leaning MEP. As a result, AD's Francisco Olivo was selected president of the CTV, while *Copeyano* Rafael León León was named to the number-two post of secretary-general. AD's proposal to create a new position of vice president in order to accommodate MEP fell through.[29] The MEPistas, who believed that their delegate strength entitled them to the secretary-generalship, decided to run a separate slate at the congress, thus departing from the tradition whereby the confederation's Executive Committee is formed on the basis of a consensus. As a result of the voting, the CTV's national committee consisted of five AD members, four MEPistas, three *Copeyanos*, two URDistas, and one member of the FDP.

MEPistas and other leftists have pointed to the pact between AD and Copei at the Sixth Congress as evidence that those two parties, as champions of the status quo, always reach an agreement in critical situations in order to block the triumph of popular interests and the Left.[30] The incident also allegedly demonstrates that AD and Copei labor leaders invariably succumb to party pressure rather than defend a truly autonomous position. Copei's trade union secretary, Dagoberto González, has presented a version both recognizing that strong political pressure was exerted and denying that the alliance was imposed on *Copeyano* trade unionists against their will:

> One year before the [Sixth] Congress, AD leaders, among them Francisco Olivo and the secretary general of that party Carlos Andrés Pérez, proposed to us that we try to reach an understanding in all the regional [state] federations in

order to unite, specifically . . . in three regional congresses that were to be held
the same weekend in the states of Trujillo, Bolívar and the other I do not
remember. They . . . raised this possibility in a meeting with Arístides Beaujón,
at the time [Copei's] secretary general, and myself. I was very categorical in
not accepting . . . this type of understanding in spite of the well-defended
position assumed by the secretary general of Copei [in favor of it] because we
had been the victim of violations . . . of previous understandings, above all the
failure to apply regulations, for example, with regard to the secret vote in
elections. I am pleased to point out that the secretary general of Copei left us at
liberty to decide on the issue, which was a magnificent demonstration of trade
union autonomy. We thus confronted AD in these elections which provoked a
situation of tension which finally forced the *Adecos* . . . to correct their
behavior. It is possible that AD . . . thought that we would accept on the basis
of political party objectives. But when we obstinately decided not to ally with
AD . . . AD had to correct their attitudes and this opened space so that in a very
free and dignified manner on our part we acceded to the agreement with Olivo
at the CTV congress.[31]

The Sixth Congress was a watershed event in Venezuelan labor history.
AD labor leaders reasserted their hegemony, which they retained throughout
the subsequent two decades. Awarded the position of secretary-general,
Copei assumed the role of loyal opposition in the CTV and soon displaced
MEP as the second largest party in organized labor. The influence of the two
main nonleftist parties in the CTV became even more marked in future
congresses. Whereas the proleftist slate headed by González Navarro received
seven of fifteen positions on the CTV's Executive Committee in 1970, the
Left's representation was greatly reduced at the Seventh Congress in 1975,
where AD trade unionists accounted for 59 percent of the delegates and
Copei another 22 percent.

The AD-Copei agreement, whereby an AD member was named CTV
president and a *Copeyano* secretary-general, was renewed in the 1975 and
1980 congresses. The accord was part of an "Institutional Pact" between the
two parties in 1970 that assigned specific positions in the National Congress
and elsewhere to AD and Copei. The pact, along with the removal of Pedro
Tinoco as finance minister, influenced AD to abandon its intransigent
position toward the Caldera administration and moderate its demands in the
labor movement, while discouraging strikes. By minimizing interparty rivalry,
the Institutional Pact would form the cornerstone of the nation's political
party system throughout the 1970s and 1980s.

The parties that supported the candidacy of González Navarro at the
Sixth Congress went on to discuss plans to put up a unity candidate for
the 1973 presidential elections. The FDP, however, withdrew from the
negotiations as a result of the inclusion of the PCV in the alliance, as did
URD when MEPista Paz Galarraga rather than Jóvito Villalba was chosen
presidential candidate. MEP's radicalization and its willingness to accept
Communist support not only strained relations with the FDP and URD but

also alienated top party labor leaders. MEP's vice president, González Navarro, was forced out of the party as a result of his criticisms of its stands. Several other prominent MEP trade unionists including Pedro Brito of the CTV's Executive Committee; José Mollegas, president of Fetrametal; and peasant leader Pedro Torres resigned in protest of the expulsion.

The internal friction in MEP was aggravated by the position on labor issues assumed by members of the national committee and student leaders, some of whom attacked party worker representatives for failing to change since their days as *Adecos* and even questioned their personal integrity.[32] MEP politicians urged the trade unionists to withdraw from the CTV in order to protest the AD-Copei pact at the Sixth Congress as well as the confederation's opposition to a strike at Sidor led by a MEPista in 1971. MEP labor leaders argued that should they leave the CTV, they would lose their *fueros* (job security and other special rights granted to officially recognized union representatives) and would thus be subject to layoffs.[33] In future years, MEP political bosses would occasionally criticize party trade unionists for failing to maintain a critical position toward AD in the labor movement. Following the initial exodus of González Navarro and others who supported him in 1972, other top labor leaders would desert MEP on an individual basis, most of them returning to the AD fold.

The emergence of MEP and the phasing out of the guerrilla struggle convinced many Communist worker activitists of the need to reexamine the Left's position toward the CTV. Eloy Torres, who had adamantly opposed dual unionism as far back as the 1940s, was one of the foremost advocates of attempting to reach an understanding with the CTV in order to facilitate the reunification of the labor movement. Torres put forward a self-criticism of the Left's labor policy in the 1960s: "The failure to follow a policy of differentiation, instead placing everybody in the same sack, when we knew full well that they were not the same, [and] the lumping together of all middle-level leaders and those in the rank and file isolated us and led to a situation of total rupture between ourselves and the unions that formed part of the CTV. This rupture even involved questions of a personal type."[34]

As a first step Torres called on Communists to merge certain unions and federations that they controlled with CTV-affiliated ones and to participate in the upcoming Sixth Congress.[35] Torres's position was accepted by Communist workers who won the elections at Atiss and went on to lead the 1969 strike at Sidor. Instead of joining the CUTV, as many expected, they retained Atiss's membership in the CTV.[36]

During the Caldera administration the CTV was receptive to efforts to cooperate with other confederations. Following MEP's founding, CTV's President González Navarro called for the creation of a Comité de Enlace consisting of the CTV, the CUTV, and Codesa to pave the way for reunification. Another MEPista, Pedro Brito, proposed an extraordinary congress open to all ideological currents in the labor movement. For the first

time, representatives of different confederations spoke at the same plat-
forms; official delegations were sent to conferences organized by rival
confederations; unified May Day marches were held; and unions affiliated
with the CTV and CUTV drew up joint proposed contracts for collective
bargaining purposes.[37]

Even after the CTV presidency reverted back to AD at the Sixth
Congress, occasional cooperation took place, as in September 1973 when
the CTV, Codesa, and the CUTV reached an agreement for a symbolic half-
hour general strike in favor of improved worker benefits. Nevertheless,
these efforts did not lead to more lasting forms of collaboration. In future
years the few instances in which the CTV was willing to consider
interconfederation understandings were in situations in which it openly
confronted the government.

Several explanations have been offered for the sharp increase and
fluctuations in the annual number of strikes during these years. Stuart Fagen
notes that there was no correlation between the number of contracts signed
and the incidence of work stoppages. He ascribes the increment in strike
activity to political motives rather than economic concerns. Fagen maintains
that rivalry with MEP and fear of losing its traditional hold over the labor
movement induced AD to harden its stands and pursue a more militant
course among workers. More important, the behavior of AD labor leaders
was determined by their party's attitude toward the Caldera administration,
which was hostile in 1969, conciliatory beginning in 1970 (as a result of the
Institutional Pact), and increasingly critical as the 1973 electoral campaign
got under way. Fagen labels the modus operandi of collective bargaining
during the middle years of the Caldera administration "programmed bargaining," and assigns the Labor Bureau of AD and the Labor Ministry key
roles in moderating worker demands and avoiding industrial conflicts.[38]

The importance of the political motives discussed by Fagen is
indisputable. Nevertheless, the statistics on strikes do not demonstrate a
ready correlation between worker conflicts and party policy toward the
government. The over threefold increase in strikes in 1971 (see Table 1), for
instance, coincided with the initiation of the Institutional Pact, which should
have diminished labor conflict, especially in light of AD's conquest of the
CTV presidency. Furthermore, although the number of strikes declined
following the election of Carlos Andrés Pérez of AD in 1973, it hardly
reverted back to pre-1969 levels.

Fagen attributes this strike activity to the militant posture of MEPista
trade unionists, but fails to take into account the fact that MEP followed a
more cautious policy in organized labor following the defeat of the Sidor
strike in 1971; in any case, the party lost a good deal of its influence among
workers during these years. The methodology employed by Fagen and
others[39] who posit a relationship between the frequency of strikes and

political party interests is marred by a major obstacle: the absence of available statistics on the number of work stoppages that were supported at higher levels in the labor movement and by opposition parties. As was the case with the shutdowns at Sidor in 1969 and 1971, many worker struggles were not endorsed by AD and the CTV.

Table 1. Strike Activity in Venezuela, 1958–1990

Year	Petitions to go on Strike	Legal Strikes	Illegal Strikes	Workers Involved (Legal Strikes)	Workers Involved (Illegal Strikes)	Man Hrs. Lost (Legal Strikes)	Man Hrs. Lost (Illegal Strikes)
1958	78	15	7	—	—	—	—
1959	63	10	5	—	—	—	—
1960	91	8	28	—	—	34,332	293,412
1961	40	5	9	2,953	11,551	178,332	214,640
1962	40	8	11	3,492	4,762	340,380	40,153
1963	24	5	4	483	2,018	105,928	117,602
1964	45	7	20	1,049	3,544	85,440	18,436
1965	52	4	20	2,225	4,680	73,912	68,493
1966	28	1	11	194	3,180	40,200	23,488
1967	59	5	29	1,154	4,227	54,638	41,327 ·
1968	78	4	9	3,054	4,473	35,038	10,757
1969	113	3	83	341	21,356	10,700	1,580,980
1970	173	2	64	902	24,836	265,502	1,874,282
1971	187	5	228	806	39,307	314,676	3,850,074
1972	257	7	172	2,069	27,263	328,068	1,169,486
1973	274	4	250	525	46,033	902,000	1,157,368
1974	236	3	116	135	17,598	19,376	1,039,824
1975	207	3	110	164	25,916	62,928	804,336
1976	210	1	178	3,000	36,932	36,000	730,123
1977	183	0	214	0	63,923	0	687,976
1978	112	0	114	0	25,337	0	318,732
1979	182	2	145	237	23,031	3,304	394,822
1980	192	4	185	494	63,844	52,592	2,431,754
1981	199	3	126	270	29,292	160,640	2,074,347
1982	158	2	102	253	14,859	31,264	329,603
1983	274	0	200	0	59,749	0	2,886,273
1984	15	0	39	0	3,767	0	50,956
1985	82	6	11	873	12,076	40,888	54,920
1986	88	2	20	1,137	—	—	—
1987	84	1	38	—	—	—	—
1988	69	2	—	—	—	—	—
1989	95	6	—	—	—	—	—
1990	134	7	—	—	—	—	—

Source: Labor Ministry, *Memoria y Cuenta, 1958–1990*. Compiled by Leonardo Rodríguez.

Another explanation not considered by Fagen goes a long way toward accounting for the increase in strikes after 1969. During the 1960s, the guerrilla struggle and resultant government repression had discouraged worker protests in opposition to the austerity measures imposed by the Betancourt and Leoni administrations. The improved prospects on the political and economic fronts at the time of Caldera's election created rising expectations among workers that were articulated by their union leaders. One political manifestation of this process was the emergence of MEP, which was spearheaded by those AD leaders who defended worker demands that had been deferred during the lean years of the early 1960s.[40]

In participating in strikes, workers were responding not so much to an imposed party line as to a new material threshold of possibilities and a changing labor environment; AD trade union support for work stoppages was not always the result of a deliberate party policy of embarrassing the Caldera administration. As political scientist Diego Bautista Urbaneja has pointed out, when Copei is in power, AD gives its trade union cadre greater autonomy in carrying out actions.[41] In the absence of the political polarization and repression of the previous decade, the number of strikes did not revert to pre-1969 levels even after Pérez assumed the presidency in 1974, although the windfall in oil income did ensure that it tapered off.

The Administration of Carlos Andrés Pérez, 1974–1979

The triumph of Pérez in the 1973 elections by a wide margin, together with the oil boom during his administration, fortified AD's position in organized labor and contributed to labor peace. In the simultaneously held congressional elections, AD received 44 percent of the vote; Copei, 30 percent; the Movimiento al Socialismo (MAS, which had split off from the Communist party three years earlier), 5 percent; and MEP, 5 percent. Relying on his party's majority in congress, Pérez passed far-reaching legislation designed to channel oil revenue into social welfare programs, ambitious development projects, and the expropriation of the iron and petroleum industries. Although various aspects of this strategy came under heavy criticism, no major party dared question a salient feature of the government's economic policy: the maintenance of a highly overvalued local currency. By failing to devalue the bolívar, the Pérez administration encouraged the mass importation of consumer goods, which seriously undermined the nation's productive capacity.[42]

To facilitate the utilization of the nation's newly acquired oil income, the congress granted President Pérez "emergency powers" that allowed him to enact his legislative package by decree. A host of "emergency decrees" were issued during his first year in office. For the first time, the government established a minimum wage, which had been authorized by the Labor Law of 1936 but never implemented. The minimum wage was set at 15 bolívares ($3.50) per day, and scaled wage increases were established (25 percent for salaries up to 1,000 bolívares, 20 percent for 1,000–2,000 bolívares, etc., up to 5,000 bolívares). Furthermore, lower-paid workers were granted *inamovilidad*, whereby they could not be laid off for 180 days. These employee benefits set a precedent in that wage hikes for low-income workers and *inamovilidad* would be decreed on various occasions by future governments.

Another novel arrangement that also became a standard feature of life in Venezuela was the government's regulation of prices—known as *precio de venta al público*—on a wide range of staples and other basic commodities. Other popular measures included the distribution of free milk to pregnant women, the condonation of debts incurred by peasants in the purchase of land, mandatory apprenticeship programs in certain trades, and the obligatory employment of personnel for building elevators and restaurant restrooms. These latter provisions were designed to guarantee full employment (*pleno empleo*), which became a catchword under Pérez.

The most controversial enactment in 1974 was the *Ley contra Despidos Injustificados*, which granted workers double severance pay when they were laid off without just cause. Various proposals designed to impede layoffs had been drawn up over the previous fifteen years but had failed to gain congressional approval. In a major innovation the *Ley contra Despidos* created statewide and regional tripartite commissions consisting of employee, employer, and government representatives to judge cases in which the origin of the layoff was in dispute. If the commission decided in favor of the worker, the company was given the option of rehiring him or providing compensation in the form of double indemnity. In future years, the Venezuelan government would utilize tripartite commissions for other diverse purposes, such as regulating immigration and controlling price and wage increases.

The original draft of the *Ley contra Despidos*, which was called the *Ley de Estabilidad Laboral*, gave workers who were unjustly fired the choice of being rehired or receiving double compensation. Fedecámaras fervently opposed this provision because it amounted to *estabilidad absoluta* in that management was deprived of the right to discharge workers under normal circumstances. Since the 1940s, when *estabilidad absoluta* was first proposed in the oil industry, company spokesmen had argued that the decision to hire and fire workers was exclusively management's prerogative. The revised version of the *Ley contra Despidos*, however, did contribute to *estabilidad indirecta* (indirect job security), whereby costly severance payments discourage layoffs. In addition, the *Ley contra Despidos* required management to replace all discharged workers, regardless of the cause of layoff, a stipulation known as *estabilidad numérica*. The law was thus designed to limit unemployment; indeed, President Pérez considered it part of his policy of *pleno empleo.*

The CTV was caught off guard in 1974 and failed to play an important role in the elaboration and presentation of Pérez's legislative program, despite its proworker content. The CTV admitted that it had no official position on how the sudden influx of oil revenue should be spent.[43] In particular, the announcement of the *Ley contra Despidos* took the CTV and other segments of national opinion by surprise.[44] The authors of the law were all AD political leaders without close ties to organized labor. (In contrast, the two previous proposals for *estabilidad* introduced in congress during the Betancourt and Caldera administrations were sponsored by trade unionists and politicians belonging to various parties.)

Furthermore, the CTV leaders bowed to political pressure by accepting and even defending the diluted version of the *Ley contra Despidos* in light of pressure from Fedecámaras. During this period the CTV limited itself to championing those aspects of Pérez's programs that came under attack from business interests. In one meeting with CTV leaders commemorating the confederation's fortieth anniversary in 1976, Pérez confessed that he had been unable to do more for the working class due to the unrelenting pressure exerted by Fedecámaras and the relative passivity of organized labor.[45]

Prior to the CTV's Seventh Congress in April 1975, uncertainty existed as to whether Copei would replace MEP as the second largest party in the labor movement. The delegate strength at the congress was as follows: AD, 59 percent; Copei, 22 percent; MEP, 17 percent; URD, 8 percent; and MAS, 1 percent. AD labor leaders maintained that rivalry between two lists of candidates for the CTV's Executive Committee should be avoided at all costs since it undermined labor unity.[46] Following conversations with representatives of other parties, AD succeeded in constituting a united slate that consisted of eight AD members, four *Copeyanos*, two MEPistas, and one URDista. Over the next fifteen years, the percentage representation of AD and Copei in CTV congresses and executive committees did not vary significantly (see Table 2).

Following the death of Francisco Olivo in 1974, José Vargas, the CTV's secretary of international affairs, and Carlos Luna, president of the graphic arts workers, aspired to occupy the confederation's presidency. Vargas was a former cigarette workers' leader who had played a prominent role in the trade union movement since the 1940s, while Luna had emerged in organized labor as a protégé of Olivo's following the overthrow of Pérez Jiménez. Luna, along with health workers' President Ismario González, formed part of a "renovation" faction, which offered a moderate critique of AD's Labor Bureau. Two other important AD leaders who supported the renovation current were Milton Carrero, who had recently been elected president of the Communication Workers Federation for his third period (after facing heavy opposition from fellow party trade unionists), and Federico Ramírez León, president of the Workers Federation of Táchira. The renovators claimed to enjoy considerable influence among middle-level labor leaders from the nation's interior, whom they purported to represent in opposition to the excessive influence of labor leaders from the capital. Luna and his followers advocated the incorporation of a greater number of trade unionists from the provinces in the CTV's national leadership. They also questioned the CTV's management of its financial resources and called for a thorough revision of the BTV and other investments.[47]

Table 2. Percentages of Delegates by Party at CTV Congresses, 1959–1990

Congress	AD	Copei	MEP	URD	MAS	MIR	PCV	Others
Third (1959)	52.2	14.5	—	10.0	—	—	23.3	—
Fourth (1961)	70.0	30.0	—	—	—	—	—	—
Fifth (1964)	70.6	14.0	—	12.5	—	—	—	3.9
Sixth (1970)	34.5	18.9	31.7	11.7	—	—	.6	14.3
Seventh (1975)	50.8	21.5	16.7	8.1	.9	.2	.5	1.3
Eighth (1980)	56.3	20.9	12.3	2.8	3.2	.6	.5	3.4
Ninth (1985)	61.3	20.8	10.2	4.0	3.7	—	—	—
Tenth (1990)	61.2	20.7	7.9	2.9	5.3	—	.9	1.1

Sources: *El Nacional* and *El Universal*.

One of the main demands of the renovators was that an AD member should be chosen CTV secretary-general, rather than a *Copeyano* or MEPista as other party labor leaders favored. Luna's group expressed discontent that the CTV was presided over by a *Copeyano*, Rafael León León, who as secretary-general of the confederation succeeded Francisco Olivo upon his death in 1974. Luna maintained that the Institutional Pact, which had led to the naming of León León as CTV secretary-general in 1970, had been justified at the time due to the fragility of AD's position both in the National Congress and in organized labor. In 1975, however, with a majority of delegates at the Seventh Congress, Luna maintained that AD should reserve for itself the top two positions in the CTV.[48] The AD delegation at the CTV congress overrode Luna's arguments and accepted the renomination of León León as secretary-general, at the same time that it selected José Vargas as president. Nevertheless, Luna was not penalized for his dissident stand on this occasion and was included along with Ramírez León on the unity slate as members of the CTV's Executive Committee.

The CTV attempted to project an image of ideological pluralism in order to avoid being branded a political instrument of AD in light of that party's expanded influence in the confederation. CTV President Olivo had been receptive to MAS's decision to seek admission into the CTV along with the unions they controlled in 1974. Despite his party's minimum representation at the CTV's Seventh Congress in 1975, MASista Jesús Urbieta was named substitute member of the confederation's Executive Committee. Following MAS's example, labor leaders belonging to the Vanguardia Comunista (formed in 1974) and MIR decided to return to the CTV fold. Leftists of all three parties, who had virulently attacked the CTV in the 1960s, justified their new policy on grounds that they were committed to criticizing the labor bureaucracy from within the confederation, especially with regard to the lack of internal democracy.

The liberalism of AD's Labor Bureau was evident in its efforts to recapture former party dissidents by offering them top positions in organized labor. Former MEPista César Gil became a member of CTV's Executive Committee, and Juan José Delpino and Pedro Brito became substitute members; José Mollegas of Fetrametal and Carlos Piñerua of Fedepetrol were allowed to retain the presidency of their respective federations. Although several AD members who had left the party in leftist splits in the 1960s became national congressmen and ministers in the cabinet of Carlos Andrés Pérez, the number of former dissidents who attained top positions in the labor movement was especially striking.

The broadmindedness of CTV leaders was also demonstrated by the invitation of Agapito Figueroa of the Confederation of Workers of Cuba to address the Seventh Congress. Figueroa was interrupted by applause on several occasions when he announced Fidel Castro's unqualified support for Venezuela's nationalization of iron and petroleum interests. He added that "the workers of Cuba reiterate their solidarity [in favor of these measures] and support the Venezuelan people in their rejection of the gross attitude of imperialism that has threatened the nation with possible reprisals."[49]

The injection of unexpected oil income into the economy and the government's costly developmental plans produced a disequilibrium that affected industrial relations during these years. As unemployment diminished, wages sharply increased and became second in Latin America only to those of Mexico. Skilled labor was in short supply and, according to the U.S. labor attaché in Caracas, salaries in that sector were competitive by U.S. standards.[50] As a result of the abundance of employment opportunities, labor discipline slackened and was reflected in absenteeism and high turnover rates. Many companies reported that the average duration of employment was a mere six months to a year.[51]

Business spokesmen blamed the *Ley contra Despidos Injustificados* and the Decree 124 (which extended severance payment to all workers whose employment was terminated, regardless of circumstances) for the lack of worker discipline that plagued industry. According to them, employees were anxious to collect their severance pay, which was now considered an "acquired right," and thus did not fear being laid off. Furthermore, the possibility of collecting double benefits induced workers to court dismissal and then claim that they had been fired without just cause.

To help overcome labor shortages, Fedecámaras called for the lifting of controls on immigration that had been in effect since 1958. These restrictions had represented a reaction to the open door policy and mass influx of the Pérez Jiménez period. During the Betancourt presidency the CTV had actually called for a temporary halt to the admission of immigrants in order to alleviate the problem of unemployment, until such a time that Venezuela "is in condition to settle them in planned fashion."[52] After 1973, Fedecámaras sponsored conferences and created a special commission designed to gain public support for liberalization. As a result of Pérez's more open policy, annual legal immigration was restored to its pre-1958 level, which was double that of the 1960s. The CTV cautioned against a massive inflow of foreigners, though it accepted the principle of selective immigration. At the same time the confederation questioned the statistics offered by Fedecámaras regarding the acute shortage of skilled workers and claimed that its real motive in lobbying for increased immigration was to create a pool of cheap labor.[53] The CTV insisted on stricter measures to clamp down on the arrival of illegal immigrants (particularly from neighboring Colombia), who during the Pérez administration outnumbered those who came in legally.[54]

The CTV also warned against the precipitous and unplanned integration of Venezuela into the economies of the Andean nations following its decision to join the Andean Pact in 1973. Labor leaders shared Fedecámaras's concern that, due to Venezuela's higher wage levels, the nation would be inundated by cheap imports, and they called for a leveling of salaries as a prerequisite for economic integration. In May 1976 the CTV, Codesa, and the CUTV met with labor leaders of the four other Andean nations in the "First Venezuelan Trade Union Conference of the Andean Pact," which issued a document demanding worker participation in the plans to establish a common market.

The CTV's criticism of the government's hastiness in promoting regional integration and immigration was part of a more thorough and basic critique of the economic policies of the Pérez administration. Not only parties of the opposition but such renowned AD figures as former Minister of Mines Juan Pablo Pérez Alfonzo attacked the much touted "Fifth Plan of the Nation," which emphasized large-scale projects designed to achieve accelerated industrial growth, as plagued by errors in judgment. Pérez Alfonzo argued that the nation lacked the infrastructure to absorb the vast sums of money that were being spent, and called for a sharp reduction in oil production and moderate growth rates to avoid imbalances and bottlenecks. He labeled the Fifth Plan of the Nation the "plan of disaster."

Although the CTV did not embrace Pérez Alfonzo's conservationist creed and his skepticism toward material progress, it shared his alarm with regard to rapid growth without planning. The CTV called the Fifth Plan "developmentalist" on grounds that, in its emphasis on economic expansion, it largely disregarded the general welfare. Along these lines, CTV leaders criticized the chaotic urban conditions in Ciudad Guayana, home of the state-run steel and aluminum industries that received priority attention under the Fifth Plan.[55]

The CTV's rejection of uncontrolled immigration fit into the framework of this critical analysis. The confederation preferred worker training programs in order to prepare Venezuelans gradually for the requirements of economic growth rather than importing skilled workers, which was considered an easy way out. The CTV also censured Fedecámaras for opposing the executive decree that forced employers to underwrite the cost of apprenticeships, even though the business sector was to be the great beneficiary of the program in the long run.[56]

Two main factions emerged in AD after 1973. President Pérez's followers, known as the *carlosandresistas*, were considered by some to represent the party's "left-wing" since they extolled the government's nationalization of petroleum and iron interests and its militant rhetoric in favor of the third world. The party's Labor Bureau was identified with the "orthodox" current, whose leading figure was Rómulo Betancourt, that stressed the issue of corruption. Some *ortodoxos* criticized the government's economic policies for favoring an emerging bourgeoisie (facetiously referred to as the "Twelve Apostles") of questionable business scruples, while others pointed to the government's inordinate reliance on deficit spending as burdening future generations.[57]

AD labor leaders, among others, were concerned with Pérez's personalistic style and his failure to consult the party, as demonstrated by the leading role played by several independents in his cabinet. AD members of the CTV's national leadership especially feared that Pérez would go over their heads and appeal directly to rank-and-file workers. This course had been followed by a friend of Pérez, Mexican President Luis Echeverría (1970–1976), whose populism resembled his own approach. Echeverría defied the top leaders of the Confederation of Mexican Workers, who belonged to the ruling PRI, by invoking the slogan "trade union democracy" and establishing close ties with unaffiliated "independent" unions.[58]

Pérez, however, a seasoned and pragmatic politician, did not copy the audacious trade union strategy of his Mexican colleague. In fact, he even failed to support *carlosandresista* Carlos Luna in his bid for the CTV presidency. According to Luna, Pérez's neutrality was due to his fear that as CTV president Luna would be difficult to control and would possibly assume militant positions and encourage worker mobilizations. Luna added that, unlike Vargas, he was accustomed to a modest life-style and was thus more responsive to the rank and file. For this reason, Pérez viewed with certain sympathy the candidacy of the more tractable José Vargas, despite his association with AD's orthodox faction.[59]

The workers' movement in the textile industry and in the heavily industrialized Guayana region (both to be examined in Chapter 7) stood out as exceptions to AD's thorough penetration of organized labor and the reduced levels of social conflict that characterized these years. In the major textile firms of the Caracas area, the AD-dominated Sindicato Unico de Trabajadores Textiles (Sutratex) was displaced by the leftist Unión de Trabajadores de la Industria Textil (UTIT). During the contract negotiations in 1977, UTIT, along with other leftist-controlled unions in Maracay, called three strikes that were illegal under the terms of Decree 440, which governed the negotiations. The government, however, did not resort to force and even permitted discussions to extend for two weeks after the expiration of the limit set for collective bargaining when, according to the decree, the contract was to be decided by compulsory arbitration. UTIT interpreted the government's restraint as evidence that worker unity and militance were the best guarantee against repression.[60]

The most serious conflict in the Guayana region was the wildcat strikes and other work stoppages carried out by iron workers at the time of the nationalization of the industry in 1975. As was the case with the oil industry employees the following year, the iron workers feared that accumulated severance and retirement benefits, which the private companies had to turn over to the new state-run Ferrominera, would be poorly invested and not be recoverable at the proper time. The situation was complicated by the existence of six unions that represented blue- and white-collar workers at the different mining sites. One of them, Soeims (which grouped employees of Bethlehem Steel's Venezuelan subsidiary), rejected the government's plan to pay each worker 25 percent of his severance benefits at the time and the remaining amount upon cessation of work. Instead the union insisted on the immediate liquidation of the one-month salary for each year of employment stipulated by labor law.[61] In addition, some labor leaders demanded double severance payment (that is, two months' salary) on grounds that the companies were supposedly prepared to pay such an amount in cases of layoffs that were considered "unjustified."

The CTV defended the government's offer and argued that experience demonstrated that when workers receive severance payment anticipatively, they tend to squander it. CTV President José Vargas condemned the demagoguery of those labor leaders who played on the workers' susceptibility to slogans that held out the immediate prospect of receiving large sums of cash. In addition, he expressed fear that unresolved conflicts in the transition to state ownership would spill over to the oil industry, which was due to be nationalized in 1976.[62]

Other AD spokesmen in the CTV accused the ultraleftist parties (such as the Liga Socialista, which had broken off from MIR in the late 1960s) of being "pseudo-socialists" since their intransigent stand in the iron workers' dispute sabotaged the process of the government takeover of the industry.[63] The PCV, on the other hand, accepted the position that the CTV ratified at its Seventh Congress on the need to play down conflict in nationalized sectors.[64] Similarly, MAS and MEP trade unionists in the CTV endorsed the iron workers' settlement.

The parties of the Left, which in general applauded President Pérez's program during his first year in office, pointed to the exhaustion of the government's reformist impulse in 1975. Leftists attributed this retrenchment to the pressure that was exerted by Fedecámaras, as demonstrated by the well-publicized campaign in opposition to the original draft of the *Ley contra Despidos Injustificados*. Leftist trade unionists attacked Pérez for his intolerant attitude toward strikes. Even more so than in previous years, almost all work stoppages were declared illegal by the government. The Left was especially critical of the *Ley Orgánica de Seguridad y Defensa Nacional*, promulgated in 1975, which contemplated the militarization of areas where labor conflicts threatened national security. The law was designed to be used as a last resort in confronting worker struggles in the Guayana region.

With the exception of Guayana's heavy industry, the textile industry, and a few other critical sectors, the Left's influence in organized labor diminished during these years. The pro-Communist CUTV failed to make significant inroads. Furthermore, MEP lost control of a number of federations, although it continued to run Fedepetrol (until the latter part of the decade) and Fetrazulia as a result of deals with *Copeyanos*. Copei, aware that MEP's losses in organized labor were usually AD's gains, followed a conscious policy of allying with MEPista trade unionists against those of AD, when possible, in union elections.[65]

Venezuela's Relative Stability, 1964–1979

The model of import substitution applied after 1958 represented a new stage based on industrial expansion that buttressed the nation's fragile democratic regime. Even leftists have retrospectively recognized that the attractiveness and relative success of these policies undermined the revolutionary movement whose decision to take up arms stemmed from the premise that the government had lost legitimacy.[66] By the end of the decade, however, economists pointed out that the "easy" phase of import substitution had reached its natural limits. Industrial production in Venezuela, as in other Latin American nations whose economies were foundering, was synonymous with assembly work, while components, machinery, and technology had to be imported. The resultant economic stagnation and failure to embark on a new model were predicaments that most Latin American nations were unable to overcome and led to coup d'états throughout the continent in the 1960s and early 1970s.[67] Those who justified the military takeovers alleged that the former democratic governments—sometimes derogatorily referred to as "populist"—were incapable of deepening the process of import substitution, had been overrun by corruption and bureaucratic inefficiency, and were unable to contain labor unrest.[68]

Venezuela, prior to reaching such a critical point, was transformed as a result of the sharp increase in oil prices after 1973. Although the nation was plagued by the same administrative deficiencies that contributed to the destabilization of other Latin American democracies, it was spared the social unrest that characterized the rest of the continent. Not only did worker participation in strikes (as measured in work hours lost) decline nearly 200 percent from the previous five-year period, but also the government party's hegemony in the CTV ensured that work stoppages did not receive firm and effective backing from higher levels of organized labor.

Venezuelans in general and political analysts in particular expressed belief that the prototypes of Latin America that emphasize political violence and instability were not applicable to Venezuela, whose tranquility was more than just a passing phenomenon. Some argued that political experiences dating back to Venezuela's struggle for independence had contributed to *social democracy* and endowed the nation with a greater degree of racial equality and upward mobility than existed elsewhere. Others saw Venezuelan stability as directly related to its privileged status as an oil producer. Nevertheless, few public commentators manifested concern that petroleum prices could decline as fast as they had increased and in the process reverse political and economic trends that were favorable to the nation. The optimism that lay at the root of the exceptionalism thesis pervaded all segments of society and manifested itself in diverse ways. Thus, for instance, the calculations of some government planners were based on the unfounded assumption that OPEC oil prices, which had increased from $2 to $36 per barrel in the course of the decade, would reach $100 in the not-too-distant future.[69]

Th exceptionalism thesis, with its auspicious implications for the nation's future development, also shaped the thinking of Venezuelan workers and their leaders. The acceptance of the claim that *pleno empleo* had been achieved, at a time when the scourge of unemployment had hardly been eliminated, was an example of the tendency to depict socioeconomic conditions in the best light. In addition, labor and political spokesmen frequently maintained that oil-induced prosperity had precluded a strategy of worker mobilization. In other nations, it was argued, scarcity had forced workers to engage in militant protests in favor of redistributive policies. In contrast, in Venezuela there were sufficient resources to satisfy the reasonable aspirations of all segments of the population.[70] These attitudes were so entrenched that, when oil prices began to decline in the early 1980s, engendering a prolonged economic contraction, discontent was slow in getting articulated; protests would break out in abrupt form only toward the end of the decade.

Notes

1. Interview no. 124, interviewee no. 142, April 2–8, 1964, pp. 29, 32, Cendes, C. C.; Donald L. Herman, *Christian Democracy in Venezuela* (Chapel Hill: University of North Carolina Press, 1980), p. 62.

2. Interview no. 125, interviewee no. 156, January 18, 1964, p. 44, Cendes, C. C.

3. M. Ignacio Purroy, *Estado e industrialización en Venezuela* (Valencia: Vadell Hermanos, 1986), p. 134.

4. Raúl Leoni, "Balance del gobierno del Doctor Raúl Leoni" [speech, December 31, 1966], in *Documentos: Revista de información política* 27 [Caracas] (October–December 1966): 610.

5. *CTV: 50 años de historia*, p. 64.

6. Clementina Acedo Machado, "Necesidades jurídicas y acceso a la justicia de un nuevo sector: beneficiarios del seguro social," in *Estudios laborales: ensayos sobre derecho del trabajo y disciplinas afines*, 2 vols. (Caracas, UCV, 1986), 1:35–66.

7. Kenneth Paul Erickson, "Labor and the Political Process in Brazil: Corporatism in a Modernizing Nation" (Ph.D. diss., University of Columbia, 1970), pp. 174–75; James Malloy, *The Politics of Social Security in Brazil* (Pittsburgh: University of Pittsburgh Press, 1979).

8. Dagoberto González, "Los trabajadores y la reforma tributaria: exposición ante el Consejo General de la CTV," July 31, 1966, pp. 5–6, MOLA Archive, vol. 12, 1964–66.

9. Interview no. 116, interviewee no. 173, April 1964, p. 45, Cendes, C. C.

10. Ibid., p. 40.

11. González Navarro, interview, April 7, 1976, Caracas: *La República*, January 3, 1966, p. 3.

12. Judith Ewell, *Venezuela: A Century of Change* (Stanford, CA: Stanford University Press, 1984), p. 160.

13. Steve Ellner, *The Venezuelan Petroleum Corporation*, pp. 15, 22–23.

14. Paz Galarraga, interview, November 26, 1986, Caracas; Moleiro, *El partido del pueblo*, pp. 240–41.

15. Comité de Obreros y Campesinos Unidos con Prieto, "Llamamento a los obreros, empleados, campesinos y demás sectores populares de Venezuela" [pamphlet], October 1968, MOLA Archive, vol. 13, 1967–1970.

16. Ellner, "Political Party Dynamics and the Outbreak of Guerrilla Warfare in Venezuela," p. 15.

17. *La Extra* [leftist newspaper], April 11, 1964, p. 2.

18. Cruz Villegas, "En marcha hacia el V Congreso de Trabajadores convocado por la C.U.T.V." (Caracas: Ediciones Mundo Laboral, 1967), p. 12, MOLA Archive, vol. 13.

19. Cartay Ramírez, *Caldera y Betancourt*, p. 310.

20. Ibid., p. 329.

21. *Daily Journal*, May 3, 1969, p. 3.

22. Dagoberto González, interview, February 12, 1987, Caracas; Andrés Mercau (after 1975, secretary-general of Fetrametal), interview, February 12, 1987, Caracas.

23. *Unidad* 1 [CUTV newspaper], November 1969), pp. 6–7.

24. *Daily Journal*, December 9, 1969, p. 1; Andreas Boeckh, "Organized Labor and Government under Conditions of Economic Scarcity" (Ph.D. diss., University of Florida, 1972), p. 242.

25. *Daily Journal*, December 4, 1969, p. 24.

26. *Unidad* 2, December 1969, p. 1.

27. Eloy Torres, interview, October 29, 1986, Caracas; Eloy Torres, "La huelga de los trabajadores de Sidor," *Documentos políticos* 22 [PCV magazine] (January 1970): 4–14.

28. Adelso González Urdaneta [secretary of organization of MEP], interview, February 26, 1979, Caracas.

29. Casto Gil Rivera [MEPista, CTV Executive Committee], interview, November 27, 1986, Caracas.

30. César Olarte [MEPista, CTV secretary-general], interview, February 3, 1987, Caracas.

31. Dagoberto González, interview, February 12, 1987, Caracas.

32. *El Nacional*, May 26, 1972, p. D-9.

33. Paz Galarraga, interview, November 26, 1986, Caracas.

34. Torres, *Ideología y sindicalismo*, p. 137.

35. Eloy Torres, "Un vuelvan caras hacia la clase obrera: resumen de intervención en el XI Pleno," 1969 (?) [mimeographed], personal archive of Arturo Tremont, Caracas.

36. *Nueva Voz Popular* [PCV newspaper], June 6, 1968, p. 7.

37. Ibid., May 23, 1968, p. 7; CUTV, "Resoluciones del Consejo General efectuado en Caracas del 14 al 16 de junio de 1968," MOLA Archive, vol. 13; *CLAT* 51 [organ of the Central Latinoamericana de Trabajadores] (June 1973): 7.

38. Stuart I. Fagen, "Unionism and Democracy," in *Venezuela: The Democratic Experience*, ed. John D. Martz and David J. Myers (New York: Praeger, 1977), pp. 174–94.

39. Jennifer L. McCoy interprets the increase in strikes after 1969 as evidence of greater labor autonomy vis-à-vis political parties. See her "Democratic Stability and Regime Change: Inducements and Constraints in Venezuela" (Paper delivered

at the 1985 convention of the American Political Science Association, New Orleans, August 29–September 1, 1985), pp. 41–42.

40. Powell, *Political Mobilization*, p. 199.

41. Diego Bautista Urbaneja, "El sistema político o como funciona la máquina de procesar decisiones," in Naim and Piñango, *El caso Venezuela*, p. 238.

42. Sergio Aranda, *La economía venezolana: una interpretación de su modo de funcionamiento*, rev. ed. (Argentina: Editorial Pomaire, 1984), p. 308.

43. *El Nacional*, August 25, 1974, p. D-1.

44. Velásquez, "Aspectos de la evolución política," p. 419; Rafael Castañeda, interview, November 18, 1976, Caracas.

45. Godio, *El movimiento obrero venezolano* 3: 116. Alain Touraine and Daniel Pecaut argue that most prolabor legislation in Latin America cannot be considered "conquests" due to the passive role played by the workers' movement in its attainment. See their "Consciencia obrera y desarrollo económico," *Revista Latinoamericana de Sociología* 2 (1966).

46. José Vargas, interview, November 18, 1976, Caracas; *El Nacional*, April 2, 1975, p. D-1.

47. *El Nacional*, April 28, 1975, p. D-7.

48. Carlos Luna, interview, January 30, 1987, Caracas.

49. *CTV: 50 años de historia*, p. 69.

50. Daniel Turnquist, "Airgram" (U.S. State Department, unclassified), Caracas, June 23, 1977, p. 11.

51. Cecilia M. Valente, *The Political, Economic and Labor Climate in Venezuela* (Philadelphia: University of Pennsylvania Press, 1979), p. 117.

52. *Antecedentes y testimonios de los congresos* 2: 128.

53. CTV, "Declaración del Consejo Directivo Nacional y del Comité Ejecutivo de la Federación de Trabajadores de la Industria de la Construcción . . . ", *Perfiles* 46 [CTV organ] (October 1976): 46–47; Saskia Sassen-Koob, "Crecimiento económico e inmigración en Venezuela," in *Migraciones internacionales en las Américas*, ed. Mary M. Kritz (Caracas: CEPAM, 1980), p. 76.

54. Susan Berglund and Humberto Hernández Caliman, *Los de afuera: un estudio del proceso migratorio en Venezuela, 1936–1985* (Caracas: CEPAM, 1985), pp. 60, 64–65. For by far the most comprehensive analysis of Venezuelan immigration in the modern period, see Susan Berglund, "The 'Musiúes' in Venezuela: Immigration Goals and Reality, 1936–1961" (Ph.D. diss., University of Massachusetts, 1980).

55. José Vargas, interview, November 18, 1976, Caracas; Manuel Peñalver, "Las recientes políticas económicas: visión sindical," *El Nacional* [special edition], August 3, 1981, p. A-14; *El Nacional* [interview with José Vargas], September 27, 1982, p. D-1.

56. *El Nacional*, April 30, 1975, p. D-16.

57. Iván Pulido Mora [AD economic adviser], interview, November 11, 1981, Caracas.

58. Jorge Basurto, "The Late Populism of Luis Echeverría," in *Latin American Populism in Comparative Perspective*, ed. Michael L. Conniff (Albuquerque: University of New Mexico Press, 1982), pp. 101–2.

59. Carlos Luna, interview, January 30, 1987, Caracas.

60. "Surge el proletariado (la lucha de los trabajadores textiles)," *Proceso Político* 7 (April 1978): 29.

61. *El Nacional*, April 8, 1975, p. D-3.

62. José Vargas, *La CTV y los problemas del hierro* (Publicaciones de la Secretaría Sindical Nacional de AD, 1975), p. 5.

63. Andrés Hernández Vásquez, *Palabras pronunciadas en ocasión del debate producido en la Cámara de Diputados el 26-5-75* (Publicaciones de la Secretaría Sindical Nacional de AD), n.p.

64. Rádames Larrazábal, *Estrategia de poder* (Caracas: Editorial Ateneo de Caracas, 1979), p. 94.

65. Dagoberto González, "Informe del Directorio Nacional del FTC ante el Directorio Nacional de Copei" [mimeographed] (Caracas, April 1976), p. 6, MOLA Archive, vol. 15, 1975–77.

66. Pedro Ortega Díaz, interview, April 22, 1989, Puerto La Cruz.

67. Guillermo O'Donnell posits a close relationship between the termination of the "easy phase" of import substitution and the military coups of the period. See his *Modernization and Bureaucratic-Authoritarianism: Studies in South American Politics* (Berkeley: University of California Press, 1973).

68. Robert Wesson defends this position in his *Democracy in Latin America: Promise and Problems* (New York: Praeger Publishers, 1982), p. 145.

69. Carlos D'Ascoli [AD member and former Finance Minister], interview, November 13, 1981, Caracas.

70. Naim and Piñango, "Conclusión," in *El caso Venezuela*, pp. 545–58.

3 Economic Contraction and Crisis in the 1980s

The Administration of Luis Herrera Campíns, 1979–1984

The performance of the Venezuelan economy underwent a dramatic turnabout during the administration of Luis Herrera Campíns, which greatly damaged Copei's prospects for the 1983 national elections. OPEC oil prices continued their upward swing by doubling in 1979, in response to the overthrow of the shah of Iran. Nevertheless, a series of international economic trends and mistaken policies subsequently took their toll on the nation's economy. The government's extrapolation of the revenue increases of the 1970s into future years led it to devise the ambitious Sixth Plan of the Nation, which had to be virtually scrapped once economic activity and oil prices began to decrease. Venezuela's public debt, which had reached $20 billion by the time Pérez left office, nearly doubled within the next few years—Herrera Campíns's condemnation of his predecessor for irresponsibly "mortgaging" Venezuela notwithstanding. With Mexico's moratorium on payment of its foreign debt in 1982, international loans dried up. Venezuelan capitalists reacted to these ominous developments by converting their bolívares into dollars to invest or deposit abroad. Capital flight was especially aggravated by the overvalued status of the bolívar and the anticipation of a devaluation.

Most economists recognize that the government was slow in responding to these predicaments.[1] It took corrective measures to control the foreign debt and modify the exchange rate only after an estimated $20 billion had left the country. On February 18, 1983, known in Venezuela as "Black Friday," the government established exchange controls and allowed the bolívar to float against the dollar. In just one day the purchasing power of Venezuelans declined by 75 percent, a trend that continued apace in the following months.

As in the first year of the Caldera administration, relations between the Herrera government and organized labor started off on a conflictive note as a result of public statements against the CTV leadership made by influential

Copeyanos. They then further deteriorated as labor leaders sharply criticized the government's economic policy and mobilized their constituents. However, as occurred during the Caldera presidency, the CTV's militance was short-lived; following a series of concessions granted by the government, the confederation modified its stands and played a major role in defense of labor harmony.

At a government-Copei conclave at the headquarters of the Christian democratic Unión de Trabajadores de América Latina in San Antonio de los Altos outside of Caracas in February 1979, President Herrera discussed the importance of dislodging AD from the CTV leadership. His comments were widely reported in the press and were interpreted by the AD Labor Bureau as a virtual declaration of war. According to Copei labor leaders, newspaper reporters had passed themselves off as *Copeyanos* and smuggled a small cassette recorder into the meeting. They then exaggerated the importance of the president's statements, and quoted him out of context. They also insinuated that the location of the meeting outside of Caracas was part of a conspiratorial plan designed to secure Copei's control of organized labor by illegitimate means. In fact, all Herrera had said was that AD labor's obstruction of the program of *Copeyano* governments made the replacement of the CTV leadership an imperative.[2]

Herrera headed a faction in Copei that accused the Caldera wing of the party of being too soft on AD and favored a confrontational approach toward AD's labor leadership. Following the gathering in San Antonio de los Altos, Senator Juan José Rachadel, who was identified with the Herrera wing in Copei, affirmed that his party was "developing a campaign and a series of actions that have as their objective the conquest of the CTV by a social Christian majority." He called on all trade unionists, other than those of AD, to close ranks under the slogan "Oust *Adequismo* [AD] from the CTV."[3]

Copei attempted to use its position in the government to gain control of the workers' movement, especially in the state sector, which had long been a bulwark of AD labor. Administrative reorganization and changes in personnel at all levels were designed to increase the number of Copei workers in order to sway the outcome of union elections. In the state-run companies of the heavily industrialized Guayana region, top executives appointed by the Herrera administration reneged on traditional practice by denouncing their predecessors for neglecting the living conditions of the workers and for engaging in corrupt dealings.[4]

As a result of controversial elections in the FVM, *Copeyano* teachers set up a rival FVM in opposition to the CTV-affiliated federation that had been controlled by MEPistas since 1967 and was backed by AD. Minister of Justice José Guillermo Andueza, whose brother headed the pro-*Copeyano* FVM, was accused of deploying the judicial police force to oust the MEPistas from the national FVM headquarters. In other sectors as well, *Copeyanos* established parallel unions that received immediate recognition from the Labor Ministry.

CTV-authorized mobilizations in 1979 and 1980 were designed to protest against the *Copeyanization* of the public sector, government-dictated price increases for regulated commodities (referred to as the "liberation of prices"), and plans to privatize the national port system. CTV worker protests during this period were thus *political* in that they centered on policy issues, particularly with regard to public employees, and were not directed against private business. The actions took the form of work stoppages—referred to as "civic protests"—in individual states, and strikes that lasted a day or two in different sectors and were meant to serve as a warning to the government by raising the threat of a general strike. (This tactic has often been used effectively in other Latin American nations, where economic and political instability obliges the government to make concessions in order to avoid the escalation of labor conflicts that may jeopardize its very existence.[5])

As had been the CTV's policy in the few instances since 1959 in which it supported mobilizations, the confederation encouraged the participation of other labor organizations, in this case the CUTV. The CTV and the CUTV drafted the Law of Salary Increases, which granted hikes of between 10 and 40 percent for wages ranging between 750 and 6,000 bolívares per month. The two organizations participated together in public meetings and issued joint declarations in favor of the proposal. Herrera Campíns, who had previously refused to enact the increase by executive decree on grounds that it would be unconstitutional, expressed reservations regarding the bill. A slightly modified version, which scaled down the increases to between 5 and 30 percent, was approved by congress and signed by the president on December 2, 1979. The CUTV hailed the passage of the law as a "historic victory" for labor, while Fedecámaras warned that mass layoffs would be forthcoming.[6]

Additional government concessions were granted in 1980. Toward the end of the year, various labor federations issued strike calls or threatened to go on strike. The Federación de Trabajadores del Transporte (Fedetransporte) demanded increases in public transportation fares. In addition, employees of the public mail and telegraph institute (Ipostel), the Instituto Nacional de Puertos (INP), the hospitals under the jurisdiction of the IVSS, and the public school system protested against layoffs that were allegedly discriminatory against AD trade unionists. In November the government announced the rehiring of discharged workers and the removal of the heads of the INP and Ipostel. For the remainder of the Herrera administration, AD's Labor Bureau opposed additional strike activity, and even took disciplinary measures against the communication workers' president, Milton Carrero, for promoting numerous work stoppages against Ipostel without consulting the CTV.

In the face of these labor controversies, the *Copeyano* workers' movement refused to commit itself to a simple pro- or antigovernment position. On the one hand, the FTC immediately criticized the Herrera administration's decision to authorize price increases, and even participated in some of the protests organized by CTV-affiliated organizations. On the other hand, the FTC recognized that the government's policies designed to cool off the economy would produce positive results in the medium-range future. Furthermore, the FTC criticized some of the CTV-sponsored mobilizations for being politically motivated.

The *Copeyanos* were reluctant to subscribe to strongly worded CTV statements in opposition to government policy. Indeed, AD labor leaders preferred to ignore the FTC, rather than encourage its participation in the antigovernment campaign, in order to profit from the administration's unpopular measures at Copei's expense.[7] If the FTC's public stands were at times equivocal, the *Copeyano* trade unionists were forceful and straightforward in their internal encounters with government and party representatives. According to them, the government had committed a major blunder in initiating its unpopular economic policies prior to the CTV's Eighth Congress in 1980, thus undermining Copei's efforts to substantially increase its delegate representation.[8]

While the strikes led by AD labor leaders involved nonindustrial employees in the state sector, leftist trade unionists planned actions among workers in public and private industrial firms. These protests, however, met limited success in large part because of leftist disunity. As a result of the meager 8 percent of the vote of the four leftist presidential candidates in the 1978 contests, the parties that backed them—the PCV, MIR, MAS, and MEP—created the "Coordinator of the Left" to facilitate the selection of a united candidacy in the 1983 national elections. Trade unionists belonging to these parties also entered into formal discussions and pledged themselves to greater combativeness and a common strategy.[9] With the Coordinator's failure to reach an agreement, however, these conversations foundered. In addition, a wide gap separated the four "established" leftist parties and a host of "marginal" leftist groups that were generally more militant and intent on fostering workers' participation and internal union democracy. These parties—which included the Causa R, the Liga Socialista, the El Pueblo Avanza (EPA), "Proceso Político," and the Grupo de Acción Revolucionaria (GAR)—embraced an analysis that viewed nationalized industries as serving the interests of international capitalism. In contrast, the established leftist parties, and the PCV in particular, concurred with the CTV position that the labor movement should wage strikes against the state companies of the Guayana region only as a last resort, due to the central role they played in the nation's development.[10]

Differences on the Left played a critical role in the two most important leftist workers' movements of these years, which occurred in the textile and steel industries. UTIT, which was controlled by Proceso Político, emerged as the largest textile union in the Caracas area. Other marginal leftist groups, along with MAS, made inroads in Maracay, the other main center of textile production. In addition to UTIT's demand for a forty-hour work week, the major issue that embittered worker-management relations centered on the sharp cutbacks in the labor force. The companies attributed the layoffs to pressing conditions in the industry due to widespread contraband and aggravated by the Law of Salary Increases. Labor leaders, however, claimed that management was carrying out a strategy of purging the work force of trade union militants and older workers.[11] Disunity in the textile workers' movement was evident in a strike in mid-1980 that was belatedly supported by pro-AD unions. Following the settlement, the refusal of unions led by the marginal Left in Maracay to order their members back to work served as a pretext for the companies to renege on their pledge to refrain from layoffs.

Dissension within one of the nation's largest unions, the Sindicato Unico de Trabajadores de la Industria Siderúrgica (Sutiss, formerly Atiss), also undermined the Left's efforts to achieve such far-reaching demands as the forty-hour work week in Sidor. Steel workers belonging to the Causa R and other marginal Left parties had formed a united slate that won a landslide victory in union elections in 1979. Nevertheless, while the Causa R was willing to make concessions by accepting the gradual implementation of the forty-hour work week, its coalition partners favored a confrontational approach. In the face of adamant company rejection of the forty-hour demand and an imminent strike, the CTV-affiliated Fetrabolívar and Fetrametal took over the union and signed a contract with Sidor, which maintained the work week at forty-eight hours (see Chapter 7).

The delegate strength of the major parties in the CTV (AD, Copei, and MEP) did not significantly change between the Seventh Congress in 1975 and the Eighth in 1980. Nevertheless, AD managed to increase its representation on the confederation's Executive Committee from seven to nine members, while Copei's was reduced from four to three. The CTV continued its "generous" policy of providing parties that had limited worker following with positions in the confederation's national leadership, a practice designed to project an image of pluralism. While this arrangement favored only MAS in 1975, it provided a host of smaller parties—MIR, the PCV, the Vanguardia Comunista, and the Morena party (a split off of URD)—regular and substitute posts on the CTV's Executive Committee in 1980.

As in 1975, many AD trade unionists objected to the overrepresentation of the allegedly right-wing Copei in the CTV's leadership. The AD trade union plenum at the time of the 1980 congress insisted that Copei accept a reduction in its representation on the CTV Executive Committee from four to three members. The *Copeyanos* were warned that if they persisted in their efforts to obtain four posts, AD would opt for a system of individual slates that would be elected on the basis of proportional representation. The AD delegation, which took in a majority at the congress, would then be able to choose for itself the leading positions on the CTV's Executive Committee in accordance with the confederation's internal regulations. Pedro Brito, who was a leading member of AD's hard-line faction (which was identified with the *carlosandresista* current in the party) admonished the *Copeyanos* to be satisfied with the secretary-generalship and to recognize that it was a "gift" granted by AD rather than won on the basis of delegate votes.[12]

Two concepts put forward at the Eighth Congress promised to provide the labor movement with considerable decision-making power in different spheres of society. Both proposals, although they were not presented for the first time at the congress, became the focus of interest for the CTV in future years. First, the CTV became a strong advocate of the model of *cogestión*. The congress made clear that worker input in the running of firms should be channeled through existing labor organizations rather than bypass them. There was widespread agreement among the delegates that, due to its overwhelming importance, *cogestión* had to be embodied in a law approved by the National Congress, rather than achieved on an individual basis in collective bargaining agreements.[13] The CTV's commitment to *cogestión* was lauded by various leading political figures, including President Herrera in his speech at the Eighth Congress, although this approval was not translated into legislation.

In the second proposal, the CTV called for the formation of various tripartite commissions consisting of labor, management, and state representatives to assume such all-important functions as the control of working conditions and the regulation of prices. For an extended period of time prior to the Herrera presidency, inflation had been kept at reasonable levels, but recent trends set in motion by the "liberation of prices" called for radical solutions. The CTV plan, in which a commission would have access to company records and would have the final word in price increases, had far-reaching implications. The proposal was approved in congress, albeit in modified form, in 1984. The term "Social Pact," which referred to this type of labor-management conflict resolution, became a slogan embraced by AD during these years. (Political analysts would point to the "Social Pact" and the tripartite commissions as evidence of the prevalence of corporatist relations because officially recognized labor and business organizations formally collaborated under the aegis of the state in order to eliminate class conflict.)

The AD Labor Bureau enhanced its influence and prestige within AD as a result of its successes in both internal party affairs and the labor movement. Despite Copei's assumption of power and its concerted effort to displace AD in the leadership of the CTV, AD labor leaders were able to increase its representation in the CTV's Executive Committee in the 1980 congress. Shortly thereafter, AD's position was further strengthened when two members of the CTV's Executive Committee belonging to Morena and one who represented the Vanguardia Comunista left their respective parties to join AD. In addition, AD labor leaders staunchly opposed the economic policies of the Herrera administration and even succeeded in wringing important concessions, at a time when the rest of AD was demoralized by the outcome of the 1978 presidential elections (as was demonstrated by the abstention during the 1979 municipal elections at the expense of AD). Internally, the Labor Bureau furthered its image by purporting to assume the position of arbiter and raising the banner of unity and consensus in the competition between the *betancourista* (or "orthodox") faction and the *carlosandresistas* for party positions.[14]

The Labor Bureau's support for Jaime Lusinchi for the 1983 presidential nomination was a master stroke. Lusinchi, who had previously been identified with the *carlosandresista*-wing of AD, was now won over to the party's "orthodox" grouping. As part of the deal, AD's trade union secretary, Manuel Peñalver (who was also the CTV's secretary of international affairs), was nominated secretary-general of the party in 1981. Lusinchi promised to consult labor and business on a regular basis in order to correct the alleged tendency of presidents Pérez and Herrera Campíns to close the doors of Miraflores to worker representatives. The Labor Bureau was given credit for having made possible Lusinchi's easy triumph in internal elections over the *carlosandresista* candidate. Following the national elections, Lusinchi proclaimed that he had been elected president "on the shoulders of the workers."

Prior to Peñalver's appointment, AD labor leaders had sought to obtain at least 30 percent of the delegates at the party's National Convention with the aim of negotiating an agreement whereby a member of the Labor Bureau would be nominated secretary-general. Some AD trade unionists viewed the selection of Peñalver as consonant with a long-range strategy of converting AD into a Labor party. Although this goal was not publicly espoused, the *Copeyanos* attempted to turn it to their advantage by raising the specter of a labor bureaucracy takeover of AD and the government.

The Administration of Jaime Lusinchi, 1984–1989

AD's Jaime Lusinchi won a near-landslide victory in the presidential election of 1983, while his party obtained half or more of the assigned number of congressmen in all twenty states. The auspiciousness of the situation on the political front contrasted sharply with the formidable economic challenges that his government faced. The price of OPEC oil, which had peaked at thirty-six dollars per barrel in 1980, declined steadily during his first two years, then nose-dived in the first half of 1986 before its partial recovery at between fourteen and seventeen dollars in 1987–1988. The problem of the nation's unfavorable trade balance was compounded by Lusinchi's decision to pay interest and a significant portion of the principal on Venezuela's foreign debt—the only major Latin American country besides Colombia to do so. By the end of the Lusinchi administration the nation's foreign exchange reserves, which were at a respectable $14 billion in 1984, were nearly exhausted.

In response to the decline in the general standard of living, the CTV hardened its stand toward the government. The CTV's new position was put forward by the outspoken Juan José Delpino, who assumed the confederation's presidency upon the death of José Vargas in September 1983. Delpino publicly affirmed that he did not consider his decision to join the left-leaning MEP in 1967 a mistake, despite his subsequent return to AD. He refused to hew closely to the party line, even on issues that were not directly related to organized labor. Thus, for instance, he criticized the terms of the refinancing of the foreign debt and denounced the corruption in the Lusinchi administration in the form of kickbacks on the sale of "preferential dollars" (at a special exchange rate) to merchants in the duty-free island of Margarita. He also broke with the tradition whereby under AD administrations (unlike Copei ones) the CTV attributed the nation's economic woes to unfavorable trends in the world economy rather than mistaken policies.

The CTV reproached President Lusinchi for failing to consult it prior to announcing policies related to the welfare of workers, a practice that ran counter to his alleged commitment to the "Social Pact." At times, Delpino assigned greater responsibility to the government than to Fedecámaras for the Social Pact's failure to resolve conflicts between workers and management. In addition, the CTV took issue with official statistics on the state of the economy. While the Labor Ministry set unemployment at 8 percent at the end of 1984, CTV figures placed it as high as 24 percent.[15] Delpino claimed that inflation in 1987 was 60 percent, three times higher than the estimates of the Central Bank.

The CTV head also pointed to the ineffectiveness of government measures for combatting unemployment. He unsuccessfully urged President Lusinchi to extend a government-decreed moratorium on layoffs from three months to a year, and pointed out that another decree that obliged companies to increase their work force by 10 percent had not been enforced. At the same time, Delpino deplored the government's failure to make good on its campaign pledge to come to the aid of CTV-owned enterprises.

Lusinchi, for instance, reneged on his promise to reopen the Workers Bank (which had been shut down by the Herrera government due to insolvency) by mid-1985. In addition, his rhetorical support for "social tourism," whereby the government built resort centers that were to be rented out to worker organizations, found expression only in small-scale construction in the coastal town of Rio Chico.

Spokesmen for the opposition parties criticized the CTV, while sometimes making a distinction between Delpino and other confederation leaders who were uncritical of the Lusinchi administration. MAS's standard-bearer, Teodoro Petkoff, depicted Delpino as an "upright and principled man" and added that he "should feel grieved, not only because of his impotence in the face of the government, but because of the heavy dinosaur which is the CTV apparatus."[16] Copei and other parties maintained that the CTV's new militant rhetoric was insincere because it did not get translated into the type of protests that the confederation had promoted under the Herrera administration.[17] Delpino himself at times threatened to call strikes, but on other occasions stated that such actions were not consonant with the Venezuelan tradition of social harmony.

The concept of the "Social Pact" was embodied in the CTV's proposal for the creation of the Commission on Costs, Prices, and Salaries (Conacopresa). The CTV recommended that labor, business, and the government receive equal representation on the commission and that its decisions on requests for price and salary increases be binding and unappealable. The CTV plan would have pegged wage hikes to the cost of living. In addition, the commission was to be given access to company records in order to determine the justification for price increases on regulated prices, a prerogative granted to unions under the Labor Law (Article 99) but one they had never exercised. Fedecámaras objected to the commission's wide range of powers and labeled the law "Red-tinted."[18]

The Lusinchi administration created Conacopresa in July 1984, but in an advisory capacity. In contrast to the CTV's original proposal, the government was given greater representation on the commission than labor and business. At first, the CTV's representatives reluctantly accepted price hikes, but subsequently they hardened their stand and vocally protested Conacopresa's failure to make recommendations in favor of across-the-board salary increases, the upturn in the rate of inflation notwithstanding. Fedecámaras reacted to the CTV's new position by withdrawing from the commission.

The CTV stressed the need to create nationwide industrial unions at its Ninth Congress, which met in May 1985. On the basis of a questionable interpretation of the Labor Law, the government had always ruled that a given union could not represent workers in more than one state. Tacit resistance to the effort to establish national unions also came from local labor leaders who feared losing their *fueros* (special privileges granted by labor legislation). The difficulty in unifying and centralizing the labor movement was compounded by the existence of parallel unions that were controlled by trade unionists belonging to different political parties. As a first step toward achieving this goal, the Eighth Congress had called for the amalgamation of CTV-affiliated parallel federations. In the case of two beverage workers' federations, one led by MEP and the other AD, the CTV's decision was complied with to the advantage of the latter party, which enjoyed majority influence in that sector. In contrast, the URD-dominated Fetrahidrocarburos refused to merge with the larger Fedepetrol led by MEP, AD, and Copei. Some opposition labor leaders were convinced that the AD-controlled CTV did not exert pressure on Fetrahidrocarburos due to the alliance between AD and URD in national politics (URD backed the presidential candidacy of Lusinchi) and in the labor movement.[19]

The Ninth Congress did not significantly alter the representation of each party in the CTV's Executive Committee, although the position of secretary-general went from a *Copeyano* to a MEPista. Partway through the period of elections for the selection of delegates to the Ninth Congress, the *Copeyanos* began to launch their own slates in individual labor federations rather than unite with AD. The FTC reasoned that this tactic would sharpen interparty differences and increase Copei's representation at all levels. Copei's go-it-alone approach was also applied at the CTV's Ninth Congress where, for the second time in the confederation's history, two slates competed for positions on the Executive Committee. Nevertheless, Copei's strategy did not pay off; in the fifty-two federations where the party launched its own slate, only in the state federations of Lara, Guárico, and Portuguesa did it come close to unseating AD as the dominant party.

The FTC's new electoral approach was consistent with its increasingly critical position within the CTV, particularly with regard to mismanagement of funds. The FTC accused leaders of thirteen federations of accepting bribes from management, disguised as payment of personal expenses in collective bargaining sessions—a practice known as *costa contractual*. The FTC's decision to present these charges was audacious for two reasons. In the first place, not all thirteen cases involved the public sector. Copei, as a staunch defender of the system of private property, was generally reluctant to attack representatives of business interests. In the second place, *costa contractual* abuses were not limited to AD trade unionists and included many *Copeyanos*. Indeed, one of the arguments offered by the FTC for eschewing alliances with AD in organized labor was the need to root out corruption in its own ranks that was purportedly fostered by electoral agreements with unscrupulous AD worker leaders.[20]

AD labor leaders made clear that their "generous" policy of accepting a *Copeyano* as the CTV's secretary-general was contingent upon Copei's participation in a united slate at the confederation's national congress. The

Copeyanos were willing to forfeit control of the secretary-generalship, in part because its powers had been whittled away since Rafael León León had first occupied the position in 1970. To avoid a repetition of what happened when CTV President Olivo died in 1974 and León León served as acting president, AD had modified confederation regulations to stipulate that vacancies of executive offices would be filled by members of the same party. In subsequent years, when CTV presidents traveled abroad, they were temporarily replaced by AD members of the confederation's Executive Committee rather than the secretary-general. Furthermore, the secretary-generalship previously acted as a controllership, but with the growth of the BTV, financial statements were signed exclusively by the CTV president and treasurer, both of whom belonged to AD. FTC leaders also objected to the pressure that AD exerted on *Copeyanos* to vote with the majority in the CTV's Executive Committee on the basis that the secretary-generalship had been a "gift."[21]

Rafael Caldera and Copei's secretary-general, Eduardo Fernández, met with members of the FTC's National Committee in an effort to convince them to form part of the AD-led slate. Ever since the overthrow of Pérez Jiménez, Caldera had consistently argued in favor of cooperation with AD and incorporation in the CTV. The FTC leaders, however, refused to reconsider their decision, even though they recognized that their defiant position in the CTV would leave *Copeyano* public employees vulnerable to layoffs.[22]

As a result of Copei's new electoral approach, AD reached an agreement with MEP whereby MEPista César Olarte, formerly of the telephone workers, was named CTV secretary-general. In accordance with AD's "generous policy" toward rival parties in the labor movement, the MEPistas were also awarded top positions in a number of federations. In return for their participation with AD in united slates, MEPistas were named to the number-two position of secretary-general in the white-collar workers' federation (Fenade), the garbage collection workers' federation (Fetrauds), and the state federation of Guárico. They also obtained the secretary-generalships of Fedepetrol and the state federations of Zulia and Trujillo, despite the fact that their slates received less votes than Copei which, in all three cases, came in second to AD. MEP's decision not to renew its long-standing alliance with Copei in Fedepetrol was particularly unfortunate for the *Copeyanos* due to its strategic importance.[23]

To many observers and even some MEPista political activists, the party's agreements with AD and Copei ran counter to MEP's leftist orientation. MEP trade unionists justified the policy—which they labeled "tactical flexibility"—on grounds that CTV regulations regarding proportional representation provided winning slates the choice of the top positions on the executive committees, thus giving smaller parties an incentive to join the majority. Although MEP's stated priority was to form alliances with other leftist parties, the meager influence of the rest of the Left in the labor movement, and MEP's own diminishing strength, encouraged it to ally with AD and Copei. Indeed, the only way MEP was able to occupy positions of president and secretary-general in CTV-affiliated federations (ten in all) was through agreements with these two parties.[24]

MEP labor leaders also defended their pact with AD by pointing out that under Delpino's leadership the confederation maintained a more critical and autonomous position in national and world politics than when José Vargas was president and Manuel Peñalver secretary of international affairs. MEPista César Olarte has stated:

> The current CTV position [on foreign affairs] is based on support for the Contadora Group, the peaceful solution of conflicts, and self-determination, and thus coincides with the Socialist International. . . . Manuel Peñalver was very anticommunist and is still living in the 1960s in the era of the guerrilla struggle whereas [international affairs head] Antonio Ríos . . . has modified the CTV's stand, although it is not altogether the progressive position that would satisfy MEP.[25]

Since the death of José Vargas, several top AD labor leaders—including Pedro Brito, César Gil, and Federico Ramírez León—aspired to be CTV president. Because of the tension generated between factions led by Carlos Luna (who supported Brito) and Manuel Peñalver, the Labor Bureau chose Delpino as a "consensus" candidate, with the understanding that he would not occupy the presidency over an extended period. Many of the members of the Luna faction had formed part of dissident groups that left AD in the 1960s (although, ironically, Brito, Gil, Ramírez León, and Delpino were all former MEPistas). While Luna's followers were identified with former President Carlos Andrés Pérez, who sought reelection in 1988, Peñalver formed part of the "orthodox" faction in the party and was mentioned as a possible AD presidential candidate.

Prior to the CTV's Ninth Congress, *carlosandresistas* Armando González and Carlos Piñerua, who had headed the FCV and Fedepetrol, respectively, since the 1960s, were voted out of office and replaced by trade unionists who would subsequently support AD's "orthodox" candidate as the nation's president. The new FCV head, Eustacio Guevara, was a personal friend of Lusinchi's and allegedly received aid from the government in his bid for the FCV presidency.[26] The AD peasants and oil workers who opposed González and Piñerua relied on the slogan "renovation" and questioned the moral integrity of both leaders (with respect to the FCV-owned company Peasant Supplies and Fedepetrol's Petroleum Financial Corporation).

Like Carlos Andrés Pérez, Armando González was known for his militant rhetoric and radical pronouncements, which evidently did not accord with his day-to-day behavior. González, whose reelection in the previous FCV congress had gone uncontested in AD, was criticized for rigging the outcome of AD-peasant plenums in various states in order to favor his candidacy. The anti-González peasant faction in AD included top national leaders and a majority in the party's Agrarian Bureau. AD's secretary-general, Manuel Peñalver, threatened to take disciplinary measures against González and appointed a special commission to investigate the charges against him.[27] Non-AD peasant leaders expressed the view that the charge of mismanagement of funds was a mere smoke screen, and that the internal opposition to González was due to his support for Carlos Andrés Pérez.[28] The fact that González was chosen first vice president of the FCV lent itself to the thesis that corruption was not the main issue at stake.

Within labor circles, Pedro Brito and Carlos Luna questioned the labor policies of President Lusinchi and called for worker mobilizations to protest the deterioration in the general standard of living. They denounced Peñalver's heavy-handed "Stalinist" methods in the shunting aside of several long-standing *carlosandresista* labor leaders in the nation's interior. They also criticized Labor Bureau chief Antonio Ríos for publicly defending the moral integrity of BTV's president, Eleazar Pinto, at the time of his conviction for the mishandling of bank funds. In addition, the Luna group argued that the CTV's secretary-general should be an AD member, since otherwise he would lack the support of the confederation majority and be virtually powerless.[29]

The Brito candidacy was formally proposed by Luna and former CTV President González Navarro. They called on Peñalver to provide "democratic guarantees" in the form of secret voting procedures in the AD plenum of delegates to the Ninth Congress, where the party's candidate for CTV president was to be nominated. They pointed out that such a method was in keeping with AD's tradition of support for democratic reforms. The dissidents noted that, prior to the recent congresses of the FCV and Fedepetrol, AD worker plenums had nominated candidates by ballot as had been recommended by top members of the party's Labor Bureau. On these two occasions, however, the Labor Bureau was intent on imposing the candidates of its choice, and thus rejected secret elections.[30]

Peñalver and his followers reacted sharply to the demands and accusations of the dissidents. Construction workers' President Juan Herrera blasted Brito for having originally belonged to URD (before joining MEP and then AD), and insisted that the dissidents be left out of the CTV's Executive Committee. In devising the slate that was submitted to the AD plenum for ratification, the Labor Bureau heeded Herrera's recommendations. In excluding Luna, Brito, and González Navarro from the CTV Executive Committee, the Labor Bureau was influenced by the possibility that the dissidents could make common cause with other parties, thus depriving AD of its majority in the confederation's national leadership.[31]

While the aging González Navarro announced that he had intended to retire from union activity all along, the reaction of Brito and Luna was less passive. They distributed leaflets at the Ninth Congress that contained the phrases "*caudillismo* does not have a place," "leadership should be collective," and "the secret vote is personal liberty." Luna maintained that, had elections at the AD plenum been secret, his group would have triumphed, or at least consolidated its power with 30 percent of the vote. Because votes were taken by hand, most of his supporters went along with the Labor Bureau's recommendations out of fear of reprisals. Luna claimed that he enjoyed widespread backing in the nation's interior from trade unionists who felt stifled by the rigid control exercised by the CTV's national leadership, and who were "purer" and more committed than their counterparts in the capital region. He added that over 30 percent of the CTV'affiliated unions had failed to hold elections to nominate delegates to the Ninth Congress.[32]

Ironically, the purge of top *carlosandresista* trade unionists facilitated labor support for the presidential candidacy of Carlos Andrés Pérez in the 1988 elections. AD labor leaders had long feared that Pérez, with minimum backing at the national level of the CTV, would attempt to build his own base of support by appealing to the rank and file, while passing over the confederation's leadership. Not only did Pérez discard this strategy, but also he was apparently willing to sacrifice his small following in the CTV in order to win over the Labor Bureau to his presidential candidacy. In a closed meeting with the dissidents in Maracay, Pérez pledged to support their efforts in favor of secret internal elections for the AD slate, but he subsequently failed to make good on his promise.

Pérez maintained a neutral stand in the factional struggle in AD labor. He also delivered a speech at the AD plenum of peasant delegates following the defeat of *carlosandresista* Armando González in which he insinuated that the former FCV president had violated electoral statutes.[33] Pérez also spoke out against teachers' strikes in universities and the public school system, which were led by labor leaders of the opposition parties and AD dissidents who were allegedly *carlosandresistas*.[34]

Pérez's strategy of moderation paid off. Most AD labor leaders, despite their long-standing association with the party's "orthodox" faction, opposed its choice for the presidential nomination, Minister of Interior Octavio Lepage. Lepage started out the campaign with the solid backing of the party's "machine" as well as the government. Indeed, Delpino, who ended up backing Pérez, protested that the Lusinchi administration was exerting undue pressure on the Labor Bureau on behalf of Lepage. Nevertheless, Lepage trailed the charismatic Pérez in public opinion surveys by as much as five to one, a margin that was not significantly reduced in the course of the campaign. Many labor leaders personally preferred Lepage but, as representatives of the workers, were reluctant to support an unpopular, and indeed lackluster, candidate.[35]

Prior to extending official support to Pérez, the Labor Bureau reached an agreement with the former president whereby the next finance minister was to be an AD member committed to the party's program, rather than a representative of big business as was usually the case. It was also decided that the BTV, which Lusinchi evidently refused to reorganize due to the deterioration in government-labor relations, would be reopened. At a special labor plenum on the eve of Pérez's nomination, the possibility was raised that a trade unionist be appointed minister, in accordance with the goal of promoting labor's input in government decision making. At the same time, AD labor leaders called for the Labor Bureau's systematic input in the formulation of Pérez's electoral platform. They also insisted on discarding the concept that an AD member who is elected president is relieved of party discipline, except in matters related to foreign policy and national defense. This revision was meant as a corrective to Pérez's overreliance on nonparty advisers during his previous administration and his failure to take the views of party leaders, and those of the CTV in particular, into consideration.[36]

Following the defeat of the Luna faction at the Ninth Congress and the Labor Bureau's endorsement of Pérez, a new division in AD pitted labor leaders previously associated with the same internal current against one another. A number of prominent AD trade unionists led by Manuel Peñalver defied the Labor Bureau by openly supporting the candidacy of Lepage. Despite their minority status, Lepage's followers convoked a national conference in the name of the AD labor movement on September 21, 1987, the day before another meeting was held that was sponsored by the Labor Bureau. They attacked the Labor Bureau for failing to consult its constituency and for creating scores of bogus labor organizations in order to inflate its representation in AD's electoral college on behalf of the Pérez candidacy.

Peñalver's group also claimed that AD statutes prohibited the Labor Bureau from taking sides in internal electoral contests. At the same time, Lepage pointed out that, with the Labor Bureau playing a key role in internal elections, AD ran the risk of being transformed into a "Labor Party."[37] Ironically, the specter of a Labor Party had previously been raised by the *Copeyanos* when Peñalver was named AD secretary-general.

Some of Lepage's labor followers were particularly scathing in their attacks on the pro-Pérez trade unionists. The president of Fetracarabobo, for instance, called on AD's Disciplinary Tribunal to sanction Delpino for breach of party discipline. This aggressiveness was intended to create the impression that AD labor was nearly evenly divided, although, in fact, Lepage's support on this front was extremely limited.

The presence of as many as 12,700 trade unionists in AD's 52,000-member electoral college facilitated Pérez's easy triumph over Lepage.

Subsequently, Labor Bureau head Antonio Ríos called for disciplinary measures against Lepage's labor followers, while Delpino insisted on the removal of Peñalver as AD's secretary-general. In a heated meeting of AD's Trade Union Secretariat in November 1987, four labor leaders—all of whom were heads or former heads of CTV-affiliated federations—were suspended from their positions for the duration of their terms; sixteen others, including several members of the confederation's Executive Committee, were censured. Lepage's followers were accused of having violated statutes in refusing to back the Labor Bureau's choice and for having utilized offensive language in the campaign against Pérez.

In the Secretariat meeting, Lepage's supporters argued that they had exercised a democratic right in working for the candidate of their preference. Furthermore, a precedent had been set fifteen years earlier when CTV President Francisco Olivo backed Reinaldo Leandro Mora for the AD candidacy for the 1973 presidential elections, despite the Labor Bureau's endorsement of Pérez. One of the four suspended trade unionists, the president of Fetracarabobo, initially refused to step down and threatened to take his case to the courts on grounds that he had been elected by the workers of his state and was thus not responsible to AD.

A hard and soft line within AD labor was discernible in the debate over the sanctions. Delpino and Federico Ramírez León favored harsh measures against their AD labor adversaries. In contrast, Antonio Ríos attempted to soften residual bitterness following the Secretariat meeting.[38] Ríos's position was shared by Pérez, who addressed the Secretariat and reiterated his policy of not interfering in internal labor disputes; at the same time, he cautioned against taking stringent measures against the minority faction.[39]

During this period the AD leadership in the CTV took steps to counter the idea that the confederation was a corruption-ridden bureaucracy that stifled rank-and-file participation. The failure to hold elections in the steel workers' union, Sutiss, after the CTV-sponsored intervention and the closing of the BTV and conviction of its president contributed to this image. The sharp attacks of Copei and the parties of the marginal Left against the CTV also undermined the confederation's prestige. At its Ninth Congress the CTV set up a five-member controllership, which included trade unionists of various parties, to oversee the ethical conduct of worker leaders. The commission investigated possible abuses in the practice of *costa contractual* on the part of the heads of Fetrasalud, Fetrametal, and the two oil workers' federations.

The CTV's national leadership ordered the Executive Committee of Sutiss, which was under the direction of Fetrametal and Fetrabolívar, to hold union elections in order to put an end to another embarrassing situation for the confederation. Delpino insisted that former Sutiss president, Andrés Velásquez, who had been ousted from the union, be given the right to vote, for which he publicly acknowledged his appreciation. Following the upset victory of Velásquez's Causa R at Sidor, Antonio Ríos attempted to distance the CTV even further from Fetrametal and Fetrabolívar. Ríos attributed AD labor's electoral fiasco to the failure to develop a capable local leadership and to the protracted duration of the intervention, which should not have lasted more than a year.[40]

AD's "generous" policy toward smaller parties in the CTV paid off in the confederation's face-lifting efforts. MAS and MEP formed part of the controllership commission and accepted the underlying principle—which only Copei increasingly disregarded—that denunciations of wrongdoings had to be presented within the CTV family rather than aired publicly. MAS and MEP members on the CTV's Executive Committee partially supported the CTV's position regarding the BTV by arguing that political considerations had induced the Herrera government to close the bank.[41] These trade unionists, along with those of Copei, publicly rejected the virulent attacks against the CTV by the Causa R and other marginal Left groups,[42] along with their view that nationalized industry did not warrant special treatment from organized labor. In short, the discretion and moderation of trade unionists who benefited from interparty deals made in the name of labor unity lent credibility to the CTV's self-portrayal as "pluralistic," and to the defense of the moral integrity of confederation leaders.

The Administration of Carlos Andrés Pérez, 1989–

The economic policies pursued by the government after 1988 and the nation's economic performance contrasted sharply with the expectations of a majority of Venezuelans, who assumed that Pérez's second term in office would be a rerun of his first. Contrary to these optimistic presumptions, the general standard of living continued to decline in the early years of the Pérez administration. According to one study, aggregate consumption decreased by 30 to 35 percent in 1989, during which time 38.05 percent of the population lived in dire poverty, and another 52.37 percent in "relative poverty."[43] In addition, Pérez's neoliberal program of austerity measures, tariff reduction, and privatization, along with the moderation of his pro-third-world rhetoric, represented a sharp departure from his former populist and nationalistic policies. Pérez's new stands were hailed by spokesmen for the U.S. government and international financial interests. In early 1991, for instance, U.S. Secretary of Commerce Robert Mosbacher wrote that the new climate of confidence generated by the easing of restrictions had encouraged the repatriation of Venezuelan capital abroad; he particularly approved of the government's decision to lift regulations that required foreign investors to associate with domestic capital in numerous sectors.[44]

AD leaders belonging to the "orthodox" faction and spokesmen for the party's Labor Bureau expressed reservations regarding certain aspects of the administration's economic policies. They questioned the appointment of "technocrats" linked with business interests to cabinet positions in charge of the formulation of economic policy. They particularly objected to the naming of Pedro Tinoco (a conservative banker who, as Caldera's finance minister, had been strongly attacked by the opposition in 1969) as president of the Central Bank on grounds of conflict of interest.

Although all AD congressmen formally endorsed Pérez's economic package when it came up for vote, many of them attempted to distance themselves from it as popular disturbances became increasingly frequent and AD suffered setbacks in the state and municipal elections of December 1989. They were particularly critical of plans to privatize some seventy public firms and to attract foreign capital to sectors that were legally reserved to the state, such as the oil industry. Some party leaders criticized the government for delivering the Banco Occidental de Descuento—the only firm that was privatized in the first two years of the Pérez administration—to the "financial oligarchy," while labor leaders expressed disappointment that the bank's employees were not granted stock participation. Leaders of CTV affiliate federations representing workers in the national port system, the public telephone company, and elsewhere were even more adamant in their opposition to privatization and were critical of confederation leaders for accepting government plans to transfer certain operations in those sectors to private hands.

The CTV's initial reaction to the spontaneous disturbances that convulsed the nation during the week of February 27, 1989 (resulting in 276 fatalities, according to official estimates) was to dismiss them as the act of "loafers, thieves and vagabonds."[45] When CTV President Delpino, who was out of the country at the time, returned to Venezuela, the confederation reinterpreted the events by viewing them as a popular reaction to the deterioration in the nation's standard of living, the hoarding of merchandise, and illegal price increases.

The CTV was especially sensitive to the charges that the occurrences of February 27 demonstrated the inefficacy of the labor movement, which failed to channel popular discontent and frustrations. At its Second Extraordinary Congress on April 25, the CTV unanimously called for a general strike on May 18 in order to pressure congress to approve the new Labor Law and other legislation dealing with consumer protection, monopolies, and housing. The nation's three smaller confederations and several independent federations also agreed to participate. The May 18 protests, which virtually paralyzed the economy including agricultural activity and air transportation, was the first day-long general strike in favor of concrete reforms in the nation's history.

The general strike signaled a measured distancing of the labor movement from AD and the government. President Pérez spoke at the Extraordinary Congress in an abortive attempt to convince the CTV to reconsider its decision. At the same time, AD President Gonzalo Barrios and Secretary-General Humberto Celli criticized party labor leaders for failing to consult the party's national committee prior to committing themselves to the strike. Nevertheless, the CTV's defiant attitude was constrained, as was its antigovernment rhetoric: it was clear that one of the confederation's objectives in calling the strike was to reassert its leadership, which had been widely questioned as a result of the February 27 disturbances.

At the Extraordinary Congress, delegates belonging to the opposition parties unsuccessfully proposed that the government's austerity program be the main target of the protests. CTV leaders did call for measures to counter the negative effects of the government's economic policies, such as a price freeze on basic commodities and the periodic revision of salaries. At the same time, however, Delpino and other AD labor leaders insisted that the protests were not directed against the government. As proof of their moderation, they refrained from raising demands for wage increases and a reduction of the work week, which may have prompted the government to assume a more hostile position. In addition, they termed May 18 a *"paro"* (work stoppage), rather than a *"huelga"* with its connotations of sharp conflict and confrontation. Also, they agreed to keep electric furnaces and other expensive equipment in state-run companies functioning in order to avoid damage, a concession that was criticized by the proleftist steel workers' union. For its part, the government pledged itself not to dock the salaries of state workers who participated in the strike.

The main targets of the CTV's attacks were business interests. Tension was especially sharpened as a result of Fedecámaras's opposition to the protest. Not only did the business organization question the legality of the strike, but also it insisted that the government guarantee the security of those employees who chose to work that day. The CTV organized "dissuasive brigades" in order to convince intransigent merchants to shut their establishments; in some cases, strong-arm tactics allegedly were used.

The CTV organized a second protest in eight cities on February 15, 1990, in opposition to announced increases in the price of gasoline. These marches, however, were less successful than the May 18 general strike. Not only was the turnout less than expected, but also the gathering in Caracas erupted in disorders, resulting in an estimated fifty nonfatal casualties and forty arrests. At the first sound of gunshots, Antonio Ríos and other top CTV leaders fled, leaving the task of negotiating with the police and trying to reestablish order to lower-ranking trade unionists. Ríos was harshly attacked and even ridiculed in the press for his behavior. Confederation leaders blamed the violence on police repression, while recognizing that they had erred in not having organized peace-keeping brigades. They also assured their followers that the CTV would continue to call mass protests in response to the nation's pressing economic conditions.[46]

The CTV, however, failed to carry through on its commitment to organize mass mobilizations. The street protests and strikes, which became frequent occurrences in the second Pérez administration, were called by labor federations—many of which were outside the CTV fold—and social movements—particularly neighborhood associations and student organizations. Those sectors of the working class that engaged in ongoing struggles during these years belonged, for the most part, to the public sphere: health workers, including doctors and laboratory technicians (who were grouped in their own federations); public schoolteachers, both at the elementary and high school levels; workers on the payroll of the National Institute of Ports; and court employees. In addition, the social movements were mainly concerned with the deterioration of public services such as education and community services. Thus, the main target of the protests was the state and not business interests, against which the CTV had concentrated its attacks in the months following the February 27 disturbances.

There are several economic explanations for this pattern. First, worker struggles were a response to the neoliberalism of the Pérez administration, which entailed reduction in federal expenditures and privatization, with their consequences of mass layoffs and cuts in real wages. Second, work stoppages against a paternalistic state were less risky than those against a private firm, which usually resulted in loss of pay and firings; this consideration was particularly important during a period of economic contraction and high levels of unemployment. Finally, the sharp fluctuations in oil prices after 1980 made it impossible for policymakers to predict government income. As a result of overly optimistic estimates of future revenue, the government was often forced to renege on benefits offered to public employees. Indeed, failure to meet contractual obligations lay behind a large number of conflicts in the public sector during this period. In contrast, the private sector was a much more reliable employer.

Government revenue also explains why so many of these labor conflicts involved professional workers and students. In the 1970s the windfall in petroleum income led to a rapid expansion in the public university system. After 1980, a glut on the market reduced many university-trained personnel to near-proletarian status, especially in the state sector, which had traditionally absorbed surplus labor.

The Tenth CTV Congress was held in May 1990. It did not signify a major shift in the correlation of political forces, although MAS nearly replaced MEP as the third largest party in the confederation (see Table 2,

Chapter 2). Despite MEP's decline and speculation that the secretary-generalship would revert back to Copei, MEPista César Olarte retained the number-two position with the backing of AD delegates.

Although non-AD trade unionists maintained that the CTV was not sufficiently aggressive in its stand against IMF-imposed economic policies, the congress did unconditionally oppose one aspect of neoliberalism that had gained wide acceptance in Venezuela: the encouragement of export-oriented industries under foreign ownership that did not integrate into the local economy, known as the *maquila*. The CTV pointed out that *maquiladora* companies were generally attracted (as in the case of Mexico) by the prospect of depressed wages and exemption from existing labor legislation, thus jeopardizing hard-fought-for worker gains. Another important resolution at the congress put the CTV on record as refusing to negotiate modifications in the practice of calculating severance pay on the basis of the workers' last monthly salary. As part of the public debate over the new Labor Law, Fedecámaras had mounted a strong campaign in favor of a complete overhaul of the system of *prestaciones sociales*, a proposal some CTV leaders had indicated their willingness to consider (see Chapter 9).

Prior to the Tenth Congress, Delpino fulfilled his original pledge to step down from the presidency, probably because he realized that, in adopting critical and intransigent positions, he was out of tune with the rest of the AD labor leadership. Indeed, after his resignation, he defended increasingly radical stands, leading to his suspension from the party's National Executive Committee. Delpino was replaced by Antonio Ríos, who was reelected president at the Tenth Congress. President Pérez threw his support behind Ríos, even though another aspirant, Federico Ramírez León, had been a loyal *carlosandresista* as far back as the 1970s. Other candidates included *carlosandresista* César Gil and *ortodoxo* Sótero Rodríguez. The pragmatic Pérez backed Ríos in hopes that his cautious and diplomatic style would foster labor peace[47]; the same concern had led Pérez to refrain from actively supporting *carlosandresista* Carlos Luna at the CTV's 1975 congress.

Ramírez León replaced Ríos as AD's labor secretary. Under his leadership the party's Labor Bureau was more forceful in its criticisms of the party and, at least initially, distanced itself from both *carlosandresista* and orthodox factions. Ramírez León insisted that the party refrain from defending members of the former Lusinchi administration who were accused of graft. The Labor Bureau also supported the proposition formulated by *carlosandresistas* that AD's national and state authorities be chosen in direct, secret elections, rather than at party conventions. Ramírez León blamed AD's setbacks in the December 1989 gubernatorial and municipal elections on the *ortodoxos* who controlled the party in most states, at the same time that he called for the replacement of the party's secretary-general, secretary of organization, and acting president—all *ortodoxos*.

Ramírez León called on AD to fulfill its role as a "governing party" by making greater efforts to defend the Pérez administration from the attacks of the opposition. Nevertheless, he recognized that the Labor Bureau was in an awkward position since it shared the objections voiced by many *ortodoxo* leaders regarding the administration's neoliberal policies. As part of the Labor Bureau's effort to assert a position of relative independence, AD trade unionists made preparations to launch their candidates for the post of secretary-general in eleven states in internal elections that were slated for the second half of 1991.[48]

Both AD Labor Secretary Ramírez León and (although to a lesser extent) CTV President Ríos realized that the widespread discontent set off by the economic crisis obliged the labor movement to harden its stands. Nevertheless, they were constrained by the imperatives of the CTV's vast economic interests and the vulnerability of the labor leadership whose ethical conduct and internal democratic practices were widely questioned, both in and out of the labor movement. One year after the reopening of the BTV in 1990, for instance, the bank was shaken by its second major scandal, which seriously compromised the reputations of top AD labor leaders, including Ramírez León, César Gil, and particularly Antonio Ríos (who had always been closely linked with the confederation's enterprises). Announced worker protests against Fedecámaras and government austerity measures were widely viewed as a ploy to divert attention from the CTV's internal economic woes.

AD's Labor Bureau faced a similar credibility gap. Ramírez León called for strict disciplinary measures against AD members who were found guilty of corrupt dealings, but at the same time expressed concern for the fate of several trade unionists who were brought before the party's Ethical Tribunal on charges of misuse of union funds. In short, AD labor leaders were not in an ideal position to articulate mass discontent and carry out militant actions. Despite this handicap, trade union challengers did not pose an immediate threat to AD's leadership position, as demonstrated by the party's majority representation at the CTV's Tenth Congress in 1990.

AD-Labor, the Economic Crisis, and the Exceptionalism Thesis

Mexico's moratorium on the payment of its external debt in 1982 interrupted the flow of foreign loans to Latin America and signaled the beginning of a protracted period of economic contraction throughout the continent. The austerity policies that were designed by the International Monetary Fund in order to regain the confidence of the international banking community hit the underprivileged classes the hardest. Resistance to these measures took the forms of frequent general strikes and urban riots. In addition, leftist-controlled trade unions and independent federations made important inroads at the expense of the more conservative established labor leadership. This new worker militance led labor historians to question assumptions regarding the alleged passivity of the Latin American working class. They challenged the thesis (associated with Gino Germani) that the recent arrival of workers from the countryside accounted for a low level of class consciousness, and the arguments of writers on corporatism that the labor movement was straitjacketed by the inducements and constraints of an omnipotent state.[49]

For most of the 1980s, writers and politicians generally viewed the Venezuelan labor movement as an exception to the combative behavior of workers throughout the continent. Although CTV heads occasionally threatened to call general strikes to pressure the government to modify economic policies, the nation was exempt from the mass protests that characterized its Latin American neighbors. Furthermore, AD managed to retain its dominant position in the CTV and, through a "generous" policy of concessions to smaller parties, avoided sharp internal conflict that would have undermined labor stability. In contrast to the acute rivalry at the level of federations and confederations in the rest of the continent, the CTV continued to nearly monopolize organized labor in Venezuela while few independent labor organizations challenged it in its traditional strongholds. Thus, the social tranquility that marked Venezuela during the oil boom period of the 1970s apparently continued uninterrupted during most of the lean years of the 1980s.

Nevertheless, those analysts who depict the Venezuelan labor movement as historically docile and emphasize AD's mediating influence present a misleading picture. Several developments raise difficult questions and place in doubt the AD government's ability to control organized labor and defuse the discontent that exists. The internal struggle in the Labor Bureau between those trade unionists who accept dictates from the AD party and government, on the one hand, and those who favor a more independent course, on the other, has characterized the post-1958 period and was only temporarily interrupted in 1967 as a result of the MEP split.

The motives of the "independent" AD trade unionists, however, have been mixed, and their future behavior is unpredictable. They can hardly be labeled "leftist." There was little possibility, for instance, that they would unite with representatives of other parties in the CTV in order to isolate the more conservative AD leaders. Furthermore, the Left has generally distrusted the AD "independents," not the least because some of them (such as future MEPistas Salom Mesa and César Olarte, former ARSista Hugo Soto Socorro, and Carlos Luna) at one point were linked with shady groups in their respective unions that used strong-arm methods against leftist trade unionists during the guerrilla period of the 1960s.

In addition, the more independent-minded AD trade unionists did not act as an organized faction; in the 1985 congress "independents" Brito, Ramírez León, and Delpino all vied for the CTV presidency. Many AD independents chafed at the deals with Copei imposed by their party in which a *Copeyano* was named CTV secretary-general in 1975 and 1980. Whether they rejected such pacts because they viewed Copei as right-wing or because they were more sectarian than the AD *ortodoxos* and resented having to concede top CTV positions to other parties was not entirely clear.

During the Lusinchi administration, the willingness of such independents as Delpino to mobilize the workers in defiance of the party's leadership was never clearly demonstrated. As CTV president, Delpino occasionally raised the possibility of calling strikes in opposition to government policy, but these warnings invariably assumed the form of empty bluffs. The events of February 27 and May 18, 1989, were also difficult to read. On the one hand, they seemed to signal a new popular militance and a move to the left on the part of organized labor. On the other hand, the CTV failed to articulate bread-and-butter grievances in the May 18 general strike and to follow up the protest with others based on concrete demands. The cynical view that AD labor leaders organized the work stoppage primarily to reassert its leadership, which had been questioned when they were taken by surprise on February 27, is plausible. Nevertheless, AD trade unionists resisted pressure from the government, as well as from their own party, to call off the strike.

AD's majority representation on the CTV's Executive Committee overstated the party's real strength in the labor movement. AD's following was most reduced in the populous region that extends from Caracas to Maracaibo, among strategic industrial workers, and in militant sectors of the working class. On the other hand, AD enjoyed disproportionate influence in the less-populated states with a traditional economy where small unions, which were easily manipulated by the national federations and the CTV, predominated.[50] AD was also markedly strong among public employees, many of whom owed their positions to party patronage. This backing was particularly significant because of the steady growth in the state sector since 1958. Eighty percent of white-collar government workers belong to CTV-affiliated unions, in a nation where only 30 percent of the working class is organized. Nevertheless, by the late 1980s, AD could no longer take for granted this base of support due to the ongoing worker conflicts that took hold of the state sector.

AD's ability to domesticate opposition trade unionists in order to maintain the CTV's image as one happy family should not be taken for granted. MEPistas and MASistas on the CTV's Executive Committee, such as César Olarte and Jesús Urbieta (who later joined AD), were severely criticized by members of their respective parties for failing to confront the

AD majority in the confederation.[51] Trade unionists belonging to MEP, MAS, and Copei have complained that AD's "generous" policy of offering them positions in the CTV always implied a tacit acceptance on their part of the unethical conduct of the confederation's AD leaders. MEPista Casto Gil Rivera pointed out that on various occasions AD threatened to expel him from the CTV Executive Committee due to his active support for rank-and-file movements that challenged CTV decisions.[52]

In short, at the outset of the 1990s, AD's hegemony in organized labor is being threatened from various positions. Since 1958 a current within the Labor Bureau has favored assuming a more critical stand toward AD governments and asserting a greater degree of independence from the party. Despite the removal of Luna and his closest supporters from the CTV in 1985, AD labor continued to be divided between hard-line and soft-line trade unionists. Furthermore, AD labor's "generous" policy toward its rivals, which was designed to curtail opposition within the CTV, did not always produce the desired results. This was especially true with the *Copeyanos* who rejected electoral pacts in the labor movement and hardened their stand toward AD after 1985. A host of smaller parties belonging to the marginal Left, which attacked AD labor leaders as veritable "sellouts," made inroads both within the CTV (in the case of the Causa R) and in the CUTV (in the case of UTIT). Finally, professional organizations largely outside of the CTV fold, including those of doctors and public school and university teachers, carried out bold actions that proved embarrassing for the confederation.

The predominately AD leadership of the CTV has also failed to channel the discontent of the nonunionized sectors of the urban poor, as it had in 1957 and 1958 immediately before and after the overthrow of Pérez Jiménez. At that time, the CTV could claim to go far beyond its immediate constituency of organized workers by representing and mobilizing the underprivileged classes as a whole in defense of the democratic system. In contrast, the CTV was completely taken by surprise by the February 27, 1989, disturbances, whose principal protagonists were members of the "marginal class" (those outside of the formal economy). The CTV failed to play any role at all in subsequent street protests led by student groups and neighborhood associations, which in the three years following the February 27 disturbances numbered five thousand, two thousand of which resulted in violence.[53] It can thus be concluded that, by the late 1980s, the CTV's sphere of influence was limited to the traditional working class belonging to the confederation's affiliate unions which, with a few exceptions (such as the textile and steel workers), were passive actors relative to other nonelite sectors of the population.

The "exceptionalism" thesis, which views Venezuela as free of the social turmoil of other Latin American nations and sees AD's control of the labor movement as a guarantee that social harmony will prevail,[54] fails to go beneath the surface to examine important trends. The internal tension in the AD leadership of organized labor is invariably passed over. No mention is made of party trade unionists' disapproval of the government's austerity policies of the 1960s, nor of the dissident group that Carlos Luna headed between 1975 and 1985. Furthermore, the exceptionalists fail to recognize that circumstantial factors played a crucial role in preserving social and political tranquility over an extended time span. These short-term considerations, corresponding to three distinct periods, can be summarized as follows:

1. The unpopular guerrilla war of the 1960s convinced many trade unionists to refrain from calling strikes.

2. The boom in oil prices in the following decade generated optimism and even euphoria among broad sectors of the population, a mood that was naturally not conducive to mass protests. (Certainly sudden increases in the world prices of the main export commodity of any third-world country would have produced a similar climate.)

3. For most of the 1980s, Venezuelans ingenuously assumed, or else wanted to believe, that the economic crisis would be short-lived; by the time of the 1988 presidential campaign, they were led to think that if Carlos Andrés Pérez were elected president, he would reimplement the policies that had allegedly made possible the prosperity of the previous decade. When Venezuelans awoke to the realization that the recession was not at all transitory, and that Pérez was determined to scrap the populist policies of his first government in favor of neoliberalism (a change that government spokesmen called *"el gran viraje"*—the great turnabout), people's disillusionment expressed itself in violent form, during the week of February 27, 1989.

The exceptionalists assume that the factors that they stress in explaining stability in the past (the absence of sharp fluctuations in oil prices and mature political culture and leadership) are constants that will ensure its continuation in the future. This unfounded optimism became especially apparent when exceptionalists writing in the mid-1980s, at a time when the recession was well under way, failed to examine the possible destabilizing effects of prolonged, acute economic problems.[55]

Much of what occurs in future years depends on whether Venezuela maintains the privileged status it enjoyed up until the mid-1980s as a result of stable oil prices and substantial foreign exchange reserves. Although the "loyal opposition"—including Copei, MAS, and MEP—plays an important role, another factor, which up until recently was latent, will determine the extent to which social conflict deepens: the spontaneous energy of the popular classes. As the disturbances of February 27, 1989, demonstrated, the popular classes can influence events in a powerful way without the leadership or guidance of political parties. With future stability shaped by such a multiplicity of variables—the internal cohesion of AD labor, the behavior of the loyal opposition in the CTV, the growth of the intransigent "marginal" Left, and the participation of the popular classes, all of which are influenced by the fluctuations in the international oil market—predictions at this conjuncture are at best tenative. This very uncertainty represents a flaw in the thinking of many analysts who, influenced by the exceptionalism thesis, optimistically assume that the maturity of Venezuela's political institutions and culture precludes social crisis and instability.

Notes

1. Oscar A. Echevarría, *Deuda, crisis cambiaria: causas y correctivos* (Caracas: Universidad Católica, 1986), p. 39.

2. Johnny Díaz Apitz (Copei, substitute member of CTV's National Committee, 1980–85), interview, November 26, 1986, Caracas.

3. *Plural* 1 [AD magazine] (December 1979): 4–5.

4. Venalum, *Venalum en 1981* (Caracas: Editorial Arte, n.d.), pp. 28–29.

5. Jose Luis Reyna, "Redefining the Authoritarian Regime," in *Authoritarianism in Mexico*, ed. Jose Luis Reyna and Richard S. Weinert (Philadelphia: Institute for the Study of Human Issues, 1977), pp. 155–71.

6. *Tribuna Popular*, November 30, 1979, p. 2, and February 1–7, 1980, p. 2.

7. "Sindicalistas copeyanos: medio de 2 fuegos," *Auténtico*, October 22, 1979, pp. 46–47.

8. FTC, "Circular No. VI — SSN-124 S NO-110 (Confidencial)," September 3, 1979, p. 2, MOLA Archive located in the UCV (hereafter cited as MOLA Archive-UCV); Dagoberto González, interview, February 12, 1987, Caracas.

9. "Primer Encuentro Sindical Nacional de la Izquierda," Caracas, September 4–6, 1981 [typewritten], MOLA Archive, vol. 16.

10. Steve Ellner, "Diverse Influences on the Venezuelan Left," *Journal of Interamerican Studies and World Affairs* 23, no. 4 (November 1989): 486–87.

11. Gustavo Landino, interview, May 24, 1989, Caracas.

12. *El Universal*, October 1, 1980, p. 1–14; Carlos Luna, interview, January 30, 1987, Caracas.

13. *El Universal*, October 11, 1980, p. 1–12.

14. *Número* 400 (May 8, 1988): 7; *El Nacional*, October 30, 1980, p. D-16.

15. Desirée Santos Amaral, "Más de un millon de desempleados," *Punto Socialista* 18 [MAS magazine] (November-December 1984): 16–17.

16. *El Nacional*, September 6, 1988, p. D-2.

17. *Frente: periódico de los trabajadores* 13 (March-April 1986): ii.

18. *El Nacional*, December 6, 1982, p. D-13.

19. Casto Gil Rivera, interview, November 27, 1986, Caracas.

20. Johnny Díaz Apitz, interview, November 26, 1986, Caracas.

21. Dagoberto González, interview, February 12, 1987, Caracas.

22. Rafael Rodríguez Acosta, interview, February 2, 1987, Caracas.

23. Johnny Díaz Apitz, interview, November 26, 1986, Caracas.

24. Jesús Paz Galarraga, interview, November 26, 1986, Caracas; Secretaría Nacional de Capacitación y Doctrina del MEP, "Cuadernos personales de los dirigentes," no. 3, Caracas, 1980, p. 10, MOLA Archive, vol. 16.

25. César Olarte, interview, February 3, 1989, Caracas.

26. Rafael Elino Martínez [FCV vice president], interview, July 1, 1989, Barcelona.

27. *El Universal*, May 4, 1985, p. 1–15; Armando González, interview, January 29, 1987, Caracas.

28. Rafael Elino Martínez, interview, July 1, 1989, Barcelona.

29. Carlos Luna, interview, January 30, 1987, Caracas; *El Nacional*, November 8, 1987, p. D-3; ibid., March 8, 1989, p. D-4.

30. *El Universal*, May 6, 1985, p. 1–17.

31. Nestor Colmenarez, *Sindicalismo irreverente* (Valencia: Raúl Clemente Editores, 1988), p. 68.

32. Ibid., pp. 71–72; *El Universal*, May 22, 1985, p. 1–14; Luna, interview, January 30, 1987, Caracas.

33. *El Universal*, May 5, 1985, p. 1–17.

34. *El Nacional*, February 1, 1987, p. C-3.

35. Rafael Castañeda, interview, December 11, 1986, Caracas.

36. *El Nacional*, September 23, 1987, p. D-2; Jesús Urbieta, interview, October 20, 1986, Caracas.

37. *El Nacional*, January 31, 1987, p. D-22; Laureano Torrealba, interview, October 27, 1986, Caracas.

38. Andrés Sánchez [former president of Fetranzoátegui; AD Trade Union Secretary in Anzoátegui], interview, April 5, 1989, Barcelona.

39. *El Nacional*, November 25, 1987, p. D-12.

40. *El Nacional*, September 3, 1987, p. D-1.

41. Jesús Urbieta, interview, September 4, 1984, Caracas; César Olarte, interview, February 3, 1987, Caracas.

42. *El Nacional*, July 31, 1988, p. D-8.

43. Study prepared for the UCV's School of Economics by Thaís Ledezma and Carlos Padrón. See *El Nacional*, June 7, 1990, p. D-1.

44. *El Nacional*, January 15, 1991, p. D-7; ibid., June 13, 1991, p. D-8.

45. Ellner, "Venezuela: No Exception," p. 8.

46. Antonio Rios, speech at the Casa Sindical of Fetranzoátegui, Barcelona, March 10, 1990.

47. "Antonio Rios: necesitamos una fedecámaras poderosa," *Número* 466 (August 27, 1989): 14.

48. Ramírez León, interview, March 10, 1990, Puerto La Cruz. See also *El Nacional*, June 18, 1989, p. D-4; ibid., December 20, 1989, p. D-11; ibid., January 21, 1991, p. D-3; ibid., July 7, 1991, p. D-6.

49. Gino Germani, *Política y sociedad en una época de transición: de la sociedad tradicional a la sociedad de masas* (Buenos Aires: Editorial Paidos, 1962). For a brief discussion of this historical debate by a critic of theories on corporatism see Ian Roxborough, *Unions and Politics in Mexico: The Case of the Automobile Industry* (Cambridge: Cambridge University Press, 1984), pp. 3–9.

50. Héctor Lucena, "La cogestión y la CTV," *Revista Relaciones de Trabajo* 1 (November 1981): 33–34.

51. Steve Ellner, *From Guerrilla Defeat to Innovative Politics: Venezuela's Movimiento al Socialismo* (Durham, NC: Duke University Press, 1988), pp. 155–57; *El Nacional*, April 3, 1989, p. D-11.

52. Casto Gil Rivera, interview, November 27, 1986, Caracas.

53. Alejandro Izaguirre provided Deputy Teodoro Petkoff these statistics for the slightly less than three years that the former was minister of interior relations. Petkoff speech in Barcelona, January 29, 1992.

54. See, for instance, James M. Malloy, "The Politics of Transition in Latin America," in *Authoritarians and Democrats: Regime Transition in Latin America*, ed. James M. Malloy and Mitchell A. Seligson (Pittsburgh: University of Pittsburgh Press, 1987), pp. 253–54.

55. Levine, "Venezuela: The Nature, Sources, and Prospects of Democracy," pp. 247–89; idem, Levine, "The Transition to Democracy: Are there Lessons from Venezuela?" *Bulletin of Latin American Research* 4, no. 2 (1985): 47–61.

4 The CTV's Strategy, Analysis, and Internal Organization

Organizations that have more than a fleeting existence invariably instill in their membership exaggerated notions regarding the importance of the role that they played in the past and the feasibility of their goals. These beliefs are designed to enhance the collective identification and commitment of those who form part of the organization both in the rank and file and at higher levels. Indeed, the group's survival is in large part dependent on the plausibility of these assertions and the leadership's credibility in making them.[1]

The CTV has achieved a surprising consensus with regard to its historical accomplishments and the attractiveness of its long-term objectives, despite the diversity of the ideological currents in the confederation. CTV leaders assign prime importance to the confederation's contribution to the establishment, consolidation, and defense of the democratic system beginning in 1936.[2] The concurrence in 1936 of the onset of the nation's modern period and the CTV's official founding buttresses the confederation's claim regarding labor's protagonistic role in shaping Venezuelan history. By dating its birth as far back as 1936, the CTV also attempts to demonstrate that it has maintained an important presence in the nation over an extended period of time.

Nevertheless, whether the CTV was founded in 1936 is a moot point. In December 1936 labor leaders established the Confederación Venezolana del Trabajo (CVT), but the organization was immediately dissolved by the government. Furthermore, its president, Alejandro Oropeza Castillo, abandoned the labor movement and became closely linked with financial interests in subsequent years. The CTV was "refounded" in 1947 and lasted but two years before it was disbanded by the dictatorship. Some writers prefer 1947 or 1959, rather than 1936, as the CTV's date of birth.[3]

The year 1936 is viewed by labor and political leaders as representing a thorough break with the past. They consider the Labor Law of 1936 as one of the great long-lasting accomplishments of the early modern period. Pro-*Copeyano* writers claim that the far-reaching implications of the Labor Law were reflections of the "lucid and progressive thinking" of its coauthor, Rafael Caldera,[4] despite the right-wing label that was tagged on him during those years. Trade unionists hail the passage of the Labor Law as evidence of the effectiveness of the mass movement and organized labor, which forced congress to promulgate it.[5] These views regarding the rupture in 1936 have been questioned by revisionist historians, who emphasize the modernizing trends of dictator Juan Vicente Gómez (1908–1935) during the previous period.[6] Some labor specialists have pointed to the Labor Law of 1928 as the "true point of departure from which our legislative tradition in social welfare stems," although their attempt to demonstrate that the law was at least partially enforced is based on tenuous evidence.[7]

CTV spokesmen argue that the labor movement was a bulwark of the democratic system during the two periods in which democratically elected governments faced serious military challenges. In 1948 the CTV favored mass mobilization in order to deter a military coup, but its plans were vetoed by AD party leaders who preferred a negotiated solution. Following the overthrow of Pérez Jiménez, labor leaders organized general strikes and mass rallies each time that right-wing officials attempted to topple the government. They also criticized the government and political leaders for failing to deal severely with military plotters and to set aside partisan interests for the sake of national unity. AD trade unionists allege that the labor movement's acceptance of austerity policies (as symbolized by the Hunger Law) during those trying years is proof of labor's willingness to make sacrifices when national interests are at stake. These same AD worker representatives point to the CTV's firm support for the government in the face of the guerrilla threat and its decision to oust leftists from union leadership positions as major contributions to the defense of the nation's fledgling democracy.

CTV leaders also maintain that the Venezuelan labor movement is more cohesive and pluralistic than its counterparts in other Latin American nations. In Colombia, Brazil, Peru, and elsewhere, several labor confederations—each loyal to a particular political party—vie for the control of organized labor, while important unions and federations maintain an independent status. In contrast, the CTV represents a large majority of organized workers and is not the exclusive preserve of any ideological current. The history of the Venezuelan labor movement is characterized by acute partisan rivalry, but trade unionists share a common heritage based on the struggle to organize workers. Martín J. Ramírez, a lifelong Communist and founder of the typographical workers' union, has stated:

> It is very interesting to see how, in spite of the differences which have always existed, during all the time after 1936 we [labor leaders] were always found together especially in the process of organizing the labor movement. There was a non-declared unity. . . . We all worked for the union movement in the first years and during a long time [thereafter] we acted together. There were always differences. That was logical. But in the first years there was a great

fraternity in spite of the internal struggle. Not a formal unity that was underpinned by any document or arrangement, but out of necessity we acted together. . . . We all had the same objective: face the past in order to correct and improve it. We did not have the least idea of exactly what we wanted and where we had to go. . . . But we can be satisfied and proud that we created a union movement throughout the country.[8]

The commitment to ideological pluralism and tolerance was reinforced during the struggle against Pérez Jiménez in the 1950s. Laureano Torrealba pointed out that, in the famed jail of San Juan de los Morros, AD labor leaders Manuel Peñalver, Luis Tovar, and José Marcano (who later joined MIR), and Communists such as Jesús Faría and himself acted collectively, at the same time that they split up in groups of two to share the tasks of cooking and presenting demands to the guards.[9] Although formal labor unity was shattered during the guerrilla period of the 1960s, personal ties were not. CTV President González Navarro, for instance, responded to the request for help from the families of MIRistas José Marcano and Américo Chacón, disregarding the criticism he received from fellow party members and the government in the process.[10]

After 1975 parties with a limited labor following were granted positions in the CTV's Executive Committee. Under the CTV's electoral rules, AD—with an absolute majority of delegates in the 1975, 1980, 1985, and 1990 CTV congresses—was entitled to the presidency and secretary-generalship, but the latter position went to a *Copeyano* on the first two occasions and a MEPista on the third and fourth. The "generosity" of AD labor was also evident in its efforts to attract trade unionists of other parties to the AD fold by allowing them to retain leading positions in organized labor. Such important labor leaders as Federico Ramírez León and César Gil (both of whom aspired to be CTV president); Carlos Piñerua, president of Fedepetrol; José González Navarro; and Juan José Delpino left MEP in the 1970s to rejoin AD. Four members of the CTV's Executive Committee— Rafael Castañeda and José Beltrán Vallejo, both members of the miniscule Morena party; Laureano Torrealba, a member of the Vanguardia Comunista; and MAS's Jesús Urbieta—joined AD in the first half of the 1980s.

Nevertheless, the image of the CTV as one happy family and the extent of AD's generosity have been overdrawn. Non-AD trade unionists have limited power in the CTV, since AD has maintained an absolute majority on the confederation's Executive Committee since 1975. AD has always retained control of three of the four positions on the CTV's Executive Committee: that of president, treasurer, and secretary of international relations. Furthermore, the influence of the number two position of secretary-general is greatly restricted by a CTV regulation stipulating that, in the absence of the president, the confederation will be presided over by a member of the same party rather than by the secretary-general.

AD labor has profited perhaps more than its rivals from its "generous" policy in the CTV. AD's concessions are part of an unwritten agreement whereby CTV members refrain from public criticisms of CTV policies and defend the confederation when under attack. In moments of difficulty, CTV leaders harp on the diversity of their internal support. Thus, for instance, when *Copeyano* Labor Minister Alfredo Tarre Murzi denounced corruption in the labor movement in 1969, trade unionists of all political persuasions— including those of Copei—closed ranks and rebuked him. Similarly, CTV leaders belonging to AD, Copei, MEP, and MAS condemned, at least initially, the government's decision to close the BTV in 1982.

Long-term Vision

At the time of its founding in 1941, AD's declared support for the system of private property and democracy was incompatible with the unstated goals of socialism and revolutionary change embraced by many of its leaders.[11] This contradiction was not completely resolved in the course of time and led to three divisions in the party in the 1960s. Labor leaders were especially attracted to long-term objectives that were not openly embraced. Thus, for instance, AD worker representatives—including many who were identified with the Old Guard such as Francisco Olivo, José Vargas, and Manuel Peñalver—defended socialism as a feasible goal. Future MEP labor leaders were particularly committed to the concept and called for programs to "educate our [AD's] rank and file regarding socialist doctrine."[12]

Parts of AD's "Labor Thesis," which was drafted by trade unionists and ratified at the party's Ninth Convention in 1958, resembled more the program of a Marxist party committed to socialism than the multiclass party that AD claimed to be. Not only did the thesis call for nationalization of basic industry, but also it insisted that those textile, food processing, and other manufacturing enterprises that were government run not be turned over to the private sector. The thesis went on to state that "cooperatives, state control, integral planning, and the participation of workers in the economy are socialist tasks that are completely compatible with the originally democratic nature of a revolution."[13]

AD trade unionists also supported an incremental strategy whereby labor gained greater power in decision making in both political and economic spheres and in the party itself. For this reason, worker representatives attached much importance to the naming of Malavé Villalba as the vice president of the Constituent Assembly in 1946, and the ever-greater number of labor leaders who were elected to legislative bodies after 1958. AD's Labor Thesis stated that "the working class has to prepare itself for the [future] management of the economy."[14] "Young workers," according to one top labor leader who belonged to the party's Old Guard, should be "trained so that tomorrow they can undertake administrative work as ministers, governors, and presidents of the Republic."[15]

AD trade unionists saw themselves as constituting a vanguard within the party. The 1958 Labor Thesis stated that "one of our [AD workers'] underlying tasks is to educate our most radicalized intellectuals in the sensibilities and thinking of workers . . . so that they dedicate themselves to the service of the working class."[16] Some party trade unionists were convinced that the end product of labor's increase in influence was the transformation of AD into a "labor party." That many of them entertained hopes regarding labor's increasingly dominant role in AD is not particularly surprising. Worker leaders of other parties in Latin America with a radical populist heritage—such as the Peronist movement in Argentina—have viewed labor as the "backbone" of their party.

The difference between trade unionists who were identified with AD's Old Guard, those who subsequently joined MEP, and those who belonged to leftist parties centered not so much on long-term objectives per se as on timing. The Old Guard labor leaders favored putting off ambitious goals until after the democratic system was thoroughly consolidated, a position they adhered to even when left-wing insurgency was brought under control in the mid-1960s. This fear of precipitating radical reforms was expressed by one veteran trade unionist who was a prominent member of AD's Old Guard faction: "The Left calls for the nationalization of the banks—and for sure it is not that I am not in agreement with the nationalization of banks— but if it is implemented today . . . , due to the correlation in favor of powerful forces in this country, the reactionaries will liquidate AD and the democratic workers' movement, so that this type of opposition [that of the Left] is more dangerous than that of reactionaries."[17]

At its Eighth Congress in 1980 the CTV declared *cogestión* a labor movement priority. At the time changing economic and political conditions had detracted from the appeal and urgency of other goals and thus created a void in the CTV's message. The defense of the democratic system was no longer a central concern once the threat of the guerrilla movement was eliminated in the late 1960s. The strategy of converting AD into a labor party lost its attractiveness, although it was not completely discarded by AD labor leaders who drew up the party's new Labor Thesis in 1980.[18] The Porlamar Manifesto, which was ratified at the CTV's 1980 congress, pointed to the limited possibilities of another strategy that had previously appealed to labor: state capitalism and government takeover of basic industry. Declining resources held back nationalization, which was a common trend during the boom period of the 1970s.[19] As an alternative to state interventionism, the manifesto proposed *cogestión*.

CTV leaders of different political parties have assumed that *cogestión* and other long-term labor goals will be achieved without recourse to forceful actions. CTV President Delpino, despite his militant rhetoric, stated on several occasions that strikes are not in keeping with Venezuelan tradition and that more effective mechanisms exist for achieving worker objectives. The president of Fetranzoátegui has pointed out that, due to the powerful influence of organized labor, *cogestión* could be established "by way of dialogue, understanding, [and] persuasion," without having to "rely on strikes or other activity that impair the nation's economy."[20] In discarding a strategy based on class conflict, labor leaders are influenced by the general optimism that prevails due to Venezuela's privileged status as an oil exporting nation where social differences are less rigid than elsewhere in Latin America.

Charles Davis, in *Working-Class Mobilization and Political Control: Venezuela and Mexico*, rejects the explanations that corporatist controls, authoritarian political culture, or the existence of a labor aristocracy accounts for the relative passivity of the Venezuelan working class. Davis interprets his survey data as showing that the main concerns of workers and their leaders are "short-term economic goals" rather than political issues or objectives.[21] It can be inferred from Davis's findings that the overwhelming influence of AD and Copei in the labor movement stems from the ability of nonleftist labor leaders to deliver the goods to the satisfaction of the rank and file.

Another empirical study that was carried out by the Centro de Desarrollo (Cendes) under the title *Conflictos y consenso* in the early 1960s pointed out that workers accepted the CTV's strategy of gradual material and social improvements since little in their past experiences would have led them to doubt its effectiveness; the Venezuelan Left has never succeeded in parlaying militant class struggle into substantial worker benefits.[22] In one lengthy unpublished interview conducted by Cendes as part of the project, one of the principal CTV leaders belonging to AD relied on the thesis of Venezuelan exceptionalism to underscore the steady political and material gains achieved by non-Communist trade unionists:

> On the social front, if you undertake an analysis of what we have accomplished . . . since we founded the first unions and political parties following the death of Gómez . . . I would say that we are among the first in Latin America. . . . It has cost us a lot but the day that an objective, sincere analysis is undertaken . . . of what AD and the democratic workers' movement have contributed, I would say gigantic steps have been taken on all fronts. There are people who have been around longer than us in Latin America, who do not have the secret universal vote. . . . And we can say that in the area of trade union liberty there is no other people in Latin America who are in the same position we are.[23]

Francisco Olivo, who was elected CTV president at the Sixth Congress in 1970, was typical of AD labor leaders who believed that progress would be achieved in the absence of internecine conflict. In private, Olivo, who was of Spanish origin, claimed to adhere to the long-term goals of anarcho-syndicalism. Nevertheless, according to his protégé, Carlos Luna, Olivo frequently used the expression *"no levante polvo"* (don't raise dust) to indicate that class confrontations in Venezuela should be put off to a future date. Although Olivo preferred to work through the system, he occasionally clashed with AD, and indeed the Labor Bureau opposed his nomination as CTV head (preferring the more tractable José Vargas). Interestingly, Luna alleged that his own behavior in opposing party interference in the choosing of CTV representatives was influenced by Olivo's views on the eventual autonomy of the labor movement.[24]

CTV leaders belonging to other parties were also reluctant to rely on militant tactics. Copei's *Tesis Sindical* explicitly rejects "class hatred," which it associates with classic Marxism.[25] Even the two leftist parties with a significant representation in the confederation, MEP and MAS, have been hesitant to call strikes, particularly because nearly all work stoppages are declared illegal. Labor leaders of both parties point to such bitter experiences as the steel workers' strike in 1971 and the textile workers' strike in 1980—as a result of which leftists lost considerable influence among the workers—as examples of the disastrous consequences of precipitous actions. One of MEP's main labor leaders, Casto Gil Rivera, who was generally more outspoken than his party companion César Olarte in the CTV's Executive Committee, defended a legalistic approach to labor conflicts:

> Based on experience we have come to view these things with much caution because in practice if we go through all the requirements contemplated by law and, in spite of this, the government refuses to grant authorization [to go on strike] it is better to carry our protest to Congress and the communications media and frankly not jeopardize our cadre with . . . [illegal] actions because we would run the risk of liquidating the forces we have in the federation. . . . If we go to the streets they will kick us out of the labor movement and jail our people and fingerprint us as conspirators; the power of the government will be brought to bear to displace us in every organization like the CTV. And so we pose the question: Are we interested in this type of politics or the alternative of struggling within the movement and raising the consciousness of the workers as a result of these denunciations?[26]

The *Conflictos y consenso* study showed that most trade unionists viewed the general strike as a weapon only to be used in extreme circumstances in opposition to political illegitimacy, such as the Pérez Jiménez government and, after 1958, the *perezjimenista* movement. Only 2.2 percent of the labor leaders surveyed by Cendes affirmed that general strikes were justifiable in order to satisfy economic demands, whereas 44.5 percent thought that they were justifiable "to satisfy important political demands," and 7.7 percent, "in the face of government injustice or illegality."[27] The May 18, 1989, general strike, which was nearly 100 percent effective, demonstrated the degree to which the attitudes of workers and their leaders had changed as a result of the economic crisis in the late 1980s.

Organized workers are not the sole beneficiaries of the reforms and changes proposed by the CTV. Confederation leaders see themselves as representing popular classes in general and not exclusively union members. This attitude is undoubtedly influenced by the fact that the CTV and its affiliate organizations are not sustained principally by union dues, but rather government subsidies and the confederation's entrepreneurial activity. Evidence of the confederation's broad social concern is its lobbying efforts in favor of across-the-board wage increases and the enactment of a new Labor Law, both of which were designed to extend the contractual benefits that organized workers have achieved to unorganized workers. The CTV also supported the controversial provisions in the proposed Labor Law that obliged companies to pay certain fringe benefits to street vendors even though they lack employee status. These salesmen belong to the informal economy that is largely outside of the confines of organized labor.

Although the CTV articulates the interests of the nonprivileged classes, it has failed to channel the discontent of the marginal class, which reached explosive proportions as the economic crisis deepened in the late 1980s and early 1990s. The CTV's awkwardness in this context was demonstrated by its reaction to the social disruptions beginning with the disturbances of the week of February 27, 1989. Initially, top CTV leaders ascribed the riots to the nihilistic tendencies of lumpen elements and denied that organized workers were involved.[28] This explanation, however, was quickly discarded as the CTV attempted to serve as spokesmen by formulating demands and attributing the event to the deterioration in living conditions. The general strike of May 18 was an attempt to reaffirm the CTV's leadership role beyond its immediate constituency. Nevertheless, the confederation has been conspicuously absent from the subsequent street protests involving students and poor people which have become daily occurrences in cities throughout the nation.

Proposed Changes in the CTV's Structure and Practices

The modernization and professionalization of the CTV have been confederation goals since the Seventh Congress in 1975. As in other Latin American nations, the Venezuelan labor movement has attempted to enhance its technical capacity and modify its internal structure and style in order to keep pace with the increasing complexity of the economy and the professionalization of the work force.[29] The CTV decided to convert its Secretariats (for example, of Propaganda, Labor, Culture, Socio-Economic Affairs, Statistics), which were tantamount to the offices of individual members of the confederation's Executive Committee, into potentially well-staffed "departments."

In addition, an advisory commission was created that included various prominent academicians of leftist leanings. The two most renowned CTV advisers have been economist D. F. Maza Zavala, who was elected national deputy on the MAS ticket, and Luis Matos Azocar, an extremely outspoken AD politician. In 1985 the CTV created the Instituto Nacional de Altos Estudios Sindicales (Inaesin) for the purpose of undertaking studies and training labor leaders, including those who were to serve in an administrative capacity under the system of *cogestión*. The following year the CTV belatedly moved into the twenty-story "José Vargas" building, which the confederation constructed with government financial support. The new headquarters, a modern structure with comfortable and spacious offices, stood in marked contrast with the run-down building that the confederation had occupied up until a few years before.

These reforms were designed to facilitate various proposals that the CTV approved at its 1975 congress and to project the image of a modern, efficacious organization. For the first time, the confederation called for a cost-of-living "escalator" clause, a demand that some labor leaders would put forward with greater insistence in the 1980s when prices rose sharply. The CTV pointed out that, for the system to be functional, it was imperative to gather reliable statistics on the rate of inflation, since those published by the Central Bank and other official bodies were notoriously inaccurate. Statistics were needed in order to fulfill another labor objective: industrywide collective bargaining agreements. Data regarding regional variations in the cost of living and company profits would allow labor negotiators to draw up separate clauses on the basis of the dissimiliar conditions in individual states and industries.[30]

Article 99 of the Labor Law provides organized labor the means to ascertain a company's capacity to pay wage increases. The provision authorizes those labor unions with over 50 percent worker backing to review company records in order to oversee the profit-sharing scheme (*utilidades*) established by labor law. Business spokesmen in both developed and underdeveloped countries have always resolutely opposed labor's demand for access to company financial information as a dangerous practice and a violation of management prerogatives.[31] In Venezuela, Article 99 is a dead letter. Some leftist labor leaders who have unsuccessfully solicited company data have objected that the Labor Inspectorate fails to enforce the provision.[32] Other worker representatives point out that the practice is virtually "taboo," and that, before labor insists on it, trade unionists have to receive training in order to interpret the information.[33] One member of the CTV's Executive Committee indicated that small firms that are near bankruptcy are only too willing to open their books to demonstrate that worker demands cannot be met, whereas larger companies falsify statistics by means of "double accounting."[34]

The "modernization" of the CTV is in large part a response to structural changes in the Venezuelan work force. Past CTV presidents Pérez Salinas, González Navarro, Olivo, Vargas, and Delpino were pioneers of the industrial labor movement dating back to the 1930s, when the overwhelming majority of the nation's workers were male, unskilled, and illiterate. In 1990, however, workers in the oil and manufacturing sectors, who represented the backbone of the traditional working class, were only 19.2 percent of the nonagricultural work force and women workers 36.2 percent (see Table 3). In addition, education was a budgetary priority of democratic governments after 1958, and received a special impetus from the windfall in oil income after 1973. As a result, the percentage of illiterates in the industrial work force declined from 20 to 8 percent in the course of the 1970s; by 1990, 35.5 percent of the work force had at least one year of high-school education. Furthermore, after 1958, university education was opened to women and working-class children.[35]

The CTV has called on university-trained employees to form unions affiliated with the confederation, while adding that they need not drop out of their professional associations (*colegios*) whose concerns are essentially noneconomic. The CTV favors the creation of *sindicatos nacionales por rama de industria* (national industrial unions) that will take in both intellectual and manual workers. Some CTV leaders have disparaged the narrow vision of professionals, urging them to "abandon their prejudice, vanity, and Spanish inheritance [with regard to] their university title and understand that they are no more than salaried workers within the productive system."[36]

Until now, the CTV's call has not struck a responsive cord. The professional associations that represent university teachers and doctors have assumed trade union functions in that they sign collective bargaining agreements and lead strikes (similar to the National Education Association in the United States), but they have not joined the CTV. Newspaper workers belong to both a professional association (Colegio Nacional de Periodistas) and a union (the SNTP), but the latter remains outside the CTV fold. Grade school teachers have established a host of organizations, many of which are unaffiliated.

The cultural and educational breach between labor leaders and professionals helps to explain why the CTV has not had greater success in attracting members of the middle class. In the early 1960s, Cendes's *Conflictos y consenso* study showed that less than 4 percent of the nation's labor leaders had any university education.[37] Twenty-five years later those top-level labor leaders (such as Jesús Urbieta of the CTV and Haydeé Deutsch of Codesa) who had university degrees completed their education only after having emerged as important labor leaders. Furthermore, the CTV failed to support strikes of public school and university teachers and doctors in state-run hospitals, which were among the longest and most conflictive labor disputes in recent years. Some CTV spokesmen actually implored the teachers and doctors to return to work on grounds that the strike jeopardized the welfare of the working class.

Table 3. Venezuelan Work Force by Sector, Age, and Sex in 1990

Activity	Female under 44	Female over 44	Male under 44	Male over 44	Total
Agriculture	21,689	19,240	478,037	253,658	808,624
Hydrocarbons and mines	6,325	972	43,062	14,087	64,446
Manufacturing	233,764	48,391	628,460	121,791	1,032,406
Food, beverage, and tobacco	38,706	9,479	119,039	22,987	190,211
Textiles and garments	105,952	28,142	78,710	17,082	229,886
Wood (including furniture)	6,562	489	63,649	14,526	85,226
Paper and printing	11,756	1,546	34,818	9,034	57,154
Derivatives of coal and oil (including chemicals, plastics, and rubber)	22,645	1,399	62,648	9,556	96,248
Fabrication of non-metallic minerals (other than coal and oil)	8,985	318	32,329	8,383	51,015
Metallurgical industry	28,227	2,106	223,940	37,331	291,604
Electricity, gas, and water	10,917	2,474	39,237	12,977	65,605
Construction	17,911	1,755	389,168	94,480	503,314
Commerce	315,602	97,324	575,284	200,595	1,189,065
Hotels and restaurants	68,106	19,188	88,650	17,879	193,823
Transportation, storage, and communication	28,244	4,860	267,849	94,939	395,892

Finance, insurance, and real estate	136,597	17,845	176,387	55,134	385,963
Public administration and defense	118,223	27,286	187,760	71,801	405,070
Health services	6,939	1,845	19,614	6,065	34,463
Social and communal services	413,181	103,442	115,963	70,021	742,607
Entertainment and amusement	21,002	4,116	58,868	12,345	96,331
Personal and domestic services	266,506	51,850	227,683	55,684	601,723
Total work force	1,668,913	401,037	3,376,300	1,082,687	6,528,937

Source: Oficina Central de Estadísticas e Informática, *Indicadores de la fuerza de trabajo* (second semester of 1990).

Some non-AD worker representatives point to the potential for intellectual workers to transform the labor movement and conclude that, for this reason, the established CTV leadership is ambivalent about drawing them into the organization. Dagoberto González, the longtime secretary-general of the *Copeyano* FTC, has stated:

> I believe that the CTV has not made any effort [to attract professionals]. It has limited itself at best to an invitation of a very general and rhetorical type. I suspect that among some trade union sectors there is an aversion to this type of proposition because the center of power in the CTV wants to maintain itself on the basis of preserving its forces; bringing in new people could change the correlation of forces. . . . Since the Third Congress [in 1959] when the CTV tried to revitalize the labor movement, the CTV has not undertaken a campaign of recruitment. On the contrary, there is a hostile attitude [which] holds back [new] contingents of workers. . . . In addition, on the part of professionals there is a type of search within their own world for an identity. The blame is not entirely with union sectors. Of course not. These sectors of workers [professionals] reject unionization and have an attitude of marginality with respect to the rest of the working class.[38]

Arturo Tremont, a leading MASista trade unionist, coincided in large part with González in his analysis:

> In MAS, we spoke a lot about the possibility that professionals incorporate themselves [in the labor movement] because [we felt] they would provide the unions with a distinct quality. . . . Our [Venezuelan] labor leaders are *obreristas*. This dates back to the strong rejection of intellectuals out of the false notion that Marxism rejected intellectuals . . . and this is still upheld by some leaders

of MAS, AD, and Copei. On the other hand, there is also much resistance on the part of intellectuals to entering [labor unions].[39]

The scarcity of women labor leaders, even in the garment industry which is predominately female, is evidence of the CTV's failure to respond effectively to the changing composition of the work force. A resolution that was ratified at the Third Congress in 1959 called for offering courses to train women for leadership positions in the labor movement. Thirty years later, however, the CTV had granted women mere token representation in the form of one regular seat on the Executive Committee of the CTV and several of its affiliate organizations.

Another challenge facing the CTV was the mounting criticism against the confederation and its federations for the misuse of funds and the unethical conduct of their leaders following the closing of the BTV in 1982. To offset these attacks the CTV created a controllership to oversee the financial activities of its members. It also formed a commission to monitor internal elections, which had been widely questioned due to the practice of selecting officers and delegates on the basis of party pacts rather than rank-and-file voting.

CTV leaders expressed concern regarding the moral behavior of local union officers. The centralization of the labor movement in the form of national unions was designed to place the activities of these trade unionists under greater scrutiny and control. CTV heads pointed to daily abuses in the practice of the *fuero sindical*, whereby elected worker representatives are given time off and other privileges in order to attend to their union responsibilities. In many places, however, it was transformed into an indefinite paid leave of absence. At an opening address at the CTV's Eighth Congress in 1985, Manuel Peñalver urged worker leaders to comply with their work schedule. He added that the *fuero sindical* originally had served to protect trade unionists from "businessmen with a *gomecista* mentality" but times had changed and "now it breeds vice that the labor movement has to eradicate."[40]

The CTV faced another predicament as a result of the practice of *costa contractual*, in which management assumes certain union expenses, including those incurred in collective bargaining. Following the intervention in the steel workers' union Sutiss, the magazine *Resumen* published a facsimile of a check for 2 million bolívares that Sidor had made out to Fetrametal President José Mollegas. The money, Mollegas claimed, was destined to reimburse labor representatives for personal expenses in the negotiation of the recently signed steel workers' contract, although he was hard put to explain why the check was for such a hefty sum. After investigating the case, the CTV's controllership denied that an irregularity had been committed.

Nevertheless, the incident unleashed a controversy regarding *costa contractual*. Copei, as part of the hardening of its stand in the CTV in the mid-1980s, revealed other cases in which the practice had apparently led to abuses. Many trade unionists admitted that they felt uncomfortable about *costa contractual* but added that it was widespread and a necessary evil as long as the union movement could not finance its expenses. The CTV attempted to limit the possibility of bribery by ordering its affiliates to specify in the contract the amount of money that the company was to turn over to the union. Other labor leaders, such as members of the leftist Causa R, opposed the practice of *costa contractual* per se on grounds that its purpose was to influence its beneficiaries to soften their positions and was thus tantamount to a payoff.[41]

At its Tenth Congress in 1990 the CTV modified its internal structure, the details of which were subsequently worked out in committee and submitted to the confederation's Third Extraordinary Congress in April 1991 (see Figure 1). The new scheme promoted centralization by allowing for the creation of national unions—which the *Proyecto Caldera* legalized for the first time—to replace the national federations. Union locals, known as *seccionales*, were to affiliate with their respective national union as well as with the statewide federation, which was now called *seccional regional*.

As part of the CTV's commitment to democratize and eradicate unethical practices, the controller and electoral commissions were removed from the immediate jurisdiction of the National Executive Committee (CEN), in the process gaining a greater degree of autonomy. The members of both commissions were to be appointed by the CTV's congress, although members of the National Electoral Commission could be removed by the newly created National Directive Council (CDN). In accordance with the CTV's commitment to pluralism, the confederation's main parties were represented on the five-member National Electoral Commission. Nevertheless, the commission's decisions had to be reached unanimously, and in cases of internal differences, the matter was to be transferred to the CEN. The creation of the CDN was designed to counter the allegedly excessive authority of the seventeen-member CEN. The National General Council (CGN) met once a year. With over half of its 250 members named by the CTV congress, the council was considered the confederation's maximum noncongressional authority, followed by the CDN, with 140 members, most of whom were designated in like fashion.

Other important steps toward internal democratization were taken. The CTV established direct elections for the Executive Committees of constituent unions and national federations and elections by second degree for the CTV's CEN. At the Third Extraordinary Congress, some delegates expressed support for the direct elections of the members of the CEN as well as forbidding their reelection for a third consecutive term. The new method of elections by second degree, however, was a significant improvement over the old system in which the selection of CEN members was five times

Figure 1. New CTV Structure Approved in 1990–91

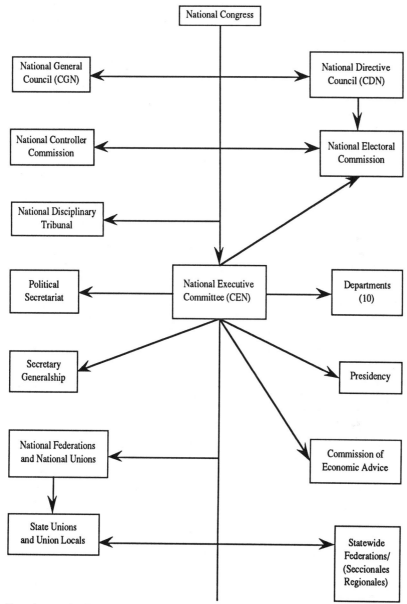

Note: Arrows signify flow of authority.

Source: Constructed with the help of Johnny Díaz Apitz and Julio Solórzano (MAS representative on CTV's National Electoral Commission).

removed from the rank and file. In an additional rectification of questionable practices, the Third Extraordinary Congress limited the FCV's representation at CTV congresses to fifty delegates, less than half the number that the confederation's old statutes assigned the federation.

The labor movement's commitment to certain stated goals and policies is open to question. In some cases, the CTV has not gone beyond rhetoric or nominal changes in its organization. Thus the CTV's insistence that women assume leadership positions and professionals enter the confederation's fold have not been translated into an active campaign or strategy. The CTV also has failed to take advantage of its financial resources and political influence to make *cogestión* a reality (see Chapter 8).

Furthermore, the CTV's efforts have lacked the necessary follow-up and evaluation to ensure its success. With the exception of the Departmento de *Cogestión*, the confederation has not publicized the work of individual departments, nor have their findings circulated within the labor movement itself.[42] Ambivalent attitudes have also impeded the CTV's efforts to eliminate corruption in its ranks and to promote internal democracy. On the one hand, CTV leaders vocally called for stringent measures against corrupt members of the Lusinchi administration and went on record supporting reforms designed to democratize the nation's political system, including primaries for the nomination of party leaders and candidates. On the other hand, the controllership failed to monitor closely the practice of *costa contractual* in order to enforce CTV guidelines designed to eliminate abuses;[43] and the CTV's Executive Committee was selected in a process that was indirect and far removed from worker members, while many delegates to confederation congresses were virtually hand chosen. These problems were addressed at the 1990 and 1991 congresses, but it remains to be seen whether the changes that were agreed upon will be effective.

In its analysis of Venezuelan history in the modern period, CTV leaders rely on the widely held thesis of Venezuelan exceptionalism, which stresses the relative degree of political stability and social harmony that the nation has achieved. The salient characteristics of Venezuela's development since 1936 according to these trade unionists—steady material progress, the gradual solidification of democratic institutions, and the absence of internecine social conflict—have both influenced and been influenced by the labor movement. As CTV leaders point out, the labor movement has traditionally rejected intransigent positions and violence and has played a major role in the fortification of democracy. Evidence of this affirmation is the absence of recurrent general strikes motivated by economic demands and labor's participation in the overthrow of Pérez Jiménez.

Nevertheless, in citing specific examples, the CTVistas often overstate their case. The general strike called by labor leaders on January 21, 1958, for instance, contributed to the overthrow of Pérez Jiménez but was not as successful and decisive as trade unionists claim. When labor leaders point to the CTV's acceptance of austerity measures to face the economic crisis and threat of insurgency in the early 1960s, they fail to mention that the confederation's leadership was highly critical of the famous Hunger Law of the Betancourt administration. AD trade unionists, who draw the picture of the CTV as one happy family that takes in worker representatives of diverse ideological convictions, have a vested interest in exaggerating the degree of pluralism that exists in the organization and downplaying AD domination. The ongoing tension that exists at all levels—within the CTV, within AD labor, and between the Labor Bureau and the party—does not coincide with the type of image that AD labor leaders attempt to project, and thus calls for a more nuanced evaluation of Venezuelan exceptionalism.

Notes

1. Many political analysts associate these imperatives with close-knit revolutionary parties, such as Marxist-Leninist ones. In fact, all organizations that have political objectives face these same challenges.
2. Charles Bergquist argues that labor's "central role" in the implantation of the democratic system in Venezuela has been "systematically ignored in U.S. scholarship on the subject." Bergquist, *Labor in Latin America*, p. 205.
3. Rafael Alfonzo Guzmán, *Estudio analítico de la ley del trabajo venezolano*, 2 vols. (Caracas: UCV, 1967), 2:181; Fernando Parra Aranguren, "La contratación colectiva y la Ley del Trabajo" [lecture], Porlamar, November 7, 1986.
4. Cartay Ramírez, *Caldera y Betancourt*, pp. 62–63.
5. This thesis is discussed by Richard Parker in "Consideraciones en torno a la Ley del Trabajo del año 1936," *Estudios laborales: ensayos sobre derecho del trabajo y disciplinas afines* . . . , 2 vols., ed. Francisco Iturraspe (Caracas: UCV, 1986), 2:201–18.
6. Typical of this revisionist approach to Gómez is Brian S. McBeth, *Juan Vicente Gómez and the Oil Companies in Venezuela, 1908–1935* (Cambridge: Cambridge University Press, 1983). For a more balanced view, see Diego Bautista Urbaneja, "El sistema política gomecista," in *Juan Vicente Gómez y su época*, ed. Elías Pino (Caracas: Monte Avila, 1985).
7. INCE, *Legislación del Trabajo* (Ri-10.2210), p. 1–14. See also Fernando Parra Aranguren, *Antecedentes del Derecho del Trabajo en Venezuela (1916–1928)* (Caracas: Universidad Católica "Andrés Bello," 1980), pp. 164–65; Julio Díez, *Estudios de Derecho Social* (Caracas: Tipografía Americana, 1940), p. 39.
8. Martín J. Ramírez, interview, October 23, 1986, Caracas.
9. Laureano Torrealba, interview, October 21, 1986, Caracas.
10. Interview no. 025, interviewee no. 074, p. 64, Cendes, C. C.
11. Steve Ellner, "Acción Democrática and the Concealment of Long Range Goals in the *Trienio* Government, 1945–1948" (Paper presented at LASA Congress, April 20, 1985, Albuquerque, New Mexico); idem, "Populism in Venezuela, 1935–48: Betancourt and Acción Democrática," in *Latin American Populism in Comparative Perspective*, ed. Michael L. Conniff (Albuquerque, NM: University of New Mexico Press, 1982), pp. 135–49.
12. Interview no. 025, interviewee no. 074, n.d., p. 106, Cendes, C. C.; "Orientación política y sindical de Acción Democrática" [typewritten], Caracas, 1964, p. 16, MOLA Archive, vol. 12, 1964–1966.

13. *Acción Democrática: doctrina y programa* (Caracas: Secretaría Nacional de Propaganda, 1962), pp. 135–36.

14. "Tesis Sindical: Proyecto" [mimeographed], Caracas, January 8, 1980, MOLA Archive, vol. 16, 1978–1982.

15. Interview no. 336, interviewee no. 287, October 15, 1963, p. 238, Cendes, C. C.

16. *Acción Democrática: doctrina*, pp. 131–32.

17. Interview no. 124, interviewee no. 142, April 2–8, 1964, pp. 61–62, Cendes, C. C.

18. "Tesis Sindical: proyecto," Caracas, January 8, 1980 [mimeographed], MOLA Archive, vol. 16.

19. *Antecedentes y testimonios de los congresos* 4: 106–10.

20. Davíd Hernández, interview, September 17, 1986, Barcelona.

21. Charles L. Davis, *Working Class Mobilization and Political Control: Venezuela and Mexico* (Lexington: University of Kentucky Press, 1989), pp. 145–46.

22. Boeckh, "Organized Labor and Government," pp. 300–301.

23. Interview no. 124, interviewee no. 142, April 2–8, 1964, pp. 63–64, Cendes, C. C.

24. Carlos Luna, interview, January 30, 1987, Caracas.

25. López Maya and Werz, *El estado y el movimiento sindical*, p. 20.

26. Casto Gil Rivera, interview, November 27, 1986, Caracas.

27. Cendes, *Estudio de conflictos y consenso*, p. 76.

28. Ellner, "Venezuela: No Exception," p. 8.

29. Robert J. Alexander, "The Latin American Labor Leader," in *Industrial Relations and Social Change in Latin America* (Gainesville: University of Florida Press, 1965), p. 82.

30. *Antecedentes y testimonios de los congresos* 3: 284–87.

31. Irwin M. Marcus, "U.S. Working Class History and Contemporary Labor Movement Symposium," *International Labor and Working-Class History* 29 (Spring 1986): 100.

32. Gustavo Landino [president of UTIT], interview, February 20, 1987, Caracas.

33. Victor Farrera [secretary-general of Fedepetrol union in Puerto La Cruz], interview, October 9, 1986, Puerto La Cruz.

34. Cupertino Peña, interview, February 23, 1987, Caracas.

35. Gustavo Escobar, "Gerentes, obreros y máquinas: la productividad industrial," in *El caso Venezuela*, p. 413; Steve Ellner, "Educational Policy," in *Venezuela: The Democratic Experience*, ed. John D. Martz and David J. Myers (New York: Praeger, 1986), pp. 296–98.

36. Buró Sindical of AD, "La clase trabajadora: poder social," p. 89.

37. Cendes, *Estudio de conflictos*, p. 25.

38. Dagoberto González, interview, February 12, 1987, Caracas.

39. Arturo Tremont, interview, August 30, 1989, Caracas.

40. *Antecedentes y testimonios de los congresos* 4: 205.

41. Andrés Mercau [secretary-general of Fetrametal], interview, February 12, 1987, Caracas; *El Nacional*, April 13, 1987, p. D-2.

42. Federico Ramírez León, interview, March 10, 1990, Puerto La Cruz; Carlos Eduardo Febres [CTV adviser], interview, March 31, 1990, Valencia.

43. César Olarte, interview, March 30, 1990, Caracas.

5 Ideological Currents and International Affiliations

Venezuela's four worker confederations are identified with ideological currents that are associated with international labor organizations. The CTV belongs to ORIT, which in turn is affiliated with the ICFTU; the CUTV is a member of the WFTU. The social Christians are grouped in three organizations, two of which are confederations: the FTC, which is Copei's fraction within the CTV; the Confederación de Sindicatos Autónomos (Codesa), founded in 1963; and the Confederación General de Trabajadores (CGT), which broke off from Codesa in 1971. Until recently, all three belonged to the Central Latinoamericano de Trabajadores (CLAT), which is the regional affiliate of the World Confederation of Labor (WCL).

The three smaller confederations have made modest inroads among sectors that are difficult to organize, such as restaurant, agricultural, and construction workers, and, in the case of the CGT, members of the "informal" economy. Membership statistics are highly unreliable since they tend to be inflated for the purpose of requesting greater state subsidies. One source breaks them down as follows: the CTV, 1,000,000; the CUTV, 80,000; Codesa, 60,000; and the CGT, 30,000. Another reference cites the CTV, 2,500,000; the CUTV, 320,000; Codesa, 200,000; and the CGT, 180,000.[1]

The CUTV, Codesa, and the CGT play a marginal role in the nation's political life and are not called upon to name members of tripartite commissions of employer, worker, and state representatives. *Copeyano* governments have been fairer than AD ones: Under Caldera, the smaller confederations were allowed to send one representative each to ILO meetings; under Herrera Campíns, the number was increased to two. The smaller confederations, particularly the CUTV, claim that their share of government subsidies is unfavorably disproportionate to their worker following.

The AD leaders who control the CTV have followed a generous policy toward smaller parties that seek representation in the CTV, but AD's spirit of unity does not include maintaining ongoing relations with the smaller confederations which, according to them, have no raison d'être. The situation in which Copei is represented in Codesa and the CGT as well as the FTC—all three of which belong to the CLAT—has no equivalent in Latin

America, and has created uneasiness among *Copeyano* labor leaders. Indeed, at international conferences, fellow Christian democratic trade unionists indicate that they consider the structure of the social Christian labor movement in Venezuela perplexing.[2]

The CTV's International Ties

During the Pérez Jiménez dictatorship, prominent CTV leaders established close ties with the AFL (and after 1955 the AFL-CIO) and the international organizations it promoted. Exiled AD labor leaders such as Malavé Villalba and Pérez Salinas occupied positions in the hemispheric labor movement. The AFL-CIO was also generous in its financial contributions—leading one PCV trade unionist to comment to Pérez Salinas that they outmatched the assistance Venezuelan Communists received from the socialist bloc.

After 1958, Pérez Salinas and others decided not to press for the CTV's affiliation with ORIT so as to preserve unity with other parties in the confederation. Nevertheless, according to Pérez Salinas, in order to avoid giving the impression that "we were brutally giving ORIT a kick after having been helped by it," AD labor leaders proposed that individual federations be given the opportunity to affiliate with International Trade Secretariats (ITS), which were closely linked with the pro-U.S. labor movement.[3] The proposition produced a heated debate at the CTV's Third Congress in 1959 and was watered down in its final version. Federations were allowed to join their respective ITS only with the approval of 75 percent of the delegates at their annual convention and the consent of the CTV's Executive Committee.[4]

With the expulsion of leftists from the CTV in 1961, opposition to affiliation with ORIT was largely removed. Although at first agreeing to seek dual membership in ORIT and the Christian democratic Clasc, the AD majority in the CTV decided at the confederation's Fourth Congress to associate exclusively with the former. In July 1963 the CTV sponsored the "First Trade Union Conference on the Alliance for Progress" where Communists and other leftist trade unionists, including the Brazilian Francisco Juliao and the Argentinian Peronists, were attacked and labor participation in the Alliance's policies was recommended.[5] Ties with the U.S. labor movement were fortified by the loan of 27 million bolívares authorized by the AFL-CIO for the purpose of setting up the CTV's Workers Bank (BTV) in 1966.

Nevertheless, various CTV leaders questioned ORIT's stands during these years. In 1960, CTV President José González Navarro criticized ORIT for ordering its affiliates to refrain from participation in the international boycott of the regime of General Rafael Trujillo, which was organized by the CTV along with various Communist-led labor organizations. Five years later, González Navarro issued a strongly worded criticism of ORIT's support for the U.S. invasion of the Dominican Republic, which received active backing from the AFL-CIO's foreign affairs department.[6] In the same year, URD trade unionists, who had recently returned to the CTV, insisted that the confederation break ties with ORIT.[7] This demand was also put forward after 1967 by several MEP labor leaders who pointed to Walter Reuthers's revelations regarding CIA funding of ORIT.[8] César Olarte and other MEPistas were particularly resentful at having been ousted from positions in the ITSs at the urging of their AD trade union rivals.

In the 1970s the AFL-CIO unexpectedly clashed with European labor organizations, leading to its temporary withdrawal from the ICFTU. The main source of contention was the decision of European social democratic trade unionists to promote unity with Communists, who controlled powerful worker organizations in France, Italy, and Spain. The conflict between the AFL-CIO and the ICFTU was reflected in many of the eighteen major ITSs where labor leaders who identified with each of the two sides jockeyed for organizational control. It also produced strains in ORIT which, although an affiliate of the ICFTU, was closely linked to the AFL-CIO due to geographical proximity and historical ties. In the 1970s and 1980s the ICFTU bypassed ORIT and established bilateral relations with organizations such as the Peronist-led Confederación General del Trabajo, the Central Obrera Boliviana (COB) in Bolivia, the Coordinadora Nacional Sindical in Chile, and the Central Unica dos Trabalhadores (CUT) in Brazil, many of which the AFL-CIO considered excessively radical and anti-North American.

On a host of important issues the positions of the CTV converge with those of European social democrats; in other cases they are closer to those of the AFL-CIO. At times, CTV spokesmen call for nonpayment of the foreign debt, while cautioning against provoking an international confrontation over the matter. Some CTVistas point out that the Europeans are more receptive to a compromise solution to the foreign debt as well as negotiations with OPEC than is the AFL-CIO. The AFL-CIO frequently employs antibank rhetoric, but its main preoccupation is that schemes to resolve the debt problem will burden U.S. taxpayers, and thus the federation shows little concern for the plight of Latin Americans. The AFL-CIO also defends U.S. commercial interests, favoring barriers against third-world imports. In at least one respect, however, CTV secretary-general César Olarte has pointed out that he concurs with the AFL-CIO:

> In a declaration of Lane Kirkland [president of the AFL-CIO] in the House of Representatives, one thing that I liked was when he talked of the problem— and in this form at least he sidetracked the issue of protectionism—of merchandise coming in from Taiwan and South Korea. He maintained that these products are subsidised not by the governments, but by the conditions of

misery of the workers—that is hunger wages—and he argued that this should not be.[9]

The CTV rejects the trade union model known as "Gomperism" promoted by the American Institute for Free Labor Development (Aifld) and the AFL-CIO. In labor training sessions, Aifld preaches that unions should restrict themselves to bread-and-butter issues and eschew ideology, political objectives, and close party ties. Naturally, this thesis clashes with reality in Latin America and particularly Venezuela, where the union-party nexus is so well established. In an indirect reference to the AFL-CIO, future CTV President Juan José Delpino wrote "to blame political parties for labor's problems is a way of dividing the workers' movement."[10] The CTV insists on overseeing Aifld-sponsored courses in order to guard against the advocacy of apolitical unionism and the questioning of its own practices. Nevertheless, AD labor leaders point out with satisfaction that the AFL-CIO has come to accept their party commitment, and thus they are frequently identified at international gatherings by their party affiliation.[11]

The CTV shares the AFL-CIO's policy of avoiding agreements with Communist-led labor organizations that facilitate organic unity. The CTV, like the AFL-CIO—and unlike nonleftist counterparts in Europe and much of Latin America—represents a large majority of the nation's organized workers. It is thus reluctant to participate with other confederations in united actions.

In the 1970s and early 1980s the conservative, orthodox current of AD, which included the CTV's Secretary of International Affairs Manuel Peñalver, dominated the confederation's national leadership and approved of the AFL-CIO's strident anticommunism and its hostility toward the Sandinistas.[12] The CTV set up training sessions for members of the two non-Sandinista labor confederations in Nicaragua at the same time that it denounced the hegemonic tendencies of the Central Sandinista de Trabajadores. Subsequently, those who led the CTV and its Department of International Affairs—Delpino, Ríos, Ramírez León, and Jesús Urbieta—belonged to the *carlosandresista* faction of AD and were more evenhanded in their analysis of Cold War disputes, although they retained ties with non-Sandinista labor organizations in Nicaragua. CTV leaders disagreed with Aifld's efforts to bolster anti-Communist unions that were linked to military regimes. This issue sometimes placed CTV and AFL-CIO representatives on opposite sides in voting at international labor meetings.

The contrast in positions assumed by the *ortodoxos* and the *carlosandresistas* was demonstrated by the different orientations of the two Venezuelan labor leaders who were designated secretary-general of ORIT in the 1980s. Juan José Delpino occupied the post at the time of ORIT's congress in Toronto in 1981. That congress's final statement bore the imprint of European social democracy in its call for a new international economic order and its defense of organized labor's political role. The pronouncement, in the words of one writer who is closely tied to the social democratic movement, "evoked great displeasure from the AFL-CIO."[13] In an oblique reference to the U.S. labor movement, Enzo Frizo, the ICFTU's adjunct secretary-general, gave Delpino credit for having initiated during his stay in ORIT "a battle in favor of the renovation of Latin American trade unionism; some organizations affiliated [with ORIT] confused anticommunism with democracy and shamefully collaborated with military dictatorships which were stained in blood."[14] After stepping down from the secretary-generalship, Delpino protested that the AFL-CIO's financial contributions served as a check on the autonomy of ORIT and called for its transformation into an exclusively Latin American organization.[15]

In April 1985, Ismael González, the former president of Fetrasalud who was identified with the U.S. position, was named ORIT secretary-general. González resented the European social democratic policy of "bilateralism," whereby large sums of money were funneled through political foundations to individual Latin American labor organizations, in the process bypassing ORIT. Consequently, he denounced the ICFTU for exerting economic pressure on ORIT in an attempt to shape its policies and resigned in protest.[16]

The CTV refused to endorse either side openly in the dispute between the U.S. and European labor movements. "We have always been extremely careful," stated Federico Ramírez León, the CTV's future secretary of international affairs, in recognizing that "each labor movement sometimes sees it in its interests to coincide with the policies of its own country. This is a type of [national] autonomy . . . and we cannot place ourselves above national concerns."[17] Often the CTV took a middle position between the social democrats and the AFL-CIO. While the AFL-CIO, for instance, urged the immediate acceptance of the Brazilian Comando Geral dos Trabalhadores (CGT) in ORIT, the ICFTU feared that the proposal would alienate the more radical rival group, the CUT, which the Europeans were attempting to woo. The CTV favored a more gradual process of admission and efforts to reconcile differences between the two organizations.[18]

AD labor leaders of both the orthodox and *carlosandresista* factions, unlike MEPistas and *Copeyanos*, regularly attended AFL-CIO gatherings. Delpino, whom European social democrats believed to be identified with their stands, maintained extremely cordial relations with U.S. labor attachés as well as with representatives of Aifld and the AFL-CIO. Such discretion goes beyond mere personal style and is typical of other labor leaders who share Delpino's orientation. While those political and labor leaders who are on the leftist fringe of the international social democratic movement, such as the Sandinistas, frequently denounce North American imperialism, mainstream groups in Latin America such as the CTV eschew a defiant or overtly critical position toward the United States.

The International Affairs Department enjoys a status of special importance in the CTV. Four of the CTV's six presidents since 1947 at one time presided over the department; another department head, Manuel Peñalver, went on to become secretary-general of AD, and still another, Ramírez León, aspires to become CTV president. The post has always been reserved for AD members. It has been conjectured that by appointing a well-tested, reliable trade unionist to the position, the AD labor leadership hopes to prevent the AFL-CIO or other international organizations from cultivating special ties with the department in order to influence the CTV's international policies and compromise its highly valued independence.[19]

The high caliber of the CTVistas who head the department also reflects the importance that the CTV assigns international relations. Additional evidence is the CTV's attendance at international labor conferences, which are frequently held in Caracas (including the world congress of the ICFTU in March 1992, the second time it took place in Latin America). Observers agree that the CTV usually sends important leaders to these meetings, who take the proceedings quite seriously.[20] International concerns are also evident among oil worker leaders, who periodically talk of the possibility of inviting their counterparts from the OPEC nations to a conference for the purpose of forming a confederation of petroleum workers. (The proposal has not materialized, perhaps due to fear of Israel's negative reaction and reluctance to associate with government-controlled unions of the Middle East.[21]) The CTV's international interest is also demonstrated by the confederation's large representation on the executive boards of the ITS. Finally, at the request of the CTV, the Venezuelan government sends labor attachés (who are selected by the confederation) to its embassies throughout Latin America and elsewhere—one of the few third-world nations to do so.

The CTV assumes credit not only for having played a decisive role in the consolidation of Venezuelan democracy but also for vigorously coming to the defense of labor movements throughout the continent that are persecuted by military regimes. The causes that the CTV champions thus go beyond the immediate concerns of the confederation's constituency of unionized Venezuelan workers. In addition to personal conviction and support for working-class internationalism, CTV leaders are guided by a pragmatic motive. The CTV's image as a guardian of democracy, which the confederation assiduously cultivates, fortifies its bargaining position in national politics. Its prestige at home and abroad has undoubtedly influenced the government, with its substantial oil-derived resources, to grant benefits not only in the form of proworker reforms but also handsome subsidies to labor organizations and economic support for the BTV and other CTV enterprises.

The Central Unitaria de Trabajadores de Venezuela (CUTV)

The strategy of creating separate labor organizations, known as dual unionism, has been the subject of extensive debate on the Left in Venezuela and throughout the world. The U.S. Marxist leader Daniel de Leon (1852–1914) defended the notion that leftists should work within their own labor unions rather than with those dominated by their adversaries. Lenin generally opposed this idea, and his *Left-Wing Communism: An Infantile Disorder* influenced the nascent U.S. Communist movement in the early 1920s to abandon dual unions and form part of the existing trade union structure. In Venezuela, a group of Communist dissidents known as the "Black Communists," who were condemned as ultraleftists by the orthodox PCVistas, set up rival unions in the 1940s with the aim of displacing the CTV, which they considered undemocratic. In the 1950s most Black Communists returned to the PCV, but their legacy of dual unionism would influence the Left in future years.

The CUTV was founded in April 1963 by PCVista and MIRista trade unionists who had been expelled from the CTV at its Fourth Congress in December 1961. The decision to establish a separate confederation met unanimous approval among leftists. Nevertheless, the move was not the outcome of a long-term strategy generally agreed upon at the time, but rather the by-product of the polarization of organized labor into leftist and nonleftist camps. A former leading Black Communist trade unionist, Horacio Scott Power, was named the CUTV's first secretary-general while another, Cruz Villegas, became its secretary of organization. In 1967, Villegas replaced Scott in the secretary-generalship, a position he would retain for the next twenty years.

The CUTV throughout its history has been subject to internal tension between trade unionists who favor making an all-out effort to reach an understanding with the CTV and those who are loath to make concessions for the sake of unity. Some of the labor leaders who left the PCV to found MAS in 1971, such as Eloy Torres, had been highly critical of the CUTV for spurning unity and harshly attacking CTVistas without distinguishing between national spokesmen and officers of individual unions, and between those who defended worker interests and those who did not.[22] Such a differentiation was made especially imperative by the emergence of the left-leaning MEP, which occupied important positions at all levels of the CTV hierarchy.

Other early MASistas, along with the MIRistas, put forward the opposite critique of the CUTV: that it was preparing for its own "liquidation" in order to coalesce with the "sell-out" CTV. In early 1971 they split off from the CUTV and founded the "CUTV-Clasista," which demanded radical reforms such as the nationalization of the iron and oil industry. The MIRistas and MASistas were encouraged by the possibility that leftist trade unionists throughout the continent, at the urging of the recently elected government of Salvador Allende, would form a new Latin American labor confederation.[23] (Since the dissolution of the Confederación de Trabajadores de América Latina (CTAL) in 1964, leftists, unlike prosocial democrats and Christian democrats, did not have their own continental labor confederation for all practical purposes.) In 1973 metal workers' leader Julio Cacique represented the CUTV-Clasista at an international conference of leftist trade unionists in Santiago, Chile, where a majority of delegates supported his call for a worldwide strike against multinational corporations.[24] Nevertheless, neither this proposal nor another that called for the creation of a new Latin American labor confederation ever materialized.

Even after the division in 1971 the CUTV did not have a uniform policy toward the CTV. Cruz Villegas, upholding the position of his earlier days as a black Communist, denied that the CTV would ever promote working-class solidarity and admitted that his own calls for interconfederation unity were merely rhetorical.[25] In contrast, President Hemmy Croes attempted to promote joint actions with the CTV under the slogan "*unidad de acción.*" Croes made considerable progress in organizing an international conference of trade unionists on the foreign debt in Caracas with the participation of the CTV. The initiative, however, was thwarted in March 1985 when he was murdered (apparently due to personal motives), although the conference was subsequently held in Havana and attended by representatives of all four Venezuelan confederations.[26]

With the deepening of the economic crisis in more recent years, the CUTV's relations with the CTV have taken on added importance. The CTV invited other confederations to participate in the May 18, 1989, general strike and the marches of February 15, 1990. The CUTV was allowed to take part in the planning of the former event and CUTV trade unionists and other leftists were included in the lists of speakers at the latter. The CUTV, however, has criticized the CTV's overly timid response to the government's austerity measures. For the first time since the 1960s, the CUTV organized separate May Day marches in all cities throughout the nation in 1990, rather than leaving the decision of whether to join those sponsored by CTV unions to its regional affiliates.

The CUTV also united with other groups in order to radicalize labor's position. The CUTV, Codesa, and the CGT, along with several nonaffiliated labor organizations and the student movement's Federación de Centros Universitarios (FCU), formed the Consejo Nacional de los Trabajadores y el Pueblo (CNTP). In early 1989 the CNTP proposed a nationwide work stoppage, and in doing so undoubtedly influenced the CTV's decision to call the May 18 general strike. The CNTP organized protests, including one in Caracas on October 14, 1989, in favor of a proposed *estabilidad absoluta* law that had been submitted to the National Congress.

Although numerical participation in these actions has been limited, the movement's potential is evident. Organizations such as the SNTP, the Association of Laboratory Analysts (Colegio de Bioanalistas), the Federation of University Professors' Associations (Fapuv), Fetramagisterio (one of the grade schoolteachers' federations), and Sutiss, which took part in these marches, have recently emerged as among the most militant and autonomous in the labor movement and have called important work stoppages. Those in the CUTV who favor a strategy of carrying out protests with groups that are independent of the CTV leadership, rather than attempting to work with the CTV itself, see these actions as leading to a radical change in the correlation of forces in organized labor, to the detriment of the nation's main confederation.[27] Nevertheless, the influence of independent labor organizations in Venezuela still pales in comparison to their counterparts in Colombia, Peru, and Mexico where the "independents" have succeeded in displacing unions affiliated with more conservative confederations.

The CUTV's young president, José Manuel Carrasquel, proposed the creation of a new organization that would take in existing confederations and independent unions and would refrain, at least at first, from affiliating with any international labor body. Carrasquel argued in favor of the model of the pluralistic Central Unitaria de Trabajadores (CUT) in Colombia, whose founding president was a former labor minister under a Conservative administration; Colombian Communists dissolved their confederation and joined the CUT, which succeeded in isolating the nation's two main proestablishment confederations. In addition to independent labor organizations, Carrasquel attempted to interest non-AD trade unionists of the CTV, including such militant unions as Sutiss and Fetramagisterio, in his plan. While fellow Communists supported the idea, many old-time party trade unionists refused to consider the elimination of the CUTV under any circumstances. Carrasquel, for his part, maintained that the close identification of the CUTV with the Communist party was a major disadvantage and contrasted with the pluralistic image that the CTV had succeeded in projecting. Carrasquel pointed out:

> They [AD leaders in the CTV] encourage a degree of pluralism. They control 70 percent of the CTV's apparatus and distribute 30 percent among the other forces . . . and thus maintain the image . . . of a pluralistic confederation. In spite of the fact that we put forward proposals which benefit the workers we do not achieve this pluralism . . . which is achieved on the basis of positions, on the basis of clientelism. . . . Obviously [other] parties are not readily going to join a confederation without resources. Therefore, in order to overcome this I say we have to create a confederation that is non-sectarian . . . and break with the practice of repeating slogans and cliches that are today irrelevant.[28]

The CUTV's structure and organizational practices have been the source of controversy within the confederation. The CUTV lost its original pluralistic character at its 1967 convention when PCVista Cruz Villegas replaced the independent Horacio Scott Power as president and the Communists insisted on selecting all the top members of the confederation's Executive Committee. The PCV also opposed the model embraced by MIR during these years of worker assemblies as a virtual substitute for the existing trade union structure.

In the 1970s the CUTV-affiliated UTIT emerged as the confederation's most important union, as textile workers in numerous companies in the Caracas area left the CTV to join it. Although the textile industry was a traditional Communist stronghold dating back to the 1940s, UTIT was led by parties of the marginal Left (Proceso Político in the 1970s and Convergencia Revolutionaria in the 1980s). UTIT leaders succeeded in pressuring the textile workers' federation to which they belonged to implement a system of direct elections for the selection of its Executive Committee, and called on the CUTV to do the same. They also demanded that CUTV congresses be held more frequently than every five years, as was the custom, and that UTIT be given greater representation in them by virtue of its increased membership. As a result of these differences, relations between UTIT and the CUTV became tense, although they eased somewhat when leadership in the union passed to the Convergencia Revolucionaria.[29] In the late 1980s the *perestroika* slogan influenced Communist trade unionists to favor greater autonomy for labor unions vis-à-vis the party and the implementation of some of the democratic reforms that the confederation's leaders had up until then resisted.

Fear of being displaced by the CTV led the CUTV to oppose the increase in the number of workers required to form *sindicatos de empresa* (unions representing workers in one company). The 1936 Labor Law set the minimum at twenty, but the proposed law that former President Rafael Caldera introduced in congress in 1985 increased it to fifty. The three smaller confederations prodded the congressional commission, which considered Caldera's *Anteproyecto*, to restore the original figure of twenty. They also opposed the *Anteproyecto*'s requirement of five hundred workers' signatures to legalize national unions (which previously had been prohibited), fearing that in certain industries they would not be able to meet this prerequisite. Although they were not opposed to the idea as were many *Copeyanos*, CUTV trade unionists were apprehensive about forming national unions since they anticipated worker distrust of labor organizations that were national in scope and whose top leaders were far removed from the rank and file.[30] In maintaining this attitude the CUTVistas diverged from traditional Marxism, which favors powerful national industrial unions over local ones.

Since its early years the CUTV has played a relatively minor role in the nation's labor movement. Two developments in the late 1980s and early 1990s have opened the possibility for dramatic inroads: the CUTV's association with other labor organizations that are among the most combative in the labor movement, and steps toward internal democratization and autonomy. There has been considerable popular pressure in favor of a militant response to the economic crisis and democratization—specifically, mass participation and the autonomy of civil society. These trends threaten to leave the CTV behind; its support for them, at least up until the 1990 congress, has been largely rhetorical. Thus, the CUTV is in a position to differentiate itself effectively from the CTV and break out of the isolation that has plagued the organization throughout most of its history.

The Social Christian Trade Unionists

Since the founding of Copei in 1946, social Christian trade unionists have been divided over whether to work within the CTV or to build their own labor movement. Following the overthrow of Pérez Jiménez in 1958, Rafael Caldera used his influence in the party to promote the former strategy. He argued that the model of collective leadership embodied in the Punto Fijo Pact, which was imperative for the survival of the democratic system, should be applied to organized labor. Other social Christians maintained that dual unionism was synonymous with "trade union democracy" in that it permitted workers to belong to the organization of their choice.[31] Those who adhered to this position established Codesa in 1963, while a majority of social Christian labor leaders belonged to the FTC, which acted as a party fraction within the CTV.

The two strategies, however, are not diametrically opposed; some FTC leaders have considered the possibility of falling back on Codesa or the CGT should relations with the AD majority in the CTV deteriorate beyond a certain point. This option in itself is a source of friction in the CTV, and AD labor leaders have sometimes insisted that the *Copeyanos* decide once and for all between the two approaches. Over the years the FTC has put forward an increasingly sharp critique of the CTV and has at times conditioned its stay in the confederation on the correction of undemocratic and sectarian practices. Behind the alternatives of accommodation, on the one hand, and differentiation and rupture, on the other, lies a fundamental question that is the source of perpetual debate among the *Copeyanos*: Which of the two will best serve their interests by allowing them to make inroads at the leadership level and increase their influence among the workers?

Political agreements accounted for the FTC's original growth in the early 1960s. The FTC collaborated with the Betancourt administration in its campaign to isolate leftists by voting for their expulsion from the CTV in 1961. The resultant vacuum in organized labor was filled by both parties. With the decline of the guerrilla threat, Copei saw fit to put forward a harsh critique of the CTV. On October 18, 1966, the FTC drafted a manifesto that was signed by *Copeyano* trade unionists and other CTVistas belonging to various smaller parties. The statement called for the democratization and modernization of the CTV and concerted efforts to unite with Codesa and the CUTV. It also questioned the CTV's financial investments on grounds that they favored individual labor leaders but not the working class as a whole.

The Institutional Pact between AD and Copei in 1970, in which the two parties reserved for themselves various congressional positions and supported certain legislation, influenced them to reach an agreement at the Sixth Congress of the CTV. In return for Copei's support for Francisco Olivo as CTV president, AD voted for *Copeyano* Rafael León León as secretary-general, even though the number-two position apparently belonged to MEP, whose delegate strength nearly equaled that of AD. The agreement was renewed at the Seventh and Eighth Congresses when Copei's representation improved significantly, and the party displaced MEP as the second largest party in the CTV. Thus, Copei's success in extending its influence at all levels of the labor movement was made possible by interparty agreements, first in the early 1960s with the expulsion of leftists from the CTV, and then in the 1970s as a consequence of the Institutional Pact.

The FTC began to harden its stand toward AD at the outset of Herrera Campíns's presidential term in 1979. *Copeyanos* utilized the slogan "trade union renovation" (previously coined by CLAT) as part of an abortive strategy to displace AD as the largest party in organized labor. In early 1985 the *Copeyanos* began to launch their own slates in the conventions of labor federations that nominated delegates for the CTV's Ninth Congress. At the same time, *Copeyano* labor leaders followed a policy of consistently putting forward the FTC's positions at labor conventions with the aim of sharpening differences with AD. As in the October 18, 1966, statement, the FTC emphasized the issue of corruption, but now it committed itself to internal confrontations and public denunciations in order to expose individual cases.[32] The *Copeyanos* insisted that the CTV's controller and electoral commissions be endowed with sufficient autonomy as well as financial and technical resources in order to act effectively. In addition, they maintained that when the electoral commission was unable to reach a unanimous decision, the case should be remitted to the CTV's Executive Committee.[33]

FTC leaders supported the *cogestión* banner, which the CTV endorsed at its 1980 congress, as a step in the direction of bringing the CTV up to date in its thinking. Nevertheless, they insisted that *cogestión* be considered a first stage that would lead to *autogestión* (workers' control). They rejected the CTV's centralist model in which the national labor movement, and not the workers themselves, would choose their representatives under the *cogestión* system. The FTC's call for the modernization and professionalization of the labor movement also represented an implicit critique of the CTV, whose leadership consisted mainly of labor leaders of old working class origin; there were few spokesmen for the professional sectors, which the confederation was allegedly intent on organizing.[34]

The autonomy of the labor movement vis-à-vis political parties and the state was another facet of the "trade union renovation" that the FTC embraced. FTC leaders pointed out that the autonomy of civil society was a cardinal precept of Christian democratic thinking, which stood in sharp contrast to Lenin's dictum that labor unions serve as a "transmission belt" for the Communist party. As an illustration of their own autonomous behavior, they frequently pointed to their opposition to the increase in prices on administered products dictated by the *Copeyano* administration of Herrera Campíns. Nevertheless, the accuracy of this example was questionable in that *Copeyano* labor leaders had wavered in their position on "price liberation" in 1980 (see Chapter 3).

The leveling off of the FTC's influence following the CTV's 1975 congress induced the *Copeyanos* to embark on a go-it-alone approach ten years later. They were convinced that running separate slates would force their cadre to work harder among the rank and file. They were also certain that AD's solid majority in recent CTV congresses was the result of its policy of avoiding union elections by creating interparty unity slates for nomination of delegates on the basis of each party's estimated following. They concluded that forcing elections by launching rival slates would shatter the myth of AD's overwhelming influence among workers.[35]

The FTC's new policy in 1985 also stemmed from its apprehension about being blamed for the CTV's mistaken policies due to association with the confederation's top leadership. The CTV's lengthy intervention in Sutiss beginning in 1981 and the government's closing of the BTV in 1982 were two painful experiences for the *Copeyanos*. In both cases the FTC initially closed ranks with AD labor leaders in the CTV, but subsequently began to question the confederation's stands. (As a result, *Copeyano* Andrés Mercau, who as secretary general of Fetrametal had endorsed the Sutiss intervention, was forced out of the FTC leadership.) Nevertheless, by the time the FTC reconsidered its positions the harm had already been done: the FTC was identified in the public mind with CTV arbitrariness and corrupt financial practices.[36]

Some *Copeyanos* wanted to go even further in solidifying differences with AD. For some time a group of FTC trade unionists, who were previously associated with the deceased party leader Arístides Calvani, favored leaving the CTV and joining the CGT should it become evident that the former confederation was not making progress toward democratization. Indeed, this option created internal tensions in the CGT where non-*Copeyanos* accused *Copeyanos* of making plans to politicize the confederation. Nevertheless, at the time of the 1985 CTV congress, FTC head Dagoberto González fervently denied that his organization had any intention of leaving the CTV.[37]

The FTC's decision to take its denunciations of financial and electoral irregularities to the public arena reflected the views of many social Christians regarding the relations between trade unions and society, which differed radically from the positions of other political parties. MEP leaders, for instance, have recognized on numerous occasions that cases of unethical behavior abound in the CTV, but maintain that the problem is internal and should not be aired in public or handled by the state. In contrast, some *Copeyano* political and labor leaders have called for the creation of a public electoral commission to supervise union elections and the designation of a nonpoliticized body such as the national controllership to monitor trade union finances. In the late 1980s a group of *Copeyanos*, including presidential candidate Eduardo Fernández, incorporated these ideas into a proposed Law of Trade Union Democracy designed to eradicate corrupt and undemocratic practices in the labor movement (although strong regulatory measures were not a feature of Caldera's proposed Labor Law).[38]

The dispute between those who call for government control and monitoring of union activity and those who view union affairs as basically a private matter has been the source of conflict in other countries; both positions cut across the political spectrum. Militant labor leaders of the CIO, for instance, favored government supervision of elections in the United States in the 1930s in opposition to the more conservative AFL.[39] In contrast, the left-leaning *peronistas* opposed government interference in Argentinian unions after 1955 while the more moderate Radical party sponsored legislation that established guidelines with regard to the political, financial, and electoral activity of labor organizations.[40] In Latin America the detractors of government intervention, such as the *peronistas*, usually champion the centralization of the labor movement in the form of strong national unions. In contrast, those who support public regulation, such as the Radical party in Argentina and the social Christians in Venezuela, are wary of excessive centralization and call on the government to defend "trade union liberty," which is often translated into the right to form local, regional, and dual unions.

Copeyano labor leaders were highly critical of the CTV plan to replace the industrial labor federations with national unions, and warned that such a process would "centralize the vices" that already existed at the local level. They pointed out that the CTV's proposal for national unions was contrary to general sentiment in favor of decentralization and out of step with the concrete measures that had been taken to increase the authority of state and local governments. As part of its proposal for "trade union renovation," the FTC called for the fusion of *sindicatos de empresa* into strong statewide industrial unions to overcome the atomization of the labor movement. The FTC protested that its proposal for statewide unions made at the CTV's 1985 congress had not been placed on the agenda of discussion in labor union meetings throughout the nation, as was agreed upon at the time. The FTC was convinced that a large number of rank-and-file workers and union officers, who ran the risk of losing their *fueros sindicales* under the system of national unions, supported the FTC's proposal.[41]

Codesa and the CGT generally defended the present structure of *sindicatos de empresa* and *sindicatos profesionales* (craft unions). Codesa's secretary-general, Haydeé Deutsch, criticized Caldera's proposed Labor Law, which increased the minimum number of members to form *sindicatos de empresa* and *sindicatos profesionales* and legalized national unions:

> We are very concerned about this because it conspires against Venezuelan reality in that the tendency here is to promote small companies. [Caldera's proposal] will mean in effect that, unable to meet legal requirements, we cease to form unions. The CTVista scheme is to absorb the largest number of workers possible and eliminate the other confederations . . . which have less economic possibilities, less logistical support and political influence.[42]

The relationship between the social Christian trade union movement and international labor organizations was another source of disagreement between *Copeyano* worker representatives and the party's major founding leader, Rafael Caldera. Both Caldera and Betancourt were members of the board of trustees of Aifld, which was created as an initiative of the Alliance for Progress in 1962 to root out communism in the hemispheric labor movement. Caldera shared the views of José Goldsack, president of the Christian democratic Clasc, regarding the desirability of joining forces with the pro-U.S. ORIT in opposition to communism.

With the ascendancy of Emilio Máspero in Clasc in the mid-1960s, however, the organization began to denounce both Aifld and ORIT as agents of U.S. imperialism. Dagoberto González and other FTC leaders sided with Máspero and informed Caldera that they rejected his position.[43] A minority of social Christian labor leaders made a distinction between Aifld—which they considered a tool of the U.S. State Department and big business—and the AFL-CIO and ORIT, which they viewed as representing labor interests. Some of these *Copeyanos* had established ties with pro-U.S. International Trade Secretariats and supported the CTV's decision to affiliate with ORIT.[44]

During the presidential term of Rafael Caldera, relations between his government and Clasc's successor, CLAT, were cool, despite the location of its international headquarters in San Antonio de los Altos, outside of

Caracas. As president, Caldera may have felt uncomfortable with Máspero's ardent anti-North American rhetoric, which led the State Department to prohibit his entrance into the U.S. In contrast, FTC leaders were in agreement with CLAT's attacks against diverse positions embraced by the AFL-CIO: the model of apoliticism ("Gomperism"), which it attempted to impose on Latin American unions; its support for protectionist measures in the United States against imports from Latin American nations; and the "Pan-American" labor movement it promoted, in the form of ORIT, that deprived Latin American trade unionists of the opportunity to group exclusively in their own international organization. At the time of the Falkland Islands War, Dagoberto González pointed to the importance of excluding U.S. unions from the continental labor movement, since while CLAT firmly supported Argentina, ORIT "failed to speak out, at least with sufficient clarity, with regard to the conflict."[45]

The failure of the social Christian labor movement to establish a single, long-term strategy and its abrupt changes with regard to relations with the CTV leadership accounted for its truncated growth. The decision in February 1985 to avoid alliances with AD, for instance, was made in midstream of the electoral process leading up to the CTV's Ninth Congress. Five years later the *Copeyanos* reconsidered their policy and joined AD slates in elections in over half of the CTV's federations prior to the confederation's Tenth Congress. The *Copeyanos* also lacked a uniform policy with regard to the smaller social Christian-led confederations. Indeed, some *Copeyanos* viewed the policy of working within three rival confederations as an unnecessary dispersion of resources. By the late 1980s they urged Codesa, which had been greatly debilitated as a result of factionalism that led to its disaffiliation by CLAT, to dissolve itself and enter the FTC. Another problem facing the FTC was its failure to match attacks against the CTV leadership with vigorous opposition to business interests. Given the severity of the economic crisis in the 1980s and early 1990s, this imbalance represented a serious error in judgment, which goes far in explaining the stagnation of Copei's influence in the labor movement.

Notes

1. Bernardo Lestienne, *El sindicalismo venezolano* (Caracas: Centro Gumilla, 1981), p. 12; *Número* 329, November 30, 1986, p. 15.

2. Johnny Díaz Apitz [former substitute member of CTV Executive Committee], interview, August 14, 1990, Caracas.

3. Pérez Salinas, interview, October 22, 1986, Caracas.

4. *Antecedentes y testimonios de los congresos* 2:197–98.

5. CTV Executive Committee, "Primara Conferencia Sindical sobre la Alianza para el Progreso," MOLA Archive, vol. 12, 1964–1966.

6. "Que presenta el comité ejecutivo de la CTV al consejo central, que comprende el período del 23 de noviembre de 1959 al 16 de diciembre de 1960," p. 9, MOLA Archive, vol. 11, 1960–1963; *La República*, May 13, 1965, p. 1.

7. *Que Pasa en Venezuela*, March 27, 1965, p. 5.

8. P.G.B., "Exigencia a la CTV: desafiliarse de la ORIT," *Perfiles* 1 (October 1970): 17.

9. César Olarte, interview, February 3, 1987, Caracas.

10. Juan José Delpino, "Caminos para la clase obrera," in *Doctrina sindical del Movimiento Electoral del Pueblo* (Caracas: n.p., 1972), p. 28.

11. Confidential interview, March 28, 1990, Caracas.

12. Peñalver, interview, April 29, 1976, Caracas; Gustavo Calleja [Aifld director in Venezuela], interview, January 30, 1987, Caracas.

13. Julio Godio and Achim Wachendorfer, "Las internacionales sindicales," *Nueva Sociedad* 83 (May–June 1986): 88.

14. *Antecedentes y testimonios* 4:212.

15. "Diálogo con Juan José Delpino: hacia una organización sindical latinoamericana," *Nueva Sociedad* 70 (January–February 1984): 30–31.

16. Francisco Iturraspe [CTV adviser], interview, February 19, 1987, Caracas; *El Nacional*, April 15, 1989, p. D-4.

17. Ramírez León, interview, March 10, 1990, Puerto La Cruz.

18. Confidential interview, March 28, 1990, Caracas.

19. Jesús Urbieta, interview, March 28, 1990, Caracas; Alfredo Padilla [director of international relations of Labor Ministry], interview, January 11, 1990, Caracas.

20. Bruce A. Jay [Aifld's Venezuelan director], interview, January 10, 1990, Caracas.

21. Confidential interview, March 23, 1990, Caracas.

22. Torres, *Ideología y sindicalismo*, p. 137.

23. José Marcano, "Problemática internacional del movimiento obrero," February 27, 1971, Caracas, MOLA Archive, vol. 14, 1971–1974.

24. *Acero* [newspaper of Sindicato de Trabajadores del Metal de la Mecánica y Conexos], July 5, 1973, p. 11; Julio Cacique, interview, February 22, 1987, Caracas. The CUTV-Clasista was short lived; MASista trade unionists reentered the CTV in 1974 and the MIRistas several years later.

25. Cruz Villegas, "Material de Organización para el Tercer Pleno del Consejo General . . . ," Caracas, February 1971, MOLA Archive, vol. 14; Cruz Villegas, interview, February 13, 1987, Caracas.

26. Francisco J. Camacaro, interview, October 27, 1986, Caracas.

27. Alexis Márquez [president of CUTV affiliate in Anzoátegui], interview, October 9, 1986, Barcelona.

28. José Manuel Carrasquel, interview, May 26, 1990, Barcelona.

29. "En lucha sindicato UTIT," April 1979 [leaflet], MOLA Archive, vol. 16; Gustavo Landino, interview, May 24, 1989, Caracas.

30. Pedro Ortega Díaz, interview, April 22, 1989, Puerto La Cruz; Luis Mariño [secretary-general of CUTV affiliate in Anzoátegui], interview, March 19, 1989, Barcelona.

31. *Copei*, September 9, 1959, p. 2.

32. Johnny Díaz Apitz, interview, February 5, 1987, Caracas.

33. *Frente* 31 [FTC newspaper], March–April, 1986, p. iv.

34. Centro de Documentación y Análisis para los Trabajadores [Cenda: social Christian labor research center], "Copropiedad social y gestión democrática:

documento preliminar de trabajo" [mimeographed], September 29, 1986; Benigno González, [CTV Executive Committee], interview, August 20, 1990, Caracas.

35. Dagoberto González letter to Imperio Rodríguez of *El Nacional*, April 19, 1985, p. 2, personal archive of Dagoberto González, Caracas.

36. Rafael Rodríguez Acosta [FTC, national deputy], interview, February 2, 1987, Caracas.

37. José Montilla [FTC national committee], interview, Barcelona, June 6, 1990.

38. Johnny Díaz Apitz, *El sindicalismo venezolano necesita una renovación* [pamphlet; reprint of speech given May 2, 1983, Los Teques], p. 17; *El Nacional*, February 11, 1989, p. D-2; Oscar Hernández Alvarez, "Comentarios al capítulo sobre organizaciones sindicales del anteproyecto de la ley orgánica del trabajo," *Revista Relaciones de Trabajo* 7 [Valencia] (1986): 333–52.

39. Cristopher L. Tomlins, *The State and the Unions: Labor Relations, Law and the Organized Labor Movement in America, 1860–1960* (Cambridge: Cambridge University Press, 1985), pp. 180–81.

40. Hipólito Solari Yrigoyen, *Defensa del movimiento obrero: debates de la Ley de Asociaciones Profesionales* (Buenos Aires: Ediciones "Librería Congreso," 1975), pp. 17, 92–93.

41. In some declarations the FTC accepted national unions for certain industries but only under the condition that they be allowed to coexist with regional and local unions. See FTC, *Manifiesto del Frente de Trabajadores Copeyanos* (Caracas: n.p., 1984), p. 6.

42. Haydeé Deutsch, interview, November 28, 1986, Caracas.

43. Dagoberto González, interview, February 12, 1987, Caracas; Francisco Lugo Urquía, interview, May 23, 1976, Caracas; Dick Parker, *El sindicalismo cristiano latinoamericano* (Caracas: UCV, 1988), pp. 129–30.

44. Andrés Mercau, interview, February 12, 1987, Caracas; Alexander, *The Venezuelan Democratic Revolution*, p. 240. Unlike those who make a distinction between the AFL-CIO and ORIT, on the one hand, and Aifld, on the other, Hobart Spalding views Aifld as the AFL-CIO's "main Latin American policy arm." Spalding, "Solidarity Forever? Latin American Unions and the International Labor Network," *Latin American Research Review* 24, no. 2 (1989): 254.

45. Dagoberto González, *Unidad de acción* [speech in Ciudad Guayana on May 2, 1982] (Caracas: Cenda), p. 13; *Cuadernos de la CLAT* 4 (July–December 1977): 54.

6 Worker Fragmentation and Transformation in the Oil Industry

A number of book-length studies that form part of the burgeoning literature on Latin America labor focus on specific industries. In some works, various sectors considered typical of the working class as a whole are analyzed.[1] Other investigations deal with one industry which, while not completely representative of conditions elsewhere, allows the author to draw broad conclusions.[2] Most of the worker movements that have been singled out for in-depth analysis are of particular importance because of their impact on the rest of organized labor and their strategic position in the economy.

The following two chapters examine labor relations and structural changes in three key industries. The oil workers have exerted a major influence on the development of the nation's labor movement since 1936. Not only did a number of trade unionists from that sector become prominent national leaders,[3] but also the oil workers played a major role in the centralization of organized labor. The textile and steel workers were the most militant unions in the 1970s when the windfall in oil income mitigated class conflict in general. Trade unionists in both industries called on workers elsewhere to copy the models that they had established for their unions, at the same time that they attempted to act as spokesmen for the entire working class. For this reason, several scholars writing on Venezuelan labor have chosen both sectors for special analysis.[4]

The Oil Workers' Movement Prior to Nationalization

The petroleum workers' movement in Venezuela has historically been a weathervane with regard to the attitudes and behavior of the rest of the organized working class. A perusal of a few of the outstanding events in the history of the oil workers' movement confirms this observation. The famous strike of 1936–37, which galvanized nationalist sentiment and isolated the oil companies, demonstrated the degree to which anti-imperialism was deeply rooted among workers in Venezuela.[5] The second major strike in the industry broke out in May 1950 and had insurrectional overtones, thus putting in evidence the hostility of workers to the military regime.

Following the overthrow of Pérez Jiménez in 1958, oil worker representatives insisted on substantial benefits in the collective bargaining sessions that were the focus of national attention. These demands reflected the impatience and high expectations of workers in general, who for the first time in over nine years were able to express openly their grievances and aspirations. In the course of the 1960s, however, leftists were purged from the industry and a number of extraordinary material concessions dampened the combative spirit of the oil workers. Their relative passivity was typical of the behavior of most of the working class during a period that was marked by the absence of general strikes and prolonged work stoppages. Only in the latter part of the 1980s, when rampant inflation and mass unemployment changed this general mood, did industrial relations in the oil industry become strained and an industrywide strike loomed as a possibility.

Certain far-reaching demands that the oil workers' movement had put forward in the 1940s were incorporated into Fedepetrol's proposed contract after 1958. At the same time, federation leaders refused to consider thirty-one proposals submitted by company representatives as counteroffers in collective bargaining negotiations and announced their intentions of discussing them in worker assemblies throughout the nation.[6] President Betancourt, who feared that an oil workers' strike would jeopardize his government's existence, pressured AD labor leaders to reach a settlement. Betancourt argued that, under the terms offered by the companies, the salaries and fringe benefits of Venezuelan oil workers would be on a par with those of their counterparts in the United States and superior to those in Mexico and the Middle East.[7] In February 1960 the AD majority on Fedepetrol's national committee agreed to a contract, which was also reluctantly signed by leftist oil worker leaders.

Foremost among Fedepetrol's original proposals was an *estabilidad absoluta* (absolute job security) clause. In addition, Fedepetrol insisted that the companies hire workers from a list submitted by the union (known as the *cláusula sindical*), and that dues be deducted from the salaries of all workers. Another proposition called for reducing the work assigned to contractor firms (*contratistas*) to a minimum. Industry spokesmen had always staunchly resisted these provisions on grounds that they infringed on the basic management prerogatives of hiring and firing workers and contracting out work. Other controversial demands included the forty-hour work week, the creation of a tripartite commission (consisting of union, company, and government representatives) to mediate disputes, and limiting those employees who were not covered by the contract (known as "*empleados de confianza*") to top executives.[8]

Although these demands were turned down in the 1960 contract, they were subsequently attained by the oil workers mostly in piecemeal and modified form. The 1960 contract lowered the work week from forty-eight to forty-four hours for most workers and to forty hours for the remaining ones. The 1963 contract established the forty-hour work week for all employees in the industry. While the petroleum companies always adamantly opposed union input in the hiring of their own workers (the *cláusula sindical*), in 1970 they accepted this arrangement for 60 percent of those employed by contractor firms. Future collective bargaining agreements also committed the companies to limiting contracted work to certain designated activities and to increasing employer obligations in the case of layoffs without just cause.

Following the expulsion of leftists from the CTV in 1961, Communists were ousted from Fedepetrol's national committee while URD's representatives withdrew voluntarily. The dissident oil workers then founded the rival federation Fetrahidrocarburos. URD favored negotiating the 1963 oil workers' contract collectively with Fedepetrol, but the PCV and MIR insisted on drawing up a separate agreement.[9] Fetrahidrocarburos's proposed contract contained many of the clauses that Fedepetrol had defended in 1959, including *estabilidad absoluta* and the creation of a tripartite commission.[10] With the purging of leftist workers from the oil industry and URD's decision to join the ruling coalition under President Raúl Leoni, Fetrahidrocarburos moderated its positions. Not only did the federation join the CTV, but also it supported a joint proposed contract in the collective bargaining negotiations in 1967, which was seen as a first step in the reunification of the oil workers' movement.[11]

Throughout the 1960s a massive reduction of the work force in the oil industry aggravated tensions between workers and management. The oil companies virtually eliminated exploratory activity and attempted to reduce their assets to a minimum due to the proximity of 1983, when oil concessions were due to expire. With the signing of the 1960 contract, nonleftist oil worker leaders ceased insisting on *estabilidad absoluta*, which they claimed was difficult to achieve and of questionable feasibility in a capitalist system. Nevertheless, they followed a strategy of obstructing and discouraging layoffs by forcing management to discuss them on an individual basis. Company representatives complained that labor leaders, in effect, were opposed to all layoffs except in extraordinary circumstances. In fact, the unions were merely attempting to block mass layoffs, a logical response to the sharp reduction in the work force during these years.

Fedepetrol leaders insisted on relocation of discharged workers, even though the contract did no more than call on management to make an effort to transfer those whose jobs had been eliminated. In cases of a serious breach in labor discipline, the oil worker representatives demanded double severance payment on grounds that "the loss of employment [in itself] constitutes sufficient punishment."[12] Following the signing of the 1970 contract, Fedepetrol unions threatened to call strikes in opposition to unilateral layoffs, forcing the companies to revoke their decision. The position of management was that it would attempt to avoid mass layoffs, but reserved the right to determine the size of its work force.

What most preoccupied the oil companies was the political support Fedepetrol received for its campaign to defer layoffs, or at least reduce them to a bare minimum. President Leoni himself called for the maintenance of existing levels of employment in the oil industry, at the same time that his labor minister argued for the extension of a company pledge to refrain temporarily from discharging employees. In the Chamber of Deputies a special commission headed by Juan José Delpino probed the matter, and subsequently a bill calling for a freeze was approved on the floor, although it later died in the Senate.

An additional arrangement designed to enhance job security, known as *estabilidad numérica* (numerical stability), was introduced in the 1963 contract. The company was obliged to replace 98 percent of all discharged workers, a percentage that was increased to 99 percent and 100 percent in the two subsequent collective bargaining agreements. *Estabilidad numérica* was hailed by AD labor leaders as a major breakthrough. Nevertheless, Fedepetrol and the AD government criticized the oil companies for granting workers special bonuses to induce them to transfer voluntarily to contractor firms, which were not covered by the *estabilidad numérica* provision. The practice, which enabled the oil companies to sharply reduce their work force, was denounced as a violation of the spirit of *estabilidad numérica*; Fedepetrol warned its workers not to be tempted by these offers.

The oil companies also attempted to reduce their responsibilities by promoting the integration of the oil worker camps into the adjacent municipalities. Under this arrangement, the fences surrounding the camps and company guards who restricted entrance were removed. The companies ceased to take charge of public services and utilities, including medical service, garbage collection, electricity, and transportation, and eliminated the commissaries, where food was sold at post-World War II prices. In return for accepting this company pullout, oil workers were given the opportunity to purchase their own houses under extremely favorable terms. Those workers who resided outside of the oil camps and thus did not receive a house were granted a bonus, amounting to over one year's salary.

In arguing for integration, company spokesmen pointed out that the special legal status of the oil worker camps demonstrated that they were originally conceived of as provisional. They added that, with the growth of nearby cities and improvements in transportation and communication, the camps were no longer isolated from the rest of the region and thus lost their raison d'être. Furthermore, not only were the communities monotonous due to the identical design of the houses, but the personal liberties of the workers were limited. Ironically, the companies benefited from the nationalistic resentment against the camps, which were viewed as constituting a "nation within a nation." While rejecting the hostility of leftist nationalists toward the oil companies, the proponents of integration accepted their assertion that the camps were based on an "obsolete paternalism."[13]

The integration plan provoked heated debate in worker assemblies throughout the nation. The opportunity to acquire a house, or substantial compensation in lieu of it, influenced a large number of workers to support integration fervently. Many union leaders, however, particularly those of the URD-controlled Fetrahidrocarburos and MEP after its founding in 1967, criticized integration on grounds that it eliminated the commissaries and other important worker gains that had been won through hard struggle. They calculated the annual value of the obligations that the companies sought to relinquish and concluded that most workers would end up losing out in the long run. While older workers who were ready to retire profited from the arrangement, younger ones, and particularly those who had yet to enter the work force, would be indefinitely deprived of important benefits. Some leaders actually accused the supporters of integration of "selling out" the younger generation. Both oil workers and municipal authorities expressed concern that the government lacked the resources to assume the tasks formerly performed by the industry.

Geographical cleavages were more important than ideological ones in explaining worker reaction to integration. The workers in the camps located in urban areas tended to support the proposal, unlike those in the small oil towns. Not only was real estate in the less-populated zones of minimum value, but public services there were highly deficient; privately run grocery stores, which the worker would have had to depend on in place of the commissary, were inferior to city ones. In the latter half of the 1960s almost all the camps near urban centers were integrated, while the workers in more remote areas, who represented less than half of the work force, rejected the arrangement.

In the 1970s, Fedepetrol reversed its position on integration. In the 1970 contract this turnabout led to the elimination of a provision in Clause 117 of the previous collective bargaining agreement in which both union and management committed themselves to integration. Two occurrences explain the change in policy. In the 1970s, for the first time in recent Venezuelan history, the nation faced a serious problem of inflation. As a result, the workers were more determined than in the past to prevent dismantlement of the commissaries. In addition, Carlos Piñerua of the moderate leftist MEP was named president of Fedepetrol at its 1969 convention and hardened the federation's position on certain matters.

In their eagerness to become homeowners, petroleum workers and their leaders underestimated the cumulative effects of inflation and the deficiency of public services. Over time, it became evident that workers who resided in the camps lived better than their counterparts elsewhere. Fedepetrol leaders of all political affiliations have recognized that acceptance of integration in the 1960s was a mistake. In the words of Carlos Ortega, one of AD's three representatives on Fedepetrol's Executive Committee, those who opposed integration in the 1960s "had a futuristic vision; time was to prove them correct."[14] Leftists have been more forceful in blaming former union leaders for failing to convince workers to resist the temptation of obtaining a house at the expense of their long-term interests.[15]

The Oil Workers' Movement and the Nationalized Industry

The nationalization of the oil industry in 1976 promised to lead to far-reaching worker gains, especially in the crucial areas of job security, the commissaries, integration, and the *contratista* system. At the time, the windfall in government revenue due to OPEC price hikes had encouraged President Pérez to embark on a program of popular reform and worker benefits. He was particularly interested in securing the active backing of oil workers for the nationalization to counterbalance the opposition's criticism that the terms of the takeover were favorable to the foreign companies. On January 1, 1976, Pérez signed the nationalization law in Zulia and then spoke to a large gathering, which was boycotted by Copei, MEP, and other parties: "The petroleum workers will be the central column that buttresses the nationalization. With their *prestaciones sociales*, retirement benefits, and rights clearly guaranteed, for them there is nothing more important than the fervent support for this audacious decision. . . . The Venezuelan people are all united around the nationalization."[16]

The nationalization law was designed to generate enthusiasm among oil workers and calm their fears regarding the possible adverse effects of the government takeover. Most important, the petroleum workers were granted the much-treasured *estabilidad absoluta*. This monumental achievement can be seen mainly as the product of government paternalism, since Fedepetrol at the time was not actively pressing for it as it had prior to 1960. The nationalization law also laid to rest worker apprehension that as state employees they would be considered part of the public sector and thus not be covered by the Labor Law. Finally, the law stipulated that the workers' *prestaciones sociales* would be deposited in the Central Bank, thus ensuring that the money would not be squandered by the government. The only major benefit demanded by Fedepetrol that was not conceded was the transfer of company houses to the workers without elimination of the commissaries and other services.[17]

During the early years of nationalization, the work force of the state oil company Pdvsa increased by an average of 10 percent annually (see Table 4). This expansion was largely due to the reinitiation of exploratory activity, but it was also undoubtedly a reflection of the state's failure to maintain existing levels of efficiency and austerity in a period of prosperity and greater resources. The increase reversed a long-term decline in the industry's labor force, which union leaders had sharply criticized for violating the *estabilidad numérica* clause.

Trade unionists applauded Pdvsa's commitment to avoid reliance on *contratista* firms for work that had been realized by the oil companies prior to nationalization (with a few specified exceptions). Pdvsa also agreed to confer with union officials about its plans to absorb gradually most contracted workers who were engaged in continuous operations. In addition, Pdvsa promised to train its own employees, when possible, for new operations, and to listen to the grievances of contracted workers.[18] In general, the state company pledged itself to improve labor relations and pointed out that, now that the industry belonged to the nation, worker-management interaction was no longer a "zero-sum game." As a demonstration of this new mentality, the Department of Industrial Relations, which was largely associated with conflict resolution, was renamed the more neutral-sounding "Department of Human Resources."[19]

The economic crisis of the 1980s and resultant government austerity policies forced Pdvsa to look for ways to cut the labor force again. The sharp increase in the work force tapered off after 1984 (particularly among blue-collar workers), despite the revised *estabilidad numérica* clause, which placed percentage limitations on the reduction of personnel due to certain causes (such as retirement) and prohibited payment of bonuses to induce workers to resign. Modifications in company structure and policy often encouraged employees to quit work, since their only alternative was to accept transfer to other parts of the country. These changes included the "rationalization" of Pdvsa, whereby the operations of its branch organizations (known as "affiliates") were relocated in order to avoid dispersion of activities; "decentralization," whereby the headquarters of the affiliates were moved out of the capital; and departmental reorganization, which transformed some workers to "floating status," without fixed responsibilities in any given area, and was often followed by their transfer to another part of the country because their services were allegedly superfluous.

Table 4. Makeup of Venezuelan Oil Work Force, 1963–1989

Year	White-collar Workers	Blue-collar Workers	Percentage of White-collar Workers	Foreign Workers	Total Work Force
1963	14,732	19,010	43.7%	2,155	33,742
1966	13,560	18,614	46.0%	1,481	29,448
1969	12,178	12,343	49.7%	1,183	24,521
1972	12,500	10,828	53.6%	856	23,328
1975	12,428	10,660	53.8%	504	23,088
Nationalization					
1976	13,307	10,517	55.9%	202	23,824
1977	13,874	11,228	55.3%	121	25,102
1978	14,382	11,738	55.1%	176	26,120
1979	17,063	13,430	56.0%	250	30,493
1980	18,671	14,753	55.9%	264	33,424
1981	20,643	15,963	56.4%	307	36,606
1982	22,782	16,407	58.1%	326	39,189
1983	23,648	15,947	59.7%	233	39,595
1984	23,655	16,450	59.0%	163	40,105
1985	23,558	14,846	61.3%	135	38,404
1986	24,320	14,604	62.5%	112	38,924
1987	24,693	14,445	62.5%	116	39,138
1988	24,362	17,597	63.1%	129	41,959
1989	25,936	13,018	66.6%	89	38,954

Sources: Ministerio de Energía y Minas, *Petroleo y otros datos estadísticos* (1989); Labor Ministry, *Memoria y Cuenta* (various years).

Pdvsa also largely reneged on its pledge to limit contracted work. Labor leaders claimed that Pdvsa had the obligation to carry out all ongoing activity, such as permanent maintenance and transportation, with its own staff. Company spokesmen, on the other hand, argued that certain tasks required sophisticated devices, such as seismic equipment for exploration, which Pdvsa did not possess. They also pointed out (as did the foreign oil companies before them) that services such as transportation were not in Pdvsa's line of business and could be better managed by specialized firms. Nevertheless, Pdvsa's main resistance to taking in contracted workers with years of service in the industry was due to the fear of bureaucratic growth in the absence of restraining mechanisms. As one company executive put it, having granted its workers *estabilidad absoluta* and *numérica*, Pdvsa was "doubly subject to the 'bureaucratic rule of proliferation' "—once positions were opened up, they could not be readily eliminated.[20]

Contratista workers naturally prefer to be on Pdvsa's payroll. Although *contratista* companies have the same contractual obligations as Pdvsa, they often take advantage of the vulnerability of their employees who must constantly reapply for work and are thus reluctant to protest unfair treatment. *Contratista* firms frequently disregard stipulations regarding overtime pay, the use of the commissaries, and other provisions; they are notorious for their disregard of occupational safety. Most important, *contratista* workers lack the job security that Pdvsa employees have.

Oil worker unions have concentrated their efforts on requiring Pdvsa to put pressure on the *contratistas* to refrain from abusive practices and to standardize working conditions and benefits in the industry. They also have attempted to oblige Pdvsa to deal with local firms, which are allegedly more reliable and responsive to union pressure than those outside of the region. Union leaders have not been particularly forceful in demanding elimination of contracted work due to their own vested interests in the system. Ever since the 1970 collective bargaining agreement, contractor firms have been obliged to hire a certain number of workers (initially set at 60 percent and increased to 80 percent in the 1973 contract) from lists submitted by the unions. This arrangement, known as *administrar el contrato*, has been sharply criticized for being conducive to unethical practices. Not only do unscrupulous union officials demand payoffs from prospective workers, but also *contratistas* collude with labor leaders by including nonworkers in employment lists in order to influence the outcome of union elections.

Fedepetrol's disciplinary tribunal has handled numerous charges against union officials who have illegally accepted fees in the hiring of *contratista* workers.[21] To avoid squabbling among oil worker leaders, Fedepetrol decided that the seven executive members of each affiliate union, rather than its secretary-general alone, would select an equal number of workers to fill its hiring quota. Fedepetrol also established an "Employment Commission" to act as a liaison between Pdvsa and individual unions, and to distribute the position openings to each one of the seven union officials (although sometimes the commission discriminates against those union officers whose party is not represented in the federation's executive committee by assigning them jobs of short duration). The practice of *administrar el contrato* has given rise to the anomalous situation in some oil towns, such as Puerto La Cruz, whereby the political parties with representation on the executive board of oil union locals have their own hiring halls. Thus, *administrar el contrato* fosters political clientelism, especially because of the widespread interest in working in the industry due to its high pay scale.

The thorniest issue in collective bargaining since nationalization has been Clause 33, which regulates the commissaries. As president of Fedepetrol, Carlos Piñerua staunchly defended the commissaries, even after he left MEP to rejoin AD in the late 1970s. Nevertheless, in the face of pressure from Pdvsa in favor of price increases, in the 1983 contract Piñerua accepted the creation of a commission to study the matter. This provision was sharply criticized by MEP oil worker leaders on grounds that the federation should have refused to negotiate any worker concession at all related to Clause 33. AD's Raúl Henríquez, who replaced Piñerua in 1985, described those trade unionists who opposed price increases as being "divorced from the economic realities of the nation."[22] At the same time, company spokesmen pointed out that many of the seventy-two products that were sold at discounts were over ten times cheaper than their going retail price. They added that numerous workers, especially unmarried ones, were entitled to purchase far in excess of their personal needs and were thus able to sell the surplus to merchants at a considerable profit.[23]

AD's three Fedepetrol representatives supported a clause in the 1986 contract that allowed Pdvsa to pass on half of the retail price increases to commissary users after an initial 40 percent increase in the cost of the product. A commission was also proposed to study changes in the types of commodities that were sold and the quotas assigned to each worker. The two *Copeyanos* and two MEPistas on the federation's Executive Committee opposed these provisions on grounds that any compromise with regard to the number of products sold and their prices would set a precedent and be the beginning of a steady deterioration that would lead to the eventual elimination of the system. Unless prices were substantially lower in the commissary, workers would prefer to shop in regular grocery stores, which had greater diversity of merchandise and superior quality and were not subject to chronic shortages. Copei's two representatives eventually agreed to sign the contract as a result of pressure from party leaders; subsequently, the MEPistas, fearful that their nonendorsement would jeopardize their right to *administrar el contrato*, also put their signatures to the contract.

In the negotiations for the 1990 contract, the AD majority in Fedepetrol again accepted price increases for commissary products. Nevertheless, AD oil worker leaders are divided over the issue. Some are resigned to the eventual dismantlement of the commissaries as a result of company pressure, while others staunchly defend the system as an effective hedge against inflation.[24]

Although the workers who have access to the commissaries represent merely one third of the oil labor force, they are particularly influential in the industry. Most of Pdvsa's twenty-two commissaries are located in isolated regions (for reasons discussed above), where labor organizations play a more important political and social role than elsewhere and attendance at union meetings is notably higher. One AD union official described the determination to defend the commissaries in particularly dramatic terms: "These men prefer to go on a general strike, burn down the industry, and not get rid of Clause 33."[25]

The workers in the integrated communities have nothing to gain materially by the maintenance of the system. Leftist labor leaders, in calling on them to support the commissaries, have invoked the slogan "working class solidarity." Pdvsa spokesmen, on the other hand, have attempted to exploit the minority status of the workers in the nonintegrated communities by claiming that they enjoy elite privileges in the industry.

At the same time, Pdvsa has pledged itself to provide financial aid in the establishment of workers' cooperatives that would sell food and other merchandise. The company, however, has made it clear that support for the venture is conditional on the elimination of the commissaries. Such a plan is designed to pit the workers in the integrated and nonintegrated communities against one another. Younger workers, who did not receive benefits at the time of integration in the 1960s, have been especially resentful of the disparities between the two communities and are anxious to see the cooperative scheme implemented. As a demonstration of its intentions, Pdvsa has carried out programs in which oil workers receive discounts in designated retail stores in the integrated communities. This initiative was welcomed by AD oil worker leaders but disparaged by leftists, who considered the discounts to be insignificant.

Since 1958 nonleftists have had the upper hand in the oil workers' movement and have been flexible on issues of major worker concern. Even when the president of the federation was a member of the left-leaning MEP in the 1970s, the more conservative AD and Copei held a majority on the federation's Executive Committee. MEP controlled the presidency as part of a deal with Copei, and its success in occupying the position of Fedepetrol's secretary-general after 1985 (as well as that of the CTV) was the result of a pact with AD. The majority of top oil worker leaders failed to oppose *integration* in the 1960s, nor did they aggressively push for *estabilidad absoluta*, the elimination of the *contratista* system, and (in more recent years) retention of the price freeze for commissary products. In contrast, leftists in the 1960s called for *estabilidad absoluta*, abolition of the *contratista* system, and the construction of new commissaries, particularly in small oil communities, in order to serve all workers in the industry.[26] They also criticized integration and reduction in the benefits and scope of the commissary system.

Most of the important gains of the oil workers have been beyond the reach of the rest of the working class (with the exception of the iron workers of the Guayana region). Thus, for instance, when the work week for oil workers was reduced in their 1960 and 1963 contracts, labor leaders were confident that other unions would emulate them.[27] Nevertheless, nearly thirty years later, no other sector of the industrial working class has achieved the forty-hour work week,[28] not even the militant steel and textile workers who faced tenacious company resistance to the proposal. The Labor Law drafted by Rafael Caldera and introduced in congress in 1985 granted far-reaching benefits, but set the work week at forty-four hours for blue-collar workers (*obreros*). In addition, the steel and textile workers' movement called on the companies to build commissaries and housing for their employees, but these demands have also been unmet to date. Finally, no other sector of the working class has achieved *estabilidad numérica* and *estabilidad absoluta*, which the oil workers have had since 1963 and 1976, respectively.

Following the decrease in oil prices after 1982, the general standard of living of petroleum workers declined noticeably. By the late 1980s strikes broke out in the industry, some of which were led by the marginal Left, which rejected MEP's nonmilitant approach. Some of the work stoppages were in opposition to the attempted elimination of the commissaries.

Significantly, another important issue behind the walkouts was the "Compensatory Bonus," which President Lusinchi decreed for all workers to help counter the effects of inflation, but which contained ambiguities with regard to its application. The CTV argued that the decree represented a salary increase and should thus be considered in the calculation of severance payments and other benefits. Pdvsa refused to accept organized labor's interpretation of the decree, particularly with regard to such nonregular compensation as overtime and vacation pay, even after the Supreme Court had decided in its favor and other employers had acceded. In doing so, Pdvsa reneged on an oil company tradition of liberally interpreting its legal and contractual obligations to the workers and of providing labor benefits far in excess of the nation's standard. In addition, the oil workers, in carrying out the protests, were taking up an issue that was of vital concern to the entire working class. Eventually, Pdvsa recognized the bonus as part of the workers' salary, although various other employers—including some in the state sector—allegedly continued to resist the court's decision.

The transformation in the relations between petroleum workers and the rest of the working population was also evident in the area of health care. Oil workers, with the exception of those in the integrated communities, now use the Social Security (IVSS) health centers, which are notoriously inadequate and far inferior to private clinics but superior to public hospitals which serve mainly underprivileged sectors that are not covered by labor law. In the 1960s leftists were in the admittedly awkward position of protesting that integration would force oil workers to rely on the IVSS centers due to the elimination of the company-managed health facilities, at the same time that they called for inclusion of workers unprotected by labor legislation in the IVSS system.[29] In fact, the IVSS centers have been deficient because professionals and other privileged white-collar workers have hospitalization insurance that enables them to be treated in private clinics. Should these sectors follow the lead of the oil workers in switching over to the IVSS, the government would be under greater pressure to upgrade the social security facilities.

The deterioration in purchasing power and fringe benefits in the 1980s hit especially hard for the white-collar workers, who constitute an increasing percentage of Pdvsa's labor force. The oil workers' movement, whose main leaders emerged from the old working class, failed to adopt itself to the changing composition of the work force (a predicament that the CTV in general faced, as was discussed in Chapter 4). The statistical contrast becomes particularly noteworthy if the number of foreign workers—almost all of whom are white-collar workers—is taken into account. As Table 4 suggests, excluding foreign workers from the figures, the proportion of white-collar workers in the industry increased from less than 40 percent to over 65 percent between 1963 and 1989.

About two thirds of the white-collar workers (sixteen thousand by 1988) have the status of "confidential" employees; they belong to the "*nómina mayor*," or upper payroll, and are not covered by the collective bargaining agreement. Many of the contractual benefits enjoyed by the rest of the work force have not been extended to the upper payroll employees. Furthermore, Pdvsa, as part of its plans to eliminate services, took away their right to shop in the commissaries. Generally, the worker who goes from the top rungs of the lower payroll to the bottom rungs of the upper payroll ends up taking a cut in salary, since he is no longer eligible for overtime pay; he is also subject to novel forms of social pressure that sometimes implies added expenses (such as formal attire) due to his changed status both inside and outside the company. As a result, white-collar workers in the lower payroll sometimes turn down promotions to the upper payroll and, in any case, lack the incentive to excel on the job. Middle-level, white-collar worker positions were not as unattractive in the past when the oil companies—whose pay scales compared favorably with all other industries—encouraged a high degree of competitiveness among their professional and technical employees.

Labor leaders have criticized management for defining such a large number of workers as "confidential" and depriving them of union benefits. Naturally, this practice debilitates the workers' movement. Most white-collar workers of the lower payroll belong to the union but resign once they ascend to upper payroll status. Not only are they under tacit pressure from their superiors to do so, but also the union ceases to represent them at the bargaining table. Trade unionists also oppose the regulation prohibiting upper payroll personnel from holding union positions. Pdvsa spokesmen, on the other hand, argue that should the upper payroll employees be allowed to act as worker representatives and take time off to attend to union matters (in accordance with the *fuero sindical*), the company would be thrown into disarray. Pdvsa has agreed, however, to accept checkoff of dues for union members who are in the upper payroll.[30]

Venezuelan Oil Workers as a Labor Aristocracy

Petroleum workers have been depicted as an elite sector of the Venezuelan working class; some politicians and political analysts have actually referred to them as a "labor aristocracy."[31] This characterization was plausible at the time of integration in the 1960s and the years immediately thereafter. Not only did oil workers enjoy a standard of living far superior to the rest of the working population, but also the most important benefits they received were not readily extended to other industries. Such company concessions as the forty-hour work week for manual labor, *estabilidad numérica* and subsequently *estabilidad absoluta*, the houses that were turned over to the workers, the special bonuses granted those who resided outside of the oil camps, the sale of commissary products at substantially reduced prices, and other services have had virtually no equivalent elsewhere in Venezuela. The uniqueness of these provisions would indicate that the oil workers, far from representing a vanguard, were an enclave in the working class. As John Humphrey discusses in his book on Brazilian automobile workers, employees in well-paying industries play a vanguard role when their demands are taken up and at least partially achieved by other sectors, but resemble a labor aristocracy when their gains, for one reason or another, are not easily copied.[32]

Another characteristic of the oil workers' movement during these years that supports the labor aristocracy thesis is its relative passivity and the affiliation of a majority of its leaders with nonleftist parties (AD, Copei, and, by the 1970s, URD). (Indeed, both Friedrich Engels and V. I. Lenin originally developed the concept of the labor aristocracy to explain why labor movements and parties—English trade unionists in the 1880s and European Social Democrats in 1914—assumed pragmatic and conservative stands and in the process disregarded revolutionary working class internationalism.) Trade unionists of the revolutionary Left in Venezuela belonging to the PCV and MIR were purged from the industry in the 1960s. Furthermore, following the 1960 contract, the oil workers lost their tradition of deciding on collective bargaining demands in assemblies throughout the nation. Not only did the union leadership fail to carry out militant actions, but also its positions on major issues of worker concern—integration, the commissaries, *estabilidad*, and the *contratista* system—were characterized by flexibility and pragmatism.[33] Nevertheless, the period of the 1960s and 1970s was not long enough to instill in petroleum workers the conservative values and attitudes that some writers maintain are the salient feature of a labor aristocracy.

The labor aristocracy thesis is completely inapplicable to the Venezuelan oil workers prior to 1960 and after 1980. Up until 1960 the oil workers' movement was in the forefront of many struggles around important political and economic issues and demands. The 1936 and 1950 strikes were monumental events in Venezuelan labor history, and an industrywide work stoppage was barely averted again in 1960. Some of the oil worker gains of these years (such as double severance pay and centralization of the labor movement) served as goals and an inspiration for other sectors of the working class.

The fragmentation of the labor force, which became especially pronounced in the 1980s, and disparities in benefits and working conditions—between workers in the upper payroll, those employed by *contratistas*, those in the integrated communities, and those in the nonintegrated ones—invalidate generalizations regarding the privileged status of oil industry employees in the present. The prolonged economic contraction of the 1980s, when for the first time oil prices plummeted, cut heavily into the purchasing power of petroleum workers. By the end of the decade, a majority of them had entered the industry following integration and were not recipients of either company houses or the commissary card. One leftist member on the executive board of a Fedepetrol local argued that prevailing notions that placed oil workers in a special social rank served to discourage them from struggling against the deterioration in their standard of living. He further added that "the view that is presented of the oil workers as a privileged group—an aristocracy of labor—this has been converted into a myth. . . . Now the salaries that the petroleum industry pays and the socio-economic benefits granted by the oil contracts in many cases are surpassed by other contracts."[34]

Those who emphasize the privileged position of oil workers, and particularly those who view them as a labor aristocracy, consciously or implicitly adhere to the thesis of Venezuelan exceptionalism. Some of these analysts point out that oil prices have not been characterized by sharp fluctuations, as have other major Latin American exports. This price behavior, it is argued, helped avoid mass layoffs and downward pressure on wages. As a result, discontent was minimized, and nonleftist reformers were able to gain control of oil workers' unions and the labor movement in general, after an initial period of autonomy and Communist predominance.[35] In short, the nation's stability—which the exceptionalism thesis highlights—was made possible by the passivity and moderate leadership of the all-powerful oil workers' movement.

The exceptionalism thesis, however, suffers from the same imprecision regarding the time span that it encompasses as does the labor aristocracy thesis. Both postulates are most convincing for the 1960s and 1970s. During these years, Venezuela's democratic political system stood in sharp contrast to the dictatorships that governed elsewhere on the continent, and the relative tranquility of the oil workers' movement was characteristic of the nation's labor movement in general. But such a period is too short and replete with circumstantial developments to draw viable conclusions regarding the broad sweep of modern Venezuelan history. Thus, the integration of the oil camps—which provided oil workers with benefits unmatched elsewhere in the nation—and the sudden increase in oil prices—which enhanced their standard of living—were transitory.

The degree of applicability of both theses prior to and following the 1960–1980 period is even more dubious. Before 1960 the oil workers' movement represented a political and trade union vanguard, which is incompatible with the labor aristocracy concept. After 1980 oil prices declined, as did the standard of living of oil workers. In conclusion, generalizations regarding the passivity and elite position of oil workers, on the one hand, and Venezuela's avoidance of the acute class conflict and political convulsions that have racked other Latin American nations, on the other, is only of limited value in explaining long-term developments in the nation's modern democratic period.

Notes

1. An example of this approach is in Joel Horowitz's forthcoming *Cooperation and Resistance: Argentine Unions and the Rise of Juan Perón, 1930–1945* (Berkeley: University of California Press).
2. See, for instance, Roxborough, *Unions and Politics in Mexico*.
3. Examples include Juan José Delpino (CTV president), Manuel Peñalver (AD secretary-general), Jesús Faría (long-time secretary-general of the PCV), Ismael Ordaz (former vice president of Fedepetrol, named governor of Zulia in 1989), Luis Tovar (Fedepetrol's first president who was a prominent AD leader), Manuel Taborda (PCV), and Martín Marval (a Communist dissident in the 1940s).
4. Daniel Hellinger, "Venezuelan Democracy and the Challenge of *Nuevo Sindicalismo*" (Paper presented at the thirteenth congress of LASA in Boston, October 23–25, 1986); Ellner, *Venezuela's Movimiento al Socialismo*, pp. 158–65.
5. Bergquist, *Labor in Latin America*, pp. 12–13.
6. *El Nacional*, November 21, 1959, p. 36.
7. Rómulo Betancourt, "La casa de Fedepetrol," in *La revolución democrática en Venezuela* (Caracas: n.p., 1968), p. 460; Ismael Ordaz, interview, August 5, 1976, Maracaibo.
8. The same issues of *estabilidad*, the commissaries, integration, and the *contratista* system are explored in my "Welfare, Oil Workers, and the Labor Movement in Venezuela," in *Welfare, Equity and Development in Latin America*, ed. Christopher Abel and Colin Lewis, to be published. Although there is naturally some overlap between the two, this chapter examines in greater detail events since nationalization in 1976.
9. Interview no. 116, interviewee no. 173, April 1964, p. 40, Cendes, C. C.
10. *Clarín*, December 5, 1962, p. 3.
11. *La República*, April 19, 1966, p. 1.
12. "Análisis de la aplicación y administración del contrato colectivo del 13-2-1960 (Confidencial)," May 1962, pp. 5–6, Pdvsa Archive, Caracas.

13. Andrés de Chene, *La transformación de comunidades petroleras* (n.c., n.p., n.d.), p. 97; Emiro Natera [Department of Municipal Affairs, Corpoven], interview, June 19, 1988, Puerto La Cruz.

14. Carlos Ortega [Fedepetrol Executive Committee, AD member], interview, January 27, 1987, Caracas.

15. Pedro Méndez [Executive Committee of Fedepetrol union in Puerto La Cruz; member of the Causa R], interview, January 23, 1990, Puerto La Cruz.

16. *El Universal*, January 2, 1976, p. 1–11.

17. Carlos Piñerua, *Los trabajadores por la nacionalización integral de la industria petrolera* [Pamphlet of speech delivered on February 16, 1975] (n.c., n.p., n.d.), p. 14–15.

18. Comité de Estudios (Pdvsa), "Confidencial: Interpretaciones de las cláusulas del contrato colectivo de trabajo," December 1976, Pdvsa Archive; *Contratación colectiva petrolera venezolana, 1946–1973* (Caracas: Litocromo, n.d.), pp. 399–447. See also Lucena, *El movimiento obrero petrolero*, pp. 421–23.

19. Cosme Trías [head of Department of Human Resources, Corpoven], interview, February 9, 1987, Caracas.

20. Hermes Morón [Human Resources, Corpoven], interview, May 23, 1989, Caracas.

21. Sulpicio Ventura Quero [Fedepetrol Executive Committee, Copei member], interview, December 10, 1986, Caracas; Jesús Márquez [Fedepetrol Executive Committee beginning in 1969, MEP member], interview, June 15, 1988, Puerto La Cruz.

22. "Noticia Hondas Porteñas," 640-AM (radio station), Puerto La Cruz, January 11, 1987.

23. Cosme Trías, interview, February 9, 1987, Caracas.

24. Luis León León [secretary of organization, Fedepetrol in Puerto La Cruz], interview, February 4, 1990, Puerto La Cruz; Arístides Bermúdez [Fedepetrol Executive Committee], interview, February 17, 1987.

25. Luis León León, interview, February 4, 1990, Puerto La Cruz.

26. *Que Pasa en Venezuela* [leftist newspaper], April 22, 1966, p. 4.

27. *El Nacional*, February 23, 1960, p. 4.

28. Asesores de Relaciones Industriales Asociados (ARIA), *Resumen de contratos colectivos en Venezuela* (Caracas, 1974?), pp. 273–84.

29. *Que Pasa en Venezuela*, March 4, 1966, p. 4.

30. "Notas de Minutas," in Fedepetrol, *Contrato Colectivo, 1983–1986 firmado con: La industria petrolera nacionalizada*, p. 26.

31. Américo Martín, *Marcuse y Venezuela: se aburguesa a la clase obrera en Venezuela?* (n.c.: Cuadernos Rocinante, 1969); Boeckh, "Organized Labor and Government," p. 310. Rómulo Betancourt justified the resistance of his administration to some of Fedepetrol's demands in the 1946 and 1948 contracts on grounds that they threatened to transform oil workers into a labor aristocracy. See Betancourt, *Venezuela: polítical y petróleo* (Mexico: Fondo de Cultura Económica, 1956), p. 284.

32. John Humphrey, *Capitalist Control and Workers' Struggle in the Brazilian Auto Industry* (Princeton, NJ: Princeton University Press, 1982), p. 232.

33. The nitrate and copper workers in Chile, for instance, have been traditional strongholds of leftist parties, which facilitated linkages with other sectors of the working class, thus ruling out their characterization as a labor aristocracy, their economic privileges notwithstanding. See Alan Angell, *Politics and the Labour Movement in Chile* (London: Oxford University Press, 1972), pp. 233–34. The

pragmatic approach to major issues of oil worker concern is explored in more detail in my "Welfare, Oil Workers, and the Labor Movement."

34. Pedro Méndez, interview, January 23, 1990, Puerto La Cruz.

35. Karl, "Petroleum and Political Pacts," pp. 70–71; Bergquist, *Labor in Latin America*, p. 14.

7 Labor Militance in the Steel and Textile Industries

Management and government strategies designed to meet international commercial competition frequently result in mass layoffs, speedups, and the elimination of job rules, which in turn generate worker resistance. This sequence is particularly notable in third-world countries where technological backwardness and inexperience make the task of catching up all the more difficult and exacting. Just as labor opposition to Taylorism in the early stages of industrialization in the developed countries has produced a body of important scholarly literature,[1] similar struggles in Latin American nations have been carefully examined by various labor historians.

The two most insightful studies of this phenomenon are *Resistance and Integration: Peronism and the Argentine Working Class, 1946–1976* by Daniel James and John Humphrey's *Capitalist Control and Workers' Struggle in the Brazilian Auto Industry*. The elimination of protectionist measures after Perón's overthrow in 1955, which was part of a strategy to go beyond the import substitution stage, and the effort of the military government and industrialists in Brazil to penetrate foreign markets after the 1964 coup are examined by the two authors. In both cases internal commissions of department delegates played an important role in channeling worker opposition to rationalization at the shop floor level and were targets of management schemes. Traditional-minded labor leaders in the national union movement were distrustful of this shop floor organization and, as James shows in the case of Argentina, held an ambivalent attitude toward company attempts to dismantle it.[2]

The most militant struggles in Venezuela since 1958 broke out in two industries that faced heavy foreign competition and greatly resembled the movements described by James and Humphrey. In the case of steel, the government committed vast resources derived from the windfall in oil income in the 1970s in an effort to go beyond import substitution by developing heavy industry. The productive capacity of steel and aluminum plants in the Guayana region was greatly expanded in order to satisfy internal demand and facilitate exports to the Andean nations and other foreign markets. The textile industry, for its part, contrasted sharply with other manufacturing sectors in the 1970s that were protected by high tariffs and thus not threatened by imports. Contraband in apparel was stimulated by overvalued currency and in large part tolerated, evidently as an official policy. Illegal foreign competition threw the textile industry into disarray, resulting in mass layoffs. In both industries, rank-and-file trade unionism based on department delegates and worker assemblies emerged in the 1970s in response to adverse management policies dictated by these market pressures.

The Steel Industry

The Corporación Venezolana de Guayana (CVG) was created in 1960 to take charge of the region's state-run industries. Over the course of the next twenty-five years, those industries would include Sidor, the Guri Dam hydroelectric installations, three aluminum companies, a bauxite company, and the nationalized iron industry. In addition to industrial development, the CVG assumed responsibility for urban planning in a metropolitan area that was beset with acute problems due to heavy in-migration and concomitant housing shortages. The election of a Communist to head the union at Sidor in 1969 marked the intensification of worker conflict in the entire region, and among the steel workers in particular.

Industrial conflict in the steel industry must be examined against the backdrop of international commercial and financial pressures. The program embodied in the Fifth Plan of the Nation to increase steel output from 1.2 billion tons in 1975 to 15 billion tons by 1990 was considered one of the most ambitious of its kind anyplace in the world.[3] Given Venezuela's limited demand for steel, the lion's share of the production was to be destined for the international market. The plan allocated a large portion of the windfall in government oil revenue to heavy industry: 19.3 percent of the national budget was to be assigned to "manufacturing industry," of which steel was to receive 67.1 percent and aluminum 24.3 percent. Some analysts pointed out that this policy fostered the growth of an "emerging bourgeoisie" that was closely linked to the administration of Carlos Andrés Pérez and stood to benefit the most from the conquest of foreign markets.[4]

The argument in favor of investing heavily in the state-owned steel and aluminum industries rested on the "comparative advantage" that the Guayana region of Venezuela had over other nations. In addition to cheap labor, the major factor was an abundance of coal, bauxite, iron, and hydroelectric power. Nevertheless, the short- or medium-term advantages of these abundant resources were exaggerated, at least in the case of steel. The coal from Naricual in the neighboring state of Anzoátegui was of questionable quality for transformation into coke, and as a result, the mine was subsequently all but closed down. Although Venezuela began to export a small amount of low-grade coal, its importation of coke for Sidor and elsewhere reached $70 million by 1990.

Cheap electricty, which was emphasized in government statements, favored aluminum more than it did steel. Furthermore, the nearby Guri Dam, in addition to providing electricity for Guayana, supplemented the oil-fired plants that supplied the central area from Caracas to Barquisimeto. Due to its potential as a substitute for gas and oil (which produced 65 percent of the nation's electricity in the 1970s), the electricity consumed by heavy industry in Guayana could not be considered intrinsically "cheap" from a macro-perspective. In effect, electricity was subsidized by the government, as was the gas that was used in some of Sidor's industrial furnaces. This point was not missed by the U.S. Department of Commerce, which pressured Venezuela to accept voluntary export quotas on grounds that artificially reduced prices for electricity and other components, which gave Venezuelan steel a competitive edge, constituted a "disloyal" trade practice.[5]

The relative advantages of Guayana's natural wealth were outweighed by the inefficiency and waste brought on by poor management. Indeed, managerial proficiency is to a great extent what allowed nations such as Japan and Italy—which are lacking in iron deposits—to become major steel producers. The Venezuelan steel and aluminum industries were plagued by the same problems of inefficiency, corruption, and clientelism as state operations such as the telephone company, the port authority, and the mail service that were not subject to sharp market pressures. They failed to emulate the high managerial performance of the state-run oil industry, the nation's only other important export sector. Sidor's attempts to reduce overhead by increasing productivity and laying off workers intensified labor conflict. These efforts came to a head in the early 1990s when the company reduced its work force by as many as three thousand workers.

In addition to market constraints, the state-run Sidor was subject to pressure from foreign creditors. Optimistic assumptions regarding continued economic growth and oil price increases led the first Pérez administration to arrange for short-term loans to finance Sidor's projects. The economic contraction in the 1980s forced the Herrera Campíns government to convert the debt into long-term loans. Subsequent administrations sought additional credit to alleviate the company's economic predicament. Although state-run enterprises in general were heavily indebted, Sidor's problems were compounded by the enormity of its financial obligations, which reflected Pérez's eagerness to convert the nation into Latin America's number-one steel producer.

Furthermore, in the course of the 1980s, international steel prices declined. As a result, aluminum replaced steel as the government's priority sector in heavy industry. By the end of the decade the World Bank rescued

Sidor from collapse but recommended "industrial conversion," which in Venezuela has become a euphemism for gradual and partial privatization, plant closings, transfer of certain tasks to contractors, and reduction of the work force.[6] This strategy was strongly endorsed by the state financial agency, the Fondo de Inversiones (FIV), which called for the immediate privatization of Sidor's pipe plant. However, the strategy was rejected by the CVG as well as the steel workers' union, which called for streamlining Sidor's upper-level bureaucracy rather than cutting the work force.[7]

The highly complex machinery acquired by Sidor for the plants it constructed during the first Pérez administration contrasted sharply with the outworn ones the company utilized in its older plants. Indeed, as a result of these procurements, the work force became sharply divided between older, unskilled employees and recently hired, skilled ones. Sidor was founded at a time when multinational corporations were loath to accept the development of steel industries in third-world countries. The machinery that Venezuela was able to obtain was inadequate and in some cases obsolete. Not only did the equipment in Sidor's old plants (such as its electric furnaces) require constant repair, but also it was accident-prone and caused numerous fatal casualties. The plant design, which was drawn up for a temperate climate, produced inordinate heat and allotted minimum space between machines.

The installations of Pérez's first administration, on the other hand, were ultramodern, and some of them were actually still in the experimental stage. Sidor's technical personnel were unprepared to operate many of these sophisticated machines. Sidor's reputation as a hazardous workplace was reinforced by the accidents in the new plants due to insufficient training. In fact, Sidor's new plants were just an extreme example of the problem of occupational safety throughout Venezuela, where abundant resources—which were suddenly and unexpectedly obtained from oil after 1973—allowed industrialists to import machinery that their work force was not adequately trained to operate safely.[8]

Sidor's employees and their militant labor leaders criticized the company's hasty expansion. Pablo Medina, a political leader with close union ties, maintained that much of Sidor's new equipment "had serious technical flaws" and several installed plants "did not get off the ground and some of those that began to produce failed to do so at required levels." Medina added that Sidor's purchase of an untested direct reduction plant from Mexico was part of Pérez's "third worldist lunacy" and that the CVG's acquisition of the Minorca Plant to produce iron briquettes (which was one of the largest and most modern of its kind) was equally ill-advised as it "never functioned and [eight years] later was sold off to the Japanese."[9]

Union representatives argued that Sidor workers should not have to suffer the consequences of this administrative incompetence. They attributed Sidor's dismal safety record to a buying spree of modern machinery without sufficient regard for technological mastery. Many of Sidor's technical employees were upset that their training lagged behind the accumulation of new machinery. One journalist wrote in the magazine *Resumen* that "Guayana's engineers in general realize perfectly well that there is no technical transfer in the mere physical transplanting of a factory"; they bitterly complained about the fortunes that "those who traffic in technological dependence" have undoubtedly made.[10]

The union was encouraged by the statements made by public authorities regarding the errors that had been committed in Sidor and other state-run companies in the Guayana region. Sidor spokesmen admitted that deficiencies in the training of personnel accounted for the failure to meet production targets and the postponement in the construction of several plants, the most important of which was to produce oil pipes. With the changeover of governments in 1979, *Copeyano*-appointed executives in Guayana, as well as spokesmen for the national government, attributed the problems of Sidor and other state-run companies in the region to administrative blunders and unprofessional conduct: mismanagement, faulty planning, failure to provide adequate housing for the workers, excessive indebtedness, and corruption.[11]

Steel Workers' Unrest and the "Causa R"

Labor tension in Sidor and neighboring companies was exacerbated by the high cost of living and lack of effective urban planning in Ciudad Guayana, which was constructed largely in response to the post-1958 government program designed to transform the region into the "Ruhr of South America." These difficulties affected workers in the area equally and thus contributed to their sense of solidarity. Militant labor leaders periodically raised the possibility that a labor conflict in one company would fuel a statewide general strike.[12] The two most important strikes at Sidor occurred in 1969 (see Chapter 2) and 1971. These strikes, led by leftists belonging to the PCV, MEP, and MAS, were accompanied by labor unrest elsewhere in Guayana. In both cases, trade unionists belonging to Copei (which was in power at the time) and AD either opposed or refused to support actively the struggle on grounds that it undermined the development of strategic state-run industries.

Following the defeat of the strike in Sidor in 1971, the discontent of steel workers was effectively articulated by the Radical Cause party, known as the "Causa R." The party was founded by a miniscule group of former Communists led by Alfredo Maneiro, a guerrilla commander who had organized a small front in Mérida even before the Left had formally committed itself to the armed struggle, and who was later jailed and exiled. The Causa R railed against other political parties, including those of the Left, for neglecting rank-and-file organizing and placing their own interests ahead of those of the workers. They were especially critical of the precipitation of the 1971 strike at Sidor, which not only ended in the firing of 514 employees but also demoralized the union and reduced its membership to several hundred workers.

Tello Benítez of the Causa R was elected to the steel workers' Executive Committee in 1977. Another party member, Andrés Velásquez, was chosen worker delegate of the conflict-ridden *Fabrica de Tubos* (Pipe Plant), which was where the strikes in 1969 and 1971 had broken out. Velásquez—young, defiant, and charismatic—was fired for having participated in marches against the company; twenty-four other workers who were dismissed for the same reason were reinstated. Velásquez fought the decision on grounds that as worker delegate he was covered by *inamovilidad* (temporary job tenure), and won. The case was highly publicized by the Causa R at Sidor and catapulted Velásquez onto center stage in the steel workers' movement.

The Causa R went to the courts over a second issue that, like the Velásquez case, held important implications for workers in other industries: the company practice of calculating retirement and severance payments on the basis of basic salary alone, without taking into account other monetary remunerations. The Causa R refused to accept Sidor's offer to pay a special bonus of a thousand bolívares if the union dropped the litigation. Arguing that the steel workers represented a vanguard and should continue the struggle to achieve demands that would benefit all workers, the Causa R transported several busloads of Sidor employees to Caracas where they rallied in front of the Supreme Court. The court decided in favor of the workers, costing Sidor an estimated 100 million bolívares.[13]

In 1979 a slate headed by Velásquez as president and Benítez as secretary-general, and including several other parties of the far Left, won a landslide victory in the steel workers' elections. As a result, leftists held eight of the eleven positions on Sutiss's Executive Committee. The reelection of Benítez broke a tradition in the steel workers' movement: In the words of one journalist, Sidor was a "tomb" for union officials, since they were always voted out of office.[14] In his inaugural speech, Velásquez set the tone for a new style of trade unionism by announcing the formation of a council of department delegates and other bodies to serve as a check on the authority of the union's executive leaders.

The new Sutiss leadership facilitated the direct participation of workers in decision making and prepared them to assume certain tasks related to the trade union movement. A new regulation allowed union members to require the presence of the union's president or secretary-general at worker assemblies. Sutiss sponsored a week of films on the life of workers and classes on such diverse subjects as occupational safety and health and writing skills. The latter course was designed to facilitate worker collaboration in the publication of the large number of newsletters and information bulletins that labor organizations in Guayana put out during these years. Finally, Sutiss helped transform the city's May Day celebration into a veritable protest, replete with political and trade union slogans and devoid of the festive atmosphere that usually characterizes the event in Venezuela.

The frequency of worker assemblies, the changes in procedures for selection of department delegates, and the redefinition of responsibilities were heavily criticized on grounds that they created new lines of authority parallel to the established union structure. MAS's Arturo Tremont, for instance, who represented Fetrametal in Sutiss's collective bargaining sessions, commented that the emphasis on open worker assemblies was ideally suited for articulate party activists but not the average trade unionist. José Mollegas, the president of Fetrametal, pointed to another possible flaw in Sutiss's decentralized structure: Each department had but one delegate, despite the fact that most of the company was on three shifts. Thus, a majority of workers did not have daily contact with their representative.[15]

Tactical differences surfaced between the Causa R and its coalition partners at the time of negotiations for the new labor contract in 1981. Sidor's firm rejection of the forty-hour work week, which had long been a major steel workers' objective, led some leftists in Sutiss to mobilize workers in preparation for a work stoppage and to call on the union to create a strike fund and take other preparatory measures.[16] The Causa R leaders, who for ten years had fervently criticized the rashness of the decision to go on strike in 1971, were reluctant to accept these plans. Instead, they favored a political strategy of rallying national sentiment in favor of worker demands. According to Benítez, the Sidor management, as in 1971, attempted to provoke a strike in order to reduce the work force and "humiliate the union." Benítez added that, had they gone on strike, "the workers' movement would have been crushed and the consequences would have been more overwhelming [than in 1971]. The steel workers at that moment [in 1981] were not in a condition to respond to the degree [that was necessary]. . . . There was no network of national solidarity nor a national workers' movement that could have backed us with sufficient force."[17]

The Causa R accepted management's request to transfer the collective bargaining sessions to Caracas in order to be in closer contact with the national press and the national headquarters of different political and trade union organizations. The decision was barely approved in Sutiss's Executive Committee by six votes to five. PCVistas and other leftist trade unionists argued that conducting the negotiations so far away would impede day-to-day worker participation in the process and contradicted Sutiss's commitment to fight against excessive national interference in regional affairs.[18]

At the outset of the conflict, Sutiss distributed ten thousand copies of its proposed contract to the workers. Thus, concessions on the forty-hour week and other key demands were difficult to make. Nevertheless, Causa R leaders realized that government resistance to the forty-hour week was hardened by the real possibility that its achievement would spill over to other industries in Ciudad Guayana and elsewhere. They proposed a compromise arrangement whereby workers in high-stress areas would be granted the forty-hour week and the remaining ones would achieve it at a later date. At the same time, however, Sutiss introduced a *pliego conflictivo* (a legal prerequisite for going on strike) in the Labor Ministry as a means to pressure management.

In an effort to avoid a strike, the AD-led Fetrametal and Fetrabolívar (the CTV-affiliated federation in the state of Bolívar) submitted a proposed contract that excluded the forty-hour demand. The steel workers' leaders rejected the move as an intrusion in the internal affairs of the union and took steps to disaffiliate from the two federations. Fetrametal and Fetrabolívar then sponsored a referendum at Sidor purportedly to measure worker support for the proposed contract. In fact, the vote was designed to authorize the two federations to replace Sutiss in the collective bargaining process. The resolutions read: "*I authorize the ratification of the contract on the basis presented by the CTV, Fetrametal, and Fetrabolívar*" and "*I endorse the legal steps taken in favor of a conflict even [if it means] going on strike.*"

The steel workers' leaders called for a boycott on grounds that the wording of the referendum was intentionally deceptive in that it reduced options and excluded mention of Sutiss. Some leftists in the CTV, such as MASista Jesús Urbieta, attempted to convince Sutiss leaders to participate in the event in order to defeat the first proposal.[19] Although the federation claimed that 4,000 workers (out of the company's 16,500 employees) voted in favor of the resolution, impartial observers—including the local press—reported that less than 400 voted and that some union members actually ripped up their ballots in protest.[20] There was little evidence to support Fetrametal's allegation that the workers were physically intimidated by leftists.

On November 13, 1981, two days after the referendum, Fetrametal and Fetrabolívar took over Sutiss and named a provisional commission consisting of AD and Copei members to run the union. The move was justified on grounds that Sutiss's Executive Committee spurned majority decision making by refusing to participate in the referendum, and that some of its members were linked to subversive activities. (The union's secretary of grievances, Gabriel Moreno, belonged to the Comité de Luchas Populares, a front group for the guerrilla organization Bandera Roja.) Concurrently, security forces entered the homes of union leaders, several of whom were jailed. The governor of the state of Bolívar justified the action as a preventive measure against terrorist activity.

Sidor failed to maintain a neutral position in the union dispute. A week after the intervention, the union's provisional commission signed a contract with Sidor that contained significant worker gains in certain areas but failed to reduce the work week to forty hours. In subscribing to the agreement, Sidor ignored a confidential report submitted by Rafael Alfonzo Guzmán, a renowned labor lawyer who was commissioned by the company, that warned that a contract lacking the signatures of the union's elected officers would not be legally binding.[21] Sidor also turned over union dues to the provisional commission, rather than to the Executive Committee headed by Velásquez that claimed to be the steel workers' authentic representatives.

Nearly a year after the intervention, Sidor fired the leftists on Sutiss's Executive Committee. Velásquez and Benítez unsuccessfully contested the decision in the courts, alleging that "Fetrametal in connivance with . . . Sidor carried out an intervention without precedence in the history of Venezuelan union struggles, creating a governing commission that was illegal and illegitimate."[22] They added that, in the case of an internal union dispute, management had to obtain court authorization in order to revoke *fueros sindicales*. Velásquez and other Causa R leaders traveled to Geneva to denounce the intervention and firings before an assembly of the International Labor Organization and succeeded in eliciting the sympathy of a number of delegates.

Contrary to the general assumption that the provisional commission would call union elections once having signed a new contract, the intervention in Sutiss lasted six years. During this period the Causa R worked in utmost secrecy to organize support in Sidor. Nearly all the party's visible leaders in Sidor, including departmental delegates, were fired. Pablo Medina, secretary-general of the Causa R, explained his party's success in winning elections in 1987—despite the repression, mass layoffs, and discriminatory hiring practices during the intervention—on the basis of the close interaction between the veteran workers of the old plants and the more technically trained younger ones:

> In [Sidor's] old plants the whole history of the workers' movement was thoroughly grasped. These are veteran workers who have a solid political formation. They are men who have passed through all the struggles of Sidor and in a certain sense they are a school. When a new worker arrives these older men grab the new worker and teach him all about the history of the workers' movement. After the intervention in 1981 in which 3,000 workers are fired . . . and Acción Democrática got 6,000 workers hired . . . in spite of the fact that they entered by way of AD, they were informed . . . about how the intervention came about and how we won in the year 1979. They [the older workers] explained how that union was unique and what the differences were with previous executive committees, and therefore when elections take place again after the intervention this great triumph occurs.
>
> With relation to the workers of the "Plan Four" [the new plants], the majority are young, but since they are involved in highly sophisticated production they have an open mentality that permits them to be receptive, to know how to adopt the best propositions and the best ideas. To a certain degree it can

be said that by now the workers of "Plan Four" and those of the old plants are evenly matched in being able to distinguish the best proposals and choose the best leadership.[23]

Differences emerged between the CTV leadership headed by Juan José Delpino, on the one hand, and Fetrabolívar and Fetrametal, on the other, with regard to elections at Sidor. Delpino vetoed the proposal made by the two federations to delay the elections, once the date of August 1987 had been fixed. He also overruled Fetrametal's José Mollegas, who ardently opposed inclusion of Velásquez and Benítez in the voting roster, by arguing that their petition for reincorporation in the union was still under consideration. Nevertheless, Velásquez was not allowed to run for the office of president, as was his announced intention.

The victory of the Causa R slate headed by Víctor Moreno with 49 percent of the vote, which gave the party six positions on the eleven-person Executive Committee, astonished the entire nation. The slates of AD and Copei received three and two positions, respectively, while a united slate of leftist parties went unrepresented. Unlike in the 1979 union elections, the Causa R refused to accept the inclusion of other leftist parties on its slate, even though it was endorsed by several groups of the far Left.

Delpino and other national AD labor leaders attributed the disappointing results to the excessive duration of the intervention. A second, albeit less convincing, explanation was offered by Federico Ramírez León, who often represented the CTV in steel workers' disputes: "There has been a management policy on the part of Sidor since its birth, a tendency that favors the union being controlled by political forces other than AD and Copei. This is due to certain lines of command in [the Department of] Human Resources which is in the hands of professionals closely linked to the ultraleft. . . . We have been denouncing this situation since 1975."[24]

The Causa R slate headed by Moreno significantly increased its vote in the subsequent union elections in 1989. While the Causa R received 71 percent, Copei's following was virtually eliminated and AD's influence also sharply declined. In the elections the Causa R members on Sutiss's Executive Committee implemented a nominal system of voting for the selection of Sidor's eighty-two departmental worker delegates. In the past, these positions had been filled by political parties, in accordance with the percentage of votes obtained by their respective slates in union elections. AD steel workers' leaders opposed the new procedure on grounds that it was not contemplated in the CTV's electoral statutes, and threatened to take the matter to the confederation's Executive Committee. In response the Causa R argued that nominal voting was being tested for the first time at other levels, such as in gubernatorial and municipal elections (which took place a few weeks after those at Sidor), as part of a national trend toward the deepening of democratic structures and practices.[25]

Causa R labor leaders have harped on the precariousness of working conditions in Sidor. In the majority of Sidor's departments, employees are subject to dangerously high levels of noise, heat, and dust. In several "critical" areas of the company, workers have been contaminated by mercury and other chemicals, and cases such as extreme nervous disorder and impotence have been detected.[26] The Causa R has constantly linked the struggle for the forty-hour work week with the issue of job risks by pointing out that worker fatigue is conducive to industrial accidents.

Ramón Machuca of Sutiss's Executive Committee has stated that "between the two struggles—the economic struggle and the struggle for the life of the worker—for us the most important has always been [the latter] . . . and with this in mind we have always fought for reduction in the work week." Machuca went on to point out that, unfortunately, many workers are singularly concerned with economic remunerations. In contrast, Velásquez and other Causa R leaders have maintained that there is a relationship between the more sophisticated skills required of company employees since the 1970s and increasing worker concern over the issue of occupational safety and health.[27]

The Causa R has forced several important concessions from Sidor on this issue. Clause 72 of the 1988 contract permitted workers to paralyze production when they had proof that the work environment was hazardous. As a result, work stoppages to protest dangerous conditions, especially in the wake of industrial accidents, have become common. In addition, the union was given access to the medical records of workers, although sometimes information considered confidential has been withheld.

Sutiss also activated the Committee of Hygiene and Industrial Security, which, although created by the 1981 contract, had been nonfunctioning prior to the Causa R's triumph in 1987. In doing so, Causa R leaders sought to enforce the *Ley Orgánica de Prevención, Condiciones y Medio Ambiente de Trabajo*, which since its promulgation in 1986 has also been a dead letter. Article 35 of the law establishes safety committees such as the one at Sidor, consisting of employer and employee representatives as well as experts in occupational safety and health. The most important provision of the *Ley de Prevención*, which Sutiss leaders have attempted to put into practice, is the establishment of civil and penal responsibilities for executives in companies that disobey the stipulations spelled out in the law.[28]

The Causa R failed to maintain cordial relations with other political parties due to its intransigent style and its harsh criticisms of the CTV, including leftists who formed part of the confederation's leadership. Causa R trade unionists attacked the CTV as a coalition of parties whose autonomy was severely limited by state subsidies and the orders it received from political leaders. MEPistas and other leftists, according to the Causa R, retained positions in organized labor as a result of bureaucratic pacts, which not only gave them representation disproportionate to their reduced worker following but also restricted their options.[29] The Causa R lashed out at labor leaders of all parties for favoring their own members in the selection of workers to fill union hiring quotas. Both leftists and nonleftists in the CTV responded to these accusations by claiming that the Causa R embraced an ahistorical vision that condemned political parties per se and dismissed all past worker struggles as the by-product of party manipulation of the working class.[30]

The Causa R blamed Delpino, along with other CTV leaders, for the protracted intervention in Sutiss, while evidently failing to recognize that he opposed the plan of Fetrametal and Fetrabolívar to further delay union elections. It also criticized the Left for failing to wage struggle against the intervention. The only exception was the presence of several nationally prominent leftist leaders in a protest march organized by the Causa R in Ciudad Guayana shortly after the intervention. (According to MEPista Casto Gil Rivera, as a result of his participation in the demonstration, AD labor leaders actually threatened to expel him from the CTV's Executive Committee.)[31]

The Causa R's influence outside of the Guayana region has been limited. The party's strategy was to emphasize the broader implications of issues related to state-run companies in Guayana in order to project itself onto the national stage. This objective was facilitated by the paramount importance of the area's heavy industry and the ministerial status of the CVG. The Causa R, for instance, attacked the *Ley de Seguridad y Defensa Nacional* (1975), which authorizes militarization in cases of labor conflicts that threaten national security. The law was designed to crack down on the labor movement in Guayana, which was considered a strategic area due to its mineral wealth and proximity to national borders. By denouncing the law, the Causa R brought attention to repression against organized labor in general and infringement on the right to strike in particular.

Another polemical target of the Causa R that transcended local concern was the CVG. During his successful campaign for governor of the state of Bolívar in 1989, Velásquez assailed the CVG for usurping the power of gubernatorial and municipal governments. In doing so, he emphasized the need to achieve municipal and regional autonomy throughout the nation. He also raised the issue of technological and financial dependency by questioning the CVG's association with multinational corporations; its decision to increase the price of steel and aluminum for the Venezuelan market, thus undermining the position of Venezuelan-owned industrial firms; and the World Bank's plans to privatize operations in Sidor and lay off 10 percent of its work force.[32]

The Causa R attempted to serve as spokesman for Guayana by denouncing the discriminatory treatment it received from the central government. Similarly, the party alleged that the intrusion of Fetrametal and the CTV in Sutiss was a blatant example of the refusal of actors at the national level to respect autonomous decision making in the region. Causa R steel workers' leaders broke the tradition whereby Fetrametal drafted the union's proposed contracts; they argued that the federation was too removed to grasp the importance of the demands that Sidor employees considered priorities.[33]

The Causa R's identification with Guayana is also reflected in its thesis that the industrial workers of the region, and the steel workers in particular, represent the vanguard of the nation's working class. Alfredo Maneiro was the first to make this assertion, and as a result he committed the nascent Causa R to concentrating its efforts in the area. Three characteristics of the steel workers' movement lend credibility to the Causa R's claim:

1. Political parties have not been able to exercise tight control in the steel workers' movement as they have in the rest of organized labor.

2. Industrial conflicts in Sidor have always threatened to spark a general strike in the entire region.

3. Steel worker slogans in favor of the forty-hour work week, occupational safety and health provisions, and other demands are stated goals of the nation's labor movement even though they have not been actively pursued by other unions. An assumption (sometimes articulated by Causa R spokesmen) behind the thesis of the steel workers as a vanguard is that their struggles serve as an inspiration for the rest of the working class, which at some future date will follow their lead.

The characterization of the steel workers as a vanguard stands in sharp contrast to the behavior of the Latin American labor movement during its formative years. The workers in the principal export sectors historically represented a vanguard as a result of their tremendous power due to the dependence of the economy on the goods that they produced. In Bolivia, for instance, the *Tesis de Pulacayo* drafted by the famed Trotskyist labor leader Guillermo Lora asserted that tin workers constituted a vanguard in the nation's revolutionary process. In Chile, nitrate and copper workers are seen as having played a similar role during the first decades of the century, although this view has recently been questioned by one U.S. historian.[34] In Venezuela the oil workers were in the forefront of the most important struggles in the labor movement until the 1960s, when they abandoned their militant tradition. The Venezuelan case is typical of other Latin American nations where certain manufacturing enterprises along with the public sector have replaced the principal export industry as the most important locus of worker unrest in recent years.

Labor Conflict in the Textile Industry

The steady growth of the textile industry in the 1950s was further stimulated in the following decade by high tariffs and generous economic assistance from the governmental Corporación Venezolana de Fomento. Between 1950 and 1964, production skyrocketed by 663 percent while registered imports actually declined by 11 percent.[35] Nevertheless, excessive protection, the government's laxness in monitoring state funds allocated to textile firms, and the traditional structure and mentality that prevailed in the industry contributed to its subsequent stagnation. Most important, textile enterprises failed to diversify beyond the production of cotton and polyester and were thus unable to produce fabrics for a wide gamut of uses, particularly costly apparel. Furthermore, most textile firms were family owned and run and were resistant to new technology and modern management techniques.

The problems that are typical of the exhaustion of the "easy" stage of import substitution were aggravated by the sudden inundation of contraband clothing during the economic boom of the 1970s. Under normal circumstances the challenge posed by foreign products to experienced local manufacturers may have induced some of them to modernize. This did not happen, however, as Venezuelan textile firms forfeited potential sales at the same time that they attained superprofits in the one captive market that was largely impervious to illegal imports: large chain stores that, unlike smaller retailers, could not run the risk of dealing in contraband items. As the crisis deepened the government attempted to rescue the industry by banning the importation of blue jeans and other key items for local production. This measure, however, was not designed to curb contraband, which was by far the major source of competition.

Business spokesmen estimate that in the 1970s national consumption broke down as follows: 40 percent national production, 40 percent illegal imports, and 20 percent legal imports.[36] These figures do not include the substantial purchases by Venezuelan consumers abroad, particularly in Miami and New York. Of the ten major manufacturing industries in Venezuela, the textile sector was the only one in which production actually declined during these years. Between 1973 and 1978 textile output decreased by 0.9 percent while total manufacturing increased by 9.1 percent.[37]

The failure of the Venezuelan textile industry to respond to market pressures was demonstrated in still other ways. In arguing for the elimination of restrictions on the importation of cotton, textile industry spokesmen pointed out that the commodity was twice as expensive in Venezuela as elsewhere. Although various large textile firms manufactured cotton, their output fell far short of national demand, and some companies—such as Telares de Palo Grande—did not produce enough even for their own needs. High cotton prices should have stimulated diversification in the production of fibers, but this occurred only in the case of polyester. Two of the three main producers of polyester were textile firms that decided to move into upstream operations. This product, however, was also expensive due to the failure to exploit the nation's petrochemical potential for the purpose of supplying the necessary raw materials.

The clothing and textile industries had markedly distinct characteristics. The former consisted mostly of small- and medium-sized businesses that were located throughout the nation and contracted out part of their work; 80 percent of their workers were female. In contrast, textile companies were concentrated in the Caracas area and Maracay, and their work force was predominately male. Labor organizations grouped both textile and garment workers together. The latter were difficult to organize due to their dispersion in small production units and possibly because of the overwhelmingly male leadership of the unions. Women sewing-machine operators who worked at home were almost totally unorganized; beginning with the famed Communist leader Olga Luzardo in 1936, efforts were made to bring them together in their own unions, but without any long-lasting success.

The greater size of textile companies and the resources at their disposal, as well as the political support they received from the workers' movement, favored them in their dispute with the garment industry over government protectionism. While textile spokesmen called for barriers on the importation of fabrics, the clothing firms favored the easing of restrictions to compensate for the textile industry's limited productive capacity. In defending their position, clothing manufacturers argued that their industry was "democratic" because it consisted of thousands of small producers and a much larger working population than in the textile sector. They added that the "textile oligarchy," in calling for import controls, sought to limit the selection of merchandise and impose a sterile criterion on the Venezuelan consumer, who aspired to "live and dress with dignity."[38]

The textile industry, while successfully lobbying for restrictions on the importation of fabrics, lacked sufficient clout to pressure the government into taking effective measures to check contraband. The resultant cutbacks in production led to plant closings and reductions in the work force. The issue of layoffs and severance payment was at the center of worker conflicts that culminated in a six-week strike in 1980.

Labor strife in the textile industry was thus due not to Taylorism and modernization but to the problems typical of an ailing industry. Despite technological backwardness and acute foreign competition, textile companies managed to earn inordinate profits due to the existence of captive markets (of large retailers), which were largely closed to contraband. The workers' movement denounced these superprofits and criticized the companies for failing to invest surplus capital and even government financial assistance in the industry.[39] The stark contrast between high returns on limited investment and cutbacks in production and employment exacerbated labor tension.

Labor leaders offered various explanations for the problems confronting the textile industry as well as possible solutions. All of them were in agreement that the companies exaggerated the extent of the crisis in order to plead before the Labor Ministry (specifically the Tripartite Commission of government, labor, and business representation) that layoffs were made necessary by "economic" circumstances. In doing so, they hoped to invoke Article 7 of the *Ley contra Despidos Injustificados*, which exempted companies facing economic difficulties from having to pay discharged workers double severance benefits (see Chapter 9).

UTIT, which had played a leading role in the two major strikes in 1977 and 1980, attributed the industry's ills to the government's support for powerful commercial interests that benefited from contraband.[40] UTIT and other unions called on the government to temporarily eliminate the duty-free status of the island of Margarita, revoke licenses for the importation of fabrics and clothes, and authorize credits to rescue the industry.[41] In contrast, other trade unionists, mostly associated with the far Left, denied that the textile companies faced any crisis at all and argued that they provoked the 1980 strike to pry concessions from the government.[42] Gustavo Landino, who was elected president of UTIT following the 1980 strike, stated:

> The *companeros* who were in the leadership of the union at the time [in 1980] maintained that it was necessary to be very careful before calling a strike because there was a crisis in the textile industry. They went on record telling the combative sector [of workers] that management was right. We opposed the "crisis thesis" because we said it was necessary to see the records of the companies. . . . An audit was required in order to demonstrate that such a crisis really existed.[43]

During this period, AD lost its majority influence among the textile workers both in the Caracas area, where its unions were displaced in many factories by the left-leaning UTIT, and in Maracay, where MAS and a number of ultraleftist groups made important inroads. The major challenge facing the textile workers' movement was the problem of disunity as a result of the large number of political organizations with an important union presence. At the time of the 1977 conflict the unions agreed for the first time to draw up a single contract for collective bargaining purposes. To facilitate this process they grouped in the Frente Sindical Unido (FSU), which was to provide leadership in the 1977 and 1980 strikes. Nevertheless, the ultraleft soon viewed the FSU as a "coalition of parties" and insisted that decisions and actions be taken directly by the workers.[44] In both conflicts, labor organizations failed to act in unison. Those controlled by AD and the ultraleft joined and abandoned the strikes at separate dates; in doing so, they facilitated employer reprisals in the form of layoffs.

In January 1980, UTIT attempted to draw national attention to the estimated 3,000 recent layoffs in the textile industry by organizing the occupation of the cathedral of Caracas by 189 workers who were discharged from Telares de Palo Grande without receiving double severance indemnification. The Tripartite Commission had recently assented to Telares's petition for reduction of personnel due to pressing "economic" circumstances, although the number of layoffs requested by the company (260 out of a total work force of 1,200) was denied in favor of 189. UTIT claimed that the economists and other experts who were consulted by the commission received bribes from the employer, as was frequently the case. The union also questioned the constitutionality of the deliberation process stipulated in the *Ley contra Despidos* in which the Tripartite Commission was not obliged to consult the union—or even notify it—concerning the company's request to reduce its work force. At the time of the occupation, UTIT organized marches in front of the Supreme Court where union lawyers appealed the Tripartite Commission's decision.

UTIT's actions had far-reaching implications. In the first place, they signified the politicalization of cases involving reduction of personnel that went before the Tripartite Commission. Although in theory any company facing economic difficulties could request exemption from double severance obligations, in practice this option was often discarded. Both leftist and nonleftist textile union leaders demanded double severance pay, at the same time that they warned that the decision in the case of Telares de Palo Grande could set a dangerous precedent resulting in a wave of layoffs.[45]

In the second place, the occupation of the cathedral took the Church by surprise. Its subsequent partisanship in favor of the union's position was criticized by textile employers. The archbishop of Caracas encouraged the occupiers and appointed a cleric to act as a liaison who played an active and supportive role. The outspoken radical Jesuit Arturo Sosa A., the son of a prominent business representative, declared that the occupation of the cathedral was shaking the Venezuelan Church out of its lethargy and encouraging it to take popular positions.

UTIT's experience with the mechanisms of rank-and-file participation based on worker delegates and periodic assemblies resembled that of the Causa R in Sidor. During the collective bargaining negotiations in 1977 and 1980, the union's proposals for the major clauses in the contract were decided upon in assemblies, which were held for individual shifts, and their texts distributed among the workers. According to UTIT leaders, the workers came to view information regarding the union, and specifically its *Boletín*

Informativo, as an "inherent right" (*derecho adquirido*). They also observed that the system of worker delegates and participation was the most firmly entrenched in those factories where the struggle led by UTIT to wrest control from AD trade unionists was the most protracted and involved the "highest levels of organization" and where "an effective leadership emerged as a product of these efforts."[46]

As in the case of Sutiss, however, UTIT leaders came to realize that worker participation had its pitfalls. Delegates often responded to party dictates, and the Council of Delegates was converted into a "parliament of leftist parties." Due to the democratic structure of the union, it was relatively easy for political cadre to gain the confidence of fellow workers and be elected delegates. In this way, leftist parties of miniscule size achieved a presence in the council disproportionate to their limited following among union members.[47]

UTIT staunchly defended the signing of industrywide contracts, a goal that was facilitated by the controversial Decree 440 (1958). This measure required business and labor representatives to negotiate a single contract (for a given region or the entire nation) whenever a majority of workers or businessmen in a given sector, or the Labor Ministry, requested it. The decree also established compulsory arbitration if an agreement was not reached after fifty days of negotiations. Since 1958, industrywide contracts had been regularly signed in both the textile and garment industries under the terms of Decree 440.

While organized labor supported industrywide contracts in theory, both textile worker leaders and companies were divided with regard to the application of Decree 440 to their industry. The Left had traditionally denounced the decree due to its compulsory arbitration provision and its restrictions on strikes. In 1977, UTIT carried out ministrikes and "slowdowns" as a means to pressure management during the negotiation process, even though such actions were strictly prohibited by Decree 440. By 1980, UTIT modified its position and criticized previously "dogmatic attacks against Decree 440,"[48] which was now viewed as a useful instrument to achieve labor unity.

In contrast, AD labor leaders had a cautious attitude toward the decree as a result of the experience of the 1980 strike, when trade unionists belonging to numerous parties and adhering to conflicting positions and strategies made unity virtually impossible. AD textile worker leaders pointed out that, in bringing such diverse currents together, Decree 440 provided a convenient forum for ultraleftists despite their relatively limited following. They also stated in private that they would only engage in industrywide negotiations when, as in the garment industry, they enjoyed an undisputable position of dominance. In 1983, AD unions refused to solicit the application of Decree 440 and signed separate collective bargaining agreements. Toward the end of the decade, they considered accepting industrywide collective bargaining but only in Maracay, where they had clearly regained the upper hand.

Cupertino Peña, a MAS labor leader from Maracay and a member of the CTV's Executive Committee, also spoke negatively about the experience with Decree 440 in the textile industry, but for opposite reasons: "440 has often been utilized to trample upon minority [unions]. . . . That is, someone gets in there and calls in the Labor Ministry to invoke 440 which is then railroaded through for everybody. Thus the tendency has been that people want to discuss their own contracts [individually]." Peña went on to state that a prerequisite for industrywide contracts in textile and other industries is the elimination of interunion discord and the establishment of national unions for all workers of the same sector.[49]

Textile worker leaders were also divided over Article 22 of Decree 440, which allowed for the exemption of smaller firms from certain clauses on the basis of their limited "economic capacity." This provision was frequently invoked in the garment industry, which contained a large number of small- and medium-sized companies. During the 1980 strike, MASistas and other moderate leftists were criticized by trade unionists to their left for insisting that unions modify their demands against smaller companies.[50] The ultraleft position was expressed by Landino: "A worker in a small shop is more exploited and the work is harder than in a large company. In the large firm the worker has less pressure from the supervisor. . . . We say that sewing machine operators in a shop are driven harder and sweat more and thus it is not justified that . . . they earn less."[51]

During the 1980 strike the unions pursued a strategy of isolating several of the largest textile companies whose owners upheld intransigent positions. In doing so, the workers' movement attempted to exploit differences within the Venezuelan Textile Association (ATV), which grouped employers. One of these businessmen, the outspoken León Mishkin, sometimes made public pronouncements in the name of the industry that contradicted the ATV's stands.[52] During the strike, UTIT protested that Mishkin called in police in an attempt to provoke confrontations with workers, even though up until then they had acted pacifically. The textile unions managed to sign contracts with a number of companies that were critical of the refusal of Mishkin and other owners to negotiate. UTIT called on the government to force Mishkin to pay back his debts to the state and, in case he was unable to, as he claimed, to take over his firms and convert them into workers' cooperatives.

In the 1980s the textile industry underwent important transformations. The exchange controls implemented in 1983 cut into consumer purchasing power in foreign currency; in doing so, they significantly reduced legal and illegal importation of clothing merchandise. In addition, the value of clothing exports jumped from $1 million to $7 million from 1986 to 1987 and reached $62 million by 1990. Textile companies attempted to meet these new market opportunities by investing in modern equipment. They also increased the labor force from fourteen thousand workers in 1982 to thirty-two thousand in 1988.

In addition to technological modernization, the textile firms modified the paternalistic attitudes toward labor that are characteristic of family-run businesses. Although the 1980 strike represented a union defeat in that numerous layoffs resulted and the workers failed to receive *salarios caidos* (interim pay), it shook the large textile companies into discarding blatantly antiunion policies. Before 1980, union leaders complained that the big firms lacked modern industrial relations departments run by trained specialists and that their owners, such as Mishkin and Esteban Zarikian, were not readily accessible. Cupertino Peña noted the effect of the strike on the mentality of these businessmen: "That [the strike] was not all negative. Following it, the *patronos* assumed new attitudes . . . and this influenced Zarikian, the elder, to abandon the business in favor of his son Marcos who has a different mentality."[53] Luis Ocar Román, president of the CTV's Federación de Trabajadores de la Industria Textil (Fetratex), noted that, whereas Esteban Zarikian refused to meet with union leaders, Marcos wines and dines them. This change, he added, is typical of other large textile firms.[54] Marcos Zarikian and other executives who emerged in the industry in the 1980s received university training in their respective fields abroad.

The expansion and modernization in the 1980s, along with the defeat of the 1980 strike, explain the reemergence of AD as the dominant party in the textile workers' movement. Nevertheless, the sharp reduction in tariffs that were part of the neoliberal policies pursued by the second Pérez administration created fears of an avalanche of textile products from abroad. In addition, the industry's productive capacity reached the limits imposed by the national market, and automation jeopardized a large number of jobs. As in the 1970s, textile employers threatened to petition the Tripartite Commission to avoid payment of double severance benefits. Labor leaders opposed this practice and insisted that management continue to reach informal agreements with the unions that specified the number of layoffs and the amount of indemnification, and committed the companies to rehire the same workers once conditions improved.

Furthermore, some of the larger textile companies that made inroads in foreign markets in the late 1980s (such as Sudamtex) talked of the need for structural changes in the work force in order to increase their competitiveness. They invoked the term "flexibility," which was a new concept in industrial relations referring to the redefinition of the traditional linkage of workers to fixed positions in the workplace. In the Venezuelan context, flexibility was a euphemism for contracting work, hiring part-time and temporary labor, and eliminating job rules and descriptions.[55] Thus, by the early 1990s the textile industry had come full circle with regard to foreign competition, pressure to eliminate hard-won worker benefits, and the possibility of mass layoffs.

Conclusion

Sutiss, under the leadership of the Causa R, and UTIT resembled one another in their internal structure and the trade union strategies they devised, at the same time that they faced similar challenges. Both unions emphasized far-reaching demands; the most important one was the forty-hour work week, a significant reduction from the forty-eight hour maximum stipulated by the Labor Law of 1936 for blue-collar workers. UTIT in 1980 and Sutiss in 1981 cautioned against calling industrywide strikes for fear that they could not be easily won due to company resistance and the disunity of the workers' movement.[56] In doing so, the leaders in both unions clashed with the ultraleft, which favored a more aggressive approach. As an alternative to the immediate calling of strikes, they pursued a policy of mobilizing the workers in their respective unions in the form of assemblies and public protests. They also attempted to secure the active support of other sectors of the working class. They argued that the forty-hour demand, given its nationwide implications, could only be achieved by broadening the scope of action.[57]

In neither of the two industries was foreign capital dominant and thus the workers' movement did not raise anti-imperialist slogans, as did the oil workers' movement in its historical struggles against multinational companies. AD, Copei, and even the main leftist parties (the PCV, MAS, and MEP), although to a lesser extent, maintained that the workers' movement should eschew excessive demands and militance in state-run strategic industries such as steel and aluminum. On this basis the CTV justified the intervention in Sutiss in 1981. In contrast, the Causa R and the leadership of UTIT concurred with ultraleftist parties, which viewed the CVG-affiliated companies and Pdvsa as closely linked to the world imperialist system and thus unworthy of special treatment by the labor movement.[58] Nevertheless, in the late 1980s, and particularly in Andrés Velásquez's gubernatorial campaign in 1989, the Causa R staunchly defended the public ownership of Sidor and other firms that were slated for partial privatization.

Sutiss and UTIT attempted to deepen internal democracy by creating mechanisms in which union officers consulted members and provided them with information regarding union affairs; the rank and file even participated in the elaboration of proposed contracts. Leaders of both unions sharply criticized the labor movement, including the Communist-led CUTV and other leftist organizations, for failing to go beyond formal democracy based on indirect electoral procedures. They viewed the activation of the council of worker delegates and the holding of assemblies on a regular basis as a check on union bureaucracy, rather than a parallel union structure (as traditional-minded trade unionists generally do).[59]

These measures, while successful in stimulating worker participation, heightened internal tensions in two unions that had attracted a host of small leftist parties seeking to carve out their own spheres of influence. Sutiss and UTIT leaders reacted to this predicament by lashing out at all political parties for placing their own interests ahead of those of the workers and limiting trade union autonomy. They also implemented additional organizational reforms such as nominal elections of worker delegates to undermine the position of parties within the union.

The antiparty rhetoric of the two unions under study, and particularly the Causa R, is reminiscent of the Syndicalist movement at the beginning of the century that viewed political parties as inherently middle class and emphasized the need to perfect working-class democracy. The Causa R's hostility toward other political parties, including those of the Left, was demonstrated by its refusal to accept their participation in its slates in the elections at Sidor in 1987 and 1989. It even rejected the endorsement of MAS and other leftist parties for the gubernatorial candidacy of Velásquez. As its name suggests, the Causa R was more *radical* than *leftist* or *socialist*; it was mainly concerned with struggling around concrete demands and denouncing corruption while its ideology and long-term goals were ill defined. The Causa R called itself a "workers' party" and boasted that its leadership was predominately of working-class origin. Causa R leaders recognized that they had had little success in attracting students and intellectuals to the party's ranks, at the same time that they criticized MAS for overemphasizing political work among the middle class.[60] The Causa R claimed that it alone respected trade union autonomy because it did not have a Trade Union Secretariat that transmitted party orders to worker cadre.

It is not coincidental that the most dramatic leftist inroads in organized labor in the 1970s and 1980s were made by movements such as the Causa R and UTIT, which rejected the traditional model of a political party and whose long-term vision was not clearly spelled out. As survey studies demonstrate, Venezuelan workers were far more concerned with the personal integrity and reformist impulse of their leaders than their commitment to profound structural transformation. The overwhelming majority of Venezuelans approved of the democratic system while they were extremely critical of the performance of politicians and skeptical about their motives.[61] The failure of political parties across the political spectrum to respect the autonomy of civil society and the unwillingness of the Left to unite around common immediate objectives added to this general mistrust.[62] The Causa R was able to capitalize on these attitudes by spurning alliances with other parties, by refusing to make compromises or tone down its rhetoric, and by harping on immediate worker demands.

Venezuela is not the only nation in Latin America where nontraditional leftist movements that emerged out of militant worker struggles have scored impressive gains in organized labor in recent years. The most striking case is the Workers Party (PT) in Brazil whose presidential candidate in 1989, Luis Ignacio da Silva ("Lula"), was a former president of the combative automobile workers. Like the Causa R, the PT has experimented with novel forms of popular decision making at the same time that it has harshly attacked the traditional Left.[63] Thus, the challenge posed by groups such as the Causa R and UTIT to the CTV and CUTV leaders has a significance that transcends the Venezuelan setting. Their successes can be interpreted as a response to the limited growth of civil society and the failure to develop a truly autonomous labor movement.

Notes

1. Herbert G. Gutman and David Montgomery have written the most outstanding literature in this vein with regard to the U.S. working class. See Ira Berlin's compilation of Gutman's works in *Power and Culture: Essays on the American Working Class* (New York: Pantheon Books, 1987); David Montgomery, *Workers' Control in America: Studies in the History of Work, Technology, and Labor Struggles* (Cambridge: University of Cambridge Press, 1979).

2. Daniel James, *Resistance and Integration, Peronism and the Argentine Working Class, 1946–1976* (Cambridge: Cambridge University Press, 1988), pp. 135–43.

3. "Perspectivas: el futuro siderúrgico," *Número* 43 (March 29, 1989): 16.

4. Purroy, *Estado e industrialización en Venezuela*, pp. 270, 282.

5. Steve Ellner, "The Venezuelan Political Party System and its Influence on Economic Decision Making at the Local Level," *Inter-American Economic Affairs* 36, no. 3 (Winter 1982): 89–91; *Gerente Venezuela*, July 1990, p. 31.

6. "Gobierno y BM preparan privatización de Sidor," *El Nacional*, October 6, 1989, p. D-7.

7. Ramón Machuca [Executive Committee of Sutiss, member of the Causa R], interview, January 20, 1990, Anaco.

8. Tello Benítez, speech delivered at "Primer Seminario sobre la Ley Orgánica de Prevención, Condiciones y Medio Ambiente de Trabajo," Puerto Ordaz, April 26, 1987.

9. Pablo Medina, interview, May 24, 1989, Caracas.

10. "La transferencia de tecnología sigue siendo un problema principal en Guayana," *El Resumen* 507 (July 24, 1983): 39.

11. *El Nuevo Metalúrgico* [Sutiss publication], June 1981, p. 2; Venalum, *Venalum en 1981* (Caracas: Editorial Arte), pp. 28–37.

12. *Clarín*, September 29, 1962, p. 5.

13. Pablo Medina, interview, May 27, 1990, Barcelona.

14. "El Mollegasco," *Resumen* 421 (November 29, 1981): 10.

15. Arturo Tremont, interview, October 16, 1986, Caracas; Andrea Mercau, interview, February 12, 1987, Caracas.

16. Andrés Pariche, "En Guayana además de mineral . . . ," *Esfuerzo* [Caracas] (August-September 1981): 8.

17. Tello Benítez, interview, February 20, 1987, Caracas.

18. *El Nacional*, October 31, 1980, p. D-20; Pablo Medina, interview, May 24, 1989, Caracas.

19. Jesús Urbieta, interview, October 20, 1986, Caracas.

20. *El Pueblo de Guayana*, November 13, 1981, p. 1; *Correo del Caroní*, November 13, 1981, p. 1.

21. Tello Benítez, interview, February 20, 1987, Caracas; Rafael Alfonzo Guzmán, interview, Ciudad Bolívar, May 18, 1990.

22. *El Recurso de Amparo y la legislación laboral* (Caracas: Ediciones del Agua Mansa, April 1985), p. 16.

23. Pablo Medina, interview, May 24, 1989, Caracas; *Matancero* 234 [Causa R newspaper at Sidor] (March 1987): 1.

24. Federico Ramírez León, interview, March 10, 1980, Puerto La Cruz.

25. Machuca, interview, January 20, 1990, Anaco; Eleazar Silva [worker delegate in Sidor's department of human resources, member of MAS], interview, March 31, 1990, Valencia.

26. "Además de acero, en Sidor se produce chatarra humana," *El Resumen* 461 (September 5, 1982): 23–24.

27. Andrés Velásquez, interview, April 26, 1987, Puerto Ordaz; Ana Brumlik de Maneiro, interview, April 2, 1987, Caracas.

28. Andrés Velásquez, interview, April 26, 1987, Puerto Ordaz.

29. *El Nuevo Sindicalismo* 2 [Causa R newspaper, Ciudad Guayana] (October 1986): 2, 8.

30. Julio Cacique, interview, February 22, 1987, Caracas; *El Nacional*, February 15, 1988, p. D-4; ibid., August 11, 1988, p. D-3.

31. Tello Benítez, interview, April 25, 1987, Puerto Ordaz; Casto Gil Rivera, interview, November 27, 1986, Caracas.

32. Steve Ellner, "Report from Venezuela: The Perils of Privatization," *Commonweal* 117, no. 12 (June 15, 1990): 375–76.

33. *Andrés Velásquez en entrevistas* (Caracas: Ediciones del Agua Mansa, 1987), pp. 49–50.

34. Peter DeShazo, *Urban Workers and Labor Unions in Chile, 1902–1927* (Madison: University of Wisconsin Press, 1983); see also Bergquist, *Labor in Latin America*, pp. 20–80.

35. Cordiplan, *Plan de la nación, 1965–1968: programa de la industria manufacturero - 23 (industria textil)* (Caracas, n.d.), p. 15.

36. Fredy Tineo [executive chief of the Venezuelan Textile Association—ATV], interview, August 30, 1989, Caracas.

37. Oscar A. Echevarría, *La economía venezolana: 1944–1984* (Caracas: Fedecámaras, 1984), p. 14.

38. *El Nacional*, December 1, 1986, p. D-29. Prior to 1973 the textile workers' movement was the only organization in the CTV to oppose Venezuela's entrance into the Andean Pact for fear that foreign fabrics, especially from neighboring Colombia, would inundate the local market. Fetrametal favored the proposal while the CTV maintained a neutral stand.

39. *Proceso Político*, "Surge el proletariado," p. 5; *El Nacional*, January 20, 1980, p. D-11.

40. *Tribuna Popular*, February 8–14, 1980, p. 11.

41. Frente Sindical Nacional, "Sin el cumplimiento," November 16, 1979, MOLA Archive, vol. 16.

42. José Ignacio Arrieta A., "Análisis del conflicto textil," *Sic* 428 (September–October 1980): 340–43; UTIT, "La ponencia sobre la huelga textil, año 1980" [mimeographed] (Caracas, December 1986), p. 2.

43. Gustavo Landino, interview, February 20, 1987, Caracas. During the 1977 and 1980 strikes, UTIT was led by a group known as "Proceso Político," which in the textile workers' movement called itself the "*tendencia clasista.*" Landino belonged to the Convergencia Revolucionaria, a small leftist party that also enjoyed some worker influence in the Guayana region.

44. Argelia Bravo, *Crisis, elecciones y violencia* (Caracas: Editorial Ruptura, 1978), p. 117.

45. *El Nacional*, January 22, 1980, p. D-13; Domingo Campos [secretary-general of Sutratex], interview, August 31, 1989, Caracas.

46. *El Nacional*, January 28, 1980, p. D-5. Arturo Sosa A. edited the Jesuit magazine *Sic*, which published articles on both strikes that were sympathetic to the workers' cause.

47. Proceso Político, "Surge el proletariado," pp. 36, 70.

48. "Compañeros de la tendencia clasista en UTIT" (Paper presented at the second conference of MOLA, Caracas, October–November 1980), p. 18. During the insurgent period of the 1960s, the CUTV condemned Decree 440 as antiworker and claimed that it bore the stamp of the most reactionary aspects of U.S. and Mexican legislation. Sometimes, the CUTV criticized CTV unions for accepting the guidelines set by 440. See *Que*, August 22, 1964, p. 10.

49. Peña, interview, August 30, 1989, Caracas.

50. Arturo Tremont, interview, October 16, 1986, Caracas.

51. Landino, interview, February 20, 1987, Caracas.

52. Fredy Tineo, interview, August 16, 1990, Caracas.

53. Peña, interview, August 30, 1989, Caracas.

54. Luis Oscar Román, interview, September 20, 1989, Caracas.

55. Osvaldo Mantero de San Vicente, "La limitación del tiempo de trabajo," in *Nuevos retos del sindicalismo*, ed. Fernando Calero (Caracas: Ildis, 1988), pp. 191–95; Consuelo Iranzo, "Las relaciones laborales y el cambio tecnológico" (Paper presented at the II Congreso Venezolano de Relaciones de Trabajo, Valencia, March 1990), pp. 11–23.

56. "Balance de la huelga textil," *Al Rojo Vivo*, pp. 4–5, MOLA Archive, vol. 16.

57. UTIT, "El papel de la contratación colectiva en la relación capital-trabajo: la experiencia textil" (Paper presented at colloquium of the UCV's Facultad de Ciencias Económicas y Sociales, June 8–9, 1979), p. 12.

58. Alfredo Maneiro, *Notas políticas* (Caracas: Ediciones del Agua Mansa, 1986), p. 131; Proceso Político, *CAP, 5 años: un juicio crítico* (Caracas: Ateneo de Caracas, 1978); Ellner, "Diverse Influences on the Venezuelan Left," pp. 486–87. Timothy Harding and Hobart Spalding point out that transnational companies have become less visible targets of labor unrest. They conclude that only a political party whose analysis links the national economy to the world imperialist system can help counter the impression that worker struggles against local, and particularly state-run, businesses are antipatriotic. See "The Struggle Sharpens: Workers, Imperialism and the State in Latin America: Common Themes and New Directions," *Latin American Perspectives* 3, no. 1 (Winter 1976): 4.

59. *Andrés Velásquez*, p. 60; Proceso Político, "Las organizaciones de masas deben ser instrumentos de la clase: el sindicato" [mimeographed] (n.p., n.d.), p. 47.

60. *Pablo Medina en entrevista* (Caracas: Ediciones del Agua Mansa, 1988), pp. 35, 81–82.

61. Davis, *Working-class Mobilization*, p. 157; Ellner, *From Guerrilla Defeat*, p. 138.

62. Ellner, *From Guerrilla Defeat*, p. 166.

63. Idem, "The Latin American Left since Allende: Perspectives and New Directions," *Latin American Research Review* 24, no. 2 (1989): 161; *La Causa R* [newspaper], April 1990, pp. 7–8.

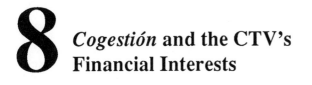

8 *Cogestión* and the CTV's Financial Interests

Since its early days the Venezuelan labor movement has embraced long-term political goals and rejected bread-and-butter trade unionism. Top AD labor leaders defended such objectives and strategies as democracy, socialism, government ownership of basic industry, and the creation of a labor party. *Cogestión* and trade union investments in important sectors of the economy were initiated in the 1960s and were later increasingly stressed by the CTV, as other goals were achieved or ceased to be sources of major concern. Following Copei's victory in the national and municipal elections of 1978 and 1979, AD labor leaders attempted to jolt the party's rank and file out of their demoralization and regain the initiative by proclaiming *cogestión* a priority of the labor movement and a viable model for Venezuela.

CTV leaders often linked *cogestión* and trade union financial investments as part of a uniform strategy to enhance labor input in economic decision making at the micro and macro levels. Direct involvement of the workers in this process, however, was downplayed in favor of the institutional participation of organized labor. Since these schemes have been pursued for a considerable period of time and labor leaders have had the opportunity to reflect upon and modify their efforts, the CTV's actions speak for themselves in indicating the extent of the confederation's commitments and in distinguishing between stated and unstated objectives.

The Model of *Cogestión*

Cogestión was proposed by *Copeyano* trade unionists at the CTV's Third Congress in 1959, but the traditional Marxist notion that the system detracted from the struggle for more authentic worker goals prevailed. Nevertheless, a resolution calling for trade union representation in state bodies in charge of policy formulation was approved. As was the case with other important worker gains in the modern period, *cogestión* received its biggest impulse by a government decree in the absence of strong worker pressure in favor of the reform. In 1966, President Leoni ordered all companies with over 50 percent state ownership and public institutes to accept one employee representative on their board of directors. Although the decree was unanimously supported in congress, national deputies of several small parties expressed fear that the government would manipulate the selection of worker representatives in favor of AD.[1]

In the following years, CTV leaders proposed the implementation of *cogestión* on a wider scale. José González Navarro, for instance, called for 50 percent worker representation in management and pointed to the positive experience of several firms, including the bus company "El Valle" in Caracas, as proof of the system's feasibility.[2] The Manifesto of Porlamar ratified at the CTV's 1980 congress committed the confederation to achieving *cogestión* in both public and private sectors. The document was drafted by a group of CTV advisers, headed by the leftist economist D. F. Maza Zavala, and was influenced by German social democrats.[3] Subsequently, Rafael Castañeda, head of the CTV's Departamento de Cogestión, and other confederation leaders lectured extensively on campuses and elsewhere to publicize the plan. The ILO and various Venezuelan universities reached agreements with the CTV to provide advice and instruction.[4] In 1985 the CTV created Inaesin, which trains *cogestores* on a continual basis.

The economic crisis that set in after 1980 presented further opportunities, but the response of the CTV raised questions regarding its true interest in making worker participation in management a reality. During this period the CTV put forward proposals to implement *cogestión* in companies that received preferential dollars from the government for payment of their foreign debts, firms that were seriously in the red and had to be bailed out by the state, and public companies that were slated for privatization. In doing so the CTV failed to heed its own warning against applying the system of *cogestión* to companies with severe economic problems, since the special difficulties they faced would discredit the system.

The most publicized experiment in *cogestión* involved the screw company Torvenca C.A., located in La Victoria in the state of Aragua. Torvenca was heavily indebted to the state-owned Industrial Bank of Venezuela (BIV). Rafael Castañeda, the CTV's representative on the BIV's board of directors, gained acceptance for a plan to convert the debt into stock, representing 20 percent of the company's ownership, that was then turned over to the workers. In 1984 the union signed an agreement with the company that created the Department of Personnel and Social Welfare, which consisted of three representatives each of the employees and management. This department was in charge of setting guidelines and planning in the areas of hiring, training, promotions, job requirements, administration of social services, and safety and health. Electoral procedures for naming employee representatives were established, but worker participation was mainly limited to the area of industrial relations; the union was entitled to only two seats on the company's board of directors.[5] Furthermore, the workplace was riddled with occupational hazards, particularly high noise levels and poor layout, leading some CTV advisers to be pessimistic regarding the plan's chances of success.[6] Although the CTV defines *cogestión* as parity between workers and owners in management and not worker ownership of stock, confederation leaders point to the Torvenca experience as proof of the system's feasibility.

Another development hailed by the CTV as an important step in favor of *cogestión* was the proposed Labor Law drafted by Rafael Caldera. CTV representatives on the congressional bicameral commission that first considered the proposal were able to increase the number of worker representatives on the boards of state companies from one to two. They also extended the system to former state companies that were privatized, as well as firms that "obtain substantial financing, either directly or through guarantees on loans, from public financial institutions." In pressing for this provision, the CTV aspired to establish *cogestión* gradually in the private sector. Fedecámaras, however, staunchly opposed the proposed arrangement on grounds that it would undermine the efforts to streamline inefficient public firms that were turned over to private interests. The business organization added that the article's ambiguous wording was dangerous since an extremely large number of firms, including all banks, that were dependent on state financial support could be included in the system. Fedecámaras succeeded in excluding nonstate companies from the arrangement in the version that was subsequently approved in congress.

The CTV was also unsuccessful in gaining acceptance for its proposal that labor representatives on the boards of directors be given veto power in certain matters related to the welfare of the workers.[7] In still another setback, the confederation was unable to defeat a proposal made by non-AD labor leaders and supported by Fedecámaras that one of the two employee representatives on the boards be elected by the workers. In effect, the new Labor Law grants the CTV the right to choose one representative, while the workers, regardless of whether or not they belong to the union, will select the other.

The CTV opposes elections to select labor representatives on boards of directors on grounds that such a procedure would create a parallel structure that would undermine union authority. CTV leaders point to the experience in Peru under the military regime of Juan Velasco Alvarado—one of the most important attempts to institutionalize worker participation in Latin America—that allegedly promoted *cogestión* to weaken the labor movement. Some CTVistas have expressed fear that worker assemblies called for the purpose of choosing employee representatives would be easily manipulated by management.[8]

Until now the CTV has submitted lists of five candidates for each state-run company and public institute to the Labor Ministry. Invariably, the ministry has accepted the CTV's first choice as the regular member and its second as his substitute on the board of directors.[9] The government has thus refrained from interfering in the selection process, contrary to what some politicians feared at the time of the 1966 decree, and what some writers who emphasize mechanisms of state control of organized labor have implied.

All labor representatives have been under the jurisdiction of the CTV's Departamento de *Cogestión* since its founding in 1977. Nevertheless, mechanisms for diffusion of information or systematic feedback have not been established, nor has the department provided the CTV with a thorough evaluation of experiences with the 1966 decree. A large number of the CTV appointees are neither employees nor former employees in the company or institute on whose board of directors they sit. The new Labor Law requires the worker-nominated representative to have been employed in the company or institute over a period of three years.

The overwhelming majority of the 200-odd labor representatives belongs to AD. *Copeyano* trade unionists have protested that their participation in the program has been reduced from about twenty to ten board-of-director seats in recent years. They claim that Copei's representatives, unlike most of AD's, are qualified in their respective fields and report regularly to the FTC.[10] Some opposition labor leaders have argued that the labor representative receives undue material benefits—personal use of a company's airplane, for instance. Labor leaders have wondered whether his first loyalty is to the workers or to management, an issue that also has been raised in other countries where *cogestión* has been implemented.[11]

Rafael Castañeda has pointed out that the limited role played by labor representatives is a consequence of the restricted scope of the 1966 decree:

> The main idea is that the labor representative [on the company board] is to serve as a liaison with the entire labor structure of the company and foster the creation of certain intermediate mechanisms of co-determination. . . . This is at the theoretical level, but this objective has not been that easy to achieve because the Law of Labor Representation does not oblige the board of directors of the state companies to create these mechanisms. The relations between the labor representative and the union operate only at times of conflict. Only after the conflict has passed through all the instances, including [the department of] industrial relations, and the president of the company has arrived at a position, does the labor representative have the opportunity to express his opinion on the basis of his dual status as a defender of worker interests and of those of the company. This participation, I would say, is quite limited.[12]

The CTV defines *cogestión* as incorporation at all levels of company decision making. As far back as the CTV's Third Congress in 1959, the confederation called for worker participation on commissions in charge of job classification.[13] Nevertheless, one study on employee training courses demonstrates that labor leaders, even in the powerful oil workers' federations, have displayed little interest in routine functions and instead are singularly concerned with selection of those workers who are to be admitted into the program.[14] In other nations (especially developed ones) where *cogestión* has been implemented over the last several decades, labor unions emphasize employee participation on commissions that directly affect the welfare of workers in such areas as health and safety, job classification, and grievances, rather than representation on boards of directors.[15]

The CTV emphatically rules out the use of force and confrontation in the implantation of *cogestión*. Ever since the Porlamar Manifesto, labor leaders have stated that such a paramount goal as *cogestión* must be incorporated into legislation rather than achieved on a piecemeal basis in individual labor contracts. At the CTV's 1985 congress, plans to gain approval for a law of *cogestión* within five years were announced, although by the confederation's subsequent congress in 1990 no such proposal had been submitted to the National Congress.[16] In calling for a legal, peaceful strategy, labor leaders frequently invoke the exceptionalism thesis, which postulates that far-reaching change in Venezuela has historically not been accompanied by sharp class conflict and violence as it has been in other nations.[17]

The response of other organizations in Venezuela to the CTV's call for *cogestión* has been less than enthusiastic. AD maintains close ties with the German social democratic party and other members of the Socialist International, which helped the CTV elaborate the Porlamar Manifesto. Furthermore, some AD leaders, such as theoretician Marco Tulio Bruni Celli, have written about and praised the *cogestión* model;[18] the party's Trade Union Bureau included a *cogestión* plank in its *Tesis Sindical* in 1980. Nevertheless, AD as a party and specifically its presidential candidates have not officially advocated workers' participation. AD's timid response to the CTV's campaign in favor of *cogestión* was noted by Castañeda:

> *Cogestión* is underpinned by a social democratic ideological credence and therefore [support for it] is an obligation from which AD cannot escape. What happens is that the levels of education and the levels of decision making operate very slowly. But if it wants to be a party of transformation, AD will have to incorporate the thesis [into its program]. . . . Up until now it has given *cogestión* its blessing but the party has failed to promote actively the project in an enthusiastic, well defined, and clear manner; it backs *cogestión* only to the degree that the workers exert pressure.[19]

Copeyano trade unionists presented a proposal in favor of *cogestión* to the party's "Ideological Congress" in 1985 for discussion. They view *cogestión* as a step leading to the more advanced system of *autogestión* (workers' control). The *Copeyanos* deny that *autogestión* is a "utopian dream,"[20] but they fail to provide a blueprint for its achievement or to explain how labor will overcome company resistance, short of reliance on force. Some AD trade union leaders have rejected *autogestión* as unfeasible under capitalism and compatible only with communist totalitarianism.[21]

The PCV opposed *cogestión* when it was first proposed by *Copeyanos* at the CTV's Third Congress in 1959, and criticized the Leoni decree in 1966 on grounds that it would only create bureaucratic privileges without benefiting the workers. Only in the late 1980s did the CUTV reconsider its traditional stand in response to plans to implement worker ownership in the Soviet Union.[22] MAS, as well as other leftist parties, has supported *cogestión* and *autogestión* as contributions to a new socialist society based on diverse forms of property relations and decision making.[23]

Fedecámaras does not have an official position on *cogestión* but some of its spokesmen, particularly industrialists, have attacked it on grounds that neither businessmen nor workers in Venezuela are even remotely prepared for it. Following the CTV's Porlamar congress, in a simultaneous broadcast throughout the nation, the Chamber of Radio Diffusion, which groups radio station owners and is affiliated with Fedecámaras, characterized the system of *cogestión* as a violation of property rights. Other business leaders claim that implementation of *cogestión* in the private sector would violate the nation's legal code, which confers decision-making authority exclusively on owners. They add that *cogestión* should be restricted to state companies, particularly those that sell stock to their workers.[24]

CTV leaders have often stated that *cogestión* is a recent proposal dating back to the Porlamar Manifesto of 1980 and that the confederation is still preparing the nation, and workers in particular, for a plan that is in its experimental phase.[25] In fact, worker participation at certain levels of company decision making, such as on the board of directors, was first raised by the CTV in the early years of the democratic period. The CTV's 1980 congress was a milestone in that the confederation called for an integral process of worker input in managerial functions. Nevertheless, sufficient time has transpired since the 1960s for the CTV to have gone beyond *cogestión*'s incipient stage.

A wide gap has always existed between plans and rhetoric in favor of *cogestión* and concrete actions to achieve it. As stated above, labor leaders pledged themselves to gain congressional approval for a law of *cogestión* by 1990, but by that date the proposed legislation had not even been drafted. At the time of his election as president, Jaime Lusinchi committed his government to selecting a pilot company in the public sphere where *cogestión* would be put into practice. His five-year term came and went, however, without carrying through on his promise. Finally, the confederation has failed to establish a linkage between rank-and-file workers and their representative on the board of directors of state companies, or to utilize him as a spokesman for employee interests. Labor leaders sometimes belittle the importance of the 1966 decree on grounds that it provides merely token representation, without recognizing the enactment's potential to foster the creation of new mechanisms of participation.

José Vargas and Manuel Peñalver were instrumental in the selection of Maza Zavala to draft the Porlamar Manifesto. That neither of the two CTV leaders were known for steering the labor movement on a militant and independent course reinforces the impression that the confederation's embracing of *cogestión* was merely rhetorical. Maza Zavala himself subsequently expressed disillusionment regarding the CTV's failure to act on his far-reaching recommendations.[26]

With the economic crisis of the 1980s, labor leaders proposed that stocks in state companies that were being privatized be turned over to the labor movement and implied that this arrangement was tantamount to worker participation. Nevertheless, the CTV has never promoted *cogestión* in its numerous companies, nor has it used the BTV's extensive resources to encourage the bank's client firms to implement *cogestión* plans. These failures leave the impression that *cogestión* is a smoke screen that disguises the CTV's interest in expanding its business holdings. It is this economic empire, and the BTV in particular, to which I will now turn.

The Workers Bank

Political scientists who write on state control of organized labor point to policies of inducement and constraint that are designed to circumscribe trade union activities. The most important areas of government action that fulfill this function are proscription of strikes, passage of legislation, and subsidies.[27] Some writers on Venezuela have argued that financial rewards have played a more significant role than reliance on force, or the threat of it, in controlling civil society and guaranteeing stability.[28] This observation is clearly applicable to the realm of state-labor relations. Venezuela contrasts with other Latin American nations where government agencies and ministries closely monitor and intervene in such union affairs as internal elections and finances, and the state frequently utilizes brute force to repress strikes. In Venezuela, abundant resources have allowed the state to achieve labor peace by offering the labor movement generous economic support under the tacit condition that it eschew activity disruptive to the economy. Indeed, subsidies from the Labor Ministry pay for over half of the CTV's expenses.[29]

Even more significant than state budgetary allocations are the special privileges granted the Workers Bank (BTV), which allowed it to become the largest private financial institution in the nation by 1980. While BTV President Eleazar Pinto claimed that the BTV was the fifth largest bank of its kind anywhere, the muckraking magazine *Resumen* affirmed that the CTV had developed the largest financial empire of any labor movement in the world.[30] The CTV's concern over its financial interests has greatly influenced the confederation's behavior, specifically its relations with the government, throughout the period under study: first, with the passage of the law that created the BTV in 1966; later, in the 1970s, when the special treatment the bank received made possible its rapid expansion; and then, following the BTV's closing in 1982, when the CTV pressured the government to reopen the bank and to provide the labor movement a share of the ownership of firms that were slated for privatization.

The initial impetus for the creation of the BTV came from abroad.[31] The idea was proposed at the Conference of Labor Ministers on the Alliance for Progress organized by the Organization of American States in Bogotá, Colombia, in May 1963. This conference was attended by U.S. Secretary of Labor W. Willard Wirtz and the vice president of the AFL-CIO, Joseph Beirne. The proposal coincided with the strategy of the Alliance for Progress that, in accordance with U.S. liberal thinking, favored the strengthening of nonleftist trade unions.

The law creating the BTV was introduced in October 1965 in congress, where it received unanimous support. Even though Copei questioned the CTV's management of various enterprises controlled by the confederation's Corporación de Ahorro y Crédito para la Vivienda (Coracrevi), the party endorsed the BTV law. *Copeyano* congressmen pointed out that their original fears that the BTV would infringe upon personal liberty had been laid to rest since there was no provision in the law that authorized the forced deposit of a portion of worker salaries in the bank.[32] Only the parties of the clandestine Left attacked the law, arguing that it was designed to create the illusion that workers would be transformed into capitalists. They also maintained that the wages of Venezuelan workers were insufficient to enable them to participate in the bank either as depositors or stockholders.[33]

The BTV law accorded the bank a privileged status as a financial institution that was not envisioned in the original Alliance for Progress proposal and was unmatched by other Workers Banks. The Workers Bank of Puerto Rico, for instance, got off the ground with a ninety-nine-day interest-free state loan. The Venezuelan government, however, was much more generous: it purchased stock in the BTV without insisting on more than minimal representation on its board of directors or the right to receive dividends. In addition, the BTV was not subject to the same legal restrictions as other banks in the nation. The BTV was unique because it was both a commercial (lending) and mortgage institution. Furthermore, the BTV was allowed to grant mortgages of up to twenty-five years (rather than the twenty years stipulated by law) and up to 90 percent (as against 75 percent for other banks) of the property value of low-income housing.

The law's framers enumerated a list of objectives to justify the BTV's special status by demonstrating that, unlike all other private banks, it would not be run on the basis of the profit motive. Among these functions were encouragement of frugality and savings habits among the workers, assistance to small- and medium-sized businesses as well as workers' cooperatives, construction of low-income housing and recreational facilities for workers, providing credit for the purchase of merchandise to counter usurious practices, and offering loans to students and underprivileged individuals who were in special need of credit. In the Chamber of Deputies, CTV Secretary-General Malavé Villalba, who was the BTV's prime mover, pointed to these goals as proof that the Workers Bank was different from its counterparts in other nations, which had all the features of an ordinary bank. Malavé Villalba went on to deny that the BTV would compete with private banks in Venezuela since its concerns were not the same and its clients were generally refused loans elsewhere.[34]

Malavé Villalba's assertion, however, was not borne out by the bank's future policies. The BTV's dramatic growth and association with companies of all sizes both at home and abroad contradicted the claim that the bank functioned outside of the realm of conventional banking and that its special status was justified by its explicitly altruistic objectives. Another affirmation put forward by Malavé Villalba in the discussion over the BTV law in the Chamber of Deputies in 1966 was also subsequently questioned. Villalba denied that the BTV would utilize its resources to finance political campaigns. At the time of the intervention in 1982, *Copeyano* National Deputy Abdón Vivas Terán, among other non-AD political leaders, argued that the BTV had been converted into an electoral and political tool of AD, and thus lessened his party's chances of winning the upcoming presidential elections.[35]

The influx of oil revenue after 1973 and the policies pursued by Eleazar Pinto, who assumed the presidency of the BTV in 1977 following the death of its first president, Malavé Villalba, set in motion the bank's rapid growth. In 1974 government deposits, which by then accounted for the lion's share of the BTV's resources, increased by 238 percent over the previous year. During the 1970s the BTV modified its original lending practices. Under Malavé Villalba the bank had fulfilled one of its original objectives by authorizing a large number of personal loans to workers, which were paid back by automatic deductions from their salaries (a procedure to which businessmen sometimes objected due to the paperwork involved). From its first year of operation in 1968 until 1970, personal loans exceeded credit granted private companies. This pattern changed in 1970 when business loans increased more than twofold, a tendency that was accelerated under Pinto.[36] Benigno González of the CTV's Executive Committee noted:

> Under Malavé the BTV extended small loans without many requirements to *compañeros* to buy a small house or for a downpayment. What happened was that people began to solicit loans for the sake of getting one and least of all for a good use. The "social portfolio" of this type of loan produced losses. Then it was decided that the Bank deal with wealthy interests and what was earned from them would compensate for the losses from underprivileged sectors. This

was more or less the thinking of Malavé. When Eleazar Pinto [became president] perhaps his first change was to review this question and he said we cannot continue losing. He was very clear on this. [He said:] "Here we have to lend to people to make money." The portfolio of personal loans of ten- or fifteen-thousand bolívares for workers was practically eliminated. Then the bank grew into a monster.[37]

Another development initiated in the early 1970s and promoted under the presidency of Pinto was the BTV's association with companies in diverse sectors of the economy. This policy shifted the BTV's priority concern away from the construction industry, particularly low-income housing. CTV leaders justified the BTV's decision to invest in new areas on grounds that it was designed to generate job opportunities to help achieve "full employment" in the nation, a stated goal of the administration of Carlos Andrés Pérez. During the period that Pinto was president, the BTV created more than a score of companies and engaged in such disparate activities as navigation, laundry service, prefabricated housing, and production of cigarette lighters, alcoholic beverages, and automobile parts. Confident that the government would bail the Workers Bank out in case of economic difficulties, CTV leaders followed a policy of retaining direct control of profitable companies through Coracrevi, while transferring those facing losses to the BTV.

The BTV became linked to diverse centers of power. It developed close ties with foreign and native capital, including the interests of AD's Leopoldo Sucre Figarella and *Copeyano* José Curiel. Enrique Delfino, who was closely tied to the Pérez government, associated with the BTV in development projects at subway station sites in Caracas. Under the administration of Luis Herrera Campíns, the BTV collaborated with the government in carrying out official economic policy, and even on occasion lent money to the state at the same time that Pinto was periodically consulted by the minister of finance.

The questions that were raised both inside and outside the labor movement regarding the BTV did not lead to a reconsideration of policies and priorities. At the BTV's fourth stockholders' meeting in 1972, MEPistas Carlos Piñerua (president of Fedepetrol), Juan José Delpino, and others walked out to protest the failure to investigate allegations of irregularities. The MEPistas decided against going to the press since they lacked concrete proof to substantiate their charges.[38] Later, several important AD labor leaders objected to the sharp reduction of personal loans granted workers.[39]

A large number of labor organizations with BTV stock selected the AD-controlled Coracrevi as their proxy. Thus, MEP, which for several years held the presidency of the CTV and Fedepetrol—both of which owned substantial shares of stock—was overruled by AD. Subsequently, both MEP and Copei, which held positions on the board of directors of the BTV and its affiliate businesses, toned down earlier criticisms of the CTV's financial dealings. MEPista César Olarte pointed out that "none of us were bankers [so that] out of ignorance when Pinto said that to do business in the capitalist system you have to go where the money is, to us it seemed logical. We had critical positions with regard to a few projects in particular . . . but with regard to the bank's general objective of grow, grow, and grow, no one was critical—neither Copei, nor AD, nor us."[40]

The BTV's status of exceptionality embodied in the 1966 law proved to be an "original sin" in that ongoing practices that violated banking legislation—and even its own legal regulations—were justified on grounds that the BTV was no ordinary bank, and thus deserved special treatment. The BTV failed to require adequate collateral on some of its loans; indeed, many of the bank's client firms were presided over by Pinto himself. Further problems were created by the BTV's sudden international commitments as well as inordinate publicity expenses, bonus payments to top employers, and investments with long-term returns.[41]

In 1981 the BTV refused to furnish information solicited by the *Superintendencia de Bancos* (General Bank Administration) regarding the bank's affiliate companies. This noncompliance, as well as other irregularities, led the *Superintendencia* to call on the government to intervene in the bank, a recommendation that fell on deaf ears in the Finance Ministry at the time. Difficulties originating from the BTV's laxness, and aggravated by its overexpansion after 1980 when the economy began to contract, forced the bank to suspend payment to creditors for several days in November 1982. At this point the administration of Herrera Campíns took over the BTV and shut it down.

Two sets of considerations explain the government's decision to reverse its previous policy of cooperation with the BTV and intervene. The BTV's insolvency convinced some government officials (particularly Leopoldo Díaz Bruzual, the polemical president of the Central Bank) that the institution was beyond repair and should be permanently closed. Nevertheless, the fact that the administration made no use of its considerable leverage to force the bank to modify ill-advised policies at any earlier date suggests that other factors were also at play. The proximity of elections undoubtedly influenced President Herrera Campíns, who had always headed a *Copeyano* faction that was particularly hostile to AD, to take the action to deprive the party of an important source of financial support and, at the same time, tarnish its image.[42]

The CTV responded to the intervention by relieving its federations and unions of "internal discipline"—in effect, allowing them to go on strike without the previous authorization of the confederation's Executive Committee. Subsequently, CTV federations drew up seventy-six sets of *pliegos conflictivos* (prestrike demands) to present to the Labor Ministry, while several unions called work stoppages. Although CTV spokesman César Gil pointed out that these measures were designed to protest government economic policy in general, he made clear that the main issue at stake was the BTV. In contrast, MAS's President Pompeyo Márquez, in an attempt to legitimize the labor unrest, claimed that worker organizations were autonomous and that the conflicts stemmed from the demands put forward by individual unions and were unrelated to the BTV.[43]

The intervention was initially criticized by labor leaders of all political parties. Nevertheless, as the seriousness of the BTV's economic predicaments and the irregularities that had been committed surfaced, public opinion shifted and the major parties were subject to internal strains. AD leaders at first asserted that the BTV's insolvency had been induced by the government, which refused to negotiate the repayment of state bonds held by the bank. They also heaped praise on Eleazar Pinto. Subsequently, however, party spokesmen hinted that no one in the labor movement other than Pinto was responsible for the problems confronting the BTV.[44] Indeed, AD National Deputy Henry Ramos Allup pointed out in congress that the CTV did not have the "faculty to supervise the BTV."[45] CTVista Carlos Luna criticized his AD labor rivals for defending Pinto, while former AD presidential candidate Luis Piñerua Ordaz unsuccessfully called on the party's Disciplinary Tribunal to investigate the ethical conduct of the former BTV president.

Differences and inconsistencies were also apparent in Copei and the government. Finance Minister Luis Ugueto, who had denied that an intervention was forthcoming in conversations with Fedecámaras, resigned, partly as a result of displeasure at not having been consulted about the decision.[46] The CTV's secretary-general, *Copeyano* Rafael León León, at first defended Pinto but then backtracked and refused to support the CTV's threatened worker mobilizations in opposition to the intervention. The *Copeyanos* were particularly resentful that the only CTVistas who were authorized to endorse BTV checks that were made out for nearly 1 billion bolívares at the moment of the intervention were the confederation's president and treasurer, both AD members. This demonstration that the secretary-generalship had been divested of real power influenced Copei to relinquish the position several years later.[47]

Spokesmen for leftist parties initially ascribed the intervention mainly to political motives, while claiming that they lacked sufficient information to judge whether the BTV had been mismanaged. Nevertheless, they affirmed that other banks, especially those of the state, were in worse financial shape due to irregular practices. They claimed that pressure from private financial institutions, which had always objected to the BTV's special privileges, also influenced the decision to intervene, thereby coinciding with an article in the *New York Times* that discussed the opposition of the banking community to the BTV.[48]

Following revelations about shady activities and the handsome remunerations that labor representatives on the bank had received, pressure mounted in MEP to condemn the bank's mismanagement and investigate the behavior of those party members who held positions in CTV financial operations. One casualty was veteran trade unionist Máximo Acuña, who represented MEP on the CTV's Executive Committee. Accusations against Acuña for having failed to share with the party income derived from the bank and from an affiliate company (of which he was president)—as stipulated in MEP's statutes—led to his permanent retirement from the labor movement.[49]

Some *Copeyano* government officials recommended elimination of the BTV's special privileges, particularly its dual status as a commercial and mortgage bank. CTV President José Vargas staunchly opposed any change in the BTV's functions, although he did accept reducing the bank's size, as did Delpino and Ríos after him.[50] Some observers pointed to the failure of the administration of Jaime Lusinchi to reopen the BTV—his campaign pledge to do so notwithstanding—as proof that the bank had been run into the ground.[51] Nevertheless, a second explanation is the friction that developed between his government and the CTV leadership, which refused to back Lusinchi's choice for AD's presidential nomination in the 1988 elections.

Carlos Andrés Pérez, whom a majority of CTV leaders decisively supported for the nomination, did make good on his promise to reopen the bank in February 1990. CTV leaders boasted that the BTV, with the help of the government, had repaid its entire foreign debt (amounting to 250 million bolívares) and was well on its way to canceling its remaining obligations—a first in the history of bank interventions.[52] Eleazar Pinto, who had received a two-year jail sentence for "aggravated fraud" in a case involving BTV credits, hailed the BTV's reopening as proof that the bank had been the "most solid in the country," despite what its enemies who were bent on destroying it thought.[53]

The BTV was reopened with only seven branches in Caracas and four other cities. Nevertheless, the 1966 law governing the BTV remained intact and the bank had no restrictions on the location and number of new offices. Similar to arrangements in effect prior to 1982, the government held 42 percent of the BTV's stock but received only six of the thirty-nine seats on the board of directors. AD again had majority control of the board, while MEP and Copei were given one seat each. Non-AD trade unionists supported the bank's reopening but favored a more definite commitment to avoid big operations and concentrate on the bank's social functions. Some of them proposed that the BTV deal only with employee deposits, such as company savings plans (*Caja de Ahorro*), pension funds, and *prestaciones sociales*. Benigno González expressed the opinion of other *Copeyano* trade unionists as well as those of the Left:

Everything [with regard to the BTV] is the same. The law is the same. What has changed is the intention to modify the bank's dimension and not continue on the same path—that is, to convert the BTV into the first bank of Latin America and the world. . . . In this sense the Executive Committee [of the CTV] is more vigilant [than before]. . . . But everything depends on the good intentions and honesty of the people who are designated.[54]

Investments in Other Sectors

Following the BTV's closing in 1982, the CTV's continued interest in financial ventures has been demonstrated by its plans to buy privatized companies, particularly hotels and sugar mills owned by the Venezuelan Development Corporation (CVF). The *Ley de Enajenación de Bienes* gives organized labor the first option in the purchase of public enterprises that are transferred to the private sector. The CTV has associated with the Spanish firm Sol Melia in the proposed acquisition of the Melia Hotels of Puerto La Cruz and Caraballeda (near Caracas) and the Hilton of Barquisimeto—which, if approved, will be the first important privatization of Pérez's second administration. The CTV claims that it intends to promote "social tourism" by renting out entire floors of the hotels to labor organizations during off-season at a substantial discount.

The deal, however, has been questioned on several grounds. First, the hotels have five-star ratings. Thus, even at discounts of 60 or 70 percent, their rooms are far out of the reach of the ordinary worker. CTV capital, it is argued, would be better employed in the renovation of nonluxury resort centers such as the famous, but run-down, "Los Caracas" (which, indeed, the CTV is also interested in administering). Second, the CTV has been criticized for failing to go beyond traditional decision-making arrangements at the executive level and, more specifically, to formulate an explicit plan of *cogestión*. Organized labor is to finance 40 percent of the purchase; of this amount, two thirds corresponds to the CTV and only one third to the federation of hotel workers. Most of organized labor's 40 percent is to be lent by Sol Melia. Thus, not only are the workers left out of the scheme, but also the CTV, which is lacking in both capital and technical capacity in the area of hotel management, is acting as a mere intermediary rather than as an active participant.

Copeyano politicians attack the sale as contrary to national interests. They maintain that a North American firm would be in a better position to promote tourism since a large majority of the tourists who travel to Venezuela are from the United States and Canada. Furthermore, other investors, such as the Holiday Inn, the Hilton (in the case of Barquisimeto), and local businessmen (in the case of Puerto La Cruz) are also interested in buying and allegedly offer the state more favorable terms. Copei argues that privatization is being discredited by a "labor aristocracy" that includes CTV congressmen who, by defending the transaction in congress, are guilty of conflict of interest.[55] As of early 1991, executives of Sol Melia who administer Venezuela's Melia hotels indicated in private that they were reconsidering the deal since it had been overly politicized.[56]

In addition to the CTV's financial interests, various affiliate federations have substantial investments, particularly Fedepetrol and the FCV. Fedepetrol, a pioneer in trade union financial activity, created the Corporación de Ahorro y Crédito Fedepetrol (Cacref) as far back as its Third Congress in May 1962 to manage the oil workers' savings plan. Cacref became closely linked to the BTV and, as a result, its activities were nearly paralyzed after November 1982. Fedepetrol's president, Carlos Piñerua, in his unsuccessful bid for reelection in 1985, was accused of being responsible for Cacref's mismanagement. His successor, Raúl Henríquez, pledged himself to creating a professional staff not directly linked to Fedepetrol to manage Cacref and its offshoot companies.

In 1965 the FCV created Suministros Campesinos C.A. (Sucam) for the purpose of importing agricultural machinery to exert a downward pressure on market prices. Sucam was granted credit facilities from large foreign industrial firms as well as the Export-Import Bank. Subsequently, the FCV founded a host of other enterprises, including Mercados Campesinos (Mercam), which established two marketplaces in Valencia and Caracas. These companies were responsible for making regular and emergency financial contributions to the FCV.[57]

Armando González, who was FCV president for nearly twenty-five years, viewed their activities as part of the Agrarian Reforms' stage of "consolidation": "The peasants for the most part now have land but there is a series of shortcomings and deficiencies in their resources; these [FCV] companies are designed to provide the peasantry services so that they do not have to depend on the services of capitalists, which are often beyond the limit of their [economic] possibilities."[58] Just as the CTV claimed that a paramount objective of the BTV was to promote *cogestión,* the peasant movement invoked the model of *cogestión* and *autogestión* to justify its interest in the creation of nonprofit commercial outfits.

The FCV enterprises, like those of other federations, faced pressing economic difficulties as a result of the closing of the BTV in 1982 and the contraction of the economy. They were heavily indebted and, as a consequence, several were forced out of business. González's bid for reelection as president of the FCV was thwarted in 1985 partly as a consequence of accusations of corruption against him. MAS peasant leader Rafael Elino Martínez noted that Sucam and other FCV operations were managed by a small clique that was loyal exclusively to González. He added, "As far as I can remember, the FCV has never been called upon to design the policies of these companies. . . . I am a vice-president of the FCV and if you ask me what the capital of Sucam is I would have to say I do not know." Martínez called on AD to monitor the FCV enterprises since they are managed in such secrecy that not even the party's Agrarian Bureau is privy to information on their financial state.[59]

Small Property Holders in CTV Unions

The FCV and Fedetransporte, which takes in public transportation drivers, represent mostly small property holders; thus, their concerns diverge in fundamental ways from the rest of organized labor. The FCV pressures for public credit facilities and the development of rural infrastructure, as does any business organization. In fact, the FCV competes with larger agricultural interests, much as small business competes with big business. Fedetransporte, for its part, lobbies in favor of transportation fare increases. Nevertheless, both the FCV and Fedetransporte take up worker issues as well. The FCV calls on the government to grant agricultural workers the full benefits of labor legislation and of the social security system (and criticizes the new Labor Law for failing to do so). Fedetransporte also demands complete social security coverage for its members.

The role of both federations is complicated by the diversity of their members. FCV peasants are, to widely varying degrees, both small landholders and agricultural workers (on nearby haciendas) at the same time. Some Fedetransporte members—many of whom occupy leadership positions in the union—own several vehicles and, thus, have the status of both employer and self-employed. In recent years, Fedetransporte has come under considerable criticism for its support of fare hikes that on numerous occasions triggered disturbances, including those of the week of February 27, 1989. In the controversies that pitted Fedetransporte against popular organizations and political parties, the CTV consistently maintained a discrete silence. Indeed, the confederation found itself in an uncomfortable position due to the attacks against an affiliate union, which was sometimes referred to in popular vernacular as a "*mafia*" due to its exclusionary character.

Although the CTV has never considered the disaffiliation of Fedetransporte, the federation does not fit the definition of a workers' organization as defined by Articles 4 and 5 of the Labor Law and, thus, has little justification for belonging to a labor confederation. Similarly, the FCV's membership in the CTV has never been questioned, even though in most other Latin American nations the peasant movement is organically independent of the workers' movement. The exceptionalism of the Venezuelan case may be explained by the fact that the FCV's historical leaders originally belonged to trade union organizations. Armando González employed a class analysis to justify the FCV's affiliation with the CTV:

> We are struggling in order to convert the peasant into an autonomous producer but without the avariciousness that the so-called capitalist businessman has in that the fundamental element in the relations of production [in his company] is exploitation. We feel that the autonomous agriculturalist should produce to obtain a satisfactory living standard but allow the prices of their products to be accessible for the urban population, and in this we coincide perfectly with the objectives of the CTV.[60]

Cogestión, the BTV, and CTV Autonomy

The CTV's financial blunders have impaired the confederation's reputation and discredited its goals. Political commentators, for instance, noted in 1982 that the closing of the BTV called into question the feasibility of *cogestión* by demonstrating the inadequacy of organized labor's managerial capacity.[61] Investments also have tarnished the image of such important veteran labor leaders as José Vargas, Juan Herrera, Antonio Ríos, Carlos Piñerua, and Armando González—resulting in the electoral defeat of the latter two in their respective federations—and have led to the jailing of Eleazar Pinto.

Margarita López, in *El Banco de los Trabajadores: algo más que un banco?*, and other scholars have concurred with José Vargas's statement at the CTV's 1980 congress that the BTV provided the labor movement "financial autonomy" vis-à-vis political parties and the state. She adds that this independence allowed the CTV to become the Herrera government's "most dynamic adversary" and to put forward far-reaching "socioeconomic alternatives to face the economic crisis" in 1980.[62] Economic autonomy, which was not incorporated into the bank's formal objectives in the 1966 law, was of prime importance to CTV leaders who always felt uncomfortable with other sources of income, such as government subsidies and the practice of *costa contractual*.[63]

Nevertheless, the BTV, if anything, increased the confederation's dependence on the government since its success as a financial institution was contingent upon state support. Had the BTV followed an explicit strategy of fortifying the labor movement by providing resources to facilitate labor objectives, the bank would have undoubtedly promoted trade union autonomy in the long run. This, however, was not the case. Some commentators have noted with surprise that the affiliate organizations of such a wealthy confederation as the CTV did not have strike funds.[64] Even the construction of the CTV headquarters, which was first agreed upon at the CTV's 1970 congress, was financed by the state rather than by the BTV and, consequently, took over fifteen years to complete. Finally, notwithstanding Vargas's statement at the Eighth Congress, government aid to the CTV and its constituent federations was not reduced after 1980.

The objections of business leaders to the BTV and the 1966 decree on labor representation went beyond the specific fears that the BTV, with its special privileges, would be able to outcompete private banks and that worker representatives on boards of trustees would press for unfair demands. In addition to these concerns, business leaders were wary that the labor movement—perhaps at a future date under a different leadership—would parlay these institutional gains into greater bargaining power and far-reaching changes that threatened company interests. The BTV's enormous resources, for instance, could have helped finance union organizing drives while the 1966 decree could have provided a stimulus to establish a system of employee elections and other mechanisms of rank-and-file input in decision making. In short, both the BTV and the 1966 decree were potentially powerful instruments for increasing labor's influence and facilitating more direct forms of worker participation and articulation of demands at all levels.

Notes

1. *Diario de Debates* (Chamber of Deputies), April 18, 1966, pp. 534–35.

2. José González Navarro, *Sindicalismo, libertad y desarrollo* [speech, October 3, 1972] (Caracas: Asociación Venezolana de Ejecutivos), pp. 15–16; Rafael Castañeda, "Participación activa en la toma de decisiones . . . ," in *20 años de la ley de representación laboral: ahora la cogestión!* (Caracas: Departamento de Cogestión-CTV, 1986), p. 17.

3. D. F. Maza Zavala, *Venezuela: Historia de una frustración* (Caracas: UCV, 1986), pp. 458–60.

4. Maria Bernardoni de Govea and Carmen Zuleta de Merchán, *Análisis sobre la cogestión y otras formas de participación obrera: Caso Venezuela* (Maracaibo: Universidad de Zulia, 1985).

5. *Convenio de cogestión laboral de Tornillos Venezolanos, S.A.I.C.A.* (1988); "Con la crisis llega la congestión [sic]," *Número* 329 (November 30, 1986): 11.

6. Iturraspe, interview, March 31, 1990, Valencia.

7. Federico Ramírez León, interview, March 10, 1990, Puerta La Cruz.

8. Pedro Castro [CTV adviser], interview, August 24, 1989, Caracas.

9. Castañeda, interview, December 11, 1986, Caracas; Héctor Lucena, "Contratación colectiva y participación en la empresa pública," *Revista Relaciones de Trabajo* 2 (1983): 47–48.

10. Johnny Díaz Apitz, interview, August 16, 1990, Caracas; Benigno González [CTV Executive Committee, Copei member], interview, August 20, 1990, Caracas.

11. See, for instance, Linda Fuller, "The State and the Unions in Cuba since 1959," in *Labor Autonomy and the State in Latin America*, ed. Edward C. Epstein (Boston: Unwin Hyman, 1989), p. 162.

12. Castañeda, interview, August 30, 1989, Caracas.

13. *Antecedentes y testimonios de los congresos de la CTV* 2:58.

14. Héctor Lucena, "Sindicatos e introducción de tecnología," *Revista Relaciones de Trabajo* 8 (1986): 394–420.

15. E. Córdova, "Workers' Participation in Decisions within Enterprises: Recent Trends and Problems," *International Labour Review* 121, no. 2 (March-April 1982): 130.

16. *Antecedentes y testimonios de los congresos* 4:247.

17. Interview, Nelson León [general coordinator of Department of *Cogestión*, CTV], August 31, 1989, Caracas. The most celebrated case of a spontaneous workers' takeover in recent times occurred in the Lip watch factory in Besancon, France, in 1973. While the Communist party spurned workers' management per se, Socialist trade union leaders warned that the model could not be achieved on a piecemeal basis and had to await legislation that would establish the system on a national scale.

18. CTV, "Intervención del Doctor Marco Tulio Bruni Celli," *Participación de los trabajadores en la dirección de la empresa* (Caracas: CTV-Ildis, 1979), pp. 112–25; Marco Tulio Bruni Celli, "Pluralismo ideológico y cogestión obrera," *Nueva Sociedad* 170 (January-February 1984): 72–81.

19. Castañeda, interview, August 30, 1989, Caracas.

20. Rito José Alvarez, *Autogestión: fórmula de progreso para los trabajadores* [pamphlet] (Caracas, Concejo Municipal del Distrito Federal, 1982), p. 11.

21. *El Nacional* [interview with Manuel Peñalver], June 1, 1980, p. C-1; Comisión de Enlace C.T.V.-ILDIS, "Lineamientos para un proyecto global de participación de los trabajadores . . ." [mimeographed], Caracas, July 1980, p. 5.

22. Hemmy Croes, "Informe de la comisión organizadora" [mimeographed], (n.d.), p. 12.

23. Ellner, *Venezuela's Movimiento al Socialismo*, pp. 75–78.

24. Bernardoni and Zuleta, *Análisis sobre la cogestión*, p. 99; Antonia Méndez de Guerra and Omaira Bello Parra, "Evolución de la contratación colectiva en Venezuela durante el quinquenio 1975–1980" (B.A. Thesis, Universidad Católica, Caracas, 1982), p. 61.

25. *Diario de Caracas*, January 6, 1987, p. 16.

26. Ibid.

27. David and Ruth Collier are most closely associated with this viewpoint regarding state-labor relations in Latin America. They favor a functional approach to state control on grounds that structural relations—which other writers of the "corporatist school" focus on—may be similar in two nations while producing widely different results. See their "Who Does What, to Whom, and How: Toward a Comparative Analysis of Latin American Corporatism," in *Authoritarianism and Corporatism in Latin America*, ed. James M. Malloy (Pittsburgh: University of Pittsburgh Press, 1977), p. 496.

28. Naim and Piñango, "El caso Venezuela," pp. 538–79; Juan Carlos Rey, "Perspectivas de la democracia" [mimeographed] (Escuela de Estudios Políticos, UCV, 1982), pp. 8–10.

29. In 1982, Codesa received 800,000 bolívares; the CUTV, 400,000; and the CGT, 100,000 from the national government. In 1985, the CTV was assigned 3,240,000 bolívares. See *Número* 329 (November 30, 1986): 15; *Diario de Caracas*, April 30, 1983, p. 14.

30. "CTV: un imperio económico de Bs. 450 millones," *Resumen* 361 (October 5, 1980): 19.

31. Leoni, as labor minister during the *trienio*, proposed the creation of a Workers Bank. See *El País*, August 28, 1946, p. 4; and Margarita López Maya, *El banco de los trabajadores de Venezuela: algo más que un banco?* (Caracas: UCV,

1989), pp. 25, 31. This book is a thorough, well-documented study of the BTV from its founding until 1985.

32. *Diario de Debates* (Chamber of Deputies), March 28, 1966, p. 369.

33. *Que Pasa en Venezuela* [leftist newspaper], May 23, 1964, p. 12.

34. *Diario de Debates* (Chamber of Deputies), March 23, 1966, p. 373.

35. *El Nacional,* December 13, 1982, p. C-1; César Olarte, interview, March 28, 1990, Caracas.

36. López Maya, *El banco de los trabajadores*, pp. 45, 49.

37. Benigno González, interview, August 20, 1990, Caracas.

38. Jesús Márquez [Executive Committee of Fedepetrol beginning in 1969], interview, October 11, 1990.

39. Carlos Luna, interview, January 30, 1987, Caracas; José Montilla, interview, June 6, 1990, Barcelona.

40. Olarte, interview, February 3, 1987, Caracas.

41. Héctor Lucena, "Experiencias de participación de los trabajadores en la gestión de las empresas en Venezuela," in *Participación, cogestión y autogestión en América Latina,* ed. Francisco Iturraspe, 2 vols. (Caracas: Editorial Nueva Sociedad, 1986), 2:234–35.

42. López Maya argues cogently that both of these factors influenced Herrera in his decision to intervene. See *El banco de los trabajadores*, pp. 87–101.

43. *El Nacional,* December 15, 1982, p. D-1.

44. *El Universal,* December 13, 1982, p. 2-1.

45. López Maya, *El banco de los trabajadores*, p. 121.

46. *El Naconal,* December 7, 1982, p. D-9.

47. Johnny Díaz Apitz, interview, August 16, 1990, Caracas; "Editorial," *Resumen* 481 (January 23, 1983): 2–6.

48. *El Nacional,* December 9, 1982, p. D-10; *New York Times,* December 16, 1982, p. IV-6.

49. "No juego a la división del MEP," *Resumen* 487 (March 6, 1983): 10–13.

50. *Número* 400 (May 8, 1988): 7; *Número* 466 (August 27, 1989): 15.

51. López Maya, "El caso de la intervención del BTV: un análisis sociopolítico" [mimeographed] (Cendes, May 1986), p. 93.

52. Antonio Ríos (Speech delivered at the Casa Sindical in Barcelona, March 10, 1990).

53. *El Nacional,* February 17, 1990, p. D-4.

54. Benigno González, interview, August 20, 1990, Caracas.

55. *El Nacional,* October 3, 1989, p. D-7.

56. Carlos Lares Cordero [former president of Hotel Melia, Puerto La Cruz], interview, December 9, 1990, Puerto La Cruz.

57. Oscar David Soto, *La empresa y la reforma agraria en la agricultura venezolana* (Mérida: FCV, 1973), p. 142.

58. Armando González, interview, January 29, 1987, Caracas.

59. Rafael Elino Martínez, interview, July 1, 1989, Barcelona.

60. Armando González, interview, January 29, 1987, Caracas.

61. *El Nacional,* December 7, 1982, p. D-9.

62. Maya López, *El banco de los trabajadores*, pp. 142–44; idem, "El caso de la intervención," pp. 41–42; McCoy, "Democratic Stability and Regime Change," p. 41.

63. Boeckh, "Organized Labor and Government," p. 202.

64. Ibid., p. 242; *Resumen* 361 (October 5, 1980): 10. Following the nationalization of iron, which produced sharp worker conflicts in 1975, Fetrametal

attempted to establish a strike fund, but quickly discarded the idea. The CTV's decision at its 1980 congress to create a strike fund based on 5 percent of the income of affiliate organizations was never implemented.

9 Labor Legislation and the Workers' Movement

One of the planks in the Common Program that supplemented the Pact of Punto Fijo signed by AD, Copei, and URD in 1958 was the promulgation of a new Labor Law to replace that of 1936. In succeeding decades, labor leaders and lawyers occasionally pointed out that a mere modification ("*Reforma*") of the existing Labor Law was insufficient due to the need to spread to more underprivileged sectors the numerous contractual benefits that relatively well-paid workers had achieved over the years.[1] Rafael Caldera introduced an *Anteproyecto* (original draft) in congress in 1985 and, after more than five years of thorough discussion in committees, the document of 666 articles was ready for ratification. That after twenty-five years the law was finally drawn up and sponsored by a leading politician and not labor leaders is a sterling example of the dependence of the labor movement on political parties, which is often translated into lack of initiative and inaction.

This chapter will examine proposed clauses and practices that have stood out as the most controversial in the nation's labor legislation: the legalization of nationwide labor unions; union participation in the hiring of workers (the *cláusula sindical*); employer severance obligations designed to discourage layoffs; and the elimination of distinctions among white-collar workers, blue-collar workers, and public employees. These propositions not only have pitted labor against management but also have produced differences and strains within the labor movement. The final subsection will deal with the *Proyecto Caldera*. Needless to say, such a discussion is in order due to the profound influence that the proposed law—effective May 1991—will have on labor-management relations. The political circumstances surrounding the national debate over the *Proyecto* also merit some commentary. Its major provisions have set off a sharp struggle between organized labor and political parties, on the one hand, and Fedecámaras and (to a certain degree) the administration of Carlos Andrés Pérez, on the other—a polarization process unique in modern Venezuelan history.

The Formation of National Unions

Two salient features of organized labor in Latin America are its fragmentation and decentralized structure, partly the result of legislation that either discourages or prohibits the creation of national unions. Military regimes have often attempted to weaken the labor movement by dismantling national unions, as occurred in Argentina after the overthrow of Perón in 1955. Historically, leftists were in the forefront of the effort to establish national unions (as were their counterparts in the United States and Europe); reformist governments, such as that of Lázaro Cárdenas in Mexico, also promoted them. Following World War II the conservative progovernment Confederación de Trabajadores de México (CTM) ceased to push for national unions out of fear that some of them would fall into the hands of Communists.[2]

In contrast to this historical pattern, opinions on national unions in Venezuela have largely cut across the left-center spectrum and obey nonideological considerations. At its Third Congress the CTV called for the creation of nationwide industrial unions and since its 1980 congress has increasingly emphasized that goal. The government has interpreted Article 180 of the 1936 Labor Law, which establishes procedures to register unions in statewide Labor Inspectorates rather than the national office of the Labor Ministry, as prohibiting national unions. Nevertheless, several labor experts have pointed out that the law does not explicitly rule out the possibility of forming national unions and have criticized the CTV for failing to question aggressively the government's position on the matter.[3]

CTV leaders argue that national unions are a necessary response to the centralization of the economy in which large companies have displaced small ones. The currently existing national federations lack sufficient strength to confront these modern corporations. Not only have the federations been unable to eliminate parallel unionism within their fold, but also they do not always receive their share of worker dues that are passed on by affiliate unions.[4] Furthermore, trade unionists point out that labor goals such as *cogestión* and union hiring of workers are virtually inoperative in some industries as a result of the fragmentation of organized labor. A hodgepodge of unions, many of which compete with one another, cannot easily reach agreements on the selection of new workers and labor representatives to serve on company boards of trustees. Finally, CTV President Delpino occasionally stated that centralization is a corrective to corrupt practices at the local level, which are currently beyond the control of national union authorities.[5]

Some labor leaders attribute the existing union structure to the practice of certain political parties of setting up parallel unions rather than ordering their worker followers to join majority unions. The government is also blamed for failing to use its influence to encourage unions in the state sector to merge. One member of the CTV's Executive Committee criticized the nation's three airlines—all of which had substantial state capital—for signing individual contracts and for negotiating separately with sectors such as pilots, mechanics, airline stewards, and clerks.[6] Another CTVista referred to the state-run metallurgical companies of Guayana and stated, "It is inexplicable that at this point the democratic state still sponsors separate discussions for these contracts."[7]

Delpino and other CTV leaders have recognized in private that the greatest resistance to national unions does not come from Copei, which favors statewide unions (see Chapter 5), or the government, but rather from local trade union officers who will end up losing out socially, politically, and economically under the new system.[8] The 1936 Labor Law grants seven members of the executive committees of each union *fueros*, thereby protecting them from layoffs without just cause (*inamovilidad*) and allowing them to attend to union matters on company time. As national labor leaders sometimes admit, the *fueros* have been widely abused; some trade unionists view them as a veritable paid leave of absence.

The new Labor Law increases the number of *fueros* to nine for unions with between five hundred and one thousand workers and to twelve for those with over one thousand members. Nevertheless, the new structure, which transforms national federations (with their scores of affiliate unions) into national unions, will reduce the number of *fueros*: twelve at the national level plus five for each state. The new law fails to incorporate the resolution passed at the CTV's 1985 congress, which called for the maintenance of seven *fueros* for each union local.[9]

Many local labor leaders stand to lose in other ways as well. Collective bargaining is a lucrative business for many worker representatives who receive money under the system of *costa contractual*, which either goes to their union's coffers or their own pockets. The creation of national unions will centralize the process and eliminate the large number of contracts signed individually with small companies. In addition, national unions will rationalize representation at conventions. Under the current system, small unions are overrepresented since, regardless of their size, they send the same number of *delegados natos* to conventions. Labor leaders are thus encouraged to form separate unions to provide increased voter strength for their party in their respective federations.

The issues of pluralism and internal democracy were raised in the debate over national unions. Originally, the CTV coined the phrase "One Union Per Industry" (*sindicato único por rama de industria*) but later dropped it after being accused of opposing the right of workers to constitute new labor organizations. During the congressional hearings over the new Labor Law, the CTV defended the first draft of the *Proyecto Caldera*, which increased the minimum number of workers needed to form plant, professional, and industrial unions from 20, 40, and 40, respectively, to 50, 500, and 500.[10] The three smaller confederations accused the CTV of trying to eliminate their organizations, which were in some cases unable to meet these requirements. Congress took into consideration this objection and, in a new draft, scaled down the numbers to 50, 300, and 300, respectively. The final version of the new law restored the original figures set by the 1936 law for company and professional unions.

MEP, MAS, and other parties in the CTV support national unions under the proviso that they guarantee worker participation and avoid a vertical line of command that delegates excessive power to a small group of national leaders. Their ideas, as well as those of Copei, were incorporated into a plan that was worked out in a special CTV commission and brought to the confederation's 1985 congress. According to this arrangement, national unions were required to hold worker assemblies throughout the country that would have formal decision-making authority. It was also proposed that a fixed percentage of worker dues be automatically assigned to union locals to avoid the withholding of funds from rebellious local leaderships. Also, sectors in each union, such as women workers and young workers, would elect their own secretariats at the national level. The AD majority at the congress, however, refused to endorse the proposal on grounds that worker assemblies would be easily manipulated by outside actors. Subsequently, AD's César Gil presented an alternative plan that centralized decision making and finances.[11]

In the 1970s and 1980s there were various important organizational fusions in the labor movement, particularly in the industrial states of Carabobo and Bolívar (Guayana). For a decade, Fetrametal attempted to promote the unification of various unions representing white- and blue-collar workers in the iron industry and finally succeeded at the time of nationalization in 1975. Furthermore, a myriad of unions in the private sector of the metallurgical industry in Guayana amalgamated to form Sutrametal.[12] Nevertheless, Table 5 demonstrates that the ratio of workers per union (excluding agricultural ones) was not only small, but also did not vary greatly throughout the 1980s, ranging from 57.0 in 1980 to 67.4 in 1987.

Table 5. Types of Unions Legalized and Worker Membership, 1980–1989

Year	Plant Unions	Professional Unions	Agricultural Unions	Industrial Unions
1980	88 (3,932)	57 (4,339)	29 (1,320)	—
1981	103 (4,789)	131 (10,541)	189 (9,636)	—
1982	79 (3,868)	114 (7,163)	65 (3,317)	—

1983	60	52	10	—
	(3,400)	(3,397)	(473)	
1984	68	42	52	7
	(3,501)	(3,181)	(2,800)	(738)
1985	71	56	157	9
	(3,193)	(4,509)	(8,660)	(561)
1986	67	67	59	10
	(3,190)	(4,476)	(3,358)	(781)
1987	79	69	66	15
	(4,229)	(5,506)	(3,465)	(1,252)
1988	98	88	76	*
	*	*		
1989	108	96	93	12
	*	*	*	*

Note: Worker membership is given in parentheses.
Source: Labor Ministry, *Memoria y Cuenta, 1980–1989*.
*Statistics are not available.

It should be noted that these statistics are deceptive in that some "professional unions" (such as the rubber workers' union of Carabobo) take in more than workers of the same profession and are really industrial unions in disguise. The fact that the Labor Law Regulation of 1973 legalized industrial unions but the Labor Ministry did not begin to register them formally until 1984 is telling; local labor leaders have not exerted pressure in favor of organizations under the official denomination "industrial unions," whose formation is a major CTV objective. Their failure to distinguish clearly between professional and industrial unions is just one more indication that they have not made a concerted effort to make the goal of trade union unification a reality.

The proliferation of small unions in Venezuela, as elsewhere in Latin America, has impeded the signing of nationwide contracts; only in Argentina, where Peronism created strong national unions, did they become prevalent.[13] Writers for the International Labor Organization (ILO) have pointed out that the success of industrywide contracts is contingent on the centralization of organized labor, an observation many Venezuelan labor leaders agree with.[14] Decree 440 (see Chapter 1) facilitates industrywide contracts at the state and national level. Although both leftist and nonleftist trade unionists have been critical of the decree for infringing on the right to strike, it is usually invoked by labor and not management.[15]

Where organized labor is powerful, such as in the oil industry, there is no need to rely on Decree 440. Table 6 shows that there has been an uneven increase in the average number of workers covered by labor contracts since the 1960s, and that the number of times Decree 440 was employed sharply rose after 1965. Although the application of Decree 440 is usually regional in scope, the contracts reached under this arrangement covered, on average, as many as 3,029 workers in 1986, 1987, and 1989, the years for which reliable statistics are available. These trends are encouraging for the CTV. Nevertheless, as Table 6 indicates, the confederation is still a long way off from achieving its goal of centralization of collective bargaining.

Table 6. Labor Contracts and Workers Covered in Venezuela, 1958–1989

Years	Contracts	Workers Covered	Average Number of Workers per Contract	Contracts under Decree 440
1958	1,016	168,883	116	3
1959	688	96,245	140	4
1960	680	98,529	145	3
1961	684	73,127	107	2
1962	642	62,509	97	6
1963	783	146,621	187	5
1964	884	102,053	115	2
1965	1,004	83,565	83	5
1966	1,066	163,474	153	15
1967	1,051	80,446	77	19
1968	1,062	202,305	190	15
1969	1,140	164,010	144	11
1970	1,422	178,207	125	13
1971	1,445	263,133	182	24
1972	1,292	98,326	76	15
1973	1,401	283,175	202	12
1974	1,171	151,812	130	15
1975	1,446	298,790	207	12
1976	1,754	333,653	190	11
1977	1,742	319,694	184	23
1978	1,681	531,187	316	15
1979	1,411	166,944	118	10
1980	1,498	391,957	262	13
1981	1,469	476,459	324	12
1982	1,329	140,943	106	11
1983	1,237	249,659	202	6
1984	1,071	268,430	251	7
1985	1,564	398,512	255	16
1986	1,427	197,361	138	21
1987	1,669	474,930	285	21

| 1988 | 1,819 | 598,156 | 329 | 14 |
| 1989 | 1,228 | 158,391 | 129 | 16 |

Source: Labor Ministry, *Memoria y Cuenta, 1958–1989*.

Mandatory Clauses on Hiring, Firing, and Payment of Union Dues

Union input in the selection of personnel (known as the *cláusula sindical*) is widespread in Venezuela and dates back to the 1940s. In 1958, Malavé Villalba called for an amendment to the Labor Law to institutionalize the *cláusula sindical* on a nationwide scale.[16] Nevertheless, labor leaders dropped this demand after the 1961 constitution (Article 90) explicitly recognized the practice without making it obligatory. The article, which also had been included in the constitution of 1947, was designed to prevent the Supreme Court from declaring the *cláusula sindical* unconstitutional.

The *cláusula sindical* takes on diverse forms. In the petroleum industry the union hires 80 percent of the employees of contractor firms, but not those on Pdvsa's payroll. Fetrametal negotiators have included in proposed contracts a clause that obliges companies to accept a union representative as a permanent employee in the Department of Industrial Relations, "with sufficient ranking to participate in decisions related to policies on subcontracting, salary increases, promotions, [and] hiring."[17] Management's acceptance of the *cláusula sindical* is usually an indication of the union's relative strength vis-à-vis the company. Thus, for instance, textile worker organizations have succeeded in including provisions regarding union hiring of between 75 to 80 percent of all employees in contracts with textile firms. Nevertheless, the same unions have been unable to gain acceptance for such an arrangement in the apparel industry, which has a stronger hold over its workers.

Latin American leftist labor leaders have been wary of union control over hiring and firing, fearing that it could result in reprisals against their own militants, but have generally not opposed the practice per se. In Venezuela, marginal leftist groups such as the Causa R objected that AD, Copei, and MEP, which held exclusive control of Fedepetrol's national leadership throughout the 1970s and 1980s, discriminated against other parties in the hiring of workers. The success of MAS in obtaining a seat on the federation's Executive Committee in 1990, with the backing of the Causa R and other leftist groups, was more significant than the one vote that it conferred. The changing composition of the committee signaled a wider distribution of benefits under the system of *cláusula sindical*.

Fedepetrol included an agency shop clause (whereby nonunion workers are required to pay union dues) in its proposed contract in 1959 that the oil companies staunchly rejected. In its place they offered to pay the dues of nonunion workers, a provision labor leaders are usually reluctant to accept since it could discourage union membership. Actually, the agency shop has generally not been favorably viewed by Venezuelan trade unionists. One top AD labor leader who later joined MEP in 1967 stated that workers could not be forced to join unions or pay dues, and that the greatest punishment of those who refused to do so was "the hostility of the great majority of fellow workers who ostracize them."[18] Even the Communist Eloy Torres characterized Rafael Caldera's proposal, made during the presidential campaign of 1968, to implement the agency shop as fascist-inspired.[19]

The original version of the *Proyecto Caldera* obliged nonunion members to pay 50 percent union dues and permitted an "exclusionary clause" in collective bargaining agreements, whereby unions could solicit the dismissal of employees whose behavior was considered antiunion. Both proposals were criticized as unconstitutional and failed to win strong backing from organized labor. Subsequent drafts eliminated the exclusionary clause, and only gave the union the right to collect special dues from nonunion members to finance collective bargaining negotiations. The CTV's lukewarm response to both articles, as well as its decision to drop the call for "One Union per Industry," demonstrates the extent to which certain notions regarding worker liberties are deeply rooted in Venezuela.

Provisions regarding Layoffs

The importance of the struggle for job security has been a long-standing source of debate among labor scholars. In the 1920s, Selig Perlman considered "job consciousness" the most pressing worker concern and praised conservative Samuel Gompers for emphasizing it, while attacking leftist intellectuals for diverting attention in favor of extraneous ideological goals. Sidney and Beatrice Webb, on the other hand, denied that trade unions represented a continuation of the medieval guild, with its ideal of absolute security for all its members. They called on unions to concentrate on wage benefits while leaving hiring and firing exclusively to management. Opposition to layoffs is a more important banner in Latin America than in developed nations where the formal economy generally absorbs discharged workers.[20] Ironically, in Venezuela and elsewhere, management has embraced the argument of the prosocialist Webbs that layoffs are a management prerogative, while leftist trade unionists have championed *estabilidad absoluta*, which is a paramount goal according to the philosophy of the ultraconservative Perlman.

There is another reason why trade unionists in developing countries are particularly eager to impede layoffs without just cause ("unjustified layoffs").

The Taylor system, which standardizes the work process, is most perfected in the United States and other developed nations. Taylorism, along with high levels of labor discipline, ensures against wide differences in output between workers who perform similar tasks. In Latin America, on the other hand, lack of standardization widens disparities in productivity and encourages management to look constantly for worker replacements. As a result, most layoffs cannot be easily classified as either "justified" or "unjustified," since such categories are based on criteria that are difficult to define. The interviews carried out for this study demonstrate that this aspect of the problem has not been readily grasped by labor leaders, or at least has not been articulated by them. The interviewees maintained that they seek to prevent layoffs stemming from capriciousness or personal motives or those in which a manager attempts to impress his own boss at the worker's expense. Worker representatives do not seem to recognize the complexity of the task of classifying layoffs.[21]

Employer obligations to discharged workers were designed to achieve *estabilidad indirecta*, whereby costly severance payments discourage layoffs. One of the two important breakthroughs dating back to the 1940s was achieved by oil workers in 1948: double severance payments (antiguedad) in the case of unjustified layoffs. The other was a clause stipulating that severance payment was an "inherent right" (*derecho adquirido*) that all workers were entitled to, regardless of the cause of separation. The white-collar workers' union (ANDE) first obtained this benefit, which was also included in proposed labor legislation drawn up by the Labor Ministry headed by Raúl Leoni in 1946.[22] In the 1960s, it was extended to iron, oil, and textile workers, among others.[23] Iron workers (unlike oil workers) succeeded in the 1960s in setting up special commissions consisting of labor and management representatives to determine whether layoffs were justified, thus sparing the worker the burdensome task of taking his case to labor court.

Two proposed laws considered by congress in the 1960s were designed to enhance worker job security. The *Ley Calvani* was drafted by *Copeyano* Arístides Calvani and sponsored by labor Deputies José González Navarro (AD) and Vicente Piñate (URD), among others. The enactment would have impeded mass layoffs and required employers who reduced their work force to give preference to Venezuelan workers as well as those with large families. In 1962 leftist congressmen took advantage of their majority in the Chamber of Deputies by strengthening the *Ley Calvani* and adding a provision for the creation of tripartite commissions of worker, company, and state representatives to handle cases of layoffs. The bill, however, was defeated in the Senate where AD and Copei retained majority control.[24]

The *Ley de Estabilidad en el Trabajo*, which was drawn up by MEPistas and introduced in congress by trade unionists and others belonging to AD and MEP in 1969, suffered a similar fate. MEP president Prieto Figueroa who, as an AD senator had helped defeat the *Ley Calvani* in 1962, hailed the proposed law in congress for promising to "place Venezuela among the most advanced nations in labor matters."[25] In 1970, however, as part of the Institutional Pact beween the governing Copei and AD, the latter party withdrew support for the proposal, and it subsequently died in committee.

The most important breakthrough in job security, and until recently the most controversial labor legislation in the nation's history, was the *Ley contra Despidos Injustificados* (1974). The original draft entitled the "Law of Labor Stability," which was introduced by Labor Minister Antonio Leidenz, left it up to the worker who had been discharged for "unjustified" reasons to choose between returning to work or receiving double severance benefits.[26] Fedecámaras sharply attacked this provision at its annual convention in San Cristóbal in July. Subsequently, the law was reworded to stipulate that the employer, rather than the employee, would have the option of rehiring the worker or paying double benefits. In cases of "justified layoffs" the worker was to receive single severance payment, which was now considered an "acquired right." In addition, tripartite commissions were established to determine whether dismissals were "justified," replacing the labor courts that had performed this task since the 1936 Labor Law. An *estabilidad numérica* clause required employers to replace all discharged workers (regardless of circumstances) at equal pay, but this provision has never been enforced.

Criticism of the *Ley contra Despidos* came from various sources. Leftist congressmen attributed the revision in the law to pressure from Fedecámaras. CUTV's vice president Américo Chacón stated that smaller companies should be exempted from the absolute job security clause but not larger ones. MAS's Germán Lairet, while on the whole supporting the law, objected to the exclusion of smaller firms of less than ten workers, and maintained that the government should provide small businessmen special credit facilities, but not privileges at the expense of their workers. At the same time, *Copeyano* congressmen argued that the government representative on the tripartite commissions would have a swing vote, and consequently the process of determining the cause of layoffs would be politicized.[27]

AD National Deputy José Vargas denied that the law had been gutted of its absolute job security provision due to pressure from Fedecámaras. Pablo Salas Castillo, a leading *Perezjimenista*, also defended the revised version of the law by insisting that in practice worker job security would be virtually absolute. Only an extremely capricious employer, he maintained, would lay off employees for "unjustified" reasons, knowing full well that he would have to provide them double severance benefits and at the same time hire other workers at the same pay. Communist Deputy Alcides Rodríguez responded to Salas's assertion by reiterating the Venezuelan Left's traditional view that *estabilidad numérica* was a "farce" since employers were left free to fire combative trade unionists and older workers, as long as others were hired in their place.[28]

Following the promulgation of the *Ley contra Despidos*, Fedecámaras initiated an ongoing campaign based on the central argument that the law undermined rather than fortified labor stability. Business spokesmen blamed the law for the high worker turnover that characterized the prosperous years of the 1970s. According to them, workers courted dismissal and then attempted to convince the tripartite commission that they had been laid off for "unjustified" reasons. Even when their cases were lost, they were still entitled to single severance pay. Fedecámaras also claimed that the money obtained was often too great to receive in one lump sum, which workers ended up squandering.

The everyday performance of the tripartite commissions has fallen far short of the high expectations that labor leaders had when the system was first implemented in 1974. The tripartite commissions—two of whose members are not public functionaries—lack judicial authority and thus can do no more than level a modest fine against those employers who refuse to obey their decisions, while penal action has to be left to the courts. Although in appearance the commissions provide the labor movement with input into the classification of layoffs, in practice the labor representative invariably sides with the worker and the business representative with management, so that it is the Labor Ministry appointee who has the final say. In addition, the latter (who is the tripartite commission's president) performs all the work while the other two commission members do no more than put their signatures on documents.

The major objective of the *Ley contra Despidos* is to induce employers to rehire employees whose dismissal is "unjustified," while the payment of double severance benefits is seen as a less desirable alternative, as is implicit in Article 6.[29] Nevertheless, the lengthy duration of the cases, which often take up to a year despite the time limits established in the *Ley*, encourages the worker who may be without employment at the time to sign a compromise agreement with the employer. The worker's lawyer, who generally does not charge (beyond an initial fee) clients of modest means who lose their case, is also favorably inclined to reach a settlement. Only in a minority of cases does the tripartite commission render a decision; however, even when it favors the worker, the company virtually never chooses to rehire him. The employer is not only convinced that the tripartite commission erred in its verdict, but he also may have developed an antipathy for the employee, especially in cases that drag on. Furthermore, the worker at this point prefers to obtain double severance pay rather than being rehired. The dilatoriness of the tripartite commissions, however, favors the worker in at least one respect: When the commission's decision favors the employee, the company is obliged to pay his salary from the time he was fired, regardless of which of the two options the employer chooses.

Labor leaders and lawyers have put forward various propositions designed to expedite the classification of layoffs. One prominent proworker lawyer advocated the elimination of the right to appeal in second-level tripartite commissions that the *Ley contra Despidos* established in each region of the country.[30] At its 1985 congress the CTV called for implementation of oral procedures (as used in the United States and England) to hasten the process. In the congressional committees that considered the *Proyecto Caldera*, CTV spokesmen suggested that the commissions be eliminated altogether and their functions assumed by "Inspectors of Labor Stability" of the Labor Ministry who would be granted judicial authority.

The CTV's proposal to eliminate the tripartite commissions was incorporated into the *Proyecto* and then modified, in accordance with Fedecámaras's position that labor courts and not inspectors should handle disputes over layoffs. The change was accepted by the CTV although, like organized labor throughout Latin America, it prefers to delegate authority to the Labor Ministry and endow its inspectors with judicial authority, at least in minor disputes.[31] The courts base their decisions on greater technical criteria and require the defendant to contract a lawyer (which, in the case of the tripartite commission, is optional), and thus the process is longer and more costly.

In the 1980s the issue of job security became a source of greater worker preoccupation in Venezuela than it was during the previous decade. As Perlman pointed out, in periods of rapid economic growth and prosperity (such as Venezuela experienced in the 1970s), workers are imbued with the same optimism as are businessmen regarding the achievement of "limitless opportunities" and are thus more concerned with income than security. Following the first signs of contraction in 1979, the attention of Venezuelan labor leaders was focused on several legal provisions whose objective was to deter layoffs. CTV President José Vargas and others threatened to organize a campaign in favor of enforcement of the *estabilidad numérica* article of the *Ley contra Despidos*, which was a dead letter.[32] In addition, trade unionists demanded that *prestaciones sociales*, a form of *estabilidad indirecta* calculated on the basis of a worker's last paycheck, take into account various monthly bonuses that the government had decreed for workers (known, for example, as the transportation bonus and the food bonus) and not just "basic salary."

Labor leaders also demanded modification of Article 7 of the *Ley contra Despidos*, which exempted employers who faced pressing economic difficulties or who introduced labor-saving devices from having to pay discharged workers double severance benefits (referred to as "reduction of personnel for economic and technical reasons"). They pointed out that the tripartite commissions, which considered these cases, should be required to examine the records of the company over a considerable period of time, and not just the previous month or two, to ascertain whether it was on the verge of bankruptcy. Furthermore, they opposed layoffs for "technical reasons" on grounds that the company was the great beneficiary of technological innovation in the long run.[33]

By the late 1980s the labor movement concurred with Fedecámaras on the need to scrap the tripartite commissions. Nevertheless, labor leaders tenaciously defended double severance pay, which had virtually no equivalent anywhere in the world. Fedecámaras, whose criticism of the *Ley contra Despidos* went beyond the practical problems inherent in the classification of layoffs, attacked the entire law when it came up in congress during discussion over the *Proyecto Caldera*. Although Fedecámaras singled out some twenty-odd articles in the *Proyecto* for criticism, its major target was the system of severance pay, and it insisted that a completely new method be devised for its calculation and implementation. The prolonged, heated debate that ensued demonstrated the extent to which the issue of job security and layoffs is a center of concern not only for workers but also for business interests in Venezuela, as in the rest of Latin America.

Distinctions among White-collar Workers, Blue-collar Workers, and Public Employees

One of the most important demands of the Venezuelan labor movement is the elimination of legal and contractual distinctions among different types of workers. All four confederations agree that the denominations of *employee* (white-collar worker) and *obrero* (blue-collar worker), which the 1936 Labor Law utilized to differentiate intellectual and manual labor, are no longer applicable due to the increasing technical capacity of the entire work force. In addition, public employees have struggled over the decades to be included in the Labor Law in order to receive the economic benefits and trade union rights it confers. FCV leaders have put forward the same demand since 1958; they criticize the new Labor Law for containing a separate chapter on agricultural workers that, among other provisions, establishes the work week at forty-eight hours, four hours above that of the rest of the work force.

Gradual trends have reduced differences between white-collar and blue-collar workers and favored their organizational unification. Most—although far from all—labor contracts combine both sectors. In the oil industry, office workers originally formed ANDE, which refrained from joining blue-collar workers in the strike of 1936–37; however, they subsequently decided to enter Fedepetrol unions. In recent years, professional workers have undertaken militant actions with other workers in the same institutions, in the process reducing their occupational isolation.

Doctors, for instance, participated with other hospital personnel in street protests in favor of improved working conditions and salaries. Some hospital doctors are receptive to the CTV's proposal for all-encompassing industrywide unions, although a majority of them indicate that they would be reluctant to join a national union of health workers. In 1990 engineers who worked for the state struck in favor of a special minimum wage, thus taking up a demand that was long associated with blue-collar workers.

Several important legal differences between blue- and white-collar workers embodied in the 1936 Labor Law have been eliminated. In the constitution of 1947, disparities in the number of annual vacation days (which in 1936 had been set at seven for the former and fifteen for the latter) were forbidden. The new Labor Law gets rid of another difference by decreasing the work week for blue-collar workers from forty-eight hours to forty-four hours. It also deletes the reference in the 1936 law to separate blue-collar and white-collar worker unions. Labor leaders, however, criticized the new law for not suppressing the distinction between the two groups altogether.[34] The law, for instance, stipulates that at least 90 percent of white-collar workers and 90 percent of blue-collar workers of all companies have to be Venezuelan; the 1936 law had established the minimum at 75 percent. By referring to the two sectors separately, the authors of the law hoped to avoid foreign domination of corporate structures.

Some labor leaders and lawyers have argued that the preservation of the distinction between *empleado* and *obrero* is designed to divide the labor movement and justify the separate and inferior treatment that the law accords public employees. Enrique Aguero Gorrín, who had been one of the CUTV's top legal advisers and later represented the CTV, stated:

> The term "worker" (*trabajador*) should be widened in scope to include public employees. The differentiation between *obrero* and *empleado* is in my opinion artificial and Venezuelan legislation goes beyond it. If you examine the Labor Law you will find that there are only 4 [or] 5 differences between *obrero* and *empleado*. . . . The differentiation is reactionary. It is a way that management has to create illusions among *empleados* on the basis that they constitute a superior stratum, an intellectual stratum, and should not form part of the union with *obreros*. . . . The differentiation is also maintained because its elimination would allow the so-called government functionaries to attain the benefits of the Labor Law.[35]

Public employees in nearly all Latin American nations have received discriminatory treatment under labor legislation, despite the ILO's recommendations in favor of equal rights and benefits. Actually, the achievement of such equality faces a structural barrier. Jobs are artificially created in the public sphere to absorb unemployment that, in third-world countries, is widespread due to economic backwardness. This objective is naturally at odds with substantial wage increases. Another reason for limiting the trade union rights of public employees is fear that political parties of the opposition will gain control of their organizations and thus be in a position to sabotage government programs.[36]

Until the overthrow of Pérez Jiménez, state workers were organizationally and legally neglected, but since then their position has steadily improved. After 1958, government blue-collar workers (including messengers, chauffeurs, and doormen) as well as employees in some fully owned state companies (such as the Banco Obrero and Aeropostal) were given the same rights as their counterparts in the private sector. White-collar workers who worked directly for the government were allowed to form the Unión Nacional de Empleados Públicos (UNEP), which called for legislation allowing state employees to establish unions and engage in collective bargaining. It also called for repeal of the Hunger Law, which lowered salaries in the public sector by 10 percent. As early as 1960, Caldera supported organizing rights for public employees, but opposed their right to go on strike.[37] By middecade the FVM was admitted into the CTV, and in 1969 it forced the government to sign a labor agreement (although it was not denominated "contract") in the wake of a two-week strike.

The *Ley de Carrera Administrativa*, which was drawn up by the Caldera administration and unanimously approved by congress in September 1970, was hailed by UNEP as a major breakthrough in its struggle for equal benefits. The AD-controlled UNEP expressed its gratitude to President Caldera and added that "we are sure that public employees will now more than ever fulfill their obligations and responsibilities to the nation."[38] Most important, the law granted public employees *estabilidad absoluta*, a privilege that virtually no other sector of the working population had at the time. They also received more annual vacation days than was stipulated in the Labor Law, and nearly the same severance benefits. On the other hand, the Christmas bonus (known as *utilidades*) was set at merely fifteen-days' pay, as against the one to two months that most workers received. Furthermore, public employees were still excluded from most of the Social Security benefits enjoyed by workers covered by the Labor Law.

The most serious shortcoming of the *Ley de Carrera* was the inadequate mechanisms it established for the defense of worker interests. Although public employees were allowed to organize unions, their activities were limited to "protection of the rights which the Law confers," as well as professional concerns. The law did not contemplate either collective bargaining or strike activity. Furthermore, each union was assigned only two *fueros*, as opposed to the seven granted by the Labor Law. To the disadvantage of public employees in the nation's interior, only one Tribunal located in Caracas was established to determine whether layoffs were justified. In addition, employees who occupied "confidential positions" were excluded from the law. In practice, this ill-defined category takes in numerous employees, leading organized labor to insist on limiting it to upper-level political appointments. In some cases, employees who are covered by the

Ley de Carrera are "lent out" in order to occupy "confidential positions," and then return to their former job once the administration's term has expired.[39] These legal provisions and practices weaken the labor movement and enhance worker dependence on the state. As a result, the nation's two political parties that have held power since 1958 have been able to maintain a near monopoly control of the leadership of labor organizations in the public administration.

The New Labor Law

The *Anteproyecto* of the new Labor Law was introduced in congress on July 2, 1985, by former President Rafael Caldera, exactly forty-nine years after the passage of the old one. The congress accepted Caldera's recommendation that a special bicameral commission be created to review the proposal. The commission invited representatives of over one hundred organizations and institutions as well as experts in different fields; after three years of deliberations, the revised version was sent to the Chamber of Deputies for consideration. At the time of congressional ratification in December 1990, President Carlos Andrés Pérez unsuccessfully called for deferment on passage of the law, while discarding the possibility of exercising a veto. Nearly all parties supported the law, although some such as the PCV believed that the advantages just slightly outweighed the disadvantages; only a handful of congressmen—including those of the ultraleftist Causa R—voted against it in congress.[40]

Perhaps more than any other piece of legislation in modern Venezuelan history, the proposed Labor Law generated a national debate that carried important implications for the nation's major political parties. On the one hand, AD and its Labor Bureau were pitted against the Pérez government, which was particularly concerned that it would be unable to meet its new financial obligations to public employees. On the other, Caldera's active role in promoting the law thrust him into the nation's limelight, thus enhancing his position as a possible extraparty presidential contender in 1993 (with the endorsement of MAS), to the detriment of Copei's aspirant Eduardo Fernández. In some of his public appearances, Caldera left the definite impression that he was pursuing a strategy of parlaying support for the Labor Law into support for his presidential candidacy. Thus, for instance, in an otherwise unemotional speech on the technical aspects of the Labor Law in Puerto La Cruz, Caldera raised his voice and emphatically stated: "If anything has brought MAS together with this fighter for social justice it was the common experience of struggling in favor of the *Proyecto* in opposition to those who defend a savage, destructive capitalism."[41]

Throughout 1990 business groups undertook an extensive campaign designed to create alarm regarding the devastating effects of the proposed

Labor Law. In full-page, often anonymous, advertisements, Venezuelans were told that the law would ruin the economy, as similar ones had in Poland, Argentina, and Peru "where social conflicts became increasingly acute day by day" at the same time that labor discipline broke down.[42] The basic thrust of Fedecámaras's argument was that the passage of the law in a period of crisis was ill timed since it threatened to disrupt the government's program of economic recovery, by discouraging private investments and privatization, and to saddle companies with onerous social obligations.

Fedecámaras pejoratively employed the word "paternalistic" to show that the law would force business to assume responsibilities for social needs, such as health care, day care, and housing, which were the natural domain of the state, and provide workers across-the-board benefits that should be attained through collective bargaining. Some employer spokesmen threatened to shut down business activity in protest and take the issue to the ILO in Geneva. In addition, representatives of leading multinational corporations in Venezuela warned that the proposed law would put a damper on foreign investments.[43]

The campaign against the Labor Law was ill conceived and proved to be counterproductive. In the first place, Fedecámaras waited until the law was about to be approved in congress, and thus failed to gradually prepare public opinion from the time the *Anteproyecto* was introduced more than four years earlier. Caldera was able to point out that the special bicameral committee that he headed had been receptive to recommendations from diverse sources, including business representatives. (Indeed, several key articles had been modified in accordance with advice from the business sector, such as the elimination of *cogestores* from the board of trustees of private companies and the naming of special judges, rather than labor inspectors, to decide whether layoffs were justified.) It was conjectured that Fedecámaras's protracted passivity was due to the assurances it received from President Lusinchi that the law would be allowed to die in congressional committee.[44]

The aggressive tenor of Fedecámaras's campaign had few precedents in Venezuela. It hardened the positions of political actors and forced their parties to define themselves either in favor of or against the law, thus ruling out compromise formulas. Some national AD labor leaders, who were closely aligned with President Pérez, initially indicated that they were willing to consider Fedecámaras's proposed plan for the annual payment of *prestaciones sociales*, which the government also viewed favorably. However, they were compelled to back down once the issue became polemical and the CTV defended the existing system as a point of honor.[45]

Fedecámaras forcefully objected to Articles 384 and 385 of the new law, which increased postnatal-paid leaves of absence from six to twelve weeks and granted one year *inamovilidad* after childbirth; previously it was limited to the duration of the pregnancy. Fedecámaras claimed that this provision would invite discrimination against women by employers who viewed it as tantamount to a year's vacation, an admonition that was echoed by President Pérez. Caldera pointed out that the argument distorted the concept of *inamovilidad*, which was hardly a license to disregard labor discipline and only proscribed unjustified layoffs. In any case, Fedecámaras's objections left the negative impression that businessmen were insensitive to the situation faced by pregnant women, and placed immediate profit before the welfare of the family and the nation.

Business representatives also were preoccupied with Articles 137 and 138—not so much due to their literal content but their implications—a concern that was aggravated by the ambiguity in the wording of the original *Anteproyecto*. Article 137 called for salary hikes in cases of increases in productivity. In the *Anteproyecto*, Article 138 stated that in situations of "notorious increases" in the cost of living, workers should receive raises to guarantee purchasing power; however, it failed to define the word "notorious." In defense of the provision, Caldera pointed out that it explicitly stated that these increases preferably should be established in collective bargaining agreements—a preference that Fedecámaras itself had always expressed—and by executive decree only in "cases of emergency."[46] He added that the president always had the power to decree across-the-board increases; the only modification was that he was now obliged to consult labor and business representatives as well as qualified economists.

Unlike business spokesmen's claims, neither article mechanically pegged wages to increases in the cost of living or productivity. Undoubtedly, Fedecámaras's real concern was that both articles would strengthen labor's position at the bargaining table. In any case, the Chamber of Deputies modified Article 138 to avoid any doubt regarding the law's intentions. The final draft merely authorized the president to increase salaries when he saw fit, while at the same time leaving open the possibility that part of the raise would not be taken into consideration in the calculation of severance pay. In another concession to business, the final version of Article 137 gave priority to increased productivity stemming from the workers' efforts, rather than the introduction of new technology.

Another aspect of the *Anteproyecto* had far-reaching implications that worried the business sector. The *Anteproyecto* defined those covered by labor legislation in broad enough terms that possibly could include self-employed workers. Fedecámaras feared that the concept of *dependence* in worker-patron relationships adhered to by the *Anteproyecto* meant that those who depended on a company for their livelihood, rather than only those who were on the firm's payroll, would be eligible for the benefits granted by the law. Thus, the employer would be obliged to pay *utilidades* and *prestaciones sociales* and grant vacation time to a broad array of workers, including street vendors who peddled the company's merchandise, as well as lawyers and other professionals (who were dealt with separately in Article 9 [47]) whose services were contracted by the firm. Fedecámaras complained that such all-inclusiveness would throw the company's planning efforts into disarray since future financial obligations would be difficult to predict.

The issue was touchy for the CTV, which was theoretically committed to articulating the interests of workers in the informal economy. Some labor leaders and writers who were closely linked to the CTV and other confederations had been calling for their incorporation into the labor movement and their coverage by existing labor legislation over the last several years.[48] The final version of the law, however, backtracked on the matter: the only workers who were completely covered were those who were *totally subordinated* to the employer, while independent workers were to receive certain benefits only gradually, beginning at an unspecified date.

The area of contention that most undermined Fedecámaras's position in the eyes of the public, and that certainly generated the most controversy, was the system of *prestaciones sociales*. Although Caldera was receptive to the annual payment of *prestaciones sociales* to the workers, the new Labor Law kept the old setup largely intact.[49] Unlike all other business objections to articles involving improvements in worker benefits, this one called into question the appropriateness of an already existing benefit that was considered virtually sacred in Venezuela. In doing so, Fedecámaras's stand clashed with the concept of the irrevocability of worker gains embodied in Article 85 of the constitution.

Fedecámaras and the government both presented proposals that scrapped the system of calculating *prestaciones sociales* on the basis of what the worker was earning at the time he left the company. Under Fedecámaras's plan, *prestaciones sociales* were computed according to the worker's salary at the end of each year; the government's plan computed them according to his monthly salary at the end of every three years. Government and business spokesmen claimed that the current system hurt workers because employers were resistant to wage increases due to their effect on *prestaciones sociales*, particularly in the case of employees serving many years with the company. They also claimed that, by taking into consideration certain special features of their plans (such as an increase in *prestaciones sociales* by one day's salary per year), the workers would end up receiving more than they do under the present system. Needless to say, this claim was open to question, particularly in the case of unjustified layoffs, which were to pay much less than what was provided under the *Ley contra Despidos Injustificados*.

Two other aspects of the proposed plans were touted as highly favorable for the workers, but were criticized by those who defended the current system. Under both Fedecámaras's and the government's plans, 50 percent of the worker's *prestaciones sociales* would be paid annually, thus leaving him with less money to face the prospects of unemployment or (as was sometimes done) to purchase a house. It was feared that in time this 50 percent would come to be considered mere wages. In addition, 10 percent of the *prestaciones sociales* was to be deposited in a special retirement fund designed to replace Social Security (IVSS), which was considered inadequate and undependable. Some labor leaders argued that the dismantlement of the social security system (or its privatization) would leave workers in the informal economy, who were striving to gain IVSS coverage, even further away from the goal of social protection.

Worker benefits under Venezuela's new Labor Law compared favorably with those of other Latin American nations. Venezuelan workers were better off than their counterparts in the rest of the continent with regard to severance payments (such as *preaviso* of up to three months), annual vacations (between fifteen and thirty days—better than most other nations except Argentina where they ranged between fifteen and thirty-five days), and the work week (forty-four hours for Venezuela and forty-eight elsewhere), to mention just a few important fringe benefits. It was unclear whether Fedecámaras's main objection to the new law was that the sum of dozens of costly worker benefits would limit profit margins, or whether it was more concerned with those articles that made it difficult for businesses to calculate future costs, such as in the case of *prestaciones sociales*. Undoubtedly, one source of preoccupation for business was that provisions such as productivity clauses, cost-of-living adjustments, and possible employer obligations to workers who were not on the company payroll would invigorate the labor movement and encourage union leaders to radicalize their positions.

The CTV failed to contribute to the national debate on the law by drawing up articles as substitutes for those of the *Proyecto*, as Fedecámaras did. The confederation did not even make good on its promise to draft an *Anteproyecto* for the system of *prestaciones sociales* to serve as the basis for public discussion along with those presented by Fedecámaras and the government. Several political analysts and actors chided the CTV for not playing a more active role. The labor movement was thus unable to exploit its advantageous position vis-à-vis Fedecámaras as a result of Article 85 of the Constitution that was affirmed in Article 3 of the new Labor Law: "In no case will the norms and dispositions which favor the workers be renounced."[50] In justifying its failure to put forward concrete proposals, the CTV claimed that any criticism of individual articles of the *Proyecto* would play into the hands of Fedecámaras by detracting from the ground swell of support for the law as a whole. Aside from this rather unconvincing explanation, the CTV's inactivity demonstrated that the confederation had failed to transform its new structure designed to enhance its technical capacity—which included Inaesin and the Executive Committee's departmental system— into effective instruments in the struggle to defend workers' interests.

Conclusion

Writers who belong to the corporatist analytical school (to be discussed in more detail in this study's concluding chapter) emphasize the constraints imposed by labor legislation on organized labor in Latin America.[51] In the case of Venezuela, the monitoring capacity of the Labor Ministry, particularly with regard to union finances and membership, is stressed. Indeed, the 1991 Labor Law includes various new provisions that are moderately restrictive, although the article limiting the consecutive reelection of the members of the union's Executive Committee to one three-year term was deleted from the *Proyecto*'s original draft.[52] In any case, until now the Labor Ministry has not played an interventionist role in organized labor and the furnishing of information is a mere formality, with which most unions do not even comply.

Writers who emphasize the close legal and institutional linkages between organized labor and the state also highlight the importance of the tripartite commissions that incorporated labor in an official decision-making capacity. Nevertheless, during their fifteen-odd years of existence, the tripartite commissions were thoroughly discredited. Labor and management representatives on the commissions played an insignificant role since their votes invariably canceled themselves, and neither of the two participated actively in the process of classifying layoffs. In addition, the uneasiness of the authors of the *Ley contra Despidos* about assigning official authority to the two members of the private sectors—that is, labor and management— led them to deny judicial power to the commissions, whose decisions were thus left unenforceable short of court proceedings. Labor leaders were clearly disappointed with the performance of the tripartite commissions, which they had hailed at the time of the passage of the *Ley contra Despidos* in 1974. So great was their disillusionment that they accepted the *Proyecto Caldera*'s reimplementation of the old system in which cases regarding layoffs are handled in the courts.

The extent of the state's control of organized labor has often been exaggerated. It is widely assumed, for instance, that the atomization of the trade union movement is due to the prohibition of national unions. Many trade unionists also blame the government for the multiplicity of contracts in such state-controlled sectors as the airlines. Nevertheless, the Labor Law of 1936 does not explicitly prohibit the existence of national unions, nor is it government policy to oppose industrywide contracts. Following the resolution in favor of national unions at the Third Congress in 1959, the CTV waited nearly three decades for politicians in congress to draft a law that contemplated the formation of unions representing workers in more than one state.

Another example of dependent attitudes that encourage labor leaders to take for granted the initiatives of a paternalistic government was discussed in Chapter 8: the CTV's failure to push ahead aggressively with *cogestión* in the private sector. Instead, it awaited labor legislation that would go beyond the limited perimeters of the 1966 decree on labor representation in state companies, as the *Proyecto Caldera* effectively did. In short, the illusion that the all-powerful government, with its abundant economic resources derived from petroleum, is the main actor in the realm of labor relations— and not the state's actual exercise of legal authority—is what holds back organized labor from acting forcefully in favor of its immediate and long-term objectives.

Notes

1. Dagoberto González, *La reforma de la ley del trabajo* (Caracas: Copei, 1964), p. 650; *El Nacional* [interview with Rafael Alfonzo Guzmán], January 27, 1960, p. 31. In contrast, some labor lawyers argued against enactment of the *Proyecto Caldera* of 1985 on grounds that the existing Labor Law should be reformed rather than replaced.
2. Richard Ulric Miller, "The Role of Labor Organizations in a Developing Country: The Case of Mexico" (Ph.D. diss., Cornell University, 1966), 215.
3. Hernández Alvarez, "Comentarios al capítulo sobre organizaciones sindicales del Anteproyecto de la Ley Orgánica del Trabajo," p. 338; Héctor Lucena, "Concertación y revisión en las relaciones laborales," *Revista Relaciones de Trabajo* 5 (1985): 16.
4. CTV, "Que presenta el Comité Ejecutivo de la CTV," p. 6. Contracts signed by larger companies generally oblige them to pay 10 or 15 percent of the workers' dues directly to the national federation. Nevertheless, in the oil industry *contratista* companies fail to comply with this procedure; for some time now, Fedepetrol has ceased attempting to collect this percentage from union locals.
5. Juan José Delpino, "La modernización del movimiento sindical," in *CTV: 50 años de historia*, p. 17.
6. Carlos Luna, interview, January 30, 1987, Caracas.
7. Rafael Castañeda, interview, December 11, 1986, Caracas.
8. Arturo Tremont, interview, October 16, 1986, Caracas.
9. *Antecedentes y testimonios* 4:279.
10. Caldera argued that the minimum number of fifty to form plant unions was actually low, since they would be left defenseless vis-à-vis management. Rafael Caldera, "Consideraciones sobre el Ante-Proyecto de la Ley Orgánica," *Revista Relaciones de Trabajo* 7 (1986): 260–61. See also *Antecedentes y testimonios* 4:392.
11. Francisco Iturraspe, interview, February 19, 1987, Caracas.
12. Héctor Lucena, "El movimiento de los trabajadores y la creación de los sindicatos nacionales," in *Estudios laborales*, pp. 457–72.
13. Arturo S. Bronstein, "Collective Bargaining in Latin America: Problems and Trends," *International Labour Review* 117, no. 5 (September-October 1978): 589; Robert Alexander, *Labor Relations in Argentina, Brazil, and Chile* (New York: McGraw Hill, 1962), p. 191.
14. Bronstein, "Collective Bargaining," p. 591.
15. González, *La reforma de la ley del trabajo*, p. 651.
16. Malavé Villalba, *Frente Sindical* 1 (August 1958): 4.

17. Andrés Mercau, *La contratación colectiva* (Caracas: Ediciones "Claridad," n.d.), p. 119.

18. Interview no. 025, Interviewee no. 074, n.d., p. 7, Cendes, C. C.

19. *Nueva Voz Popular*, October 10, 1968, p. 6.

20. See, for instance, Manuel Barrera, *El sindicato industrial: anhelos, métodos de lucha, relaciones con la empresa* (Santiago: Universidad de Chile, 1969), pp. 52–54.

21. Ellner, "Welfare, Oil Workers, and the Labor Movement." See also Ministerio del Trabajo, *Memoria y Cuenta*, 1959, pp. xi–xii.

22. Dorothea Melcher, "Estado y movimiento obrero en Venezuela (represión e integración hasta 1948)" [unpublished paper] (Mérida: Universidad de los Andes, 1984), pp. 139–40.

23. These contracts generally provided greater benefits to workers who voluntarily withdrew from the company than those who were laid off for "justified reasons." Thus, the oil workers' contract of 1946 provided workers with over three years with the company *antiguedad* (two weeks' salary for each year of work) in cases of voluntary withdrawal, but not those who were laid off for "justified reasons." The 1972 contract of the Iron Mines Company recognized *antiguedad* as a *derecho adquirido*, but granted those who voluntarily withdrew additional payments.

24. Francisco Hung Vaillant, *Contribución al estudio de la Ley contra Despidos Injustificados* (Caracas: Editorial Jurídica Venezolana, 1979), pp. 16–17; Pedro Ortega Díaz, interview, August 14, 1990, Caracas.

25. Luis Beltrán Prieto Figueroa, "Estabilidad en el Trabajo" in *Proyecto de Ley de Estabilidad en el Trabajo* (Caracas, 1969): p. 12.

26. Like Prieto Figueroa, Leidenz helped defeat the *Ley Calvani* in congress in 1962, even though he had cosponsored the original proposal.

27. *Diario de Debates* (Chamber of Deputies), July 25, 1974, pp. 1022–23.

28. Ibid., July 3, 1974, p. 835; ibid., July 25, 1974, pp. 1034, 1038.

29. Rafael Caldera, *Derecho del Trabajo*, 2d ed., 3rd printing (Buenos Aires: Editorial "El Ateneo," 1972, p. 471.

30. Enrique Aguero Gorrín, interview, April 30, 1987, Caracas.

31. *Antecedentes y testimonios de los congresos* 2:93.

32. *El Universal*, October 10, 1980, p. 1–12.

33. The *Ley contra Despidos* has also been criticized for not requiring management to consult the union prior to laying off workers for "economic or technical reasons," as is recommended by the ILO. See Edward Yemin, "Job Security: Influence of ILO Standards and Recent Trends," *International Labour Review* 113, no. 1 (January–February 1976): 19.

34. *Fragua* [CTV periodical], October 1986, pp. 50–52.

35. Aguero Gorrín, interview, April 30, 1987, Caracas. This same point was made by *Copeyano* Rafael Rodríguez Acosta, interview, February 2, 1987, Caracas.

36. Efrén Córdova, "Labour Relations in Public Service in Latin America," *International Labour Review* 11, no. 5 (September 1980): 584.

37. *La Esfera*, October 16, 1960, p. 13; *La República*, January 18, 1965, p. 4.

38. *El Nacional*, September 6, 1970, p. D-12.

39. Manuel Rachadell, "Aspectos políticos de la carrera administrativa," in *Estudios Laborales*, p. 265. Unions have faced a similar problem in the private sector where management also loosely defines the term *empleado de confianza*. Confidential employees are not covered by the *Ley contra Despidos* and are thus not eligible for double severance pay.

40. Pedro Ortega Díaz, interview, August 14, 1990, Caracas; *Tribuna Popular*, May 1–7, 1987, p. 3.

41. Rafael Caldera, Inauguration of the conference "La Nueva Ley del Trabajo," sponsored by the Colegio de Abogados of Anzoátegui in Puerto La Cruz, April 6, 1991.

42. *El Nacional*, June 20, 1989, p. D-5.

43. *El Nacional*, November 1, 1990, p. D-9. The proposal for a business strike was formulated by the Asociación de Industriales Metalúrgicos de Minería (AIMM) and presented to Fedecámaras for consideration.

44. *El Nacional*, July 2, 1989, p. D-2; Johnny Díaz Apitz, interview, August 14, 1990, Caracas.

45. *El Nacional*, July 2, 1989, p. D-2; Federico Ramírez León, interview, March 10, 1990, Puerto La Cruz.

46. *Anteproyecto de Ley Orgánica del Trabajo presentado por el Senador Vitalicio Dr. Rafael Caldera* (Caracas: Ediciones del Congreso, 1985), pp. 91–92.

47. For a discussion of the ambiguity of the term "liberal professionals," specifically with reference to the public administration, see Enrique Marín Quijada, "Problemas jurídicos del Proyecto de Ley del Trabajo," in *Las relaciones de trabajo en los noventa: desafíos y propuestas*, ed. Héctor Lucena and Fernando Calero (Caracas: Ildis, 1990), p. 143–52.

48. Orangel Rivas, "Sindicalismo y sector informal urbano," in *Nuevos retos de sindicalismo*, ed. Fernando Calero (Caracas: Ildis, 1988), pp. 127–58; CGT, "Antiproyecto Ley Orgánica del Trabajo: propuestas y modificaciones" [mimeographed] (Caracas: Cenda, n.d.), p. 4.

49. The new Labor Law increased *preaviso* (whereby the employer had to notify employees prior to laying them off, or else pay an indemnity) for workers with more than five years with the company from one to two months, and to three months for those with more than ten years of service.

50. Ricardo González, "El derecho del trabajo y la crisis económica," *Revista Relaciones de Trabajo* 7 (1986), p. 284.

51. The importance of labor legislation in facilitating state control is discussed by Ruth Berins Collier and David Collier in "Inducements versus Constraints: Disaggregating 'Corporatism,' " *The American Political Science Review* 73, no. 4 (December 1979): 971.

52. The most controversial provision that was approved in the final version of the *Proyecto* was Article 442 whereby 10 percent of a union's membership could request a federal probe into their organization's finances undertaken by the Controllership of the Republic. In addition, Article 446, which allowed unions to collect extraordinary dues from nonunion members to cover collective bargaining expenses, opened the doors for government intervention on grounds that the state needed to defend those workers who were obliged to make these periodical payments but were ineligible to vote in union elections.

Conclusion

As may be expected of any large, influential organization, the CTV maintains an active presence in various institutions, where it pursues a multiplicity of short- and long-term objectives. Its most important activities and functions include participation in government-created commissions concerned with diverse problems such as inflation, immigration, and labor legislation; serving as spokesman for popular interests, which frequently leads it to oppose price increases on regulated goods and other austerity measures; the financial operations of the BTV and its affiliate companies in different sectors of the economy; training sessions sponsored by Inaesin designed to capacitate labor leaders as *cogestores*; the frequent hosting of international labor conferences, which contributes to the confederation's marked presence in the continental workers' movement; and mediation in disputes between worker organizations (not all of which belong to the CTV) and management to avoid work stoppages.

An underlying concern of the CTV that manifests itself in these activities is the avoidance of sharp confrontations. The CTV has seldom, if ever, extended decisive support to the workers for the purpose of winning a strike. On the contrary, the confederation invariably either condemns work stoppages or maintains a neutral stand. On the international front, the CTV also upholds a discrete uncommitted position with regard to the dispute between U.S. and European labor movements (see Chapter 5). Finally, the CTV's strategy to achieve *cogestión* is based on persuasion and consensus rather than on conflict, even though business interests have been unreceptive to the idea. Only in its daily public pronouncements does the CTV consistently criticize Fedecámaras, but such rhetorical opposition rarely gets translated into vigorous action.

Until the economic crisis in the late 1980s, the labor movement and Fedecámaras had never been locked into irreconcilable positions on major issues over an extended period. Most labor gains (the passage of the law establishing the BTV in 1966, the reforms dictated by Carlos Andrés Pérez in 1974, and the granting of *estabilidad absoluta* to the oil workers in 1976, to name but a few) were not the outcome of protracted worker struggles; in some cases, these concessions actually took the labor movement by surprise.

On May 18, 1989, the CTV launched a general strike, which was resolutely condemned by the business community at the same time that the confederation called for the prompt ratification of the new labor law, one that Fedecámaras predicted would bring economic disaster on the nation. These disagreements marked the beginning of a new era in labor-business relations.

The historical behavior of the CTV has influenced political spokesmen, trade unionists, and social scientists—all of whom utilize a variety of conceptual frameworks—in their depictions of the role of labor in national politics. They concur that the reduced levels of labor conflict in Venezuela have ensured against violent and brusk political change. Venezuelan exceptionalists view labor as contributing to the social stability and durability of the democratic system, which stands in marked contrast to other Latin American nations since the late 1950s. Other writers use a corporatist frame of reference to show that the Venezuelan workers' movement, like its counterparts throughout the hemisphere, is straitjacketed by policies and structures imposed by the state that restrict autonomy and encourage labor passivity.

AD trade unionists and writers of a social democratic orientation also downplay social conflict in their interpretations of recent Venezuelan history. They credit the workers' movement with having constituted the main bulwark of the democratic system since 1958 and for acting as the major agent in socioeconomic transformation. The social democrats attribute AD labor's growing influence within the party to its cohesiveness, its conscious embracement of long-term objectives such as *cogestión*, and its role as mediator in intraparty disputes that enhance its prestige. They also extol the efforts of AD labor leaders to transform the CTV into a truly pluralistic organization by offering small parties and individual trade unionists positions on the confederation's Executive Committee. The social democrats envision AD, with its labor leadership in the forefront, as serving as a vehicle for far-reaching change in the absence of violence at a future date. They argue that AD's mass base and the nation's well-established democratic tradition rule out the need to rely on force.[1]

Many of the defenders of these varied theses (exceptionalism, corporatism, and social democratic doctrine) underestimate the tension that has existed among rank-and-file workers and take at face value the overt objectives of the party's labor leadership without considering possible unstated motives. AD, as a mass-based party, has always felt the discontent of the popular classes at all levels of the organization. Its labor leaders are particularly subject to this pressure from below, as is shown by the number of them who have left the party or have been shunted aside as a result of political disputes. Due to AD's vertical structure and extreme internal discipline, however, differences are usually suppressed and only come to the surface following the consummation of a division. This dynamic, in which concrete political differences were not apparent prior to party splits, has misled political analysts; many of them erroneously deny that programmatic or ideological conflict lay behind the various schisms in AD, which they ascribe exclusively to personality differences and internal power struggles.[2]

Social democratic writers who stress AD labor's central role in party affairs since 1958, particularly in favor of the maintenance of unity, overlook its failure to parlay this internal influence and prestige into worker gains. AD trade union leaders have ended up disillusioned with the performance of the nation's three presidents who owed their nomination to labor backing: Leoni, whose selection as candidate was an initiative of the Labor Bureau, but who subsequently sided with the conservative *betancourista*-wing of the party; Lusinchi, who was nominated and elected "on the shoulders of the workers"; and Carlos Andrés Pérez, who triumphed over Lepage thanks to the solid backing of the Labor Bureau.

The gap between rhetoric and reality is evident in the social democratic portrayal of the role of organized labor in the years immediately following the overthrow of Pérez Jiménez, when the democratic regime was threatened by right- and left-wing insurgencies. Labor leaders are praised for having subordinated bread-and-butter demands to political imperatives by signing the *Pacto de Avenimiento Obrero Patronal* in 1958, which discouraged strikes, and for accepting the Betancourt administration's austerity policies. In fact, the pact did not commit labor to refrain from work stoppages, as was underlined in a resolution at the CTV's Third Congress the following year. Furthermore, many top AD labor leaders called for modification of such government measures as the Hunger Law, although they did not go as far as leftists in calling for its repeal. The armed struggle placed these critical trade unionists in an awkward position, since the questioning of government policy was interpreted by some as tacit support for the leftist subversives. Only after the guerrilla threat subsided did internal tensions crystallize, giving rise to the MEP split in 1967.

The increase in strike activity after 1968 has been attributed to the emergence of the left-leaning MEP and the manipulations of AD, which for the first time since 1958 found itself in the opposition. Although these party factors were undoubtedly influential, the new setting created by the virtual elimination of subversive activity was also important. Not only did trade unionists have greater liberty to call work stoppages as a result of the lifting of restrictions, but also rising expectations spurred workers to action after a decade of government pleas to accept sacrifices for the sake of the nation's fledgling democracy. After the election of Pérez in 1973, strike activity tapered off, although it did not return to pre-1969 levels. The same combination of party factors and general environment explained the relative passivity of workers. On the one hand, AD was back in power and had recouped most of its influence in organized labor at the expense of MEP. On the other hand, the windfall in oil revenue brought with it a sudden prosperity and created a veritable euphoria among the general populace. This aura of bonanza was not conducive to social protests, as was recognized by labor and leftist leaders alike. Economic difficulties set in, in the early 1980s, but there was a time lag in popular reaction. AD politicians assured the public that their return to power would trigger a restoration of the prosperity of the 1970s. Furthermore, substantial government financial reserves accumulated during the previous decade helped mitigate the initial impact of the recession. By the end of the 1980s, however, these public savings had been unwisely exhausted, and most Venezuelans showed signs of impatience at the steady deterioration in living standards.

The social scientists and labor leaders who emphasize the prevalence of social harmony in Venezuela were undoubtedly taken by surprise by the violent events of February 27, 1989, as was the nation as a whole. The increase in labor unrest and social tension in general since the mid-1980s demonstrates that *"el 27 de febrero"* was not an anomaly and that the case for Venezuelan exceptionalism has been overstated.

It is true that the Venezuelan political culture and mentality were shaped over a period of several decades by a particular set of conditions that channeled grievances through electoral politics rather than in the form of street actions. Nevertheless, from the perspective of the early 1990s, it is evident that many of the explanations of Venezuelan stability that have been offered by exceptionalists do not give sufficient weight to circumstantial factors. Two stand out as particularly important: the widespread repudiation of the armed sruggle in the 1960s, which influenced Venezuelans to refrain from protests that could be confused with leftist-inspired political disruptions; and the oil-induced prosperity of the 1970s, which also discouraged popular mobilizations.

The social unrest of recent years demonstrates the relativeness and fluidity of factors that the exceptionalists posit as long-lasting and enduring. The stability of oil prices, for instance, which differentiated Venezuela from other single-product exporting nations, was interrupted in 1986 when OPEC prices nose-dived to one third their previous levels. Furthermore, the allegedly "responsible" leadership of moderates who reached consociational arrangements excluding Communists—which are highlighted by some of the exceptionalists—apparently did not outlast the decade. The administration of Jaime Lusinchi was riddled by corruption, leading to the subsequent arrests of several of its top members and imputations against the former president himself. At the same time, the formal agreements among nonleftists (the Punto Fijo, *Ancha Base*, and Institutional pacts), which in various forms had guided Venezuelan democracy for three decades, also ran their course; in 1989 the *Copeyanos* allied with parties to their left in several state and municipal elections. Another unpropitious trend developed beginning in 1988. Venezuela's tradition of mass participation in voting, which has been emphasized by political scientists who praise the nation's political system, was severed when levels of abstentionism dramatically increased. Equally significant is the emergence of the intransigent Causa R—a party that owed its initial growth to worker struggles in heavy industry—as an important point of political reference. Finally, the AD leadership of organized labor hardened its stance by calling protests and openly criticizing the economic measures taken by AD governments, unlike in the past when important policy differences surfaced only at the time of party schisms.

Alongside the particular characteristics that set off the nation from its neighbors, Venezuela remains as dependent as ever before, with all the socioeconomic problems that dependent status implies. Most important, in Venezuela, as on the rest of the continent, more than half the population belongs to the marginal class and is trapped in dire poverty.[3] As was the case with other dependent nations that enjoyed transitory prosperity as a result of favorable market conditions for its main export product,[4] the experience of Venezuela following the oil price hikes in 1973 demonstrates that a sudden influx of revenue does not in itself guarantee structural transformation, nor does it necessarily help lessen social inequality. Thus, the affirmations of the exceptionalists regarding Venezuela's uniqueness should not divert attention from the common challenges and problems that, to a greater or lesser extent, all Latin American nations face.

An analysis of the structural transformation of the petroleum industry— and specifically its labor force—demonstrates the need to qualify or refine generalizations regarding the exceptionalism of the Venezuelan workers' movement and its ongoing passivity. Until 1960 the oil workers had constituted a vanguard; their militant struggles in favor of union recognition, *estabilidad absoluta*, and the overthrow of the Pérez Jiménez dictatorship had served as an inspiration for the rest of the working class. Subsequently, however, the oil workers refrained from strikes, and their leaders accepted a flexible policy of piecemeal negotiations as individual problems arose rather than embracing such banners as *estabilidad absoluta*, defense of the commissaries, and elimination of the *contratista* system. After the purging of trade unionists of the proscribed MIR and PCV from the industry in the early 1960s (allegedly at the instigation of the government), majority representation in the oil workers' leadership was retained by moderate AD and *Copeyano* trade unionists. This political pattern contrasted with the main raw material export industries in other Latin American nations, such as Bolivia (tin) and Chile (copper), that were dominated by militant and leftist labor leaders over an extended period of time.

Nevertheless, the stereotype of oil workers as an elite sector is misleading. As discussed in Chapter 6, both material and nonmaterial benefits in the oil industry have not been evenly distributed among all workers, and the resultant fragmentation of the labor force has facilitated nonleftist control and discouraged industrywide strategies and protest. Thus, for instance, one third of the work force are contracted workers who are easily manipulated by the dominant sector in the union and who are denied the most important oil workers' gain, *estabilidad absoluta*. Furthermore, the sharp fluctuations and uncertainty in the oil industry, which had such a devastating effect on the Venezuelan economy as a whole in the 1980s, have particularly hurt oil workers, whose living conditions have deteriorated even more than their counterparts in other major industries. As a result of growing discontent, militant leftists made inroads in several important oil camps throughout the nation.

The exceptionalism and social democratic theses take for granted AD's overwhelming strength in the labor movement. The party's consistently large representation at CTV congresses and its control of the confederation's Executive Committee, however, exaggerate its real influence among workers. AD has been strongest in sparsely populated states and among public employees who are often hired on the basis of clientelistic considerations; the Left's following is greatest in highly concentrated, strategic sectors such as petroleum (although MEP's influence has always fallen short of the majority needed to set policy), steel, and textiles. Furthermore, the electoral procedures of some of the CTV's affiliate organizations have been highly questioned. Sometimes elections are not widely publicized among the workers, and the process of nominating delegates takes on the form of a caucus. Various federations have been overrepresented in the CTV as a result of inflated membership figures. The representation of the FCV, for instance, which was highly controlled by AD, was not readjusted in accordance with the declining size of the nation's peasantry; the FCV is the only federation whose officials—in addition to those on its Executive Committee—receive automatic delegate status (*delegados natales*) at CTV congresses. Finally, important strikes have been carried out in recent years by state-employed professionals (such as doctors, grade-school and university teachers, laboratory analysts, and engineers) who are grouped in professional associations (*colegios*) that are outside the fold of the AD-dominated CTV.

Some writers and AD trade unionists have painted a picture of the CTV as pluralistic, internationally prestigious, and concerned about the well-being of the popular classes in general. Indeed, this image has been carefully cultivated by the CTV leadership. Small parties, for instance, that agree to form part of united slates in trade union elections have been rewarded positions beyond what their limited worker influence warrants. This "generosity" is designed to lend credibility to the claim that the CTV has achieved a consensus of politically and ideologically diverse currents. The CTV's active participation in and frequent sponsorship of international conferences also enhance the CTV's reputation, contributing to its status as one of the outstanding labor organizations in Latin America (see Chapter 5). Finally, the CTV has arrogated to itself the role of spokesman for the popular classes.

The hiatus between the CTV's claim to represent broad segments of the population and its day-to-day behavior must be examined against the backdrop of the economic crisis of the 1980s and 1990s. During these years the CTV failed to live up to its historical role as defender of the nonprivileged classes, a position it had most clearly assumed at the outset of the modern, democratic period. The CTV and its precursor organizations had been instrumental in channeling popular sentiment in favor of democracy, in the form of the January 21, 1958, general strike and subsequent mobilizations that served as warnings to military conspirators. Throughout the years, the defense of the interests of broad sectors of the population—and not just those of unionized workers—was a major CTV goal. The wide scope of the CTV's concerns was demonstrated by its adamant support for increases in the minimum wage and the application of the benefits of the labor law to workers in the informal economy.

The mass protests of the recent past, however, left the CTV largely on the sidelines. The initially hostile position of the CTV toward the February 27, 1989, disturbances was representative of the gap between the confederation and those students and poor people who participated in the protests that became a daily phenomenon in cities across the nation. Worse still for the CTV, a large number of these street actions were in opposition to the increase in public transportation fares and were directed against the CTV-affiliated transportation workers' unions, thus placing the confederation in an extremely awkward position. Finally, the growth of the CTV's economic empire and charges of flagrant misuse of funds leveled against top CTV officials only widened the distance between the CTV and the popular classes and undermined the credibility of the confederation's effort to pose as a champion of the latter.

Despite this shortcoming, which was of no small concern for labor leaders, the CTV continued to represent the attitudes and priorities of its major constituency. Rival militant confederations and independent unions did not make significant inroads in traditional sectors of the working class, which was the CTV's stronghold, as occurred in Colombia, Peru, and elsewhere. The success of the CTV leadership in retaining a hold over its rank and file was due not only to dubious electoral practices, but also to the positions it assumed. In the face of the economic crisis, the CTV skillfully disassociated itself from the AD governments of Jaime Lusinchi and Carlos Andrés Pérez. Most AD labor leaders refused to endorse President Lusinchi's choice for the presidential nomination of 1988, and under the second Pérez administration, they became firm critics of the government's neoliberal economic policies. The CTV called several national political strikes and protests that were opposed by the AD government and party. These mobilizations were certainly no more than a moderate response, given the intensity and duration of the crisis. Nevertheless, the traditional working class was reluctant to follow the lead of other sectors, such as public workers who were mainly outside the CTV's fold, in calling work stoppages and pursuing a more militant course. The only important industrial unions whose behavior departed from this general pattern were the textile and steel workers, for reasons related to the rather unique market conditions in those industries (see Chapter 7).

The CTV's efforts to pose as a paladin of the popular classes in general and not just organized workers is perhaps meant to impress the state more than the confederation's own members. On the basis of the CTV's claim to represent workers of all ideological convictions, and even those who are outside the confines of organized labor, the government grants the confederation and its affiliate organizations the lion's share of the subsidies earmarked for the labor movement. In addition, the government has provided special treatment to the CTV's enterprises, particularly the BTV. Indeed, the dues collected from CTV worker members are insignificant in comparison to this direct and indirect financial aid. The CTV's claim to near-monopoly status also helps to ensure that its appointees serve as the exclusive representatives of the workers on government commissions, tripartite commissions under the direction of the Labor Ministry, and the executive boards of state companies and institutes.

The need to go beyond appearances and stated objectives is illustrated by the CTV's assertion that the BTV has provided the labor movement with an autonomous status that both business organizations and political parties find threatening. Some writers take at face value CTV President José Vargas's claim that his organization had achieved "financial autonomy." As discussed in Chapter 8, the BTV was initially endowed with temporary privileges that were not contemplated in existing banking legislation. The bank's rapid growth in the 1970s and early 1980s was made possible by this special treatment and the state's tolerance of practices that were not even authorized in the law creating the BTV. Thus, exemptions originally designed to get the BTV off the ground were extended indefinitely, allowing the bank to become the largest in the nation. Far from ensuring the CTV's autonomy, the BTV increased the confederation's dependence on the state.

Scholars who accept a corporatist paradigm attribute labor stability to the tight control exercised by the state in trade union affairs. Corporatist models and policies were originally analyzed in depth in the 1970s to explain the linkages between civil institutions, particularly organized labor, and the state in Latin America. Those who point to the applicability of corporatism in Venezuela emphasize the following features of state-labor relations: the government's recognition of the CTV as the sole representative of the working class; the creation of tripartite commissions to discuss aspects of government policy that relate directly to worker interests and to settle disputes involving worker severance pay; certain articles of the labor law authorizing the Labor Ministry to monitor and control union activities; the system of worker representation on the board of directors of all state companies and public institutes; severe restrictions on the right to strike; efforts to implement a "social pact," whereby employee and employer organizations are in constant communication and guidelines for price and salary increases are mutually set at the macro level; and worker achievement of their most important gains in the absence of militant struggle.[5] Political scientist Jennifer McCoy has argued that the state's assumption of an interventionist role in union affairs and labor relations—a basic characteristic of corporatism—was closely related to the state capitalist model, which was made possible by the windfall in oil revenue in the 1970s. According to McCoy, interventionism was also a reaction to the labor movement's efforts to assert its independence, as manifested by a marked increase in strike activity and the financial leverage provided by the BTV.[6]

Statements regarding the dependent status of the Venezuelan labor movement and other corporatist features need to be qualified. Many of the mechanisms and legal provisions that appear to facilitate state domination have not been effectively utilized. Thus, for instance, some writers have noted that the Labor Ministry's monitoring and information-gathering faculties intimidate and constrain unions.[7] Nevertheless, in practice, the ministry does not interfere in union decision making, not even in the delicate areas of union elections (as does the U.S. government) or finances, nor does it ever revoke the legal status of labor organizations. In general, the Labor Ministry lacks the resources and influence of its counterparts in Latin American nations that were clearly subject to corporatist structures, such as the governments of Getulio Vargas in Brazil and Juan Domingo Perón in Argentina. In addition, the "social pact" and policy of "concertation," which suggests an ongoing harmonious interaction between business and labor—a hallmark of corporatism—were largely dropped from political vernacular by the early 1990s, having failed to withstand the test of a difficult economic period. Finally, the system of labor representation on the executive boards of state firms, which also has corporatist implications, has not been developed by the labor movement into a meaningful mechanism of input into decision making at the micro level (see Chapter 8).

This is not to argue that the duality of state incentives and constraints, which some writers point to as corporatism's modus operandi designed to ensure labor docility, has not played an important role. Support for the BTV was a particularly effective incentive since the bank received multiple official and extraofficial exemptions from legal requirements, thus placing the labor movement at the mercy of the government. An example of a major constraint is the limitation on the right to strike. Most work stoppages are declared illegal, although more coercive measures are generally not employed; the degree to which failure to gain legal recognition restrains workers from going on strike is worthy of further inquiry.

Political party ties, however, are a more important locus of labor constraint. The Labor Bureau of AD, and its equivalent in other parties, links the party's national leadership to its worker fractions. This bond is reinforced by the positions that worker leaders occupy in the party's hierarchy, their selection as candidates to legislative bodies, and in numerous other ways. More important than state domination are these vertical lines of command in which the party's commitment to labor peace is transferred to organized labor.

The relative importance of party as against state control can be illustrated by the following example. Writers who argue in favor of the application of the state-mediated model to Venezuela point to the promulgation of the *Ley de Seguridad y Defensa* in 1975 as a powerful tool to repress militant worker struggle in the strategic Guayana region. Nevertheless, the law has never been invoked. At the moment that a general strike loomed as a real possibility in the area as a result of apparently insurmountable differences in collective bargaining in the steel industry in 1981, AD and Copei intervened in the dispute. In agreeing to the takeover of Sutiss, the two parties adhered to a tradition dating back to 1958 of closing ranks in the face of threats to stability. The measure, however, was not successful in the long run. In the first place, Copei reconsidered its support for the intervention and, in the second, the Left triumphed when elections were finally held six years later. The incident shows that most of the important instruments of control originate in the party, but that their utilization is risky and not always effective in the long run.

Political analysts have not paid sufficient attention to the internal tension and ongoing strains in organized labor and specifically the AD workers' movement. This neglect is understandable given the tendency of some writers (those who accept exceptionalism and corporatist assumptions) to depict labor as a passive actor in the political life of the nation or, in the case of the social democrats, as constituting a powerful bloc whose cohesiveness and uniformity of objectives have allowed it to play a major role in national politics. The ongoing internal conflict in the labor movement demonstrates its unpredictability and radical potential. Both characteristics are important in explaining the reaction of powerful sectors to certain policies and projects embraced by the CTV, such as the Workers Bank. The BTV was not in itself threatening to the status quo since its CTV architects did not design a strategy to utilize the bank's enormous resources to enhance union bargaining power or to confront business interests. Nevertheless, at a future date, perhaps in the hands of a different leadership, a radicalized CTV would be able to use the BTV to finance strikes. It is this potential, rather than the BTV's present functions or short-term prospects, that explains the reservations of the business community toward the bank ever since its founding in 1966.[8]

The ability of AD and CTV leaders to avoid internal confrontations and disunity will be a major factor in ensuring Venezuela's ongoing stability. It is unlikely that AD—with its mass base—and the CTV—with its tradition of near-monopoly status in organized labor—will be easily displaced or eclipsed by leftist groups. Nevertheless, an erosion of their influence will undoubtedly create internal strains that may represent a more serious challenge for them than opposition from the Left. A host of variables will enter into play in determining whether the proestablishment parties and the CTV are able to check internal discord and retain hegemony. Leadership skill is just one factor—the writing of the exceptionalists who stress statecraft notwithstanding. The weight of political culture and general attitudes in avoiding breakdown is also quite relative, especially because thirty years of political stability is not sufficient time to instill in the general populace a deep-seated rejection of mass protest and popular resistance.

The arguments of Venezuelan exceptionalism that have influenced scholars, and even more so the general populace and its leaders, are not as plausible in the context of the early 1990s as they were in the past. The circumstantial developments of the 1960s and 1970s have run their course, and a multiplicity of new factors—such as the sharp fluctuations in the price of oil, the volatility of the underprivileged sectors, and the surge in strike activity—has emerged, making predictions hazardous. The optimistic assumptions regarding the future of those exceptionalists who defend the status quo, and the pessimism of those exceptionalists who favor radical change, have been undermined. Specifically, in the case of organized labor, its docility and role as a major prop of the established system—a cornerstone of Venezuelan exceptionalism—cannot be taken for granted.

Notes

1. Julio Godio defends this thesis in *El movimiento obrero venezolano*, p. 3.

2. In 1967, Rómulo Betancourt fervently argued that the dissident leaders who formed MEP and ARS were motivated exclusively by personal ambition. This position subsequently influenced many writers on the period. Similar accusations were leveled in private at Carlos Luna by fellow AD labor leaders. ARSistas and MEPistas have maintained that programmatic and ideological issues were at the root of the divisions they led. See, for example, Manuel Alfredo Rodríguez (former ARSista), "Ramos Giménez," *El Nacional*, May 11, 1990, p. A-4. This issue is explored in Ellner, "Political Party Dynamics and the Outbreak of Guerrilla Warfare," pp. 12–20.

3. For a descriptive account of the living conditions of underprivileged classes in Venezuela, see George W. Schuyler, *Hunger in a Land of Plenty* (Cambridge, MA: Schenkman, 1980).

4. Andre Gunder Frank calls this phenomenon "the development of underdevelopment" in his *Capitalism and Underdevelopment in Latin America: Historical Studies of Chile and Brazil* (New York: Monthly Review Press, 1967).

5. Luis Salamanca analyzes these characteristics in "La incorporación de la Confederación de Trabajadores de Venezuela." For references to other writers who attempt to demonstrate the influence of corporatism in Venezuela, see Ellner, "Organized Labor's Political Influence," pp. 115–16.

6. Jennifer L. McCoy, "Labor and the State in a Party-mediated Democracy: Institutional Change in Venezuela," *Latin American Research Review* 24, no. 2 (1989): 35–67.

7. Ibid., p. 55; Salamanca, "La incorporación de la Confederación de Trabajadores," p. 188.

8. The unpredictable nature and radical potential of the reforms and programs embraced by AD during an earlier period are explored by Steve Ellner in "The Venezuelan Non-Communist Left in Power, 1945–1948," in *Latin American Labor from the Second World War to the Cold War*, ed. Leslie Bethell and Ian Roxborough, to be published by Cambridge University Press. Other authors have discussed this characteristic with reference to populist and corporatist policies in third-world nations. See Ernesto Laclau, *Politics and Ideology in Marxist Theory: Capitalism, Fascism, Populism* (London: NLB, 1977), chap. 5; John D. French, "Workers and the Rise of Adhemarista Populism in Sao Paulo, Brazil 1945–47," *Hispanic American Historical Review* 68, no. 1 (1988): 1–43; Geoff Hodgson, "Communication," *New Left Review* 128 (July-August, 1981): 97.

Selected Bibliography

Abente, Diego. "Politics and Policies: The Limits of the Venezuelan Consociational Regime." In *Democracy in Latin America: Colombia and Venezuela*. Edited by Donald L. Herman, 133–54. New York: Praeger, 1988.

Alexander, Robert Jackson. *Rómulo Betancourt and the Transformation of Venezuela*. New Brunswick, NJ: Transaction Books, 1982.

————. *The Venezuelan Democratic Revolution*. New Brunswick, NJ: Rutgers University Press, 1964.

Alfonzo Guzmán, Rafael. *Estudio analítico de la ley del trabajo venezolano*. 2 vols. Caracas: UCV, 1967.

Basurto, Jorge. "The Late Populism of Luis Echeverría." In *Latin American Populism in Comparative Perspective*. Edited by Michael L. Conniff, 93–111. Albuquerque, NM: University of New Mexico Press, 1982.

Belmonte Guzmán, Amalio; Briceño Reyes, Dimitri; and Urbano Taylor, Henry. *Ensayo sobre historia política de Venezuela (1917–1968)*. Caracas: Academia Nacional de la Historia, 1981.

Bergquist, Charles. *Labor in Latin America: Comparative Essays on Chile, Argentina, Venezuela, and Colombia*. Stanford, CA: Stanford University Press, 1986.

Bernardoni de Govea, Maria, and Zuleta de Merchán, Carmen. *Análisis sobre la cogestión y otras formas de participación obrera: caso Venezuela*. Maracaibo: Universidad de Zulia, 1985.

Betancourt, Rómulo. *La revolución democrática en Venezuela*. Caracas: n.p., 1968.

Boeckh, Andreas. "Organized Labor and Government under Conditions of Economic Scarcity." Ph.D. diss., University of Florida, 1972.

Bruni Celli, Marco Tulio. "Pluralismo ideológico y cogestión obrera." *Nueva Sociedad* 70 (January-February 1984): 72–81.

Caldera, Rafael. *Derecho del Trabajo*. 2d ed., 3d printing. Buenos Aires: Editorial "El Ateneo," 1972.

Calero, Fernando, ed. *Nuevos retos del sindicalismo*. Caracas: Ildis, 1988.

Centro de Desarrollo (Cendes). *Estudio de conflictos y consenso: muestra de líderes sindicales*. Vol. 1. Caracas: Imprenta Universitaria, 1965.

Chene D., Andrés de. *La transformación de comunidades petroleras*. N.p.: n.d.

Collier, Ruth Berins, and Collier, David. *Shaping the Political Arena: Critical Junctures, the Labor Movement, and Regime Dynamics in Latin America.* Princeton, NJ: Princeton University Press, 1991.

Colmenarez, Nestor. *Sindicalismo irreverente.* Valencia, Venezuela: Raúl Clemente Editores, 1988.

Confederación de Trabajadores de Venezuela. *Antecedentes y testimonios de los congresos de la CTV.* 4 vols. Caracas: Inaesin, n.d.

———. *Participación de los trabajadores en la dirección de la empresa.* Caracas: Ildis, 1979.

———. *20 años de la ley de representación laboral: ahora la cogestión!* Caracas: Departamento de Cogestión [CTV], 1986.

Contratación colectiva petrolera venezolana, 1946–1973. Caracas: Litocromo, n.d.

Davis, Charles L. *Working-class Mobilization and Political Control: Venezuela and Mexico.* Lexington, KY: University of Kentucky Press, 1989.

Delpino, Juan José. "Diálogo con Juan José Delpino: hacia una organización sindical latinoamericana." *Nueva Sociedad* 70 (January–February 1984): 23–33.

Departamento de Cogestión [CTV]. *20 años de la ley de representación laboral: ahora la cogestión!* Caracas: Editorial Gente, 1986.

Díaz Apitz, Johnny. *El sindicalismo venezolano necesita una renovación* [speech in los Teques, May 2, 1983]. Guarenas: Formateco.

Ellner, Steve. *From Guerrilla Defeat to Innovative Politics: Venezuela's Movimiento al Socialismo.* Durham, NC: Duke University Press, 1988.

———. "Organized Labor's Political Influence and Party Ties in Venezuela: Acción Democrática and Its Labor Leadership." *Journal of Interamerican Studies and World Affairs* 31, no. 4 (Winter 1989): 91–129.

———. "Venezuela." In *Latin American Labor Organizations.* Edited by Gerald Michael Greenfield and Sheldon L. Maram, 727–60. New York: Greenwood Press, 1987.

Ewell, Judith. *Venezuela: A Century of Change.* Stanford, CA: Stanford University Press, 1984.

Fagen, Stuart I. "Unionism and Democracy." In *Venezuela: The Democratic Experience.* Edited by John D. Martz and David J. Myers. New York: Praeger, 1977.

Frente de Trabajadores Copeyanos. *Manifiesto del Frente de Trabajadores Copeyanos.* Caracas: Talleres Gráficos, 1984.

Fuenmayor, Juan Bautista. *Historia de la Venezuela política contemporánea, 1899–1969.* Vol. 12. Caracas: Miguel Angel García, 1985.

Godio, Julio. *El movimiento obrero venezolano, 1945–1980.* 3 vols. Caracas: Ildis, 1980–1985.

González, Armando. *Grava de una misma cantera.* Caracas: Editorial Arte, 1977.

González, Dagoberto. *La reforma de la ley del trabajo.* Caracas: Copei, 1964.

González Navarro, José. *Sindicalismo, libertad y desarrollo*. 2 vols. Caracas: Asociación Venezolana de Ejecutivos, n.d.

Herman, Donald L. *Christian Democracy in Venezuela*. Chapel Hill, NC: University of North Carolina Press, 1980.

Hernández Alvarez, Oscar. "Comentarios al capítulo sobre organizaciones sindicales del anteproyecto de la ley orgánica del trabajo." *Revista Relaciones de Trabajo* 7 (1986): 333–52.

Hung Vaillant, Francisco. *Contribución al estudio de la ley contra despidos injustificados*. Caracas: Editorial Jurídica Venezolana, 1979.

Karl, Terry Lynn. "Petroleum and Political Pacts: The Transition to Democracy in Venezuela." *Latin American Research Review* 22, no. 1 (1987): 63–94.

Lestienne, Bernardo. *El sindicalimso venezolano*. Caracas: Centro Gumilla, 1981.

Levine, Daniel H. "Venezuela: The Nature, Sources, and Future Prospects of Democracy." In *Democracy in Developing Countries: Latin America*. Edited by Larry Diamond, Juan J. Linz, and Seymour Martin Lipset, 247–89. Boulder, CO: Lynne Rienner Publishers, 1989.

———. "Venezuela since 1958: The Consolidation of Democratic Politics." In *The Breakdown of Democratic Regimes: Latin America*. Edited by Juan J. Linz and Alfred Stepan, 82–109. Baltimore: Johns Hopkins University Press, 1978.

López Maya, Margarita. *El banco de los trabajadores de Venezuela: algo más que un banco?* Caracas: UCV, 1989.

———, and Werz, Nikolaus. *El estado y el movimiento sindical (1958–1980)*. Caracas: Cendes, 1981.

Lucena, Héctor. *El movimiento obrero petrolero: proceso de formación y desarrollo*. Caracas: Ediciones Centauro, 1982.

———. "Concertación y revisión en las relaciones laborales." *Revista Relaciones de Trabajo* 5 (1985): 6–28.

———. "Contratación colectiva y participación en la empresa pública." *Revista Relaciones de Trabajo* 2 (1983): 29–48.

———. "El movimiento de los trabajadores y la creación de los sindicatos nacionales." *Estudios laborales: ensayos sobre derecho del trabajo y disciplinas afines. . . .* Edited by Francisco Iturraspe, 457–72. Caracas: UCV, 1986.

———. "Experiencias de participación de los trabajadores en la gestión de las empresas en Venezuela." In *Participación, cogestión y autogestión en América Latina*. Vol. 2. Edited by Francisco Iturraspe, 199–240. Caracas: Editorial Nueva Sociedad, 1986.

———. "La cogestión y la CTV." *Revista Relaciones de Trabajo* 1 (November 1981): 15–36.

———, and Calero, Fernando., eds. *Las relaciones de trabajo en los noventa: desafíos y propuestas*. Caracas: Ildis, 1990.

McCoy, Jennifer L. "Democratic Stability and Regime Change: Inducements and Constraints in Venezuela." Paper delivered at the 1985 convention of

the American Political Science Association, New Orleans, August 29–
September 1, 1985.

————. "Labor and the State in a Party-mediated Democracy: Institutional
Change in Venezuela." *Latin American Research Review* 24, no. 2 (1989):
35–67.

Maneiro, Alfredo. *Notas políticas.* Caracas: Ediciones del Agua Mansa,
1986.

Martín, Américo. *Marcuse y Venezuela: se aburguesa a la clase obrera en
Venezuela?* N.p.: Cuadaernos Rocinante, 1969.

Martz, John D. "The Growth and Democratization of the Venezuelan Labor
Movement." *Inter-American Economic Affairs* 17, no. 2 (Autumn 1963).

Maza Zavala, D. F. *Venezuela: historia de una frustración* [interviews by
Agustín Blanco Muñoz]. Caracas: UCV, 1986.

Medina, Pablo. *Pablo Medina en entrevista.* Caracas: Ediciones del Agua
Mansa, 1988.

Mercau, Andrés. *La contratición colectiva.* Caracas: Ediciones "Claridad,"
n.d.

Moleiro, Moisés. *El partido del pueblo: crónica de un fraude.* 2d ed.
Valencia, Venezuela: Vadell Hermanos, 1979.

Naim, Moisés, and Piñango, Ramón. "El caso Venezuela: una ilusión de
armonía." In *El caso Venezuela: una ilusión de armonía*, 538–79. Edited
by Moisés Naim and Ramón Piñango. Caracas: Ediciones IEASA, 1986.

Parker, Richard. "Consideraciones en torno a la ley del trabajo del año
1936." *Estudios laborales: ensayos sobre derecho del trabajo y disciplinas
afines. . . .* Vol. 2. Edited by Francisco Iturraspe, 201–18. Caracas: UCV,
1986.

Peñalver, Manuel. "No existe conquista social o económica que no tenga
huella cetevista." In *CTV: 50 años de historia, 1936–1986*, 35–37. N.p.:
CTV, n.d.

Piñerua, Carlos. *Los trabajadores por la nacionalización integral de la
industria petrolera* [speech delivered February 16, 1975]. N.p.: n.d.

Pla, Alberto J.; Castro, Pedro; and Aizpúrua, Ramón, et al., eds. *Clase
obrera, partidos y sindicatos en Venezuela, 1936–1950.* Caracas: Ediciones
Centauro, 1982.

Powell, John Duncan. *Political Mobilization of the Venezuelan Peasant.*
Cambridge, MA: Harvard University Press, 1971.

Prieto Figueroa, Luis Beltrán. "Estabilidad en el trabajo." In *Proyecto de ley
de estabilidad en el trabajo*, 5–12. Edited by Antonio Espinoza Prieto,
Prieto Figueroa, and Jesús Angel Paz Galarraga. Caracas: n.p., 1969.

Proceso Político. "Surge el proletariado (la lucha de los trabajadores textiles)." *Proceso Político* 7 (April 1978): 1–70.

Quijada, Ramón. *Reforma agraria en Venezuela.* Caracas: Editorial Arte,
1963.

Rachadell, Manuel. "Aspectos políticos de la carrera administrativa." In
*Estudios laborales: ensayos sobre derecho del trabajo y disciplinas
afines . . .*, 252–72. Edited by Francisco José Iturraspe. Caracas: UCV,
1986.

Romualdi, Serafino. *Presidents and Peons: Recollections of a Labor Ambassador in Latin America.* New York: Funk and Wagnalls, 1967.

Salamanca, Luis. "La incorporación de la Confederación de Trabajadores de Venezuela al sistema político venezolano, 1958–1980." Caracas: UCV, 1988.

Soto, Oscar David. *La empresa y la reforma agraria en la agricultura venezolana.* Mérida: FCV, 1973.

Torres, Eloy. *Ideología y sindicalismo.* Caracas: Cantaclaro, 1970.

Valente, Cecilia M. *The Political, Economic and Labor Climate in Venezuela.* Philadelphia: University of Pennsylvania Press, 1979.

Velásquez, Andrés. *Andrés Velásquez en entrevistas.* Caracas: Ediciones del Agua Mansa, 1987.

Velásquez, Ramón J. "Aspectos de la evolución política de Venezuela en el último medio siglo." In *Venezuela moderna: medio siglo de historia, 1926–1976,* 13–433. Caracas: Editorial Ariel, 1979.

Index

Acuña, Máximo, 187
AD (Acción Democrática), 1, 87–91,
    169, 222, 223, 226, 230, 231;
    during Betancourt period, 9–29,
    96; and BTV, 98, 181–88; during
    Caldera period, 42–50; and
    cogestión, 178, 179, 181;
    factionalism in, 7, 16–17, 28–29,
    40–41, 76–80, 85, 97; during
    Herrera Campíns period, 65–71;
    influence in CTV, 20–21, 39, 52,
    53, 69, 74, 84–85; international
    ties of, 14–15, 21, 114–18;
    during Larrazábal period, 5–9;
    during Leoni period, 37–42;
    during Lusinchi period, 71–81;
    among oil workers, 17–18, 131–
    43, 225; during Pérez period,
    (1974–79) 50–58, (1989–94) 81–
    86; position on labor legislation,
    199, 200, 205, 206, 211; among
    steel workers, 44, 80–81, 156,
    157, 158; in struggle against
    Pérez Jiménez, 2, 3, 4, 7; among
    textile workers, 164, 166; trade
    union strategy of, 98–102. See
    also Labor Bureau; Old Guard
AFL (American Federation of Labor),
    114, 126
AFL-CIO, 15, 20, 21, 115, 116, 117,
    118, 127, 128, 130n. 44; support
    for CTV, 38, 114, 117
Agency shop, 203–4
Agrarian Bureau, 26, 77
Agrarian reform, 25–29, 34n. 104,
    189, 190
Aguero Gorrín, Enrique, 210

Aifld (American Institute for Free
    Labor Development), 116, 127,
    130n. 44
Alexander, Robert Jackson, 34n. 90
Alfonzo Guzmán, Rafael, 157
Allende, Salvador, 120
Alliance for Progress, 114, 127, 182
Anarcho-syndicalism, 100–101, 170
ANDE (Asociación Nacional de
    Empleados), 17, 44, 205, 209
Andean Pact, 22, 55
Andueza, José Guillermo, 66
Anzoátegui, 3
Armed forces, 4, 5, 10, 16, 23, 30n. 6,
    33n. 90, 63n. 67, 96
ARS Group, 7, 10, 16, 37, 45, 87;
    political stands, 28, 29, 35n. 119,
    231n. 2
Association of Laboratory Analysts,
    121
Atiss (Asociación de Trabajadores de
    la Industria Siderúrgica), 43–44,
    47
Autogestión, 124, 179, 180, 189

Banco Occidental de Descuento, 82
Bandera Roja, 156
BAP (Banco Agrícola y Pecuario), 25,
    29
Barrera, Carlos Luis, 26
Barrios, Gonzalo, 42, 83
Beaujón, Arístides, 46
Beirne, Joseph, 182
Benítez, Tello, 154, 155, 157, 158
Bergquist, Charles, 111n. 2
Betancourt, Rómulo, 1, 7, 8, 9–29,
    32n. 69, 33n. 90, 37, 38, 40, 44,

Betancourt, Rómulo (*continued*)
52, 55, 123–24, 132, 147, 231n.
2; austerity measures and, 11, 18,
21–22, 50; labor and left
criticisms of, 9–10, 11, 16, 18,
22, 26, 56; relations with
international labor, 15, 127
Beverage workers, 74
Bras, Marcel, 14
Brito, Pedro, 23, 47, 54, 70, 76, 77,
78, 88
Bruni Celli, Marco Tulio, 179
BTV (Banco de los Trabajadores)
(Workers Bank), 73, 79, 118,
181–88, 189, 221, 228, 229,
230; closing of, 80, 81, 98,
125, 185–86, 189; founding of,
38, 114, 182; mismanagement
of, 53, 77, 86, 107, 183–85
Burelli Rivas, Miguel Angel, 42

Cacique, Julio, 120
Cacref (Corporación de Ahorro y
Crédito Fedepetrol), 189
Caldera, Rafael, 7, 13, 37, 42–50,
113; dealings with organized
labor, 42–44, 65, 75, 123, 127–
28; labor legislation and, 95,
122, 197, 204, 211, 212, 214,
216, 217n. 10
Calvani, Arístides, 125, 205
Cárdenas, Lázaro, 25, 198
Carrasquel, José Manuel, 121
Carrero, Milton, 52, 67
Castañeda, Rafael, 23, 97, 176, 178
Castro, Fidel, 9, 15, 31n. 26, 54
Castro León, Jesús María, 10, 17
Catholic Church, 5, 10, 165
Causa R (Causa Radical), 68, 69, 108,
153–62, 203; attacks against
CTV, 81, 89, 159–60
CDN (Consejo Directivo Nacional),
108, 109
Celli, Humberto, 83
Central Bank, 72, 82, 103, 136, 185
Central Sandinista de Trabajadores,
116
CGN (Consejo General Nacional), 20,
108, 109
CGT (Confederación General de
Trabajadores), 113, 120, 125,
126, 127

Chacón, Americo, 4, 17, 23, 97, 206
CIA (Central Intelligence Agency),
115
CIO (Congress of Industrial
Organizations), 126
Ciudad Guayana, 56, 156
Clasc (Confederación
Latinoamericana de Sindicalistas
Cristianos), 21, 31n. 47, 39, 114,
127
CLAT (Central Latinoamericana de
Trabajadores), 113, 124, 127,
128
Cláusula sindical, 132, 133, 139, 197,
203
CLP (Comité de Luchas Populares),
156
CNT (Confederación Nacional de
Trabajadores), 3
COB (Central Obrera Boliviana), 115
Codesa (Confederación de Sindicatos
Autónomos), 43, 48, 55, 104,
113, 120, 123, 127
Cofetrov (Comité Pro-Federación de
Trabajadores de Venezuela), 12
Cogestión, 16, 99, 100, 124–25, 175–
81, 189, 198, 221, 222; CTV's
department of, 110, 178;
legislation on, 38, 70, 177, 179,
180, 213
Collier, David, 193n. 27, 220n. 51
Collier, Ruth, 193n. 27, 220n. 51
Colombia: illegal immigrants from, 55
Comando Geral dos Trabalhadores
(CGT) (Brazil), 117, 123
Commissaries: in oil industry, 136,
139, 140, 144
Communists. *See* PCV
(Conacopresa) Commission on Costs,
Prices, and Salaries, 73
Confederación General del Trabajo
(Argentina), 115
Conflictos y consenso (Cendes study),
100, 101, 104
Contratistas: in oil industry, 139, 141,
144, 145, 218n. 4, 225
Convergencia Revolucionaria, 122,
173n. 43
Coordinadora Nacional Sindical
(Chile), 115
Copei (Comité de Organización
Política Electoral Independiente),

2, 4, 7, 9, 39, 50, 58, 75, 88, 89, 90, 117, 169, 188–89, 203, 206; during Betancourt period, 9, 13, 15–16, 19, 20, 21; during Caldera period, 42, 44, 45, 46, 47; doctrine of, 101; during Herrera Campíns period, 66, 67, 68, 124, 125; influence in CTV, 13, 39, 45, 46, 52, 53, 69, 70, 71, 74; international affairs and, 127–28; during Leoni period, 37, 39, 124; during Lusinchi period, 75, 76, 80, 81, 107–8, 224; among oil workers, 44, 58, 74, 136, 140, 141, 144, 225; during Pérez period, (1974–79) 50, (1989–94) 85; position on BTV, 98, 125, 182, 184, 185, 186, 187–88; position on *cogestión*, 175, 178, 179, 180; position on labor legislation, 126–27, 197, 199, 200; among steel workers, 44, 153, 158, 230. *See also* CGT; Codesa; FTC

Coracrevi (Corporación de Ahorro y Crédito para la Vivienda), 182, 184

Corporatism theory, 70, 87, 92n. 49, 100, 193, 217, 222, 228, 232n. 8

Costa contractual, 74, 80, 107–8, 110, 191, 199

Croes, Hemmy, 120

CSU (Comité Sindical Unificado), 5, 6, 11, 12

CTAL (Confederación de Trabajadores de América Latina), 120

CTC (Confederación de Trabajadores de Cuba), 15, 21, 54

CTM (Confederación de Trabajadores de México), 25, 198

CTV (Confederación de Trabajadores de Venezuela), 59, 86–91, 95–98, 221–31; during Betancourt period, 13–24; during Caldera period, 42–50; Eighth Congress, 68, 69, 70, 74, 99, 107, 124, 191, 192; Fifth Congress, 38, 39; Fourth Congress, 20, 21, 22, 24, 119; during Herrera Campíns period, 65–71; International Affairs Department, 71, 76, 116,

118; international ties, 14–15, 21, 114–18; investments, 188–90; during Leoni period, 37–42; during Lusinchi period, 71–81; National Directive Council, 108, 109; National Electoral Commission, 108, 109; National General Council, 108, 109; Ninth Congress, 73, 74, 77, 78, 79, 80, 88, 124, 127, 128, 179; organization, 107–10; during Pérez period, (1974–79) 50–58, (1989–94) 81–86; position on labor legislation, 198, 199, 200, 201, 204, 208, 210, 213, 215, 216, 217; Second Extraordinary Congress, 82, 83; Seventh Congress, 46, 47, 52, 54, 58, 85, 102, 103, 124; Sixth Congress, 45, 46, 47, 48, 100, 124; strategy, 98–102; structure and practices, 102–11; Tenth Congress, 84–85, 86, 108; Third Congress, 13–16, 17, 27, 33n. 90, 38, 106, 114, 175, 178, 180, 198, 217, 223; Third Extraordinary Congress, 108, 110. *See also* BTV; Causa R; *Cogestión*; Executive Committee; Fedepetrol; Sutiss; Textile workers

CTV-No Oficialista, 22, 23

Cuba, 9, 16, 54, 120. *See also* Castro, Fidel; CTC

Curiel, José, 184

CUT (Central Unica dos Trabalhadores) (Brazil), 115

CUT (Central Unitaria de Trabajadores) (Colombia), 121

CUTV (Central Unitaria de Trabajadores de Venezuela), 23, 41, 43, 44, 45, 47, 67, 89, 113, 119–23, 169–70, 171, 173n. 48; following, 41, 113; founding of, 22; united efforts with CTV, 41, 47, 48, 55, 67, 119–20, 124

CUTV-Clasista, 119–20

CVF (Corporación Venezolana de Fomento), 38, 162, 188

CVG (Corporación Venezolana de Guayana), 150, 160, 169

CVT (Confederación Venezolana del Trabajo), 95

Davis, Charles, 100
Decree 440 (1958), 6, 41, 57, 166–67, 173n. 48, 201
De Leon, Daniel, 119
Delfino, Enrique, 184
Delpino, Juan José, 15, 54, 73, 76, 85, 88, 97, 104, 134, 146n. 3, 158, 184, 187, 198; criticism of government, 72, 88; on February 1989 disturbances, 82; position on strikes, 83, 88, 99–100; role in internal AD affairs, 78, 79, 80; role in international affairs, 76, 116, 117
Deutsch, Haydeé, 104, 127
Díaz Bruzual, Leopoldo, 185
Digepol: human-rights violations and, 42
Dominican Republic: U.S. invasion of, 115

Echeverría, Luis, 57
Elino Martínez, Rafael, 189
Emergency Measures (1962), 18, 22
Emergency Plan (1958) 7, 8, 11, 18
Empleados de confianza, 132, 143, 211–12, 219n. 39
Engels, Friedrich, 144
EPA (El Pueblo Avanza), 68
Exceptionalism thesis, xv–xxiii, 5, 60, 86–91, 110–11, 145–46, 221–31
Exclusionary clause: in collective bargaining, 204
Executive Committee (CTV), 13, 17, 46, 52, 54, 69–70, 71, 74, 75, 77, 88, 97, 102, 114, 185, 222, 226; CTV restructuring and, 108, 109, 124, 216
Export-Import Bank, 189

Fagen, Stuart, 48–49
Falkland Islands War (1982), 128
(FAPUV) Federation of University Professors' Associations, 121
Faría, Jesús, 97, 146n. 3
FCU (Federación de Centros Universitarios), 120
FCV (Federación Campesina de Venezuela), 13, 17, 23, 25, 28, 76, 77, 110, 190–91, 209, 226; on

agrarian reform, 26, 27, 29, 189; economic interests, 189, 190; ethical conduct questioned, 43, 76
FDP (Fuerza Democrática Popular), 39, 42, 45, 46
Fedecámaras (Federación de Cámaras de Industria y Comerico), 10, 55, 58, 73, 86, 180, 221; opposition to 1989 general strike, 83; position on labor legislation, 51, 52, 67, 85, 177, 197, 206, 207, 213, 214, 215, 216, 220n. 43, 222
Fedepetrol (Federación de Trabajadores Petroleros), 39, 74, 80, 135, 136, 139–40, 145, 147n. 31, 209; party influence in, 44–45, 58, 76, 141, 203; struggle for job security and, 18, 133–34
Fedetransporte (Federación de Trabajadores del Transporte), 67, 190. See also Transportation workers
Fernández, Eduardo, 75, 126, 212
Ferrominera, 57
Fetrabolívar, 69, 80, 81, 156, 158, 160
Fetracarabobo, 79, 80
Fetrahidrocarburos (Federación de Trabajadores de la Industria de Hidrocarburos), 39, 41, 74, 80, 133, 135
Fetramagisterio, 121
Fetrametal, 44, 47, 69, 80, 81, 107, 125, 155, 156, 158, 160, 161, 172n. 38, 194n. 64, 203
Fetrasalud, 80, 117
Fetrazulia, 45, 58, 75
Fifth Plan of the Nation, 56, 150
FND (Frente Nacional Democrático), 37, 39, 42
Frizo, Enzo, 117
FTC (Frente de Trabajadores Copeyanos), 39, 44, 68, 123, 124, 125, 126–28, 130n. 41, 178; hardening of position, 74, 125–26, 128. See also Copei
Fuero sindical, 47, 73, 107, 127, 143, 157, 188, 211
FVM (Federación Venezolana de Maestros), 43, 66–67, 211

GAR (Grupo de Acción Revolucionaria), 68
García, Eduardo, 39
Garment workers. *See* Textile workers
Germani, Gino, 87
Gil, César, 54, 76, 85, 86, 97, 186, 200
Gil Rivera, Casto, 89, 101, 160
Goldsack, José, 127
Gómez, Juan Vicente, 1, 96, 111
Gompers, Samuel, 204
González, Armando, 29, 76–77, 78, 189, 191
González, Benigno, 183, 187
González, César, 30n. 7
González, Dagoberto, 4, 45, 106, 126, 127, 128
González, Ismario, 52, 117
González Navarro, José, 19, 20, 22, 41, 44, 46, 104, 205; chosen CTV president, 14, 15; on *cogestión*, 38, 176; on international affairs, 14, 114–15; with Luna faction in CTV, 77, 78; membership in MEP, 40, 47, 97
Guayana region, 18, 66, 68, 141, 149, 151, 155, 199, 200; labor conflicts in, 6, 57, 58, 160, 230
Guerrilla warfare, 24, 33n. 73, 37, 40, 41, 47, 90, 153, 156, 223
Guevara, Eustacio, 76
Guri Dam, 150, 151

Henríquez, Raúl, 140, 189
Herrera, Juan, 5, 11, 19, 24, 77, 113, 191
Herrera Campíns, Luis, 65–71, 124, 125, 151, 184, 185
Hotels: CTV acquisition of, 188–89
Humphrey, John, 144, 149
Hunger Law (1961), 18, 22, 40, 96, 111, 211, 223

IAN (Instituto Agrario Nacional), 26, 27, 28, 29
ICFTU (International Confederation of Free Trade Unions), 14, 21, 113, 115, 117
ILO (International Labor Organization), 6, 113, 157, 176, 201, 202, 210, 213

IMF (International Monetary Fund), 85, 86
Immigration, 51, 55, 56
Inaesin (Instituto Nacional de Altos Estudios Sindicales), 176, 221
Inamovilidad, 51, 154, 199, 213, 214
Informal economy. *See* Nonunionized workers
Institutional Pact (1970), 46, 48, 53, 124, 206, 224
Ipostel (Instituto Postal Telegráfico), 67–68
Iron workers, 44, 57, 58, 141, 200, 205, 219n. 23
Israel: OPEC and, 118
ITS (International Trade Secretariats), 114, 115, 118, 127
IVSS (Instituto Venezolano de Seguro Social), 14, 38, 67, 142–43, 211, 216

James, Daniel, 149
Jauregui, Arturo, 39
Job security, 14, 39, 44, 52, 136, 144, 204–9; *estabilidad absoluta*, 17, 24, 40, 43, 51, 121, 132, 133, 136, 138, 141, 144, 204, 211, 221, 225, 226; *estabilidad indirecta*, 51, 205, 208; *estabilidad numérica*, 51, 134, 137, 138, 142, 144, 208
Juliao, Francisco, 114
Junta Militar, 5, 6
Junta Patriótica, 4, 6, 10, 12

Kirkland, Lane, 115

Labor aristocracy, 100, 144–46, 147n. 31, 147n. 33, 189, 231n. 2
Labor Bureau (AD), 21, 37, 48, 54, 66, 67, 179, 212, 223, 230; internal party affairs and, 17, 56, 70, 71, 76, 77, 78, 79, 80, 85, 86, 87, 111, 212, 223, 230
Labor Law (1928), 96
Labor Law (1936), 1, 4, 51, 73, 95, 103, 169, 190; on layoffs, 204–9; on national unions, 198–203; on public employees, 210–12; Regulation (1973), 201; on union hiring, 203

Labor Law (1991), 82, 102, 126, 142,
    177, 197, 204, 212–18; on
    layoffs, 85, 208, 209, 215–16; on
    union classification, 108, 122,
    127, 199–200
Lairet, Germán, 206
Landino, Gustavo, 164, 167
Lares Ruiz, Gustavo, 7
Larrazábal, Wolfgang, 5, 8, 37
Law of Workers' Representation
    (1966), 38, 178, 180, 192
Leandro Mora, Reinaldo, 80
Leidenz, Antonio, 206, 219n. 26
Lenin, V. I., 119, 125, 144
León León, Rafael, 45, 53, 75, 124,
    186
Leoni, Raúl, 37–42, 50, 133, 134, 175,
    193n. 31, 205, 223
Lepage, Octavio, 78, 79, 80
Ley Calvani, 206
Ley contra Despidos Injustificados
    (1974), 51, 52, 55, 58, 164, 165,
    206, 207, 217, 219n. 33, 219n. 39
Ley de Carrera Administrativa
    (1970), 39, 43, 211
Ley de Estabilidad Laboral, 39
Ley Orgánica de Prevención,
    Condiciones y Medio Ambiente
    de Trabajo (1986), 159
Ley Orgánica de Seguridad y Defensa
    Nacional (1975), 58, 160, 230
Liga Socialista, 58, 68
López, Margarita, 191
Lora, Guillermo, 161
Luna, Carlos, 76, 87, 90, 101, 186,
    231n. 2; aspires to CTV presi-
    dency, 52–54, 57, 85; at 1985
    CTV congress, 77–78, 79
Lusinchi, Jaime, 71–81, 88, 110, 142,
    180, 187, 223, 224, 227
Luzardo, Olga, 163

Machado, Eduardo, 28
Machuca, Ramón, 159
McCoy, Jennifer L., 61n. 39, 229
Malavé Villalba, Augusto, 14, 15, 21,
    38, 98, 114, 183, 184, 203
Maneiro, Alfredo, 153, 161
Maquilas, 85
Maracay: unions in, 69, 164
Marcano, José, 17, 41, 97
Margarita: duty-free status, 72

Márquez, Pompeyo, 186
Marxism, 4, 9, 14, 16, 17, 98, 101,
    106, 122, 175
MAS (Movimiento al Socialismo), 50,
    58, 68, 73, 81, 88, 89, 90, 169,
    180, 203, 212; anti-CTV position
    of, 119–20; attitude toward
    strikes, 101, 153; decision to join
    CTV, 54, 69, 119; influence in
    CTV, 52, 53, 69, 84; position on
    BTV, 81, 98, 186; position on
    labor legislation, 200, 212;
    among textile workers, 69, 164
Máspero, Emilio, 127–28
Matos Azocar, Luis Raúl, 103
Maza Zavala, D. F., 103, 176, 181
Medina, Pablo, 152, 157
MEP (Movimiento Electoral del
    Pueblo), 42, 45, 47, 48, 50, 52,
    58, 66–67, 72, 81, 88–89, 90, 98,
    99, 119, 126, 159, 169; attitude
    toward strikes, 101, 223;
    founding of, 21, 40, 41, 87, 231n.
    2; influence in CTV, 45, 53, 69,
    84–85, 124; interparty relations,
    42, 44–45, 46, 68, 75–76, 141; on
    international affairs, 115, 117; in
    oil workers' movement, 135,
    136, 139, 140, 141, 142, 203;
    policy toward BTV, 98, 184, 187;
    position on labor legislation, 200,
    205–6; among steel workers, 43,
    44, 47, 153; among teachers, 66–
    67
Mercados Campesinos (Mercam), 189
Mercau, Andrés, 125
Mesa, Salom, 87
Ministry of Agriculture, 27, 29
Ministry of Labor, 30n. 13, 41, 48, 67,
    72, 166, 177, 181, 185–86, 198,
    201, 205; limited role of, 38–39,
    217; role in classifying layoffs,
    164, 208, 229
MIR (Movimiento de Izquierda
    Revolucionaria), 17, 18, 20, 33n.
    90, 42, 58, 68; expulsion from
    CTV, 21; founding of, 16, 18;
    membership in CUTV, 41, 119,
    122; in oil workers' movement,
    18, 39, 133, 144, 225; reenters
    CTV, 54, 69
Mishkin, León, 167, 168

Mollegas, José, 44, 47, 54, 107, 155, 158
Morena party, 69, 71, 97
Moreno, Gabriel, 156
Moreno, Víctor, 158
Mosbacher, Robert, 81

New York Times, 186
Nonunionized workers, 16, 89, 102, 113, 214–15, 227, 228

OAS (Organization of American States), 182
Occupational safety and health, 152, 154, 159, 179. *See also* Sidor
O'Donnell, Guillermo, 63n. 67
Oil workers. *See* Petroleum workers
Olarte, César, 75, 76, 85, 87, 88, 101, 115, 185
Old Guard (AD), 8, 10, 28, 29, 35n. 119, 99
Olivo, Francisco, 37, 45, 52, 53, 54, 75, 80, 98, 100–101, 104, 124
OPEC (Organization of Petroleum Exporting Countries), 18, 65, 72, 115, 118, 136, 224
ORIT (Organización Regional Interamericana de Trabajadores), 14, 15, 21, 31n. 47, 39, 115, 116, 117, 127, 130n. 44; criticism of, 114, 115; CTV affiliation with, 38, 113
Oropeza Castillo, Alejandro, 95
Ortega, Carlos, 136
Ortega, Pedro, 24

Pacto de Avenimiento Obrero Patronal (1958), 6, 9, 10, 14, 223
Paz Galarraga, Jesús, 35n. 119, 37, 40, 46
PCV (Partido Comunista de Venezuela), 1, 9, 10, 13, 16, 31n. 30, 42, 46, 58, 69, 114, 169, 212, 224; expulsion from CTV, 20, 21, 23; leftist unity and, 68; among oil workers, 39, 133, 144, 225; opposition to Betancourt, 11, 12, 18, 24; opposition to Pérez Jiménez, 2, 4, 97; position on *cogestión*, 180; role in CUTV, 22, 41, 44, 119, 121, 122; among steel workers, 150, 153, 155,

169; support for democracy (1958), 6, 7, 8
Pdvsa (Petróleos de Venezuela), 137, 138, 139, 140, 142, 143, 169, 203
Peña, Cupertino, 167, 168
Peñalver, Manuel, 9, 71, 97, 98, 107, 116, 118, 146n. 3, 181; AD orthodox faction and, 76, 77, 79
Perestroika: influence of, 122
Pérez, Carlos Andrés, 42, 45, 48, 50–58, 81–86, 90, 150, 151, 152, 168, 184, 187, 223, 227; AD renovation faction and, 56–57, 76–79, 85–86; on labor legislation, 197, 212, 213; oil nationalization and, 136; reformist program, 50–52, 58, 221
Pérez Alfonzo, Juan Pablo, 18, 56
Pérez Jiménez, Marcos, 2, 3–5, 6, 7, 9, 11, 12, 14, 55, 101, 110
Pérez Salinas, Pedro Bernardo, 8, 14, 104, 114
Perlman, Selig, 204
Perón, Juan Domingo, 149, 198, 229
Peronists, 99, 114, 115, 126, 201
Petkoff, Teodoro, 73
Petroleum workers, 3, 12, 17, 24, 131–48. *See also* Fedepetrol; Fetrahidrocarburos
Piñate, Vicente, 4, 19, 205
Piñerua, Carlos, 44, 54, 97, 135, 139–40, 184, 189, 191
Piñerua Ordaz, Luis, 186
Pinto, Eleazar, 77, 181, 183, 184, 186
Pinto, Luis, 18
Porlamar Manifesto (1980), 99, 176, 179, 180, 181
Prieto Figueroa, Luis Beltrán, 35n. 119, 40, 42, 206, 219n. 26
Privatization, 81, 152, 176, 177, 181, 182, 188–89, 213; opposition to, 67, 82, 160, 169, 216
Proceso Político, 68, 69, 122, 173n. 43
Profit sharing, 43–44, 103, 211
Proyecto Caldera. *See* Labor Law (1991)
Public employees, 38, 39, 40, 43, 67, 88, 197, 209–12
Punto Fijo Pact (1958), 123, 197, 224

Quijada, Ramón, 13, 16, 23, 26–27, 28, 29, 35n. 119
Quintero, Rodolfo, 10, 23, 31, 33n. 73

Rachadel, Juan José, 66
Radical Party (Argentina), 126
Ramírez, Martín J., 23, 96
Ramírez León, Federico, 80, 86, 88, 97, 116, 117, 118, 158; AD renovation current and, 53–54, 76, 85
Ramos Allup, Henry, 186
Ramos Giménez, Raúl, 37
Rangel, Domingo Alberto, 18
Reciprocal Commerce Treaty (1952), 22
Ríos, Antonio, 76, 80, 81, 83–84, 85, 86, 116; CTV investments and, 77, 86, 187, 191
Rodríguez, Alcides, 206–7
Rodríguez, Sótero, 85
Romualdi, Serafino, 15, 24

Salas Castillo, Pablo, 206
Sandinistas, 116, 117
Scott Power, Horacio, 22, 41, 119, 122
Self-employed workers, 102, 215–16
Sidor (Siderúrgica de Orinoco), 43–44, 47, 48, 49, 69, 107, 150–62; hazardous conditions in, 152, 159
Sixth Plan of the Nation, 65
Skilled workers, 55, 56, 104, 152
SNTP (Sindicato Nacional de Trabajadores de la Prensa), 4, 104, 121
Socialist International, 179
"Social Pact": conflict resolution and, 70, 72, 73
Social Security. See IVSS
Sosa A., Arturo, 165
Soto Socorro, Hugo, 45, 87
Soviet Union: worker ownership in, 180
Spalding, Hobart, 130n. 44, 173n. 58
Strikes, 19–20, 30n. 13, 37, 42, 49, 57, 67–68, 96, 100, 101, 191, 194n. 64, 227; general strike of January 1958, 4, 5, 110, 227; general strike of 1989, 83, 102, 120; incidence of, in 1960s and

1970s, 48–50, 59, 61n. 39, 223; of iron workers, 57; of oil workers, 3, 131–32, 142, 145; of steel workers, 43–44, 153, 155; of teachers, 43, 78; of textile workers, 57, 164, 166, 167; threats and unsuccessful calls of, 19, 44, 88, 134
Sucre Figarella, Leopoldo, 184
Suministros Campesinos C.A. (Sucam), 76, 189–90
Superintendencia de Bancos, 185
Sutiss (Sindicato Unico de Trabajadores de la Industria Siderúrgica), 69, 80, 121, 125, 230
Sutratex (Sindicato Unico de Trabajadores Textiles), 57

Táchira: transportation strike in, 19
Tarre Murzi, Alfredo, 43, 98
Taylorism, 149, 163, 205
Teachers, 43, 78, 84, 89, 104, 226. See also Fetramagisterio; FVM
Telephone workers, 19
Textile workers, 6, 105, 107, 122, 131, 142, 162–71, 172n. 38, 205, 226
Tinoco, Pedro, 42, 46, 82
Torrealba, Laureano, 23, 97
Torres, Eloy, 4, 11, 17, 21, 23, 47, 119, 204
Torres, Pedro, 25, 47
Torvenca C.A., 176
Tovar, Luis, 44, 97, 146n. 3
Transportation workers, 5, 19–20, 105, 217. See also Fedetransporte
Tremont, Arturo, 106, 155
Trienio government (1945–1948), 2, 6, 37, 193n. 31
Tripartite commissions, 51, 133, 164, 165, 168, 205, 206, 207, 228; functions other than classifying layoffs, 70, 132
Trujillo, Rafael, 114
Turén: conflict at, 3

Ugueto, Luis, 186
UNEP (Unión Nacional de Empleados Públicos), 211
Union hiring practices. See Cláusula sindical

Unions: national, 6–7, 14, 73, 104, 108, 109, 122, 198–203, 204, 217. *See also* Nonunionized workers
United States, 9, 22; Máspero denounces, 127, 128; opposition to Pérez Jiménez, 5, 30n. 7
Urbaneja, Diego Bautista, 50
Urbieta, Jesús, 54, 88, 97, 104, 116, 156
URD (Unión Republicana Democrática), 2, 7, 8, 9, 12, 13, 19, 42, 45, 52, 69, 115, 133, 197; among oil workers, 39, 41, 74, 135, 144; opposition to Betancourt government, 10, 11, 16, 18; relations with left, 20, 22, 23, 46; in struggle against Pérez Jiménez, 2, 4
Uslar Prieti, Arturo, 28, 37
Utilidades. See Profit sharing
UTIT (Unión de Trabajadores de la Industria Textil), 57, 69, 89, 122, 164, 165, 166

Vallejo, José Beltrán, 97
Vanguardia Comunista, 54, 69, 71, 97
Vargas, Getulio, 229
Vargas, José, 58, 72, 76, 98, 104, 181, 206, 208; aspires to CTV presidency, 52, 57, 101; BTV and, 187, 191, 192, 228
Velasco Alvarado, Juan, 177

Velásquez, Andrés, 80–81, 154, 157, 158, 159, 160, 169
Velásquez, Ramón J., 19
Venezuelan Petroleum Corporation, 40
Venezuelan Textile Association, 167
Villalba, Jóvito, 7, 37, 46
Villegas, Cruz, 33n. 73, 41, 119, 120, 122
Vivas Terán, Abdón, 183

WCL (World Confederation of Labor), 113
Webb, Beatrice, 204
Webb, Sidney, 204
WFTU (World Federation of Trade Unions), 14, 113
Wirtz, W. Willard, 182
Women workers, 104, 105–6, 107, 110, 163, 200; labor law and, 213–14; organizing attempts, 163
Workers Bank. *See* BTV
Workers Bank Law (1966), 38
Workers' law. *See* Law of Workers Representation (1966)
Workers Party (Brazil), 171
Work week, 14, 69, 83, 84, 132, 133, 141–42, 155, 156, 159, 161, 169, 210, 216
World Bank, 151, 160

Zarikian, Esteban, 168
Zulia, 3, 18, 45, 46. *See also* Fetrazulia

Latin American Silhouettes
Studies in History and Culture

William H. Beezley and
Judith Ewell
Editors

Volumes Published

William H. Beezley and Judith Ewell, eds., *The Human Tradition in Latin America: The Twentieth Century* (1987). Cloth ISBN 0-8420-2283-X Paper ISBN 0-8420-2284-8

Judith Ewell and William H. Beezley, eds., *The Human Tradition in Latin America: The Nineteenth Century* (1989). Cloth ISBN 0-8420-2331-3 Paper ISBN 0-8420-2332-1

David G. LaFrance, *The Mexican Revolution in Puebla, 1908–1913: The Maderista Movement and the Failure of Liberal Reform* (1989). ISBN 0-8420-2293-7

Mark A. Burkholder, *Politics of a Colonial Career: José Baquíjano and the Audiencia of Lima*, 2d ed. (1990). Cloth ISBN 0-8420-2353-4 Paper ISBN 0-8420-2352-6

Kenneth M. Coleman and George C. Herring, eds. (with Foreword by Daniel Oduber), *Understanding the Central American Crisis: Sources of Conflict, U.S. Policy, and Options for Peace* (1991). Cloth ISBN 0-8420-2382-8   Paper ISBN 0-8420-2383-6

Carlos B. Gil, ed., *Hope and Frustration: Interviews with Leaders of Mexico's Political Opposition* (1992). Cloth ISBN 0-8420-2395-X Paper ISBN 0-8420-2396-8

Charles Bergquist, Ricardo Peñaranda, and Gonzalo Sánchez, eds., *Violence in Colombia: The Contemporary Crisis in Historical Perspective* (1992). Cloth ISBN 0-8420-2369-0 Paper ISBN 0-8420-2376-3

Heidi Zogbaum, *B. Traven: A Vision of Mexico* (1992). ISBN 0-8420-2392-5

Jaime E. Rodríguez O., ed., *Patterns of Contention in Mexican History* (1992). ISBN 0-8420-2399-2

Louis A. Pérez, Jr., ed., *Slaves, Sugar, and Colonial Society: Travel Accounts of Cuba, 1801–1899* (1992). Cloth ISBN 0-8420-2354-2 Paper ISBN 0-8420-2415-8

Peter Blanchard, *Slavery and Abolition in Early Republican Peru* (1992). Cloth ISBN 0-8420-2400-X   Paper ISBN 0-8420-2429-8

Paul J. Vanderwood, *Disorder and Progress: Bandits, Police, and Mexican Development*. Revised and Enlarged Edition (1992). Cloth ISBN 0-8420-2438-7   Paper ISBN 0-8420-2439-5

Sandra McGee Deutsch and Ronald H. Dolkart, eds., *The Argentine Right: Its History and Intellectual Origins, 1910 to the Present* (1993). Cloth ISBN 0-8420-2418-2   Paper ISBN 0-8420-2419-0

Jaime E. Rodríguez O., ed., *The Evolution of the Mexican Political System* (1993). ISBN 0-8420-2448-4

Steve Ellner, *Organized Labor in Venezuela, 1958–1991: Behavior and Concerns in a Democratic Setting* (1993). ISBN 0-8420-2443-3

Paul J. Dosal, *Doing Business with the Dictators: A Political History of United Fruit in Guatemala, 1899–1944* (1993). ISBN 0-8420-2475-1

Marquis James, *Merchant Adventurer: The Story of W. R. Grace* (1993). ISBN 0-8420-2444-1

John C. Chasteen and Joseph S. Tulchin, eds., *Problems in Modern Latin American History: A Reader* (1993). Cloth ISBN 0-8420-2327-5 Paper ISBN 0-8420-2328-3